SMOKY MOUNTAIN MAGIC

The Junior League of Johnson City, Tennessee, Inc.

P.O. Box 1082

The Association of Junior Leagues, Inc. is an international organization of women committed to promoting voluntarism and leadership of trained volunteers. Its purpose is exclusively educational and charitable.

The proceeds from the sale of **SMOKY MOUNTAIN MAGIC** will support community projects sponsored by the Junior League of Johnson City, Tennessee.

To order additional copies of:

SMOKY MOUNTAIN MAGIC
or
TREASURES OF THE SMOKIES,
Tempting Recipes from East Tennessee
write to:

High South Publications
P.O. Box 1082
Johnson City, Tennessee 37605

1st Printing November 15, 1960—1,000 copies
2nd Printing October 1, 1961—5,000 copies
3rd Printing October 1, 1969—5,000 copies
4th Printing July 1, 1971—10,000 copies
5th Printing August 1, 1974—10,000 copies
6th Printing March 1, 1979—10,000 copies
7th Printing June 1, 1983—5,000 copies
8th Printing July 1, 1986—5,000 copies
9th Printing July 1, 1989—5,000 copies
10th Printing June 1, 1991—10,000 copies
11th Printing April 1, 1995—5,000 copies

ABOUT THE COVER:

Special thanks to J. Scott Graham/Scott's Shots for providing the front and back cover photographs. With an eye for the unusual, Graham travels from nearby sites around his home in East Tennessee to numerous locations throughout the Blue Ridge Mountains to record the beauty and uniqueness of this region on film. His images of wildlife, beautiful mountain scenery, and wonders of nature have gained national recognition by demonstrating an artistic viewpoint and revealing a unique ability to bring a fresh focus to familiar subjects. For more information on award winning images in the Scott's Shots collection of photographs, or for a free catalog of limited edition prints, please call (615) 854-9435.

Printed in the USA by

WIMMER
The Wimmer Companies, Inc.
Memphis • Dallas

TABLE OF CONTENTS

Preface

In the hills of Tennessee there is a tradition that lives on: true natives appreciate and value good friends and good food. Without the one, life is empty; without the other, one is empty. To fill the void, Tennesseans for generations have cultivated friendliness and culinary arts.

Believing in this tradition, the Johnson City Junior League has accumulated a collection of recipes, gleaned from its many families and friends. From pioneer game dishes to modern frozen foods, these recipes, favorites, if not originals with the donors, have been time tested, dining room tested, and gastronomically tested. Each recipe in this book has been served to friends without losing a friend, to families without provoking a quarrel, and to acquaintances, who sometimes have become fast friends!

We hope that you, our friends who acquire this book, will enjoy our gleanings from the coves and ridges of this beautiful countryside. We trust that you will relish the varied dishes and find some of our Smoky Mountain Magic!

The Johnson City Junior League has contributed, for a number of years, sizeable sums of money to its Community Welfare Fund. The proceeds from the sales of this book will be designated, in part, to the specific service project, The Mental Health Association of Washington County. The remaining funds from this project will be given to other worthy welfare work in which the organization is now engaged.

Acknowledgments

The Junior League wishes to express its appreciation to the following people who have assisted the organization in the compilation of this book: Mr. Ray Chalker and his staff, who have worked untiringly with the editors of this book; Mrs. Frank Collins, who has given professional help in the organization of the Calorie Chart; Miss Mary Eleanor Prentiss and Miss Margaret Dugger, who have given significant editing advice; Mr. Herb Shulman, who has donated the mailing cartons; Mr. George Brandt, who has served as legal advisor; and our many friends and relatives, who have contributed their favorite recipes.

APPETIZERS

ANCHOVY CHEESE DIP

8 ozs. cream cheese	1 t. onion juice
1½ t. Anchovy Paste	¼ C. coffee cream
1 T. Worcestershire sauce	Salt
	Cayenne pepper

Mash cheese and thin to dipping consistency with cream. Add seasoning, using more or less anchovy paste as desired. Beat until smooth and serve with potato chips or crisp crackers.

MRS. JAMES H. EPPS, JR.

APPETIZER PUFFS

¼ C. butter	½ C. flour
½ C. milk	2 eggs, unbeaten

Add butter to milk. Bring to boil and while hot, add flour all at once. Stir until ball forms in center of pan. Add eggs, one at a time — beating after each addition. Drop by teaspoonfuls onto greased cooky sheet. This will make about 30 small appetizer size puffs. Bake 40 to 45 minutes in 375 degree oven.

TANGY HAM SALAD FILLING:

1 C. ground ham	1 T. ground onion

Add mayonnaise to desired consistency for filling puffs.

MRS. JAY GUMP

AVOCADO SAUCE FOR SHRIMP COCKTAIL

1 C. mashed avocado	1 C. mayonnaise
Dash of tabasco	½ C. catsup
	2 T. Worcestershire sauce

Mix all ingredients together and chill. Place shrimp in cocktail glasses with lettuce leaves around edges. Drop a spoonful of sauce on each serving.

This sauce is delicious with all seafood cocktails and ½ as much mayonnaise and catsup makes it a fine dip for crackers or chips.

MRS. E. R. BAYLOR

BLEU CHEESE SALAD DRESSING OR DIP

1 pkg. bleu cheese	1/3 C. grapefruit or orange
1 pkg. cream cheese with	juice
chives	1/3 C. mayonnaise
1/3 C. salad oil	1 t. grated onion (optional)

Increase or decrease half and half mixture of salad oil and fruit juice to obtain desired consistency.

MRS. E. W. POTTS, JR.
Abingdon, Va.

HOT CHEESE APPETIZERS

1 lb. sharp cheddar cheese   Worcestershire sauce
mayonnaise   loaf sandwich bread
red pepper

Grate cheese and soften to spreading consistency with mayonnaise.
Add red pepper and Worcestershire sauce to taste (several dashes
of each needed for good sharp flavor). Trim the crusts from the
slices of bread, and spread each slice generously with the cheese
mixture. Roll up and secure with toothpicks and bake in hot (450
degree) oven for 15 to 20 minutes. Serve hot.

These are very easy rolls to prepare, but oh! so good!

MRS. ALFRED ABERNETHY

REFRIGERATOR CHEESE CHIPS

1½ C. Flour   ¾ C. grated American cheese
½ t. salt   Dash of cayenne
¼ t. paprika   Enough cold water to make
½ C. shortening   stiff dough

Sift dry ingredients together and blend with shortening. Add water
to make stiff dough. Add cheese last. Mold into rolls, wrap in wax
paper, and place in refrigerator until ready for use. When ready,
slice, brush tops with milk and sprinkle with caraway or celery seeds.

Bake 10 minutes at 400°

MRS. JOE B. JARED

HOLIDAY CHEESE DIP

1 3-oz. pkg. cream cheese   2 T. chopped, stuffed olives
1 T. milk   2 T. chopped walnuts
½ t. grated onion   Dash of tabasco sauce
          Dash of Worcestershire sauce

Add milk to cream cheese and mix until soft and creamy. Add remaining ingredients and blend. Use potato chips, pretzels or small
crackers to scoop up mixture.

MRS. E. R. BAYLOR

CHEESE PUFFS

1 C. water   1 C. sifted flour
½ C. butter   4 eggs

Let water and butter come to a boil. Add flour and stir briskly.
This makes a white, pasty batter. Take it off the stove and let it
cool. Beat eggs until they are very thick. Combine eggs and paste
and mix thoroughly with electric mixer. Drop on greased pan in
½ t. sizes. Bake in hot oven 450° for 10 to 15 min. When done,
split and fill with cheese filling.

CHEESE FILLING
Mix 3 3-oz. packages cream cheese with ¼ lb. Roquefort cheese.
Moisten with cream to make a good consistency. Fill puffs with a
half teaspoon or so of cheese filling. Makes about 70.

MRS. HARRY CRUMLEY

CHEESE ROLL

Mix 1 jar of Roko cheese, 1 large pkg. of cream cheese with 1 t. Worcestershire sauce and 2 t. minced onion. Add chopped chives, then roll in crushed pecans to form a log roll. Serve with crackers.

MRS. GEORGE BRANDT

TEXAS CHEESE STICKS

1 lb. longhorn cheese	2 pkgs. cream cheese
2 small cloves of garlic	Mayonnaise (as needed to mix)
2/3 C. pecans	

Put first 3 ingredients through food chopper, then mix all ingredients thoroughly. Spread on waxed paper which has been thickly sprinkled with chili powder. Remove and roll as for cinnamon roll. Chill thoroughly before slicing to serve. This will keep for a month wrapped in waxed paper in the refrigerator.

MRS. ALLEN HARRIS, JR.

CHEESE STRAWS

1 C. sharp cheese (pack tightly)	½ t. baking powder
1 C. flour	1 t. salt
1 lump butter, size of small egg	Little bit ice water
	Dash of red pepper

Roll out and cut into thin strips. Bake at 350° F.

MRS. ADAM BOWMAN

SESAME CHEESE STRIPS

1 C. sifted flour	¼ C. toasted sesame seeds
½ t. salt	1 slightly beaten egg yolk
½ t. monosodium glutamate	1/3 C. melted butter or margarine
½ t. ginger	1 T. water
½ t. sugar	½ t. Worcestershire sauce
1 C. grated sharp American cheese	

Sift together dry ingredients; then stir in cheese and sesame seed. Combine remaining ingredients. Add to first mixture and stir to form a ball. On lightly floured surface, roll to ⅛ inch thickness. Cut in 1 x 3 inch strips. Bake on ungreased baking sheet in 350 degree oven for 10 to 15 minutes. Cool and serve.

A flaky pastry with cheesy nut-like flavor!

MRS. KYLE WILLIAMS

CLAM CANAPES

½ lb. cheese (mild)	2 t. mayonnaise
1 can minced clams	1 t. minced onions

Mix and let stand in ice box several hours before serving.

Heap on rounds of toast or crackers and brown slightly under broiler.

MRS. WILLIAM G. PREAS

CLAM DIP

Melt in a double boiler:

3 T. butter
1 chopped onion
1 chopped green pepper
One 10½-oz. can of minced
   clams which have been
   drained

½ lb. diced cheese
4 T. catsup
1 T. Worcestershire sauce
1 T. milk
½ t. cayenne pepper

Cook over water until cheese melts. Serve hot from chaffing dish with crackers, chips, etc.

MRS. DON KING
Bristol, Tennessee

CRAB MEAT CANAPES

6½-oz. crab meat
½ lb. saute'ed mushrooms
¾ C. cream sauce

1 T. finely chopped green
   peppers
1 T. chopped pimiento
1 t. Worcestershire sauce

Heap the mixture on rounds of toast. Sprinkle tops with grated parmesan cheese and bread crumbs. Dot with butter and heat under broiler until very hot.

MRS. GEORGE DOUGHTY

DATE CONFECTION

1 C. flour
¼ C. butter

13-oz. package cream
   cheese

Mix into a pastry. Wrap pitted dates with pastry.

Dip each wrapped date in unbeaten egg white. Roll in ½ C. sugar and ½ C. finely chopped walnuts. Bake on ungreased cooky sheet at 325 degrees for 15 minutes.

This is a delicious tea time confection.

MRS. G. K. SCHOLL

DATE CHEESE DREAMS

2 C. flour
1 lb. cheddar cheese
¼ lb. butter

1 t. salt
1 t. red pepper

Mix together into a dough. Roll out about ¼ inch thick.

Stuff one package pitted dates with pecan halves. Wrap each stuffed date in the cheese dough. Bake on ungreased cooky sheet at 375 degrees until brown, about 15 minutes.

This is a tart pastry and perfect for cocktail or tea time.

MRS. J. B. THOMAS

HAM CANAPES

Cookie sheet — Preheat oven to 400°

¼ lb. grated American cheese	¼ t. monosodium glutamate
¼ C. deviled ham spread	6 T. flour
2 T. cornstarch	½ t. Worcestershire sauce

Mix all ingredients thoroughly. Pinch off bits and shape into balls ½ inch in diameter. Place on ungreased cookie sheet and flatten with a fork dipped in flour, to about 1½ inches in diameter. Cover with waxed paper. Chill 1 hour. Bake in 400° oven for 10 min.

May be frozen for as long as several weeks before baking.

MRS. ROSS SPEARS

CHOPPED LIVER SPREAD

1 lb. veal liver or chicken livers, cooked with enough water to cover until done. 3 hardboiled eggs. Grate liver and eggs on fine grater.

Melt chicken fat or butter in pan. Add 1 white onion minced fine and cook slowly until done. Add to liver and egg mixture. Add salt and pepper to taste.

Makes a wonderful appetizer. Use on rye bread or thin crackers. Keep spread in refrigerator.

MRS. PHIL SCHARFSTEIN

HORS D'OEUVRES—MEAT BALLS

1½ lb. ground round steak	2 t. salt
½ lb. pork sausage	½ C. beer
1 C. dressing mix or bread crumbs	½ C. chopped onion
2 eggs	1 t. ground ginger

Mix all together. Roll into small balls. Bake on cookie sheets in 425° oven for 10 minutes. Serve hot!

Vary seasoning — add Worcestershire, Tabasco, etc.

MRS. JOHN DILLON
San Francisco, Cal.

BARBECUE OYSTERS

24 selected oysters
Salt and pepper lightly, dredge with flour and broil on lightly buttered grill in 400° oven until crisp and brown on both sides.

Combine:

3 T. melted butter	1 T. Worcestershire sauce
2 t. lemon juice	1 jigger sherry or maderia wine

Heat this mixture in sauce pan over low heat. Place freshly broiled oysters on hot plate and pour over hot sauce.

Serve immediately on frilled toothpicks.

MRS. MALCOLM CAMPBELL

PEANUT BUTTER DIP

Blend together ¾ C. peanut butter, ¾ C. thick dairy sour cream, 5 T. finely chopped sweet pickle, 2 T. vinegar and 3 T. chili sauce.

Fry or broil 5 thin strips of bacon, drain on paper and crumble into the peanut butter mixture.

Add salt as needed. This can be made the day before but let stand at room temperature a while before serving, so it will not be too stiff. Serve with potato chips. Can be used as a dip, but have a couple of small knives for those who want to spread it.

MRS. FORREST MORRIS

SHRIMP DIP

½ lb. (chilled, drained and deveined) shrimp or 1 5-oz can shrimp

1 pt. cottage cheese	½ t. lemon juice
3 T. chili sauce	¼ t. Worcestershire sauce
½ t. onion juice	4 T. milk

Chop shrimp fine. Add cottage cheese, stir in chili sauce, onion, lemon juice and worcestershire sauce. Gradually beat in enough milk for dipping consistency. Serve on crackers.

MRS. CHARLES P. LEWIS
Reidsville, N. C.

PICKLED SHRIMP

BOIL: 2 lbs. shrimp for 10 minutes in water with ½ C. celery tops, 4 t. salt and ¼ C. mixed pickling spices.

Drain shrimp, peel under cold running water and remove vein.

MIX SAUCE: 1¼ C. salad oil, ¾ C. white vinegar, 1½ t. salt, 2½ t. celery seed and dash tabasco. Mix well and pour over shrimp. Add onion rings and 8 bay leaves. Cover and store in refrigerator 24 hours before serving.

MRS. THOMAS J. ELLIS

HOT SHRIMP CANAPES

1 lb. cooked and drained shrimp, broken into small pieces	½ lb. sharp cheese (grated) Red pepper Salt
3 hard boiled eggs	1 T. Worcestershire sauce
1 small bottle olives	

Chop first four ingredients. Mix well and wet with mayonnaise. Spread on rounds of bread. Bake 15 minutes. Serve hot.

MRS. ALLEN HARRIS

BACON WRAPS

1 small jar sharp cheddar cheese (room temperature)

white bread, crusts off
1 lb. bacon, cut in half

Spread several slices of bread with cheese. Cut bread in strips (3). Roll up and then roll in bacon slice, secure with pick. Use until cheese is gone. Bake at 350 about 45 minutes or until golden brown. Serve with hot mustard. They freeze unbaked well. May bake unfrozen also.

Mrs. A. E. Miller

SOUR CREAM BEAN DIP

1 can black bean soup
Scant ¼ soup can water
½ t. cayenne
2 garlic cloves, pressed
1 T. vinegar

1 can bean with bacon soup
1 t. dry mustard
½ t. chili powder
4 or 5 drops tabasco
½ C. sour cream

Heat soup slowly, stirring constantly, adding water gradually. Combine mustard, cayenne, chili powder, garlic, tabasco with vinegar. Stir into sour cream. Then add to soup. Over very low heat, simmer 10 minutes. Cool at room temperature. Then chill. Good served with fritos.

Mrs. Tom Happel

MRS. O. E. POWELL'S CEREAL CANAPES

¼ lb or 1 stick margarine
2 T. Worcestershire sauce
few drops Tabasco sauce
3 cups bite-sized cereal

2 cups broken pretzels
1½ cups nuts
1 t. garlic salt
1 t. seasoned salt (or substitute ¼ cup grated cheese for salts)

Melt the margarine and add the Tabasco and Worcestershire sauce to it. Mix cereal, pretzels, and nuts together in a large, flat baking pan or cookie sheet, and pour margarine mixture over all, stirring to coat each piece. Heat in 300° oven for 30 to 45 minutes, stirring often. Add salts immediately upon removal from oven. This keeps well in a covered container. (NOTE: The amounts of cereal, pretzels, and nuts are not arbitrary. You may add or subtract from each ingredient to suit your own taste, but the entire quantity should be about enough to fill one average- sized cereal box.)

Mrs. James R. MacLean

CHEESE BALL

½ lb. roquefort	1 clove garlic, grated
1 lb. cream cheese	2 T. wine
1 jar very sharp cheese	½ C. chopped nuts
1 jar snappy or smoked cheese	½ C. parsley
	1 T. Worcestershire sauce

Soften cheese by leaving at room temperature for about an hour. Then combine cheeses with Worcestershire sauce, garlic and wine. Mix well. Roll on wax paper and shape into ball. Combine nuts and parsley, and roll cheese ball in it.

Mrs. C. E. Jacobs, Jr.

CHEESE PUFFS

BLEND:	ADD:
2 C. grated sharp cheese	6 T. soft margarine (1-stick)
1 C. flour	1 t. paprika
	½ t. salt

Mix well. Work dough around olives, ham, Vienna Sausage. Freeze-Bake at 425 degrees for 10 to 15 minutes.

Mrs. Mark Hicks

HOT CHILI DIP

2 lbs. loaf Velveeta cheese	1 lb. sharp cheese
2 (small) cans pickled green peppers	1 large onion
	3 T. cooking sherry
	1 large tomato

Grate cheese; grind peppers, onion and tomato. Mix and melt in double boiler. Add sherry 30 minutes before serving. Serve hot (in chafing dish).

Mrs. C. E. Goulding, Jr.

PIZZA APPETIZERS

1 No. 2½ can tomatoes	1 C. cubes sharp cheddar
1 C. dried beef	black pepper

Pour boiling water over beef and drain until dry, then cut into small pieces. Simmer tomatoes about 1 hour slowly until very thick. Add cheese, stir until melted. Season with pepper. Add salt if needed. The dried beef will probably furnish enough salt.

Pile on toast rounds or lightly toasted English muffins and sprinkle with a little grated parmesan cheese. Heat in slow oven and serve hot. Makes about 18 pizza appetizers.

Mrs. W. S. Sells

SWISS SANDWICH PUFFS

16 slices tiny rye bread	2 T. parsley
½ C. mayonnaise	8 slices Swiss cheese
¼ C. finely chopped onion	

Toast bread on both sides. Combine mayonnaise, onion, and parsley; spread on toast. Cut out rounds of cheese to fit toast; place a cheese round on top of each slice, covering mixture. Broil 3 or 4 minutes until cheese is puffy. Trim with olive slice. Serve hot.

Mrs. A. E. Miller

GUACAMOLE (WAC-A-MO-LE)

2 ripe avacados	dash garlic salt
1 small onion	dash Tabasco
½ t. lemon juice	1 small tomato

Peel—then mash avacados into paste. Mix in finely chopped onion. Add lemon juice, tabasco and garlic salt to taste. This makes a rather thick paste which should be refrigerated (under cover) for several hours. Just before serving, dice unpeeled tomato into smallest possible pieces and mix into paste. The resulting dip is extremely tasty with crisp fried tortillas.

Mrs. G. E. Oldham, III

RUM TUM DITTY

1 can tomato soup	1 C. water
2 med. onions (optional)	1 lb. American cheese or
1 t. salt	½ lb. American cheese and
3 eggs	½ lb. Sharp Cheese
1 t. Worcestershire sauce	1 t. paprika
1 t. dry mustard	½ t. white pepper or black

Add water to soup and bring to boiling point. Add onions which have been thinly sliced and let cook about ten minutes or until onions are tender. Add cheese which has been cut in thin slices, stirring constantly until cheese is thoroughly melted. Separate eggs; beat yolks with salt, Worcestershire sauce, paprika, pepper, and mustard. Add seasoned yolks to cheese mixture. Beat egg whites until stiff and fold them into the hot cheese mixture, blending thoroughly. Serve on toast or crackers. May be prepared several hours before needed. Keep warm in a double boiler and reheat thoroughly before serving. Makes a delicious dip hot or cold, using tiny hot franks, small toast rounds, crackers or triscuits.

Mrs. Jackson Trethaway

LIVER PATE'

1½ lbs. calves' liver	1½ C. heavy cream
1 med. onion, chopped (½ C.)	7 slices bacon
1 can anchovey fillets in oil	1 envelope plain gelatin
1 T. salt	1 can consomme
¼ t. ginger	¼ C. cold water
⅛ t. ground cloves	truffles or ripe olives
Dash of cayenne	water cress
	¾ C. flour

Soak liver in cold water to cover, 6 to 8 hours or overnight; wipe dry. Put liver, onion, anchovy fillets, and oil through food chopper, using fine knife; grind 4 or 5 times more or transfer to blender and mix until smooth. Mix in salt, ginger, cloves, cayenne, flour; blend in cream, beat well. Line loaf pan, 9" x 5" x 3", with bacon slices; pour liver mixture carefully into pan; set pan in pan of hot water. Bake in slow oven (275 degrees) 1 hour and 50 minutes or until firm in center. Chill several hours or overnight. Remove thoroughly chilled pate' from pan; discard bacon slices; wash and dry pan. Soften gelatin in cold water; dissolve over hot water; combine with consomme'. Spoon ¼" layer of gelatin mixture into loaf pan; chill until set; arrange cut pieces of truffles or ripe olives on top; cover with 2nd layer of gelatin mixture; chill until set. Place pate' in loaf pan: Carefully spoon remaining gelatin mixture around the sides. Chill until set. When ready to serve, unmold; garnish with watercress. Freezes well.

Mrs. Sidney MacLean

PATE' PINEAPPLE

2 C. (1 lb.) butter	2 lb. chicken livers
2 med. onions, quartered	1 t. curry powder
1 t. paprika	2 T. cognac
¼ t. freshly ground black pepper	1¼ C. sliced pimento stuffed olives

Melt ½ cup butter in a saucepan. Add the chicken livers, onions, curry powder, paprika, salt, and pepper. Cover and cook 8 minutes. Blend the mixture in a blender until smooth. Add cognac and rest of the butter and blend well. Chill. Mold into a pineapple shape. Cover with sliced olives. Cap with a real pineapple top. Yield 5 cups.

Mrs. Norton Beach
Chapel Hill, North Carolina

SHRIMP SPREAD

Cooked cleaned shrimp
(½ to one pound)
3 small pkgs. cream cheese
½ small jar of India relish

1 t. catsup
Tabasco and Worcestershire
sauce to taste

Mash shrimp as fine as possible. Add cream cheese thinned to spreading consistency with evaporated milk. Add relish (you may prefer less than ½ jar)
Add catsup, Tabasco and Worcestershire to taste. Chill well and serve with crisp crackers or chips.

Mrs. Calvin Morgan

SAUSAGE PINWHEELS

2 C. sifted flour
2 t. baking powder
1 t. salt
2 T. shortening

⅔ C. milk (if buttermilk is
preferred, us ¾ C. and add
½ t. soda)
1 lb. sausage

Sift flour, baking powder and salt together in bowl. Add shortening and blend with pastry blender. Add milk, blend lightly until mixed. Turn on floured board. Knead about 20 strokes. Divide dough. Place half on board. Roll ¼ inch thick into a rectangle. Pat ½ lb. sausage on top of dough. Roll dough and sausage like jelly roll. Repeat with other half of dough and sausage. Roll each in waxed paper and refrigerate or freeze until needed. When ready to bake, slice ¼ inch thick with sharp knife. Bake on ungreased cooky sheet at 425 degrees until brown—10 to 12 minutes. Serve hot.

Mrs. Harry D. Miller

ICE BOX CHEESE WAFERS

1 (10 oz.) pkg. extra sharp
cheddar cheese
1 stick butter or margarine
Pinch cayenne and pepper

½ t. salt
2 T. Worcestershire sauce
2 t. chopped chives (optional)
1½ C. flour

Cream cheese, butter, salt, cayenne and Worcestershire. Add flour; mix well. Make into rolls size of quarter, wrap in wax paper and chill. Slice ¼ inch thick and bake in slow oven at 325° until very light brown.

Mrs. Sam W. Mitchell

SKEWERED OYSTERS

2 doz. oysters
24 strips bacon

lemon juice
freshly ground black pepper

Drain oysters and discard liquor. Season with lemon juice and pepper. Wrap each oyster in a strip of bacon & thread on skewer, (or stick with pick) leaving some space between wrapped oysters. Broil under moderate heat turning frequently for 15 minutes or until bacon is crisp and thoroughly cooked or rest skewers on rim of baking pan and bake in 425 degree oven for 15 minutes.

Mrs. A. E. Miller

SHRIMP DIP

1 can of shrimp
½ C. sour cream
1½ t. Worcestershire sauce

2 small pkgs. of Philadelphia
cream cheese
1 medium onion

Grind shrimp and onion; add cheese and seasoning. Serve with potato chips.

Mrs. Charles Hillman

BEVERAGES

FRENCH CHOCOLATE

2½ squares unsweetened chocolate, cut in pieces
½ C. cold water
¾ C. sugar

Dash of salt
½ C. cream, whipped
6 C. hot milk

Cook chocolate with water over direct heat, 4 minutes, stirring constantly. When creamy and smooth, add sugar and salt. Return to fire and cook 4 minutes longer. Cool.

Fold this mixture into whipped cream. Place 1 rounded tablespoon of this mixture in each cup. Pour hot milk over it and stir well. Serves 8. This is very festive and good for get-togethers where sandwiches are served. Guests can enjoy serving themselves.

MRS. R. S. SWAIN

HOT CHOCOLATE

3 squares Baker's chocolate. Add ½ C. cold water. Put into sauce pan over low heat and stir until smooth. Add ½ C. sugar and pinch of salt. Blend and boil five minutes. Flavor with ½ t. good pure vanilla (still better, a small piece of vanilla bean). When cool, fold in ½ C. heavy cream, whipped stiff.

Heat milk and add heaping t. of syrup to each cup. This is good with coffee flavored milk also.

JANE BOWMAN FORT

BUTTERED SPICED HOT CIDER

2 3-inch sticks cinnamon
4 qts. good apple cider

¼ C. brown sugar
3 T. butter

Place stick cinnamon in kettle, add cider and bring almost to boiling point. Do not let the mixture boil! Stir in sugar and when dissolved, add butter. Serve in heated jug. Pour into small mugs or punch cups and sprinkle with powdered nutmeg and cinnamon.

JANE BOWMAN FORT

CIDER ICE

Melt 1 pt. of sugar in 1 qt. of water. When cool, add 3 pts. of bottled cider and a wine-glassful of cognac.

Freeze like ice cream, but when about half-frozen add the whites of 3 eggs that have been beaten to a stiff froth.

L. C. WHITE

MULLED CIDER

½ t. allspice
2 sticks cinnamon
6 whole cloves

1 qt. cider
1/3 C. brown sugar

Tie whole spices in cheesecloth bag. Drop bag into kettle of hot cider with sugar added and let it simmer until cider is spicy enough. Serve in mugs with dash of nutmeg. Serves 6.

MRS. W. E. KIBLER

HOT SPICED CRANBERRY PUNCH

3 C. cranberry juice
1 C. water
½ C. sugar
¾ t. nutmeg

1 1-inch stick cinnamon
6 whole cloves
¼ C. lemon juice
¼ C. orange juice

Combine cranberry juice with the water and sugar. Heat to boiling. Tie spices in bag and add to the juice. Let simmer 20 minutes. Remove spice bag. Just before serving add fruit juices. Serve steaming hot. Garnish with orange and lemon slices, cut very thin. This is enough for 12 cups.

MRS. MAUDE ANDREWS

ICED TEA FOR PUNCH BASE

2 qts. water
2 lemon rinds

1 orange rind
1½ C. sugar

Boil above ingredients for 10 minutes. Strain.

1 C. boiling water

4 heaping t. tea

Let these ingredients stand 5 minutes. Strain.

Combine strained mixtures, cool and add fruit juices. The orange is optional. Other juices may be added for punch base.

MRS. BLAINE SHELL

LEMONADE — SERVES 100

4 C. water
8 C. sugar
7½ C. lemon juice

Sliced lemon rinds
4 gals. water

Boil the 4 C. of water and 8 C. of sugar for 10 minutes. Cool. Add lemon juice, lemon rinds and remaining 4 gallons of water.

MRS. TOMMY GALLAGHER

MOCHA PUNCH

1 C. heavy cream	1 qt. chocolate ice cream,
½ t. almond extract	(vanilla may be used)
1 qt. cold strong coffee	Pinch of salt
	Dash of nutmeg

Whip cream and add flavoring. In a three quart punch bowl, blend coffee and half of ice cream. Fold in whipped cream and remaining ice cream. Dust with ntumeg. Serves 12.

MRS. KENNETH SCHOLL

SPRING WINE

1 pkg. lemon-lime Kool-Ade	1 tall can pineapple juice
1 C. sugar	1 or 2 trays of ice

Mix together and serve ice cold.

MRS. TOMMY GALLAGHER

WEDDING PUNCH — SERVES 100

Juice of 2 doz. oranges	2 qts. water
Juice of 2 doz. lemons	4 C. sugar
2 large bottles ginger ale	

2 large cans crushed pineapple	½ gal. peach ice cream (or
1 large jar red cherries	any kind of sherbet)
½ gal. vanilla ice cream	50 lbs. crushed ice

Boil water and sugar and let cool.

Mix juices of lemons and oranges with sugar mixture (this can be done the night before). Add crushed pineapple, cherries (cut in half, if desired), ginger ale to first mixture and stir well. About ½ hour before serving, add ice cream and stir well. Just before serving, add some crushed ice. Keep plenty of ice in mixture as it is much better ICE COLD.

MRS. MADGE M. LEWIS

WINE PUNCH

1½ C. raisins (if desired)
4 C. water
2 C. sugar
1 T. grated lemon rind

2 C. fresh or frozen lemon juice
2 C. (1 pt.) red wine

In a covered saucepan, cook the raisins and water for 20 minutes. Strain and reserve liquid, discarding the raisins. Stir the sugar and lemon rind into the liquid; boil for five minutes. Cool. Add the fruit juices and wine (use a good tasty red wine). Serve over ice cubes. Garnish with thinly sliced orange slices.

AUGUSTA O. WOLFF

HOT PARTY TEA

Make tea of 4 C. water and 6 t. of tea
Boil 2 C. water and 2 C. sugar. Remove from heat and add **1 t. whole cloves** and **1 stick of cinnamon.** Let stand for 20 minutes and then strain the mixture.

Squeeze and strain 4 lemons and 6 oranges. Add 1 large can of pineapple juice. Place in a glass or enamelware pan.
Mix tea, sugar, water and juice and heat, but do not boil. Keep on low heat to keep warm.

MRS. HARRY GASTEIGER

RUSSIAN TEA —SERVES 20

1 C. sugar
¼ C. tea leaves (or
    6 tea bags)
5 sticks cinnamon
2 t. whole cloves
4 pieces ginger root

1 gal. water
3 C. orange juice (1 can
    frozen orange juice)
½ C. lemon juice
Any other fruit juices

Place spices and sugar in ½ gallon water — boil for 5 minutes; simmer for 30 minutes. Make tea with remainder of water. Strain spice solution, mix with fruit juices and tea. Serve hot.

MRS. DALE CORNETT

CHILDREN'S PUNCH

2 C. sugar
1 carton of 7-up
(regular size)
1 large can pineapple
and grapefruit juice

4 C. water
2 pkg. lemon — lime koolade

Mix and serve.

Mrs. William Blackard

DESSERT DRINK

1 pt. vanilla ice cream
2 jiggers Brandy

1 jigger creme de menthe

Mix in blender and serve in champagne glasses in living room after dinner for dessert.

Mrs. Al Costner

WHISKEY SOUR PUNCH

1 (6 oz.) can frozen orange
juice
1 qt. sparkling water or
ginger ale

1 (6 oz.) can frozen lemonade
½ C. maraschino cherry juice
1 fifth bourbon

Mix orange juice and lemonade with water according to directions on the can. Pour this, cherry juice, sparkling water and bourbon over a block of ice in a punch bowl. Garnish with cherries and orange slices. Serves 15-20.

Mrs. Bill Stevens

INSTANT RUSSIAN (OR SPICED) TEA

2 C. Tang
1 (10 oz. pkg.) lemonade
(dry mix)
½ C. instant tea

1¼ C. sugar
1½ t. cinnamon
½ t. ground cloves

Combine and place in air tight jar or other container. Use 1 to 3 tsp. per cup of boiling water according to taste.

Mrs. E. C. Sellers

MOCK WHISKEY SOUR

1 small can frozen lemonade
1 can light rum

1 can dark rum
1 can bourbon

Serve over crushed ice. Use lemonade can for measuring rum and bourbon.

Allen Harris, Jr.

BREADS

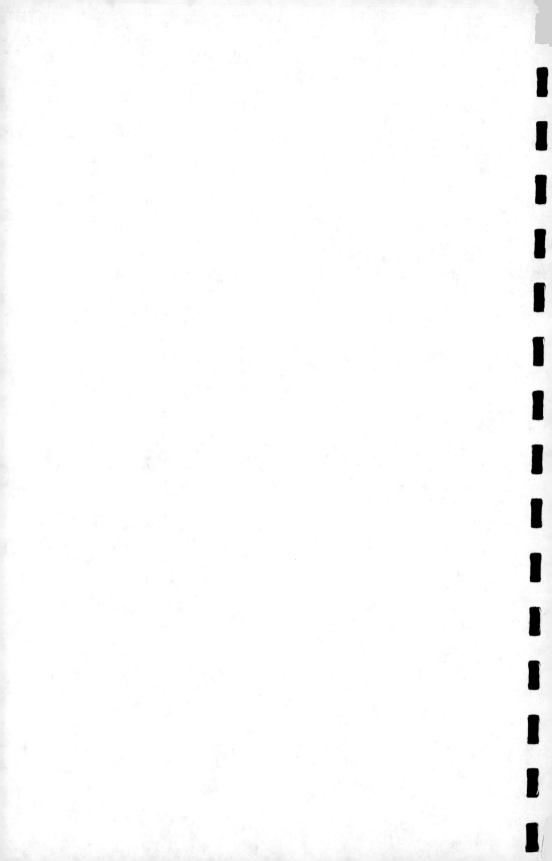

RICE BATTERBREAD

4 eggs	1 t. baking powder
1 teacup cooked rice	1 t. salt
4 T. corn meal	1 T. melted butter
1 pt. milk	

Beat eggs separately. Mix egg yolks with other ingredients. Fold in beaten egg whites. Bake in greased casserole for 30 to 40 minutes at 425° F. or 450°F. Good and rather like a rice pudding.

MRS. PRESTON W. CAMPBELL
Abingdon, Va.

CHEESE BISCUITS

½ lb. sharp grated cheese	Dash salt
2 C. flour	2 drops Tabasco
½ lb. butter	Dash paprika

Cream butter and work in grated cheese. Add flour and seasonings and work together with hands. Let stay in icebox over night. Roll out and cut. Roll in powdered sugar and put nut on top.

MRS. B. W. HARRIS, JR.
Durham, N. C.

CHEESE BISCUITS

½ lb. butter	2 C. flour
½ lb. sharp cheese	

Cream butter and cheese together and add flour. Roll thin and cut with small biscuit cutter. Sprinkle with crushed almonds. Bake in moderate oven until light brown (golden). Sprinkle with powdered sugar when cool. Rated very good and easy.

MRS. GEORGE DOUGHTY

WHOLE WHEAT BISCUITS

1½ C. whole wheat flour	3 t. baking powder
1¼ C. white flour	6 T. shortening
1¼ C. milk	1 t. salt

Sift white flour. Measure and sift with baking powder and salt. Add whole wheat flour; cut in shortening; add milk; stir until blended. Drop by teaspoonfuls on to well oiled baking sheet. Bake at 450° for 12 - 15 minutes.

MRS. RENO BURLESON

YEAST BISCUITS

Cook one medium sized potato in 2½ C. water. Run potato and water through strainer, let cool and add:

1 cake yeast	½ C. shortening
1 egg	1 t. salt
¼ C. sugar	5 C. flour

Put in large bowl and keep in refrigerator, taking out enough dough each time to make the number of biscuits desired. Brush with melted butter and let rise one hour before baking at 450°F. Good—like rolls.

MRS. W. P. GOVER, SR.

EASY BANANA BREAD

2 C. flour
3 t. baking powder
½ t. salt
1 C. chopped pecans
½ C. shortening

1 C. sugar
2 eggs, beaten
1 C. mashed bananas
1 t. lemon juice

Sift dry ingredients. Add nuts. Cream shortening and sugar and add eggs, bananas and lemon juice. Bake at 350° about 50 minutes.

MRS. TOMMY MILLER

BANANA NUT BREAD

2 C. flour
1 t. soda
½ t. salt
½ C. shortening
¼ C. chopped nut meats

1 t. vanilla
1 C. sugar
2 eggs
3 bananas, medium size

Sift together flour, soda and salt. Blend together shortening and vanilla. Gradually add sugar, creaming until light and fluffy. Add eggs, one at a time, beating well after each addition. Mash bananas, add alternately with dry ingredients. Add nut meats. Pour into greased loaf pan. Bake at 325° for 1 hour and 15 minutes.

MRS. FRANK LOWRY

BISHOP'S BREAD

1 C. butter
2 C. brown sugar
1 egg
¾ C. sour milk
2½ C. flour

1 t. salt
1 t. cinnamon
1 t. baking powder
½ t. soda

Mix sugar and butter and divide in half. Add egg to half of creamed butter mixture. Mix dry ingredients and add alternately with milk to butter and egg mixture. Spread in loaf pan. Crumble other half of sugar and butter over top of cake and bake at 300°F. for 30 minutes.

MRS. C. T. HERNDON, III

BOSTON BROWN BREAD

2 C. white flour, sifted
2 C. corn meal
2 C. graham flour
2 t. salt

2 C. molasses
2 C. buttermilk
2 t. soda
2 or 3 T. shortening, melted

Mix all dry ingredients except soda, which is added to buttermilk. Combine dry ingredients and liquids. Melt shortening in cans and then put most of it in batter. Fill cans with batter three-fourths full. Put lids on and place in steamer or pan of hot water. Steam 3½ to 4 hours. Add raisins if desired.

MRS. BURR HARRISON

BOSTON BROWN BREAD

3 C. graham flour
1 t. baking powder, rounded
1 t. soda, rounded
1 C. raisins
½ C. brown sugar, packed

2 C. buttermilk
1 C. white meal
1 egg
¾ C. molasses

In large bowl mix flour, meal, soda, baking powder and raisins. In small bowl beat egg, add brown sugar, molasses and milk. Pour liquid into dry ingredients and mix quickly. Grease coffee cans (1 lb. size), pour batter into them and cover tightly with lids. Steam in boiling water 1½ to 2 hours.

MRS. RUSSELL BARRINGER
Durham, N. C.

APPLE BUTTER BRAN BREAD

1 C. All-Bran
1½ C. apple butter
1 t. lemon juice
¼ C. shortening
½ C. sugar
1 egg

1½ C. flour
½ t. baking powder
½ t. soda
½ C. seedless raisins
½ C. nuts (if desired)

Combine bran, apple butter and lemon juice. Let stand 5 minutes. Cream shortening and sugar. Add bran mixture, then add flour with salt, baking powder and soda. Stir until dry ingredients are moistened but not smooth. Add raisins. Put in loaf pan lined with waxed paper. Bake at 325°F. for 1 hour.

MRS. E. H. SILER

BANANA BRAN BREAD

¼ C. shortening

½ C. sugar

Cream together and add following:

1 egg
1 C. All-Bran
1½ C. mashed bananas
1 t. vanilla
1½ C. flour

2 t. baking powder
½ t. salt
½ t. soda
½ C. nuts

Bake in greased loaf pan at 350°F. for 1 hour.

MRS. FRANK EDMONDS

CHEERIE CHERRY BREAD

1 C. sugar
2 eggs, beaten
1½ C. flour
1½ t. baking powder
¼ t. salt

¾ C. nut meats, chopped
1 6-oz. glass red maraschino
cherries, quartered
Juice from cherries

1. Beat sugar and eggs together.
2. Sift flour. Measure. Sift with baking powder and salt.
3. Add nuts and cherries. Alternately add flour and cherry juice.
   Use part green cherries for a Christmas bread.
4. Bake for 1 hour at 350°F. in 1-lb. loaf pan.

MRS. ALICE FRIBERG

DATE BREAD

1 8-oz. pkg. dates, chopped	2 t. soda
1½ C. boiling water poured	2¾ C. flour
over dates	½ t. salt
1 T. butter	1 t. vanilla
1 C. sugar	1 C. nuts
1 egg, well beaten	

Bake in loaf pan in moderate oven for 45 minutes.

MRS. BURR HARRISON

DATE BREAD

1 8-oz. pkg. dates, pitted	1 lump butter, size of egg
1 C. sugar	1 C. hot coffee
1 C. nuts	2 C. flour
1 t. soda	Dash salt
1 egg	

Pour coffee over dates. Add soda and cool. Alternately add flour and other ingredients. Line loaf pan with waxed paper. Bake at 350°F. 50 to 60 minutes.

MRS. JOHN WILSON

PRUNE NUT BREAD

¼ C. shortening	1 t. baking powder
¾ C. sugar	¼ t. soda
2 eggs, beaten	¼ C. buttermilk
½ t. cinnamon	¼ C. cream
½ t. nutmeg	½ t. vanilla
½ t. allspice	½ C. chopped nuts
1¼ C. flour	½ C. chopped, cooked prunes
½ t. salt	

Cream thoroughly shortening and sugar. Add beaten eggs and beat well. Sift all dry ingredients together. Add to sugar mixture alternately with the milk, cream and vanilla, which have been stirred together. Then stir in nuts and prunes. Pour in greased 5"x9" loaf pan and bake in 350°F. oven for 50 to 60 minutes.

MRS. ROBERT N. DOSSER

SALLY LUNN HOT BREAD
(Over 100 Years Old)

4 eggs	3 T. sugar
1 C. butter, melted	¼ C. warm water
1 yeast cake	4 C. sifted flour
1 t. salt	1 C. milk

Soak yeast in luke warm water. Beat eggs well — until light in color. Add milk and butter (after milk has been heated to lukewarm temperature). Add sugar, salt, yeast and flour. Pour in bowl and let double in size. Beat well and pour in oiled angel food cake pan and allow 1¼ hours to rise. Bake 40 minutes at 350°F. Serve hot.

MRS. LEWIS COSBY

SPOON BREAD

2 C. yellow corn meal	2 eggs
1½ t. salt	1 t. soda
2 C. boiling water	2 C. buttermilk
1 T. drippings or butter	

Sift meal and salt together into mixing bowl. Add water and make stiff dough. Stir in drippings and beaten egg yolks. Combine soda and buttermilk; add to meal mixture, stirring until smooth. Fold in stiffly beaten egg whites. Pour into hot, greased baking dish and bake in 400°F. oven for 40 minutes.

MRS. ALFRED W. JONES

VIRGINIA SPOON BREAD

1 pt. milk	1 large lump butter
1 C. corn meal, sifted	3 or 4 eggs
½ t. salt	

Warm milk and add meal, stirring constantly and cooking until it makes a mush. Remove from stove. Add salt and butter. Add egg yolks and stir. Fold in stiffly beaten egg whites. Put in greased casserole and bake in moderate oven for 40 minutes.

MRS. E. T. WEST

SWEDISH COFFEE BREAD

2 C. warm water	24 cardamon seeds, finely
1 C. sugar	crushed
2/3 C. powdered dry milk	2 yeast cakes
1 t. salt	

Mix above ingredients together.

Crumble yeast into mixture, stir, and then add:

2 eggs	6½ C. flour
½ C. shortening	

Knead. Let rise twice. After second rising, knead again. Then divide dough into two equal parts. Divide each part into three. Roll each into rope shape and braid. Place in 14"x10½" pan. Let rise about 30 minutes. Bake in 350°F. oven 40 minutes. After first 15 minutes brush tops with milk and sprinkle with sugar.

NOTE: Cardamon seeds come in pods. Remove the seeds from the pod and crush finely before adding. This recipe calls for 24 of the seed pods. Powdered Cardamon can be used but it does not give the flavor that freshly crushed seeds will give.

MRS. EDGAR STOHLER

POTATO BUNS

1 cake yeast	½ C. mashed potatoes
1 T. sugar	4½ C. sifted flour
1 C. milk, scalded and cooled	½ C. shortening
1 C. sugar	1 egg

Dissolve yeast and sugar in lukewarm liquid, add potatoes and 2 cups sifted flour. Stir well; let rise about ½ hour. Add shortening, sugar and egg creamed together, and about 2½ C. sifted flour, or enough to make dough that can be handled. Cover, let rise 2 hours, or until dough has doubled in bulk. Form into buns, place in well-greased pans and let rise about 1½ hours. When light, bake for 25 minutes in 425°F. oven.

MRS. J. L. WOOD

HUNGARIAN BUTTER HORNS

1 cake yeast, crumbled	½ t. salt
4 C. flour	1 C. butter

Mix like pie crust and add:

3 egg yolks, beaten	1 t. vanilla
½ C. sour cream	

Mix thoroughly. Divide dough into 6 parts. Roll each part like pie crust and divide into 8 wedges, using confectionary sugar on the board. Filling: Beat 3 egg whites very stiff and add 1 C. sugar. Fold in ¼ lb. chopped nuts (walnuts have more flavor).

Spread 1 t. filling on each wedge. Roll like butter horn and begin rolling from wide end. Place on greased cookie sheet and bake at 375°F. for 20 minutes.

MRS. M. A. BITZER

BUCKWHEAT CAKES

1 cake yeast	2 C. water
½ C. warm water	1 t. soda
2 C. buckwheat flour	2 T. molasses
1 C. corn meal	4 T. milk
1 t. salt	

Dissolve yeast cake in warm water. Sift flour, corn meal and salt. Add dissolved yeast and 2 C. water. Let stand in warm room for 2 hours, then add soda, molasses and milk. Stir well. Keep in cool place. Cook on slightly greased griddle.

MRS. GEORGE BRANDT

OVERNIGHT BUCKWHEAT CAKES

2 C. buckwheat flour	1 C. white flour

Sift together

3 t. salt	½ cake yeast
1/3 C. sugar	1 qt. warm water

Dissolve yeast in warm water. Add all other ingredients to make batter. Add ½ C. bacon drippings. Set at room temperature for 1 hour. Put in refrigerator overnight. Add small amount of soda to portion to be used next morning to leaven sourness of yeast. Fry on hot griddle. Serve with whipped butter if you like.

MRS. W. D. GRINDSTAFF

COWBOY COFFEE CAKE

2 C. brown sugar	½ t. soda
2½ C. flour	½ t. cinnamon
½ t. salt	½ t. nutmeg
2/3 C. shortening	1 C. sour milk
2 t. baking powder	2 eggs, well beaten

Combine sugar, flour, salt and shortening. Mix as a pie dough, with blender, until mixture is consistency of coarse meal. Reserve ½ C. to sprinkle over batter. Add baking powder, soda, cinnamon and nutmeg and mix thoroughly. Add milk and eggs. Pour into greased pan and sprinkle with crumbs (chopped nuts and cinnamon if desired). Bake at 375°F. for 25 to 30 minutes.

MRS. WALTER HAMMOND WILEY

"CUTCHA" COFFEE CAKE

8 C. flour	1 egg
2 cakes yeast	2 C. milk
4T. warm water	1 T. salt
½ C. sugar	½ C. shortening

Scald milk; add shortening, salt and sugar. Cool. Add yeast which has been dissolved in warm water. Then add well beaten egg and flour. Mix and knead well. Roll out in a sheet. Spread with shortening, sugar and cinnamon. Roll up like jelly roll and twist around tube in angel cake pan. Let rise double in size. Bake in 300°F. oven for 1 hour. Makes two coffee cakes.

MRS. IVA BIDDLE

QUICK COFFEE CAKE

2½ C. flour	1 T. butter, melted
2 t. baking powder	1 or 2 eggs
1 t. salt	1¼ C. milk
3 T. sugar	

Sift flour, baking powder, salt and sugar. Then add melted butter and milk. Beat eggs and add; mix together to a soft dough. Flavor with a little nutmeg. Raisins may be added.

Put in a well greased pan and sprinkle with sugar and cinnamon, or use sliced peaches or apples. Bake in moderate oven (350°F.) about 25 minutes.

MRS. LEE G. COCHRAN

FLAWLESS CORN BREAD

1 egg	½ t. salt
1 C. buttermilk or sour milk	1 t. baking powder
1 C. cornmeal	½ t. soda
1 T. melted shortening	½ C. flour

Mix and put in greased pan. Bake at 400°F. about 30 minutes.

MRS. LORA DAVIS

CORN CAKES

1 egg, separated	1 handful flour
1 pt. sour milk	2 C. cornmeal
1 t. soda	Dash of salt

Mix soda and milk and add to beaten egg yolk. Add remainder of ingredients. Fold in stiffly beaten egg white. Fry on hot griddle.

MRS. J. H. WINSTON

CORN MEAL SHELLS

1 C. flour, sifted	¼ C. shortening
3 T. corn meal	3 to 4 T. ice water
1 t. celery salt	

Combine flour, meal and celery salt. Cut in shortening. Add only enough water to make mixture hold together. Roll thin and cut in circles. Shape over back of custard cups. Prick with fork and bake in hot oven (425°F.) for 15 to 20 minutes. Makes 6 shells. Delicious filled with your favorite creamed tuna or chicken.

MRS. J. R. WOLFF

CORN STICKS

1 egg, well beaten	1 T. sugar
1 C. milk	1 t. baking powder
1 T. cream	1 C. white corn meal
1 T. Wesson Oil	

Mix well. Bake in 450°F. oven. Have pan piping hot when batter is dropped in.

MRS. J. R. SIMMONDS

DANISH RINGS

½ C. butter	1 t. baking powder
½ C. sugar	1 t. vanilla
3 egg yolks	1 T. cream
2 C. flour	

Mix ingredients like a butter cake and after working thoroughly, roll out like a pencil. Cut in 2″ or 3″ lengths to form rings. Dip first in melted butter, then a mixture of sugar and cinnamon. Bake at 325°F. until golden brown.

MRS. VIRGIL (NANCY SMATHERS) HARTLEY
Atlanta, Ga.

DOUGHNUTS

Sift together:

2 C. flour	**1 t. salt**
¼ C. sugar	**1 t. nutmeg**
3 t. baking powder	

Add at one time:

¼ C. Wesson Oil	**1 egg**
¾ C. milk	

Stir with fork and drop by teaspoonfuls into hot fat (375°F). Cook approximately 3 minutes. Drain and shake into a bag of sugar and cinnamon.

MRS. OWEN CRUTCHER

DANISH DOUGHNUTS

6 egg yolks	**1 t. brandy**
2 whole eggs	**3 C. flour**
1 C. sugar	**2 t. baking powder**
6 T. cream	**½ t. cardamon seed**
1 t. butter, melted	

Beat eggs very well; add sugar and other ingredients. Roll **thin** on floured board and cut in 1½" wide by 3" long strips. Twist and drop in deep fat. Turn and brown. Place on brown paper when done and sprinkle with powdered sugar.

MRS. JOHN WILSON

MATZOS DUMPLINGS

2 T. chicken fat or butter	**meal can be used)**
1 egg, sligtly beaten	**1 C. boiling water**
1 t. salt	**Pepper and nutmeg to taste**
1 C. matzos meal (corn	**½ t. chopped parsley**

Pour boiling water over meal and stir until water is absorbed. Add fat, then egg and seasoning. Mix well. When cool, place in refrigerator for 1 hour or longer. Roll dough into balls the size of a walnut. If sticky, grease palms of hands or moisten with cold water occasionally. Drop into boiling soup 15 minutes before serving. Boil gently uncovered.

MRS. JACK BROAD

COTTAGE CHEESE FRITTERS

1. Sift together:

1 C. flour	**2 t. baking powder**	**½ t. salt**

2. Cut in **1 T. butter or margarine**
3. Combine:

1 egg, beaten	**1 C. cottage cheese**	**¼ C. milk**

4. Add dry ingredients to egg mixture.
5. Heat shortening in deep fryer to 375°F.
6. Drop batter from teaspoon into hot shortening.
7. Fry until golden brown 2 to 4 min. Serve with honey or maple syrup.

MRS. RAY SMITHEY

CORNMEAL GRIDDLE CAKES

½ C. cornmeal	1 T. molasses
2 T. shortening	1 C. flour
1 C. boiling water	1 t. salt
½ C. milk	3 t. baking powder
2 eggs	

Combine cornmeal and shortening; scald with boiling water. Cover and let stand 5 minutes. Add milk and when cool, add eggs, molasses and then beat in flour, salt and baking powder. If batter seems thin, more flour may be added.

MRS. WILBUR KENNEDY

HUSH PUPPIES

2 C. white cornmeal	½ t. soda
2 t. baking powder	1 egg
1 t. salt	½ C. minced onion
1 C. buttermilk	

Mix first three ingredients in bowl. Add soda to buttermilk. Stir into dry ingredients. Add whole egg and beat well. Lastly, stir in finely chopped onion. Drop by teaspoonfuls into hot oil and cook to golden brown.

MRS. W. T. WOOD

QUICK LIGHT BREAD

2 C. milk	2 C. lukewarm water
5 T. sugar	12 - 13 C. flour
2 T. salt	5 T. shortening, melted
2 yeast cakes	

Scald milk, add sugar and salt. Cool to lukewarm. Add yeast dissolved in lukewarm water. Add half the flour and beat until smooth. Add melted shortening and remaining flour. Place dough in greased bowl and set in warm place until double in bulk. Divide and shape into 4 loaves in greased bread pans. Let rise again and bake at 375°F. until brown on top — 30 to 40 minutes.

MRS. DON SNYDER

BLUEBERRY (HUCKLEBERRY) MUFFINS

4 T. shortening	1 egg
4 t. baking powder	2 C. flour
4 T. sugar	½ C. berries
½ t. salt	¾ to 1 C. milk

Blend shortening, sugar and eggs. Mix 1½ C. flour, baking powder and salt, and add alternately with the milk to first mixture. Mix lightly. Dredge berries with ½ C. flour and stir in gently. Bake in greased muffin pans in hot oven (400°F.) for 25 to 30 mins. Makes 12 muffins.

MRS. EARL MILLER

EXTRA GOOD CORNMEAL MUFFINS

2/3 C. corn meal
1 1/3 C. flour
Sift together

3 t. baking powder
½ t. salt

2 eggs, beaten
2/3 C. milk
Mix

1/3 C. maple syrup
½ C. shortening, melted

Add liquid mixture to dry ingredients. Stir (not beat) to mix well. Bake about 30 minutes at 400°F. Serve hot.

MRS. FRED BROWN

HOTEL PEABODY VANILLA MUFFINS

1 lb. flour (4 C.)
¾ lb. sugar (2 C.)
1 pt. sweet milk (2 C.)
4 eggs

1 T. vanilla
1 T. baking powder
4 oz. melted butter
(1 stick)

Beat sugar and eggs together. Add flour, milk, baking powder, butter and vanilla. Mix thoroughly and bake in hot muffin pans, well greased. Makes 36 muffins. Bake at 350° for 15 or 20 minutes. Good basic muffin for marmalade filling, nuts, blueberries, etc. Would make a good muffin for strawberry shortcake.

MRS. C. R. SMATHERS

FEATHERWEIGHT PANCAKES

3 eggs, separated
¼ t. salt

¼ C. flour
¾ C. cottage cheese

Heat griddle slowly. Beat egg whites until stiff. Beat egg yolks until lemon colored. Stir in salt, flour and cheese. Fold in whites. Drop by spoonfuls on lightly greased griddle. Bake until golden brown on both sides. Serve with butter and maple syrup.

MRS. FRANK ERB

RAW POTATO PANCAKES

4 medium potatoes, grated
4 T. canned milk
4 T. flour

1 egg
Salt and pepper to taste

Fry in ¼" of hot shortening. Serve with sour cream. This can serve as a substitute for bread or French fries.

MRS. D. M. CHAMBERS, JR.

SCANDINAVIAN PANCAKES

3 eggs
1 C. buttermilk
2 T. butter, melted
1 C. flour

1 T. sugar
⅛ t. salt
1 t. baking powder
¼ t. baking soda

Beat eggs, add buttermilk and continue beating. Then add cooled melted butter. Sift all dry ingredients into liquid mixture and beat only until thoroughly mixed. Fry on hot greased griddle. About 1 T. of mixture will make the dollar sized pancakes for which Scandinavians are noted.

MRS. ORLAND OLSEN

POPOVERS

3 eggs
½ t. salt
1 t. sugar
1 C. flour

1 C. milk
2 t. salad oil or melted
    shortening

Directions are given here for making popovers in the electric mixer, although this same recipe can be used for making them by hand. Before starting to make popovers, put greased muffin tins or custard cups into a very hot oven (450°F.) and heat until they are sizzling hot. Beat eggs at medium speed a few minutes until frothy. Now add salt, sugar, flour and half the milk and mix again at medium speed until smooth. Then add remaining milk and salad oil or melted shortening and beat at low speed just until blended. Pour batter into hot muffin tins or custard cups, filling each about half full. Bake in 450°F. oven for 15 minutes. Reduce heat to 400°F. and continue baking for 15 minutes longer. Do not open oven while baking. Makes 12 popovers.

SENA TATE

ROLLS

¼ C. shortening
1½ C. buttermilk
¼ C. sugar
1 t. salt

1 yeast cake
½ t. soda
3 C. flour

Gradually warm buttermilk and add shortening, sugar and salt. Then add yeast cake. Sift soda and flour together and stir into buttermilk mixture. Cover and let rise until double in bulk. Make out into rolls and let rise again 1 hour. Bake 15 minutes at 450°F. Yields 3 dozen rolls. Rolls may be frozen before last rising.

MRS. TOLBERT KITTS, JR.

ROLLS OR HOMEMADE BREAD

1 C. boiling water
1 C. shortening
½ C. sugar
2 t. salt

1 yeast cake, dissolved in 1 C.
    cool water
2 eggs, beaten
6 C. flour

Pour water over shortening, sugar and salt. Let cool. Add yeast mixture and eggs. Stir together and add flour. Mix well and place in refrigerator at least 6 hours. This dough will keep for 2 or 3 days. Make out rolls and let rise 1½ or 2 hours before baking. Or make out 2 loaves of bread and let rise 3 hour, or until double in size. Bake at 400°F. for 10 minutes. Reduce heat to 350°F. for additional 30 min.

MRS. ALFRED ABERNETHY

BRAN ROLLS

½ C. boiling water
½ C. shortening
½ C. bran
3 T. sugar
¾ t. salt

Combine, cool and add:
½ C. water with 1 yeast cake
1 egg
3 C. flour

Place in refrigerator up to 24 hours. When you make out rolls, let rise for at least 1½ hours. Bake at 400 to 450° F. for 30 minutes.

MRS. KENNETH MATTHEWS

ALL - BRAN ROLLS

Combine the following ingredients:

½ C. All - Bran	3 T. sugar
½ C. boiling water	1½ t. salt

Mix and add to above ingredients:

1 yeast cake, dissolved in ¼ C. warm water	½ C. shortening
	½ C. warm water

Add:

1 egg, beaten	3½ C. flour

Do not make dough too stiff. Let rise; turn out and roll lightly. Cut out rolls. Let rise and bake at 425°F. Can be kept in refrigerator a week.

MRS. L. E. MITCHELL

ICE BOX ROLLS OR BREAD

Mix and let stand 20 min:

2/3 C. warm water	1 yeast cake
1 t. sugar	

Cream the following:

2/3 C. sugar	2 eggs, beaten
¾ C. Crisco	

Combine above mixtures and add:

2 C. warm water	8 C. flour
2 t. salt	

Work into dough. Let rise overnite in refrigerator. Make into rolls or loaves and let rise in warm place 2 or 3 hrs. Bake at 400° till brown. Makes 75 rolls or 3 loaves.

Mrs. Frances Carr

QUICK CHEESE ROLLS

¾ C. milk, scalded	½ T. salt
1 T. sugar	3 T. shortening

Combine and cool

1 cake yeast	2 C. flour
½ C. cooking cheese	

Add yeast to cooled mixture and stir until dissolved. Add cheese and 1 C. flour. Beat smooth with beater. Add one more cup flour, or enough to make soft dough. Brush dough and inside of bowl with salad oil. Let rise in warm place (80° to 85°F.) until double in size, or about 30 minutes. Toss on floured board and cut into 10 equal pieces. Place in greased muffin pans and let rise about 10 minutes. Bake at 450°F. about 15 minutes.

MRS. ELMER LUCAS

REFRIGERATOR ROLLS

1 cake yeast
½ C. lukewarm water
2/3 C. shortening
½ C. sugar
1 t. salt

1 C. mashed potatoes
1 C. scalded milk
2 egg whites
6 to 8 C. flour

Thoroughly mash hot potatoes; add shortening, sugar, salt, and cream well. Beat egg whites until stiff and fold into the creamed mixture. Dissolve yeast in lukewarm water; add to lukewarm milk and then add to potato mixture. Add sifted flour to make a dough. Toss on floured board and knead. Put into large bowl and let rise until double in bulk. Knead slightly. Shape into rolls as desired, or cover tightly and place in refrigerator until ready to bake. About 1 hour before baking time, pinch off dough and shape into rolls as desired. Cover and let rise until light. Bake at 400°F. for 15 to 20 minutes.

ADA HORNSBY EARNEST

WAFFLES

1 C. buttermilk
½ C. cold water
2 C. flour
½ C. melted butter or
    salad oil
1 T. sugar

1 egg
1 t. salt
4 t. baking powder
½ t. soda dissolved in
1 T. cold water

Beat egg and add milk, melted butter or oil, salt and flour. Thin batter with half cup water. When ready to bake, add soda and sift in baking powder. Mix thoroughly and pour into pitcher. Do not beat any more. Pour in center of hot waffle iron until half full. Spread batter and close iron. Bake until crisp and golden brown.

MRS. ADAM BOWMAN

CORN MEAL WAFFLES

1 egg
1 C. buttermilk
1 C. corn meal
1 C. flour
¼ C. boiling water

½ t. soda
1 T. sugar
3 T. salad oil
½ t. salt

Mix corn meal and hot water. Beat egg. Sift dry ingredients and alternately add dry ingredients and liquids to corn meal and water. Pour on pre-heated waffle irons. Bake until golden brown.

MRS. FERDINAND POWELL, JR.

FLUFFY WAFFLES

3 eggs
2¼ C. milk
3 C. flour

6 t. baking powder
½ t. salt
9 T. shortening, melted

Separate eggs; beat egg yolks until light; add milk. Sift flour and measure. Add baking powder, salt and sift this mixture into milk mixture. Add melted shortening and fold in stiffly beaten egg whites. For variety add chopped nuts, chips of bacon, etc.

MRS. ALFRED COSTNER

BISCUIT ROLLS—MAKES 6

1 C. self-rising flour   ½ C. milk
2 T. mayonnaise

Mix all ingredients. Grease and fill muffin tins ½ full. Bake 30 minutes at 350 degrees.   Mrs. Bill Lancaster

BRAN MUFFINS BY THE PAIL FULL

4 C. All Bran   1 C. shortening
2 C. 100% Bran   4 eggs
1 t. salt   5 C. pre-sifted flour
2 C. boiling water   5 t. soda
1 qt. buttermilk   3 cups sugar

Combine Brans and salt. Stir in water and then buttermilk. Cool to lukewarm. Cream sugar and shortening; add eggs, one at a time, beating well after each addition. Stir into Bran mixture. Combine flour and soda. Add to Bran mixture and stir to just dampen dry ingredients. Store in refrigerator until ready to use. TO BAKE: Fill greased muffin tins 2/3 full and bake 20-25 minutes, in pre-heated 375° oven. If desired, add dates, raisins or blueberries just before baking. Makes 72 muffins.   Mrs. Dudley Evans

BUTTER DIPS

⅓ C. butter   3½ t. baking powder
2¼ C. flour   1½ t. salt
1 T. sugar   1 C. milk

Heat oven to 450°. Melt butter in oven, removing pan as soon as butter is melted. Sift flour and other dry ingredients. Add milk, turning slowly with a fork until dough just clings together. Knead lightly. Roll out ½" thick and cut ½" lengthwise, then crosswise into 16 strips. Dip each strip in the butter and bake 15-20 minutes and serve hot.

Mrs. Charles Smith

CHEESE PUFF

8 slices bread, trimmed and   ½ lb. cheese, grated (2 cups)
   buttered on both sides   3 eggs
2 C. milk   pepper, paprika, dry mustard,
½ t. salt   if desired

Fit four bread slices into the bottom of a greased baking dish. Sprinkle with half the cheese and cover with remaining bread. Beat eggs, add milk and seasonings, pour over the bread and cheese mixture, and cover with the remaining cheese. Set baking dish in a pan of hot water and bake in a moderate oven (350°) for about 40 minutes or until the custard is set and the bread is puffed up.   Mrs. Bill Stevens

CORN PONES

COMBINE:

1 C. corn meal	1 t. salt
1 T. of bacon drippings	

BOIL:

1 C. water

Pour water over the dry ingredients. Beat until blended. Drop the batter from a spoon onto a greased sheet. Bake in 450° oven for 25 minutes then put under broiler a few seconds to brown.

Mrs. Burgin Dossett, Jr.

SPIDER CORN BREAD

1 C. sifted all purpose flour	⅔ C. yellow corn meal
1 T. granulated sugar	¼ C. shortening (butter or
2 t. baking powder	bacon grease)
1 t. salt	2 eggs
½ t. baking soda	1 C. buttermilk

Into bowl, sift together flour, sugar, baking powder, salt and soda; stir in corn meal. About ½ hr. before serving, start heating oven to 400°. Melt shortening in 9" iron skillet. With egg beater, beat egg; stir in buttermilk, then dry ingredients. Add melted shortening; mix well. Pour batter into hot greased skillet.

Bake 20–25 minutes or until nicely brown.

Mary Will Morgan

SPOON BREAD

1 heaping C. corn meal	½ C. sweet milk
2 C. sweet milk	3 heaping t. baking powder
½ stick butter or oleo	1 t. salt
3 eggs	1 t. sugar

Bring to boil 2 cups milk. Add meal, then add butter. Stir together and set aside to cool. Separate 3 eggs, beat whites very stiff, when they begin to foam, add pinch of cream of tartar. Beat egg yolks and ½ cup sweet milk together then add baking powder, salt and sugar. Fold egg yolk mixture into mush. Then fold in egg whites. Bake at 350° for 45 minutes until golden brown on top.

Mrs. D. M. Chambers, Sr.

MOTHER'S NUT BREAD

3½ C. flour	1 T. melted butter
1 C. sweet milk	3 t. baking powder
1 egg	1 C. sugar
1 C. broken nut meats	½ t. salt
(English walnuts are best)	

Mix well. Pour into a well greased pan and bake in a 350 degree oven.

Mrs. Wm. P. Bailey

DILLY CASSEROLE BREAD

1 pkg. dry yeast	1 T. butter
¼ C. warm water	2 t. dill seed
1 C. cream cottage cheese heated	1 t. salt
	¼ t. soda
2 T. sugar	1 egg
1 T. minced onion	2¼ to 2½ cups flour

Mix yeast in water, add cottage cheese. Combine remaining ingredients except flour. Add yeast mixture and blend well. Add flour to make sticky dough, a little at a time, beat well after each addition. Cover, let rise in warm place until light and double in size (1 hr.) Punch down and turn into well greased casserole or bread pan, let rise again. Bake at 350° for 40-50 minutes or until goden brown. Brush with butter. Yields 1 round loaf.   Mrs. D. M. Chambers, Jr.

ONION-CHEESE SUPPER BREAD

½ C. chopped onions	1 C. grated sharp American Cheese
1 beaten egg	
1½ C. biscuit mix	1 T. poppy seed
1 T. fat	2 T. melted butter
	½ C. milk

Cook onion in fat until tender and light brown. Combine egg and milk. Add to biscuit mix and stir only until the dry ingredients are just moistened. Add onion and half of the grated cheese. Spread dough in greased 8" round baking dish. Sprinkle top with remaining cheese and poppy seed. Drizzle melted butter over all. Bake 20-25 minutes at 400°. Serve hot with cold meat slices and tossed salad.

Mrs. Phil S. Barksdale, Jr.

PAT'S BUSY DAY BREAD (NO KNEADING)

Soften 3 envelopes of dry yeast in 4 cups warm water.
Mix in large bowl:

14 C. self-rising Red Band Flour (pre-sifted)	3 t. sage
	2 t. dill seed
2 C. whole wheat flour	1 t. salt

Pour in yeast - water mixture. Stir in enough more water to make a soft dough (start with 1 cup and add second cup gradually.) Sprinkle in ¼ cup sugar & mix well. Separate into 3 large greased bowls. Grease top of dough with oil. Cover with linen or light cotton towels. Allow to rise until double in bulk. (About 2 hrs.) Beat down by hitting with hand. Divide into 6 loaf pans. (May be baked in round casseroles but loaf pan makes bread slice more easily). Cover and let rise to top of pans (about 1 hour). Bake at 375° for 30 to 40 minutes. Brush top of loafs with melted butter immediately after removing from oven. Cool in pans 10 minutes. Remove to cutting board. May be sliced as soon as it is cool enough to handle. Mrs. Everett Lee

OATMEAL BREAD

2 C. rolled oats, uncooked	1 T. butter
2 t. salt	2 C. boiling water
1 pkg. yeast	¼ C. lukewarm water
¾ C. brown sugar, packed	½ C. warm water
5 to 5¾ C. flour, sifted	

Lightly grease 1 mixing bowl and 2 loaf pans. Now in another mixing bowl, combine oatmeal, butter, salt and boiling water. While this is cooling slightly, soften the yeast in the ¼ cup warm water and stir the brown sugar until melted in the ½ cup warm water. Then add yeast to oatmeal mixture. Add brown sugar mixture. Now in 2 additions stir in flour - first with a spoon and then when dough becomes too stiff, by hand. Turn out on floured board and knead till smooth and elastic (3 to 4 minutes), add more flour to make a stiff dough. Now put the dough into greased mixing bowl turning once to bring greased side up. Cover with a damp cloth and set in warm, draft-free place to rise till double again (about 1½ hours). Punch down and allow to rise until double again. Turn out on lightly floured board and divide into two portions with a knife. Place damp cloth over them and let them rest for 10 minutes. Then form into loaves and place in loaf pans. Allow to rise until near top of pan. Bake at 350° for about 50 minutes. Done when sounds hollow when tapped. Remove immediately from pans and allow to cool on rack before serving. Mrs. Al Costner

PEGGY'S EASY REAL FRENCH BREAD

1 pkg. quick acting yeast	1 T. sugar
1¼ C. lukewarm water	2 t. salt
4 C. sifted all purpose flour	

Dissolve yeast in one cup of lukewarm water. While yeast softens stir flour, sugar and salt together in a large bowl, then stir in the dissolved yeast. Add just enough of the second cup of water to hold dough together. Mix until you have a soft rather sticky dough. Cover with a clean cloth, set bowl in a warm spot (not near direct heat) and let rise until double in bulk. This takes two to four hours depending upon warmth of kitchen.

When dough is high and spongy, punch it down with your fist and give it a good sound beating with your hand. Divide bread into two parts and place each part in a greased round 6" baking dish (glass casserole is perfect). Cover again and let rise until it reaches top of baking dish. At this point start oven at 400° or moderately hot, brush top of bread with butter (gives lovely flavor to crust) and bake one hour. You'll love the fine flavor and crustiness of this real French Bread. Mrs. T. D. Evans, III

PUMPKIN BREAD

3 C. sugar
1 C. salad oil
4 eggs, beaten
1 can (1 lb.) pumpkin
3½ C. flour
1 t. baking powder
2 t. baking soda
2 t. salt

½ t. cloves
1 t. cinnamon
1 t. nutmeg
1 t. allspice
2/3 C. water
½ t. almond flavoring
1 C. golden raisins

Glaze for Tops of Loaves:
1 C. sifted powdered sugar
3 to 4 t. water

½ t. vanilla extract
½ C. grated nuts

Combine sugar, oil, and eggs. Add pumpkin. Sift together dry ingredients and add to pumpkin mixture. Stir in the water, almond flavoring and raisins. Line the bottoms of 3 - 5" x 9" loaf pans with waxed paper and grease and flour the pans. Pour the batter in the pans and bake at 350° for 50 to 60 minutes. When cool, glaze each loaf with a mixture of the powdered sugar, vanilla and water. Sprinkle gra ed nuts over the tops. This bread stays moist for days.

Mrs. James R. MacLean

PUMPKIN BREAD

2 C. white sugar
1 C. brown sugar, packed

4 eggs
1 C. salad oil

Combine above and add: 2 C. pumpkin (1 can)
Sift together and add:

3½ C. flour
1 t. baking powder
2 t. soda
½ t. ground cloves
Pinch ginger

1 t. nutmeg
1 t. allspice
1 t. cinnamon
2 t. salt
2/3 C. water

Bake in two greased and floured loaf pans for 1 hour at 350°.

Mrs. Walter Robinson

YEAST BISCUITS

5 C. sifted flour, plain
3 t. baking powder
1 t. salt
¾ C. shortening
¼ C. sugar

2 C. buttermilk
1 t. soda
2 yeast cakes dissolved in 3
T. warm water

Stir into stiff batter or dough. Put in covered bowl and store in refrigerator and then take out what you want to use. Roll out on floured board. Cut out biscuits. Let rise until double in bulk. Bake in hot oven at 375°. Remainder will keep in refrigerator several days to use when you like.

Mrs. Earl Cloyd

CAKES & ICINGS

ABRAHAM'S CAKE — (JEWISH RECIPE)

8 eggs	1 tart apple, grated with peel
1¾ C. sugar	2 T Sherry or Port wine
1 lemon, juice & grated rind	Do not use Sauterne
1 C. cake meal or	½ C. grated nuts
vanilla wafer crumbs	

Beat yolks and sugar together. Add lemon juice, rind and wine. Add cake meal and fruit alternately. Fold in the stiffly beaten egg whites. Add nuts. Bake in an ungreased angel food cake pan at 350° for 50 to 55 minutes. Cool upside down in pan.

MRS. LEE G. COCHRAN

APPLESAUCE CAKE

½ C. butter	½ t. nutmeg
¾ C. white sugar	½ t. allspice
½ C. brown sugar	2 C. sifted flour
1½ C. unsweetened	1½ C. raisins
applesauce	1½ C. nuts (pecans
1 egg	preferred)
1 t. soda	½ t. baking powder
½ t. ginger	1 t. salt
1 t. cinnamon	

Sift together flour, baking powder, salt and spices. Add nuts and raisins to flour mixture, making sure each piece is coated with flour. Cream butter and sugar and add the egg to this mixture. Add soda to hot applesauce and add alternately with flour mixture. Mix the cake just as quickly as possible since the leavening agents start acting in the hot applesauce.

Bake in a loaf pan which has been greased and floured. Bake at 275° for 45 muintes, then at 325° for 30 minutes. To have a moist cake, place a pan of water in the oven.

MRS. ROBERT E. DODSON, JR.

CHOCOLATE CUP CAKES

Cream together well:

1 egg, beaten	4 rounded T. butter and
1 C. sugar	1 t. soda, dissolved in
1 C. buttermilk	about 1 T. warm water
1½ C. flour	Vanilla
2 squares chocolate, melted	
with;	

Mix in usual cake batter manner. Bake 25 minutes at 350°.

MOCHA CHOCOLATE ICING

Cream 2 T. butter. Add 1 C. of sifted confectioners sugar gradually; blend thoroughly. Add ⅛ t. salt and 3 squares of sweetened melted chocolate. Mix well. Then add 4 C. sifted powdered sugar, alternately with ½ C. **strong** coffee. Beat after each addition until smooth.

MRS. T. F. BECKNER, JR.

BLACKBERRY CAKE

2½ C. flour
2 C. sugar
2 C. blackberries
½ C. vegetable oil

2 eggs
1 t. allspice
1 t. nutmeg
1 t. soda

vanilla

Mix the eggs with the oil, and add the sugar. Mix well and add the sifted dry ingredients. Fold in the berries and juice. Bake at 300° for 1½ hours.

Blueberries or any other berries may be substituted for the blackberries.

MRS. INA BUCKLES

CHOCOLATE CAKE

2 sticks butter
2 squares chocolate
2 C. sugar
4 eggs (separated)
2½ C. flour (sifted cake flour)

1 C. buttermilk
1 t. soda
½ t. salt
½ t. lemon flavoring
1 t. vanilla

Cream butter and sugar. Add beaten egg yolks. Next add alternately milk (with soda in it) and sifted cake flour. Add melted chocolate and flavoring. Fold in beaten egg whites.

Pour into 2 greased 9 inch layer pans. Bake in a moderate oven, 350° for about 35 minutes.

MRS. W. T. WOOD

TOASTED COCONUT CAKE

1 T. butter, melted
1 C. sugar
2 beaten eggs
½ C. hot milk

1 C. flour
¼ t. salt
1 T. baking powder
1 T. vanilla

Combine sugar and melted butter. Add beaten eggs. Add hot milk. Let cool while sifting flour with salt and baking powder. Add this to other mixture. Add vanilla. Bake in a greased and floured pan at 325° for 25 minutes.

TOPPING

1/3 C. butter
1 C. brown sugar

1 C. coconut
4 T. cream

Mix all ingredients and spread on top and put under broiler until brown on top.

MRS. L. E. FAULK

BANANA CAKE

½ C. shortening
1 C. sugar
2 eggs, unbeaten
1 t. salt
2½ t. baking powder
1 t. soda

1 t. cinnamon
½ t. nutmeg
2 C. flour
¼ C. milk
1 T. lemon juice
1¼ C. mashed ripe bananas

Cream shortening and sugar, add eggs and beat. Sift all dry ingredients together and add alternately with milk. Mix and gently stir in lemon juice and banana. Bake at 350° in loaf cake pan, approximately 13" x 9", for 30-40 minutes. Coconut topping above would do well on this cake.

MRS. CHARLES BOLTON, JR.

ANGEL FOOD

¾ C. sifted cake flour
¾ C. plus 2 T. sugar
1½ C. egg whites
1½ t. cream of tartar

¼ t. salt
1½ t. vanilla
¾ C. sugar

Keep egg whites at room temperature until ready to beat. Sift the flour and sugar together three times and set aside while you beat the egg whites, cream of tartar, salt and vanilla together until foamy. Gradually add the last ¾ C. sugar, 2 T. at a time, and beat about 10 seconds after each addition, until meringue is firm and holds stiff peaks. Sift dry ingredients 3 T. at a time over the meringue, folding in gently after each addition. Continue folding until the flour and sugar are all used, and mixture is thick. Push gently into an ungreased tube pan and cut through the batter with a knife to eliminate air bubbles. Bake in preheated 375° oven for 30 to 35 min. Angel Food Cake Fillings listed in the back of this chapter could be used with this cake.

¼ C. cocoa may be sifted with flour and sugar to make a Chocolate Angel Food.

MRS. BEN D. HALL

DEVIL'S FOOD CAKE

2 C. flour
1 t. soda
¼ t. salt
½ C. shortening
1 1/3 C. sugar

2 eggs
2 squares of chocolate
1 C. plus 2 T. milk
1 t. vanilla

Sift flour once. Measure and add soda and salt. Sift together three times. Cream shortening; add sugar gradually and cream together until light and fluffy. Add eggs one at a time, beating well after each one. Add melted chocolate and blend. Add flour, alternately with milk, beating well after each addition. Add vanilla. Pour into two 9 inch pans, lined on bottom with waxed paper. Bake at 350° for 30 minutes. When cool spread with creamy chocolate icing.

———o———

CHOCOLATE ICING

2 C. sugar
¼ C. white corn syrup
½ C. milk
½ C. shortening

2 squares of chocolate
½ t. salt
1 t. vanilla

Combine ingredients and stir over low heat until chocolate and shortening are melted. Bring to boil and boil one minute, stirring constantly. Remove from stove and beat until lukewarm. Add vanilla and beat until of spreading consistency.

MRS. VIRGIL T. GUTHRIE

FLOWERING FIG CAKE

½ C. sugar	3 t. baking powder
½ C. molasses	½ t. salt
½ C. butter	½ t. nutmeg
3 eggs	2 t. cinnamon
1 C. milk	1 t. almond flavoring
3 C. flour	1 C. finely cut dried figs

Cream butter and sugar. Add beaten eggs and molasses. Beat until creamy. Sift dry ingredients together, and add alternately with milk. Add flavoring and figs. Pour into two 9-inch lightly greased and floured cake pans, and bake in 350° oven 25 minutes.

FIG ICING

1½ C. powdered sugar	6 T. milk
1 C. brown sugar	6 whole dried figs
½ C. butter	6 candied cherries

Boil butter, brown sugar and milk together a minute and cool. Add powdered sugar and stir until ready to spread. Ice cake. To make fig "flowers," cut down through each fig four times, leaving bottom portions joined. Spread out in a fan shape. Arrange on cake as desired, then place cherries beside each fig to form "flower" centers.

MRS. HUNT W. ARCHER

FRUIT CAKE

1 C. white sugar	1 lb. candied pineapple
½ lb. butter, creamed	cut in large pieces
5 eggs	1 lb. candied cherries, whole
2 C. flour	Vanilla extract (about 2 T.)
4 C. pecans, cut	Lemon extract (about 2 T.)

Cream butter and sugar. Add eggs, one at a time, beating well each time. Add vanilla and lemon extract. Mix fruit and nuts with flour until thoroughly coated; then add to butter mixture.
Line pans with brown paper, greased and floured.
Bake in moderate oven, 350° for 1 hour and 15 minutes in a large tube pan. If using small pans or 1 lb. cans bake at 300°. Recipe will make 3 1 lb. cakes.

MRS. T. V. McCOWN

WHITE FRUIT CAKE

1½ C. white sugar	1 lb. white raisins
½ lb. shelled pecans	½ lb. butter
½ lb. crystallized pineapple	6 eggs
½ lb. crystallized cherries	2½ C. flour
½ lb. citron	1 T. vanilla
½ lb. shredded coconut	1½ T. cinnamon

Cream sugar and butter. Add beaten eggs. Add fruit and nuts which have been mixed with the flour. Mix in coconut and add cinnamon and vanilla. Bake at least 3½ hours at 300°. For best results, grease brown paper and line cake pan. Place pan of water on rack under cake, to steam cake as it bakes.

MRS. RALPH E. CROSS

FUDGE CAKE

Melt together:
    1 stick butter   2 squares chocolate
Add to:
    2 eggs and 1 C. sugar which have been beaten together
Sift together:
    ½ C. flour   1 t. baking powder

Add flour to first mixture and mix well. Stir in 1 C. chopped nuts. Bake in greased loaf cake pan at 350° for 30 min. Cut ½ pkg. marshmallows over the cake while it is hot. Ice cake, while still in pan, with fudge frosting.

MRS. DEE DONALDSON
Rome, Georgia

FANCY GINGER BREAD

1 C. butter or shortening	4 eggs
1 C. sugar	2 t. soda
1 C. molasses	1 t. cinnamon
1 C. buttermilk	1 t. allspice
1 C. chopped dates	1 t. nutmeg
1 C. shredded coconut	2 t. ginger
1 C. nuts, broken	2 t. salt
4 C. flour	

Cream butter and sugar. Add eggs ,one at a time, beating thoroughly. Add dry ingredients, that have been sifted together, alternately with the milk. Add molasses; then dates, coconut and nuts. Bake in a 350° oven from 30 to 45 minutes. This will serve about 36. Half of the recipe can be made successfully.

MRS. FRANK LEE

TOP DRESSING FOR FANCY GINGER BREAD

2 C. sugar	3 T. flour or cornstarch
1 can shredded coconut	Juice and grated rind of 2 lemons
2/3 C. water	1 grated apple (do not peel)
½ C. broken pecan meats	

Mix together and cook until it thickens. Add nuts after cooking. If you want a thicker topping, double the recipe.

MRS. FRANK LEE

MOLASSES GINGER BREAD

	1 t. soda
2 C. molasses	1 t. ginger
¾ C. butter	½ t. grated nutmeg
2 eggs, well beaten	4 t. baking powder
3 C. sifted flour	1 C. milk

Heat molasses. Add butter and beat well. Stir in sifted soda and spices. Add eggs, flour and milk alternately, having first sifted baking powder with flour. Pour in greased and floured pan and bake at 350° in shallow bread pan for 15 minutes. Serves 24.

MRS. W. T. MATHIS, JR.

GOLD CAKE

Sift together:

2½ C. flour	8 egg yolks
¼ t. salt	¾ C. milk
2½ t. baking powder	½ t. lemon extract
¾ C. butter	1 t. vanilla
1¼ C. sugar	

Cream butter with sugar. Add well beaten egg yolks; add flour and baking powder mixture, alternately with milk. Beat thoroughly 1 minute. Bake 350° about 1 hour in a loaf pan or tube pan. This cake resembles a pound cake.

MRS. R. H. OTTINGER

GRAHAM CRACKER CAKE

½ C. shortening	¼ t. salt
1 C. sugar	24 graham crackers (crushed)
3 beaten egg yolks	¾ C. milk
½ t. vanilla	¼ C. walnuts
¼ C. flour	3 beaten egg whites
1½ t. baking powder	

Cream sugar and shortening. Add egg yolks and vanilla. Add dry ingredients, alternately with crackers and milk. Add nuts and fold in egg whites. Bake in layer pans at 350° for 25 minutes. Place cream filling between layers.

———o———

CREAM FILLING

5 T. flour	2 C. scalded milk
½ C. sugar	2 slightly beaten egg yolks
½ t. salt	(use whites in frosting)

Cook like pie filling. Ice cake with brown sugar frosting.

———o———

BROWN SUGAR FROSTING

1 C. brown sugar	2 beaten egg whites
¼ C. cold water	1 t. vanilla

Cook sugar and water until it forms a soft ball. Add to egg whites and beat until smooth. Add vanilla and mix well.

MRS. ROBERT TEGARDEN
Indianapolis, Indiana

JAM CAKE

1 C. shortening	1½ t. nutmeg
1 C. sugar	1½ t. cloves
4 whole eggs	1½ t. cinnamon
3 C. flour	1 C. buttermilk
2 C. jam	1 C. raisins
½ t. salt	1 C. nuts
1½ t. soda	

Cream shortening and sugar. Add eggs and jam. Sift together dry ingredients; add alternately with buttermilk. Dust raisins and nuts with flour and add to mixture. Bake in a tube pan at 275° for 1½ to 2 hours.

MRS. A. H. ABERNETHY, SR.

KENTUCKY BURNT SUGAR CAKE

1½ C. sugar	2½ C. soft wheat flour
¾ C. butter	1 t. baking powder
4 eggs, separated	¾ t. soda
1 C. milk	1 t. vanilla

Caramelize ½ C. sugar. Add ¾ C. water and boil mixture to a heavy syrup. Cool. Cream butter; add remaining sugar — cream until light. Add beaten egg yolks and mix well. Add soda and baking powder to flour and sift three times. Add flour to butter mixture alternately with milk and vanilla. Mix thoroughly. Add caramel syrup and beat well. Fold in beaten egg whites. Mix well. Pour into greased, paper lined cake pan. Bake 40 minutes in moderate oven 350°.

MRS. KATHERINE K. MEREDITH

LANE CAKE (White Cake)

1 C. butter	1 C. milk
2 C. sugar	1 t. vanilla
3¼ C. sifted flour	8 egg whites
2 t. baking powder	

Cream (soft) butter and sugar together until **very** light and fluffy. Sift dry ingredients and add them alternately with milk, into which you have put the vanilla. Begin with the dry ingredients and then add the liquid. Fold in the beaten egg whites. Pour into 3 greased and floured layer cake pans and bake in 350° oven about 30 minutes.

FILLING

½ C. butter	1 C. seeded raisins
1 C. sugar	1 t. vanilla
8 egg yolks	1 wine-glass of brandy
1 C. chopped pecans	

Cream butter and sugar. Add well beaten egg yolks and cook in top of double boiler until thickened. Add nuts and raisins, which have been soaked in brandy for an hour or so. Add vanilla and spread between layers of the cake. Frost the cake with a boiled frosting.

MRS. EUSTIS A. LANCASTER, JR.

MAHOGANY CAKE

½ C. cocoa	3 eggs, beaten
1 C. milk	1 t. soda
½ C. butter	½ C. buttermilk
1½ C. white sugar	1 t. vanilla
2½ C. flour	

Boil milk and cocoa together until thick. Cool. Cream butter and sugar; add eggs, vanilla, soda mixed with buttermilk and flour. Mix well and add cooled chocolate. Bake at 350° 30-35 minutes.

MRS. NEILL A. BEASLEY

MAYONNAISE CAKE

Mix together:

1 C. mayonnaise	2 t. jelly (any kind)	1 C. sugar

Sift together and add to mayonnaise mixture:

2 C. flour	2 t. soda	4 T. cocoa

Add:

1 C. water	1 t. vanilla

Beat thoroughly and bake in two 9-inch cake pans at 350° for 30 minutes or until cake is spongy. Use 7 minute frosting on cake.

MRS. B. F. PORTER

ORANGE CAKE

1 C. sour milk	¼ t. almond extract
1 C. sugar	1 t. vanilla
¾ C. shortening	Dash of salt
2 eggs	½ C. chopped cherries
2 C. flour	¼ lb. pineapple
1 t. soda	¾ C. pecans
1 t. baking powder	1 C. chopped dates

Cream sugar and shortening. Add eggs, then add dry ingredients alternately with sour milk. Cream well. Add vanilla and almond flavoring. Chop fruit and nuts very fine and add ½ C. flour. Add fruit to mixture and bake in a greased loaf pan. Bake 30-40 minutes at 350°. While baking, mix juice of 2 oranges and 1 C. of sugar. When dissolved, pour over warm, baked cake.

MRS. ANNE B. CHAMBERLIN

ORANGE DATE CAKE

1 C. white sugar	2 eggs
½ C. butter	2 T. ground orange peel
2/3 C. sour milk	1 pkg. pitted, chopped dates
1 t. soda	1 C. chopped nuts
2 C. flour	

Cream sugar and butter; add orange peel. Add well beaten eggs. Dissolve soda in sour milk and add alternately with sifted flour to first mixture. Stir in chopped dates and nuts that have had a small amount of the flour dusted over them. Bake in a well greased and floured shallow pan about 12"x8"; 30-35 minutes at 350°. While still warm and before taking from pan, pour the following topping over the cake.

TOPPING

1 C. orange juice	2 heaping T. ground
1 C. brown sugar	orange rind

Place this mixture in a sauce pan and stir often until sugar is thoroughly dissolved.

MRS. W. L. SISK
Elizabethton, Tennessee

PECAN CAKE

1 C. shortening	1 t. salt
1½ C. sugar	1 t. nutmeg
5 eggs	2 t. lemon juice
2 T. milk	1 t. grated lemon rind
2 C. flour, sifted	1 C. pecans, toasted

Cream sugar and shortening. Add whole eggs (one at a time until thoroughly mixed). Add 2 T. milk. Next add dry ingredients, which have been sifted together. Add lemon juice, lemon rind and 1 C. pecans. Put into greased and floured tube pan and add a few whole pecans to top of cake mixture. Bake in a 350° oven for about 1 hour.

MRS. FORSTER MILLER

PINEAPPLE CAKE WITH PINEAPPLE FROSTING

½ C. shortening	½ t. salt
1¼ C. sugar	¾ C. pineapple juice
1 egg yolk	¼ C. water
3 t. baking powder	4 egg whites
3 C. flour	

Cream shortening and sugar well. Add egg yolk and beat. Sift dry ingredients together. Add, alternately with diluted pineapple juice, to first mixture. Fold in stiffly beaten egg whites and ½ t. grated lemon rind (if desired). Bake in two layers. Time: 35 to 40 minutes. at 350°. Cool and frost.

PINEAPPLE FROSTING

2 unbeaten egg whites	5 T. pineapple juice
1½ C. sugar	⅛ t. cream of tartar

Place all ingredients in top part of double boiler over boiling water. Beat constantly with electric beater until mixture holds peak (about seven minutes). Remove from heat. Add ¼ t. grated lemon rind, if desired and beat until thick enough to spread. Frost cake above.

MRS. J. J. BROWN

PINEAPPLE NUT UPSIDE - DOWN CAKE

4 T. butter	1½ C. sifted flour
1 C. brown sugar	2½ t. baking powder
4 slices canned pineapple	¼ t. salt
1/3 C. whole pecans	¼ C. evaporated milk
¼ C. shortening	diluted with ¼ C. water
¾ C. sugar	½ t. vanilla
1 egg, beaten	

Melt butter in 9-inch cake pan. Add brown sugar and stir until blended. Remove from heat and spread in an even layer over the bottom of the pan. Arrange the pineapple slices with pecans, in an even layer. Cream shortening and sugar. Add egg and beat well. Sift dry ingredients together and add alternately with diluted evaporated milk. Mix thoroughly. Stir in vanilla.

Pour batter carefully over fruit in pan. Bake in moderate oven 350° about 45 minutes. Remove from oven and invert onto a serving plate immediately.

MRS. F. B. SMITH

AUNT ANNIE BRENNAN'S OLD FASHIONED POUND CAKE

1 lb. pulverized sugar	1 doz. eggs
1 lb. butter	7 drops oil of lemon —
1 lb. flour, well sifted	no more

Cream butter and sugar thoroughly. Add egg yolks which have been beaten thoroughly and are very light. Mix well. Sift approximately 2 or 3 T. of flour into this mixture and continue mixing. Add 2 T. of the beaten whites of eggs; mix. Add remainder of flour, oil of lemon and mix well. Lastly, fold lightly into the above the remainder of whites. Drop off, a spoonful at a time, into a regular greased pound cake pan; cover and bake 250° for 2 hours. Remove cover and if not brown enough let stay in oven for a little while longer.

MRS. THOMAS McKEE

NEVER - FAIL POUND CAKE

¾ C. butter—room temperature	1¾ C. sugar

Beat these two thoroughly.

6 eggs, add one at a time— mix well	2 C. flour
	¼ t. baking powder
1 T. rich milk or cream	Vanilla, lemon or any flavoring

Pour into a greased tube pan, or a regular pound cake pan. Start in cold oven — set at 325°. Bake 1 hour.

MRS. M. A. BITZER

PRUNE CAKE

3 eggs	1 t. nutmeg
1½ C. white sugar	1 t. allspice
1 C. buttermilk	1 t. soda
1 C. vegetable oil	1 t. vanilla
2 C. flour	1 C. nuts, chopped
1 t. salt	1 C. prunes, cooked, pitted
1 t. cinnamon	and diced

Use mixer:

Mix eggs, buttermilk and vegetable oil together. Add sugar and mix. Sift flour, salt, spices and soda together. Add to egg mixture and mix well. Stir in prunes, nuts and vanilla. Pour into a well-greased pan (about a 13″ oblong pan — this makes a big cake). Bake in medium oven 300° to 325° until sides begin to leave pan and it springs back when touched in center (About 30 minutes)). As soon as cake is in oven put this sauce on to cook:

½ C. buttermilk	¾ stick butter
1 C. sugar, brown or white	½ t. soda

Cook sauce until it forms soft ball in water. When cake is done, pour sauce over cake at once. If you want to remove cake and have sauce go over sides by spreading with a knife, place a cookie sheet or large bake pan on top of cake pan and turn upside down. Then pour sauce and spread down the sides with knife.

MRS. A. H. McANNALLY

RAINBOW CAKE

Measure into bowl:

3 C. sifted flour	1 t. salt
2 C. sugar	1 C. milk
¾ C. shortening	

Mix thoroughly by hand or mixer. Stir in 3 t. double acting baking powder. Add 4 egg whites (save yolks for icing); ½ C. milk and mix 2 minutes.

Divide batter into three parts. Add ½ t. vanilla or almond flavoring to 1 part for the white layer. Add 4 drops yellow food color and ½ t. lemon extract to another part and for the dark layer add ½ t. cinnamon, ⅛ t. cloves, ⅛ t. soda and 2 T. cocoa blended with 2 T. water. Bake in greased and floured layer pans at 375° for about 25 minutes. Cool before icing.

ICING

Combine 4 egg yolks, 3 C. powdered sugar; ½ t. salt with 1½ t. vanilla and ½ C. cream. Add ½ C. shortening or oleo and beat until creamy.

MRS. INA BUCKLES

SOUP CAKE

1 C. brown sugar	1 t. nutmeg
½ C. shortening	1 C. nuts, chopped
1 can tomato soup	1 C. raisins, cut in half
1 t. soda dissolved in soup	Pinch of salt
1 t. cinnamon	2 eggs
1 t. cloves	2 C. flour

2 t. baking powder

Cream the shortening and sugar together. Add the eggs. Add alternately the soup with all the dry ingredients which have been sifted together.

Bake in greased and floured layer pans 20 minutes or loaf pan for about 40 minutes, at 350°.

MRS. JOE J. BROWN

MERINGUE SPICE CAKE

5 T. shortening	½ t. soda
1 C. dark brown sugar	½ t. cinnamon
1 egg yolk	½ t. cloves
1¼ C. flour	2/3 C. sour milk
½ t. salt	½ t. vanilla
½ t. baking powder	

Cream shortening and sugar and egg yolk together. Sift dry ingredients and add alternately with the milk. Add vanilla. Beat after each addition. Pour into a greased and floured 8"x8"x2" pan. Cover with meringue as follows:

MERINGUE

1 egg white, beaten	½ C. light brown sugar
½ C. chopped nut meats	

Slowly add sugar to egg white and continue beating until smooth. Spread meringue over cake batter and sprinkle with nut meats. Bake about 35 minutes in a 350° oven.

MRS. PAUL PERRY

ENCHANTED CREAM SPONGE CAKE

1 C. sifted cake flour	1 t. grated lemon rind
1 t. baking powder	¾ C. sugar
¼ t. salt	1 t. lemon juice
2 eggs, separated	2 T. sugar
½ C. cold water	

Sift flour once and measure. Add baking powder and salt and sift together three times. To egg yolks, add water and lemon rind — beat with rotary egg beater until light and foamy. Add sugar gradually, beating well after each addition; then add flour in small amounts beating with beater to blend. Beat egg whites until foamy throughout; add lemon juice and 2 T. sugar and beat until stiff peaks form. Fold into flour mixture. Pour into two 8-inch ungreased cake pans. Bake in moderate oven 350° 25 minutes or until done. Invert on rack until cakes are cold.

Spread lemon cream filling between layers and sprinkle top with powdered sugar.

———o———

FILLING

Combine 1 C. sugar and 5 T. cake flour in top of double boiler. Add 1 slightly beaten egg, 1/3 C. lemon juice, 2/3 C. water and 2 t. butter; mix thoroughly. Place over boiling water and cook 10 minutes, stirring constantly. Chill. Divide in half. Fold in 1 t. grated lemon rind and ¼ C. whipped cream and spread between layers. Using other half, add ¾ C. whipped cream to serve on top of each slice.

MRS. R. H. OTTINGER

ORANGE SPONGE CAKE
(Made with Mixer)

5 egg yolks	¼ t. salt
2 C. sugar	½ C. water
2 C. flour	½ C. orange juice
2 t. baking powder	4 egg whites

Place egg yolks in bowl and beat well; gradually adding sugar. Sift dry ingredients 3 times. Combine liquids. With mixer at high speed alternately add dry ingredients and liquids. Beat egg whites stiff and fold in last by hand. Bake in ungreased tube pan at 350° for 60 minutes. Invert pan and let cake cool in pan.

———o———

ORANGE BUTTER FROSTING
(Made with Mixer)

1 C. butter	4 T. orange juice
6 C. powdered sugar, well sifted	1 T. grated orange rind

Cream butter well with mixer. Add sugar and juice alternately. Beat, by hand, the orange rind into mixture. Beat until well blended and fluffy. Will cover sides and top of cake above.

MRS. FERDINAND POWELL, JR.

STRAWBERRY SHORT CAKE

2 C. sifted flour	1 scant t. salt
1 level t. baking powder	2 heaping T. sugar

½ C. shortening, or shortening and butter mixed
Add milk until dough leaves sides of the bowl (about ½ C.)

Sift dry ingredients. Work in shortening and milk. Roll as thin as possible and cut with a large cutter. Butter one round, place another on top. Butter again and sprinkle on a little sugar. Continue until all rounds are used. Place on greased cookie sheet and bake at 450° until browned. Remove from oven. Separate rounds immediately. When ready to serve, place sugared strawberries between rounds and serve with thick cream. Fresh peaches may be substituted, in which case a few chopped pecans are good added to the dough. Serves about 8 or 9.

MRS. CALVIN MORGAN

SWEET STORY CAKE

2½ C. sifted cake flour	½ C. pecans, finely chopped
3½ t. baking powder	(¾ C. may be used)
½ C. butter	1½ C. sugar
¼ C. maraschino cherry juice	1 t. salt
2 t. almond extract	¾ C. milk
18 maraschino cherries,	1½ t. vanilla
drained & finely chopped	4 egg whites

Cream sugar and butter well. Sift dry ingredients three times and add alternately with combined milk and cherry juice. Add extracts. Next fold in beaten egg whites, (beat whites if mixed by hand — add unbeaten if electric mixer is used). Add cherries and nuts. Bake at 375° for 25 minutes.

PINK ICING FOR SWEET STORY CAKE

2 T. butter	½ t. salt
2 T. shortening	4 C. sifted powdered sugar
1 t. vanilla	9 T. scalded cream (more or
½ t. almond extract	less as needed)

Combine shortening, butter, vanilla, almond and salt and blend. Beat in ½ C. sugar. Add hot cream alternately with remaining sugar; beat well after each addition. Add only enough cream to give a nice spreading consistency. Finally, add a few drops of red coloring to tint frosting a delicate pink.

MRS. ALFRED COSTNER

WHITE CAKE

3 egg whites	¼ t. almond extract
½ C. shortening	3 C. flour
1¾ C. sugar	3 t. baking powder
½ C. water	¼ t. salt
1 t. vanilla	½ C. water

Beat egg whites until stiff. Mix shortening and sugar well. Add ½ C. water, vanilla and almond. Sift together dry ingredients and blend in alternately with ½ C. water. Fold in the egg whites. Bake at 375° for 25 to 30 minutes.

MRS. CHARLES ROLLER

WHITE CAKE

2½ C. flour
2½ t. baking powder
1¼ C. sugar
5 egg whites
1 t. salt

½ C. sugar
2/3 C. vegetable shortening
1 C. milk
1 t. vanilla

Sift flour once and measure into sifter with baking powder, salt and 1¼ C. sugar. Beat egg whites until foamy. Add ½ C. sugar gradually, beating until mixture will hold up in soft peaks. Have the shortening at room temperature in a large bowl — stir to soften. Sift dry ingredients and add ¾ C. milk and vanilla. Mix until all flour is dampened. Beat 1 minute and add remaining milk. Beat 2 minutes longer. Add beaten egg whites. Beat one minute. Bake at 350°, about 25 minutes for layers and 35 minutes for a loaf cake.

ICING

2 C. sugar
¾ C. water
2 stiffly beaten egg whites
1 T. corn syrup (light)

1 t. vanilla
1 t. lemon juice
Dash of salt

Cook sugar, water, corn syrup and salt over low heat, stirring until sugar dissolves. Cook until soft ball forms. Gradually add hot syrup to egg whites, beating constantly. Add vanilla and lemon juice. Continue beating until frosting is of spreading consistency. Cover frosting with coconut (fresh coconut is best).

MRS. JOHN HOWREN

YELLOW CAKE

½ C. butter
1 C. sugar
2 C. flour
2 t. baking powder

2 eggs
1 t. vanilla
½ C. milk

Cream butter and sugar. Add eggs. Sift flour and measure — add baking powder and sift again. Add alternately with the milk. Mix well. Add vanilla. Bake in a tube or loaf pan at 350° for about ½ hour.

MRS. WALTER HEEB

ALMOND SAUCE TOPPING

Melt in double boiler; 1 T. butter. Stir in 3 T. flour. Add ½ to 1 C. heavy cream. Cook until it thickens.
Add 1 C. sugar and 5 egg yolks, one at a time. Beat well after each addition. (Be sure water isn't boiling too hard in bottom pan of double boiler.) Cook 2 or 3 minutes.

Add almond flavoring to taste (about ¼ t.) or vanilla (about 1 t.). Slivered ,blanched almonds may be added to sauce. Serve over angel food cake, vanilla cream, spice cake, etc.

MRS. GEORGE E. MILLER
Eau Claire, Wisconsin

RHUBARB CAKE

1½ C. brown sugar
1 egg
1 C. buttermilk
1½ C. fresh rhubarb,
  cut up

½ C. shortening (Crisco)
1 t. soda
2 C. sifted flour
1 t. vanilla flavoring

Mix sugar and shortening and egg in mixer. Dissolve soda in buttermilk. Mix in flour, rhubarb, and buttermilk alternately. Pour into sheet pan. Make a topping of ¾ cup brown sugar and 1 tsp. cinnamon. Sprinkle on cake and bake at 350 degrees for 40-45 minutes. 1 tsp. cinnamon may be added to the cake if desired.

TEA CAKE

½ C. shortening
1 egg, beaten
rind of 1 orange
¾ C. sour milk

1 C. brown sugar
2 C. sifted flour
1 t. baking soda

Cream sugar and shortening, add egg, rind, put soda in sour milk and add alternately with flour. Bake in greased 9" x 9" pan for 25 to 30 minutes in a 325 degree oven. When baked, take ½ cup orange juice and fill cup with granulated sugar, let set awhile to dissolve. Pour over cake while hot, let set until ready to serve.

Mrs. Alfred Bolton

VANILLA WAFER CAKE

1 C. or 2 sticks oleo
CREAM WITH:
  2 C. sugar
BEAT & ADD:
  1-12 oz. box crushed
    vanilla wafers
  1 C. pecans

6 whole eggs

½ C. milk
1- 7 oz. can coconut (flaked)

Bake at 275 degrees for 1½ hrs. in greased tube cake pan.

Mrs. Leland Lancaster

FRESH APPLE CAKE

MELT: 2 sticks margarine
  Blend in 2 unbeaten eggs
ADD: 2 C. sugar   3½ C. finely chopped apples
                                              (uncooked)
MIX: in separate bowl
     3 C. sifted flour   1 t. cinnamon
     ½ t. salt   1½ C. chopped pecans
     2 t. soda   1 C. seedless raisins
     1 t. nutmeg

Add these ingredients to the first mixture - a small amount at a time and mix well. Pour into large oblong greased and floured pan and bake for 1 hour at 375 degrees. While cake is still warm make a syrup of 1 cup brown sugar and 1 cup orange juice. (firmly pack brown sugar.) Bring to a boil, remove from heat and drip syrup over cake and let soak in. Top with whipped cream for dessert or serve plain for morning coffee.   Mrs. Vance Cheek

APRICOT NECTAR CAKE

MIX: ½ C. white sugar   ½ C. cooking oil
       4 eggs   1 C. apricot nectar (canned)

Add mixture to: One regular size box of yellow cake mix. (Duncan Hines)
Mix well.
Bake in 13″ x 9″ pan at 350 degrees for 30 to 40 minutes.
TOPPING:
Add 3 cups powdered sugar to juice of 3 lemons. Pour over warm cake. Prick top of cake with fork while pouring on topping. This cake may sink slightly in center. Is excellent for freezing or will keep approximately one week in refrigerator.   Mrs. Ray Chalker

BUGABOO ROAD CAKE

       3 C. sugar   6 eggs, separated
       1 C. butter   2 t. maple flavoring
       3 C. flour   1 t. vanilla
       ½ t. soda   1 C. pecans
       1 C. buttermilk

Cream one cup of butter with three cups of sugar. Add yokes of six eggs, one at a time. Cream well. Add 3 cups of flour and 1 cup of buttermilk to which you have added ½ tsp. of soda. Chop 1 cup of pecans very fine and add, along with 2 tsp. maple flavoring and 1 tsp. vanilla, to the creamed mixture. Beat the 6 eggs whites until stiff and fold into the mixture. Line the pan with waxed paper and pour in batter. Bake at 300 degrees for 1½ hrs. Cool on rack.
                                         Mrs. Bill Meredith

CARAMEL FUDGE CAKE

Combine a 1-lb. box brown sugar with ½ cup white sugar, 2 sticks margarine, melted; and 4 eggs, added one at a time and beaten well after each addition.

Add 2 cups flour, sifted with 1 tsp. baking powder and a pinch of salt. Add 1 tsp. vanilla flavoring. Bake in a large baking pan, 9 x 13 at 300 degrees for 45 minutes. When cool cut in squares and roll in powdered sugar.

Mrs. James Coleman

CARROT CAKE

2 C. sugar	2 t. soda
1½ C. Wesson oil	2 t. cinnamon
4 eggs, well beaten	3 C. carrots (grated)
1 t. salt	½ C. chopped walnuts or
2 C. sifted flour	pecans

Bake at 300 degrees for 1 hour.

Icing: Blend together one 8 oz. pkg. of Philadelphia cream cheese, ½ stick butter or margarine, one box 10X powdered sugar and 2 tsp. vanilla.

Spread on cake after cake has thoroughly cooled.

Mrs. Harry Fortune

CHEESE-CAKE

Bake 325 degrees for 40-45 minutes.

CREAM:

1 C. cream cheese (8 oz.)	⅔ C. sugar
½ C. sour cream	1 t. vanilla

BLEND IN:

2 unbeaten eggs	set aside

Mix together:

1 C. flour	1 t. baking powder
½ t. salt	

CREAM:

½ C. butter	⅔ C. sugar
2 unbeaten eggs	

Put into 10" pie pan that is well-greased and lightly floured. Spread: Batter over bottom and sides, thinner on sides. Spoon: Cream cheese mixture over batter. Put in oven and bake. Remove from oven-spread with topping, baking 5 minutes more. Chill at least 4 hours.

TOPPING:

1 C. sour cream	2 T. sugar
1 t. vanilla	

Mrs. Fred Lenz

DIBBY'S CHOCOLATE CAKE

CREAM:

1 stick butter	1 box brown sugar-dark

ADD:

3 eggs, one at a time	3 sq. bitter chocolate, melted
2¼ C. sifted flour	2 t. soda
½ C. buttermilk	

Alternate 3 times ending with flour mixture

1 t. vanilla
Little salt

Pour over all the dough—1 cup boiling water - fold in and be sure it is thoroughly mixed. Oil pan and put wax paper on oiled pan. Bake at 350 degrees for 40-50 minutes in a 9" X 12" pan.

Mrs. John Wilson

GERMAN CHOCOLATE CAKE

1 pkg. sweet cooking choco-	1 t. vanilla
late of German's chocolate	2½ C. sifted cake flour
½ C. boiling water	1 t. baking soda
1 C. butter	½ t. salt
2 C. sugar	1 C. buttermilk
4 egg yokes, unbeaten	4 egg whites, stiffly beaten

Melt chocolate in ½ cup boiling water. Cool. Cream butter and sugar until light and fluffy. Add egg yokes one at a time, beating after each. Add vanilla and melted chocolate and mix until blended. Sift flour with soda and salt. Add sifted dry ingredients alternately with buttermilk, beating after each addition until batter is smooth. Fold in stiffly beaten egg whites. Pour batter into 3 - 8 or 9 inch layers pans, line on bottom with paper. Bake in moderate oven (350 degrees) for 35 or 40 minutes. Cool. Frost top and between layers with coconut-pecan frosting.

Mrs. Norman Thomas

COCONUT PECAN FROSTING FOR GERMAN CHOCOLATE CAKE

Combine 1 cup evaporated milk, 1 cup sugar, 3 egg yolks, ¼ lb. butter and 1 tsp. vanilla in sauce pan. Cook over medium heat 12 minutes, stirring constantly, until mixture thickens. Add 1 can chopped pecans. Beat until cooled and of spreading consistency. Makes enough to cover tops of three 9" layers. Do not frost sides of cake.

Mrs. Norman Thomas

NEVER-FAIL CHOCOLATE FROSTING

Mix the following in saucepan:

2 C. sugar	1 stick margarine
½ C. milk	3 T. cocoa
Pinch salt	

Let come to rolling boil. Boil 1 minute - Set off to cool. Add 1 tsp. vanilla. Set sauce pan in larger pan of cold water - Beat 3 or 4 minutes until right consistency to spread. If cools too quickly, thin with a little milk.

Mrs. Ed Parker

CHOCOLATE SPONGE ROLL

Bake at 350 degrees in a 10" x 15" Jelly Roll pan for 8 to 10 minutes.

¾ C. sugar	6 T. all-purpose flour
4 eggs, separated	¼ t. salt
1 t. vanilla	½ t. baking powder
2 (1 oz. sq.) melted unsweetened chocolate	

Beat egg whites stiff. Fold in sugar to this mixture, add egg yolks which have been beaten and vanilla. Add sifted flour, baking powder and salt, slowly. Stir in melted chocolate and pour into waxed paper lined pan.

CHOCOLATE FILLING:

1 (1 oz.) sq. unsweetened melted chocolate	½ C. sugar
	1 t. vanilla
1/3 C. evaporated milk	1 T. water
2/3 C. oleo or butter	¼ t. salt

Mix ingredients together and at high speed beat 10 min. Cool chocolate roll and spread and roll. Store in refrigerator.

Mrs. Robert L. Hodges, Jr.

CREOLIA CAKE

2 C. sugar	1 C. vegetable oil
2 C. plain flour	1 t. vanilla
2 T. cocoa	1 t. soda
½ t. salt	1 C. boiling water
2 eggs	

Sift dry ingredients. Dissolve soda in boiling water. Combine all ingredients and beat one minute with mixer. Turn into greased pan 9" X 12". Bake 25-30 minutes at 350 degrees.

Topping recipe next page.

TOPPING FOR CREOLIA CAKE:

1½ C. brown sugar	1 C. chopped nuts
½ C. butter	1 t. vanilla
pinch of salt	1 C. evaporated milk
1 C. coconut	

Heat sugar, butter and milk. Add rest of ingredients and spoon over cake. Return to oven for 10 minutes or until topping is light brown.

Mrs. Kelver Willis

COFFEE CAKE

SIFT TOGETHER:

2 C. flour	1 t. baking powder
1 t. soda	1 pinch of salt

CREAM:

1 stick butter	1 C. sugar
1 t. vanilla	2 eggs

Add small carton sour cream then flour mixture. Grease tube pan and alternate cake mixture with filling - ending with filling on top.

FILLING:

½ C. brown sugar	½ C. broken pecans
1 t. cinnamon	1 t. flour

Bake 30-35 minutes at 375 degrees.

Mrs. Al Costner

JELLY ROLL

3 large eggs	1 C. flour
1 C. sugar	1 t. baking powder
5 T. water	¼ t. salt
1 t. vanilla	

Beat eggs and sugar, add water and vanilla. Sift together and add dry ingredients. Grease and flour pan (oblong shallow bread pan) Bake at 375 degrees for 12-15 minutes. Turn out immediately on towel covered with confectioners sugar. Spread with jelly and roll up. Keep covered with towel until cool.

Mrs. Douglas Sizemore

KENTUCKY BOURBON CAKE

¾ lb. (3 sticks) butter
2¼ C. light brown sugar
  (firmly packed)
5½ C. sifted all-purpose
  flour
3½ C. (1 lb.) pecan meats

2 C. white sugar
6 eggs
¼ t. salt
1 t. mace (nutmeg)
2 C. Bourbon Whiskey

Cream butter until soft in your largest mixing bowl. Combine white and brown sugar thoroughly. Gradually work half the sugar mixture into butter, keeping it as smooth as possible. In a separate bowl beat eggs until light and fluffy. Then gradually beat in remaining sugar until you have a smooth, creamy mixture. Stir into butter mixture thoroughly. Sift flour, salt, and mace together. Add flour combination and whiskey to batter, alternating them and beginning and ending with flour. Break pecans into pieces and stir into batter. Pour into a well-greased 10 inch tube pan (batter should almost fill the pan), and bake in a pre-heated 300 degree oven for 1½ to 1¾ hrs. or until cakes shrinks slightly from pan. Allow cake to cool in pan about 15 minutes, then turn out onto cake rack and cool completely.

Bourbon Cake improves with age. It should be well-wrapped in foil and stored in refrigerator.

DO NOT FREEZE!   Mrs. David Johnson—Mr. Herman Jenkins

LEMON JELLO CAKE

1 pkg. Duncan Hines Cake
  Mix (white)
1 pkg. lemon jello

½ C. cooking oil
½ C. water

Juice of 1 lemon - add enough water to make 1/3 cup (This gives you the 1 1/3 cups of liquid called for on the cake mix box)
4 eggs - Add the grated rind of the lemon to the batter. Bake 1 hour at 350 degrees in a well greased and floured loaf pan (Mix by directions on box.)

Ida Ramsey

LITTLE JESUS CAKE

Cook 1 cup seedless raisins in 1 cup water until tender. Pour into pan to cool. While hot add ½ cup oleo. Beat 1 egg and add ½ cup water. **In a Pan Mix:**

1 C. sugar
1½ C. flour
1 t. soda
½ t. cinnamon
¼ t. cloves

Pour egg mixture and raisin mix together, and pour on flour and sugar mixture. Stir out all lumps. Pour into a greased and floured pan. Bake at 350 degrees for 20 to 25 minutes.

Mrs. Kelver Willis

ORANGE ICE BOX CAKE

½ C. sugar   2 t. flour
3 egg yokes

Mix above ingredients together.

ADD:

1 t. butter   1 C. milk
1/3 C. orange juice   1 t. grated orange rind

Cook until thick. Remove from heat and fold in 3 beaten egg whites. Alternate layers of split lady fingers or sponge cake with orange filling - beginning and ending with lady fingers. Top with whipped cream.

Put in a 9 X 5 X 3 inch loaf pan. Chill 6 to 8 hours or overnight.

Mrs. C. E. Jacobs, Jr.

CHOCOLATE POUND CAKE

2 sticks margarine   1 C. sweet milk
1 C. shortening   ½ t. salt
3 C. sugar   ½ t. baking powder
5 eggs   3 C. sifted flour
1 t. vanilla   ½ C. cocoa

Cream margarine and shortening with sugar. Add eggs one at a time. Sift dry ingredients together 3 times then add alternately with milk. Add vanilla. Bake in greased paper lined tube pan for 1½ hrs. at 325 degrees. Cool slightly before removing from pan.

Mrs. William C. Stevens

COCONUT POUND CAKE

CREAM:

2 sticks butter	**3 C. sugar**
½ C. shortening	

Beat and add 6 eggs, one at a time, beating 2 minutes after each one. Sift 3 cups flour and add alternately with one cup milk and ½ tsp. almond flavoring and 1 tsp. coconut flavoring. Add 1 can coconut. Beat well. Put in tube pan which has been greased and floured. Put in cold oven and turn to 325 degrees. Bake 1½ to 2 hours.

Mrs. John Hayes

POOR MAN'S POUND CAKE

3 C. sifted flour	**1 stick margarine**
1½ t. baking powder	**6 eggs**
2¼ C. sugar	**1½ t. vanilla**
1 C. shortening	**¾ C. milk**

Beat altogether 10 minutes at highest mixer speed. (Start on low-increase gradually) Pour into ungreased tube pan. Place in cold oven. Bake at 350 degrees for 1 hour and 15 minutes approximately.

Mrs. Ed Parker

SHERRY POUND CAKE

1 pkg. yellow cake mix	**¾ C. sherry**
1 pkg. instant vanilla pudding	**1 t. vanilla**
4 eggs	**1 t. nutmeg**
¾ C. oil	

Beat 5 minutes medium speed - grease angel food cake pan. Cook at 350 degrees for 45 minutes.

Mrs. Dwight Runge

ANGEL FOOD CAKE FILLING

3 egg yolks	3 t. melted butter
1 C. sugar	Juice of 1½ lemons
4 t. cornstarch	Juice of ½ orange
Pinch of salt	1 C. water

Cook in a double boiler until thick, all the above ingredients. Chill well and then add ½ pt. whipped cream. Slice Angel Cake in two layers and ice entire cake with remainder of filling. Refrigerate.

MRS. J. H. WINSTON

BOILED ICING

3 C. white sugar	4 stiffly beaten egg whites
½ C. water	1 scant C. powdered sugar
¼ C. syrup (white)	1 t. vanilla flavoring
½ t. cream of tartar	

Combine white sugar, water and syrup. Boil until it spins a thread. Take off heat and beat in ½ t. cream of tartar. Pour slowly over stiffly beaten egg whites. Beat in scant cup of powdered sugar. If all isn't needed at once, put in covered dish in refrigerator and use when desired.

MRS. D. M. CHAMBERS

BUTTER CREAM ICING

1 C. milk	1 T. plus 1 t. cornstarch

Cook the above until thick and then let cool.

Cream 1 C. butter and 1 C. sugar. Add cold mixture and 1 t. vanilla. Beat until fluffy — 10 or 15 minutes.

MRS. CHARLES PARKER

BUTTERSCOTCH SAUCE

2 C. brown sugar	½ C. flour

Mix the above together. Add:

2 C. water	2 T. butter

Cook until thick over slow heat, stirring all the time. Cool until luke-warm. Add 1 t. vanilla and ½ C. canned milk.

To keep warm, set saucepan in hot water.

This is delicious for gingerbread, cupcakes, etc.

MRS. R. H. OTTINGER

CARAMEL ICING

1 box brown sugar, plus 1 C. (¼ lb.) butter and enough canned milk to mix well.

Bring to slow boil. Cook until icing forms soft ball in cold water. Cool and beat until consistency to spread.

MRS. BRUNICK DEREN

CARAMEL ICING

Boil together for two minutes:

1 C. brown sugar   **¼ lb. butter**

Add ¼ C. milk and bring to a good boil. Take off stove and let stand until cool. Then add:

2 C. powdered sugar   **1 t. vanilla**

Beat until of spreading consistency. This icing never gets hard.

MRS. ROBERT GRIFFITH

CARAMEL ICING FOR JAM CAKE

1½ C. brown sugar (firmly   **2 T. butter**
      packed)   **1 T. vanilla**
¼ C. top milk or cream

Bring to boil for 3 minutes. Remove and beat until creamy. Add a little cream if icing gets too hard.

MRS. FRANK POTEAT

CHOCOLATE FROSTING

2 squares unsweetened chocolate
1 C. powdered sugar   **3 T. boiling water**

Melt chocolate squares over hot water. Add sugar gradually, stirring thoroughly. Add hot water and continue stirring. Cook until smooth, adding more hot water, if necessary, for spreading consistency. Ice cake immediately. Cut into squares when icing has become firm.

MRS. LILLIAN FIELDS

CHOCOLATE FROSTING (EASY, QUICK)

2 squares chocolate   **1/3 C. milk**
¼ C. butter   **¼ t. salt**
1 C. sugar   **¼ t. vanilla**

Melt chocolate. Add remaining ingredients and bring to boil. Let boil one minute. Remove from heat. Beat and spread.

MRS. FORREST TRAYLOR

CHOCOLATE FUDGE ICING

2 C. white sugar   **½ C. butter**
2 squares chocolate   **2/3 C. milk**
      (cut up)

Combine all ingredients in a saucepan. When ingredients come to a full boil, cook for 2 minutes. Remove from heat and beat until right consistency to spread.

MRS. PAUL MALLORY

CHOCOLATE FUDGE FROSTING WITH PEANUT BUTTER

3 squares unsweetened   Dash of salt
   chocolate   1 T. light corn syrup
1¼ C. milk   3 T. smooth peanut butter
3 C. sugar   1½ t. vanilla

Add chocolate to milk and salt and place over low heat. Cook until smooth, stirring constantly. Add sugar and corn syrup and stir until mixture boils. Boil, stirring occasionally, until mixture reaches the very soft ball stage (234°).

Remove from heat. Add peanut butter and vanilla. Cool to lukewarm. Beat until of right consistency to spread.

MRS. BRUCE THOMPSON

CHOCOLATE ICING

1 box powdered sugar
3 squares melted chocolate or 9 T. cocoa
Soften 1/3 stick of butter and add cocoa (less for chocolate)
Add 4 egg yolks   1 t. vanilla

Mix and add hot water to spreading consistency desired. Takes more hot water in winter than the summer. Add little at a time until icing is spreading consistency. This icing will freeze well.

MRS. DAN WEXLER

HUNGARIAN CHOCOLATE FROSTING

4 squares cocolate   2 eggs
1 C. powdered sugar   6 T. butter
1 T. hot water   Vanilla

Melt chocolate in a double boiler. Remove from heat. Add sugar and water and blend. Add eggs, one at a time, beating well after each addition. Add butter and blend to spreading consistency. Perfect for Boston Cream Pie, cream puffs or eclairs.

MRS. ROGER HENDRICKS
Seattle, Washington

LEMON FROSTING

½ C. butter   4 C. sifted powdered sugar
Dash of salt   4 or 5 t. lemon juice
1 t. grated lemon rind   1/3 C. milk (approximately)

Cream butter, salt and lemon rind. Add part of sugar **gradually,** blending after each addition. Add remaining sugar alternately with lemon juice, then with milk, until right consistency to spread. Be sure it is smooth.

MRS. GEORGE PARKERSON
Winder, Georgia

MARSHMALLOW ICING

1¼ C. sugar
2 T. white corn syrup
½ C. cold water
Pinch of salt

1 egg white
5 marshmallows, chopped
4 or 5 drops of vanilla

Boil sugar, syrup, salt and water until it forms almost a hard ball in cold water. Beat egg white until stiff. Continue beating and pour syrup over egg white slowly. Add marshmallows and vanilla. Continue beating until icing forms a peak when lifted with spoon. Double this recipe for a three layer cake or a larger cake.

MRS. FRED BROWN

EASY PENUCHE ICING

½ C. butter
1 C. brown sugar (firmly packed)

¼ C. milk
1¾ to 2 C. sifted powdered sugar

Melt butter in sauce pan. Add brown sugar. Boil over low heat for two minutes, stirring constantly. Stir in milk. Bring to boil, stirring constantly. Cool to lukewarm.

Gradually add powdered sugar, beating until thick enough to spread. If icing gets stiff, add a little hot water.

MRS. ROBERT UPCHURCH

RUM FILLING (FOR ANGEL FOOD CAKE)

Scald 2 T. Knox gelatin with 2 C. of milk in top of double boiler. Beat ½ C. of sugar slightly with 4 egg yolks. Add rum to taste.
Combine the ingredients and return to double boiler. Cook a few minutes. Cool in ice water. Then add 1 pt. of whipped cream, stirring until cool but not stiff.

Cut Angel Food Cake crosswise. Spread filling, to which has been added 1 small bottle maraschino cherries and two small packages of pecans. Cover cake with filling. Garnish with whole cherries and pecans.

MRS. BAILEY WILLIAMS, SR.

SEA FOAM ICING

1½ C. brown sugar
5 T. cold water
1½ t. white syrup

⅛ t. salt
2 egg whites

Beat all ingredients together over boiling water until mixture stands in peaks. Remove from heat. Add 1 t. vanilla and beat until consistency to spread.

MRS. JACK WHAREY

NEVER - FAIL WHITE ICING

2 egg whites
1½ C. sugar

2 t. white syrup
5 T. water

Mix together in double boiler. Place over heat and beat with rotary beater until icing stands in peak. Take off heat immediately. Spread on cake.

MRS. FRANK FLOYD

CANDY

DATE LOAF CANDY

1 C. milk	½ C. nuts
2 C. sugar	1 C. coconut
¼ C. butter	2 pkgs. dates

Cook milk, butter and sugar until it will form a soft ball in water. Add chopped dates, cook, stirring constantly until mixture leaves sides of pan. Remove from heat; add nuts and coconut. Beat until firm. Pour out on a damp cloth and roll into a loaf. When cool, cut in slices.

MRS. W. D. PATRICK

PENUCHE CANDY

2 C. light brown sugar	2 T. butter
½ C. milk	½ lb. nuts
⅛ t. cream of tartar	

Mix the sugar with the milk. Add cream of tartar and boil gently to soft boil stage. Before removing from heat, add butter and nuts. Beat until mixture thickens. Pour into buttered pan and cut in squares.

MISS ROSE BAUM

SEAFOAM CANDY

3 C. white sugar	¾ C. hot water
¾ C. white syrup	1 t. vanilla

Stir together and cook until hard ball forms when put in water. Beat 3 egg whites until stiff. After syrup cools, beat egg whites in slowly until mixed. Nuts may be added after cooling if desired. Beat mixture until thick (stands up). Spoon out. Makes 25 - 30 pieces.

MRS. CLIFFORD JOHNSON

SPIRIT CANDY

1 lb. pitted dates	¼ C. sugar
1 C. pecan or walnut meats	¼ C. whiskey
1 4¾-oz. box vanilla wafers	2 T. light corn syrup
(about 30)	2 C. shredded coconut

Put first 3 ingredients through a food chopper — using fine blade. Add sugar, whiskey and syrup; blend well. Form a layer ½ inch thick on a baking sheet. Cut in 1 inch squares. Coat on all sides with coconut. Store in tightly covered container until ready to use.

MRS. RENO BURLESON

FRENCH CHOCOLATES

2 pkgs. semi-sweet chocolate bits	1 t. vanilla
	1 C. chopped pecans
1 can sweetened condensed milk (1-1/3 C.)	Coconut or chopped nut meats

Melt chocolate over hot water. Stir in milk and add vanilla and pecans. Let mixture cool. Grease hands and form into balls. Roll in coconut or chopped nuts.

MRS. G. E. CREGAR

SMALL CHOCOLATE KISSES

1 lb. granulated sugar   ¼ lb. bitter
Whites of four eggs   chocolate

Beat egg whites and sugar for 30 minutes or with mixer until **very** stiff. Then add grated chocolate, stirring as little as possible. Using two teaspoons, drop about 1/3 teaspoon of mixture at a time on greased cookie sheet. Bake in very slow oven about 275 degrees until light and dry.

MRS. J. D. McQUILKEN

GLAZED FRUITS OR NUTS

¾ C. boiling water   Vanilla
2 C. sugar   Fruits or nuts

Boil water and sugar rapidly until syrup begins to turn brown. Add a little vanilla. Put fruit or nuts into the syrup; take out with fork and drop on marble slab.

NOTE: Nuts and the following fruits can be used: Dates, cherries, and white grapes with stems left on.

MRS. WILLIAM G. PREAS

CHOCOLATE FUDGE

3 C. white sugar   enough to mix well
2/3 can of cocoa, sm. size   ½ stick butter
1 T. cornstarch   Pinch of soda, baking powder
½ can condensed milk, or   and salt

Cook until mixture will form a soft ball in ice water. Remove from heat. Add butter, soda, baking powder and salt. Set in pan of cold water to cool and then beat. Pour into greased platter.

MISS EMILY BECKNER

MILLION DOLLAR FUDGE

(From The White House)

4 sqs. cooking chocolate   2 T. cream
4 T. butter (⅛ lb.)   1 lb. confectioners sugar
1 egg   1 C. nut meats
1 t. vanilla

Melt chocolate and butter together over hot water. Combine egg, vanilla, cream and sugar. Add to chocolate mixture; knead in nut meats. Turn into greased platter and chill several hours in refrigerator before cutting.

NOTE: If sweet butter is used, add a pinch of salt.

MRS. DWIGHT DAVID EISENHOWER

HARRIET'S MINTS

½ C. boiling water
2 C. sugar
⅛ lb. butter

Few drops oil of peppermint
Food coloring

Boil water. Add sugar and butter. Cover and cook until candy has boiled almost to top of pan. Uncover during remainder of cooking time. Cook until small amount of mixture forms a hard crack in ice water (290°F. on candy thermometer). Pour onto ice cold but dry buttered marble slab. In a few minutes take up and pull. Work peppermint and coloring into candy now and pull until almost all the gloss is gone. Twist and pull into long string and cut with shears. Will keep in closed tin for several weeks.

NOTE. Chill marble slab beforehand with ice, being sure to dry well before buttering.

MRS. CHARLES GORDON

MINTED NUTS

3 C. pecans
1 C. sugar
½ C. water
1 T. white Karo

⅛ t. salt
6 marshmallows
½ t. essence of peppermint

Cook sugar, water, Karo and salt slowly. Remove from heat just before mixture forms a soft ball when tried in cold water. Add marshmallows. Add peppermint and nuts and stir until every nut is coated and the mixture begins to harden. Pour out on wax paper.

MRS. HARRY CRUMLEY

CREOLE PECAN PRALINES

3 C. light brown sugar
¼ C. butter
1 C. cream

1½ C. chopped pecans
⅛ t. ground cinnamon

Mix sugar, butter and cream; cook until a small quantity dropped in cold water forms a soft ball. Add the chopped pecans and cinnamon. Beat until almost cold, then drop by spoonfuls onto waxed paper.

MRS. PAUL COLEMAN

PECAN PRALINES

2 C. sugar   ¾ C. milk

Boil gently until soft ball stage.

Then add 1 C. sugar which has been carmelized, 2 T. butter, and at least 2 C. pecans. Let cook a few minutes. Stir well. Put spoonfuls on greased pan. After hardening, remove with spatula.

MRS. EARL MILLER

SUGARED PECANS

2 C. pecans   ½ C. milk
1 C. sugar

Combine ingredients and let it boil until a soft ball forms in water. Remove from heat and beat. Keep stirring until the pecans take up all the sugar.

MRS. EARL MILLER

OLD FASHIONED POPCORN BALLS

1 C. white sugar   ¼ t. salt
½ C. light molasses   3 T. butter
½ C. white corn syrup   1 t. vanilla
¼ C. water   4 qts. popped corn, unsalted

Mix sugar, molasses, syrup, water and salt in 3-qt. saucepan. Cook over medium heat, stirring constantly until mixture boils. Boil gently until small amount of syrup forms a hard ball in cold water (about 250°F.) Remove from heat and add butter and vanilla. Stir thoroughly. Pour evenly over popped corn and mix well with wooden spoon. Form quickly into balls, using butter on hands. Makes 12 medium balls.

Variation: SQUARES OF POPCORN. Add 1 C. plain roasted peanuts. Pack corn in buttered oblong pan. Cool and cut in squares.

MRS. LEE G. COCHRAN

DIVINITY

2½ C. sugar	½ C. corn syrup
1/8 t. salt	1/3 C. water
2 egg whites	1½ C. chopped nuts
1 T. vanilla	3 drops almond extract

Cook sugar, corn syrup, salt and water until a small amount forms a soft ball (234 degrees to 240 degrees) when tested in cold water. Take out ½ cup of this mixture and cook the rest until it forms a hard ball (250 degrees to 265 degrees) when tried in cold water. Pour the ½ cup of syrup slowly over the beaten egg whites, beating constantly. Continue beating and add the remainder of the syrup. Add nuts, vanilla, and almond and keep beating until mass thickens and becomes heavy and dull in color. Drop with a teaspoon on wax paper. NOTE: Do not make on a rainy day.

Mrs. Bill Stevens

ENGLISH TOFFEE

½ lb. butter	Ground black walnuts
1 C. white sugar	1 can (4 or 5 oz.)
Large milk chocolate bar	blanched almonds

Melt butter **slowly**. Add sugar and almonds. Turn heat up until sugar and butter are blended, but be careful it does not smoke. Then cook slowly until a rich golden brown, for approximately ½ hour. Pour into tins. Rub on chocolate white hot and sprinkle with walnuts, using wooden spoon. Makes about 1½ lbs.

Mrs. T. A. Webster

FRUIT FANCIES

3 C. sugar	1 C. brazil nuts
1½ C. cream	1 C. whole pecan halves
1 C. white Karo	1 C. walnuts, broken
1 t. vanilla	1 C. candied cherries
1 C. candied pineapple	

Cook first 3 ingredients to soft ball stage. Remove fom heat and beat until thick. The color changes slightly. Add 1 tsp. vanilla and continue beating. Now add slowly, brazil nuts cut in half, whole pecan halves, walnuts, candied cherries cut in half and candied pineapple cut up. Mixture will be thick and sticky. Pack into loaf pan and chill. After a few hours the sticky syrup becomes firm and creamy. Store in refrigerator 24 hours. Slice ½" thick and cut each slice into finger lengths. Will keep for months and is most delicious.

Mrs. Phil Barksdale

NEVER FAIL FUDGE

1 C. Carnation milk	2 T. Karo syrup
2 sq. chocolate	3 T. butter
3 C. sugar	

Cook until mixture forms a soft ball or until temperature reaches 225 degrees on candy thermometer. Beat slightly. Add chopped nuts and 1 tps. vanilla. Pour in shallow dish to cool. Cut into squares.

ORANGE CANDY

1 C. sugar, melted in skillet until brown	1½ C. milk, scalded
	2 C. sugar
grated rind of 2 oranges	Pinch of salt
½ C. butter	1 C. nuts

To carmelized sugar add scalded milk; add remaining sugar. Cook to almost hard ball stage. Add salt, butter, orange and nuts. Cool. Beat, until creamy and drop from spoon.

Mrs. Vernon Wilson
Mrs. R. S. Shell

PEANUT BRITTLE

1½ C. sugar	2 C. raw peanuts
½ C. Karo syrup	2 T. butter
½ C. water	1 t. soda

Cook sugar, syrup and water until it spins a thread (on high heat). Turn to medium heat, add peanuts and cook 10 minutes or until peanuts are brown. Add butter and let come to boil. Add soda. Pour onto well greased cookie sheet. When cool, break into pieces.

Mrs. Harriet B. Nachman

SEAFOAM CANDY

1 C. white sugar	1 C. brown sugar
½ C. hot water	¼ t. cream of tartar
Pinch of salt	2 egg whites, beaten
1 t. vanilla	

Mix sugar, salt, cream of tartar and water. Bring to a boil, cover and turn heat down. Boil for 5 minutes or to 248 on candy thermometer. Pour syrup into well-beaten egg whites and beat until candy stands in a peak. NOTE: Make only on a sunny day. Drop with a teaspoon on waxed paper.

Mrs. Buddy Price

SPICED NUTS

½ C. sugar	½ t. salt
1 t. cinnamon	¼ t. cloves
2 T. water	¼ t. nutmeg
¼ lb. pecans (shelled)	

Combine all ingredients except pecans and cook until mixture forms a soft ball in cold water. Remove from heat, add nuts. Stir until turns to sugar; pour in buttered pan. When cool, break apart.

Mrs. R. E. Dodson, Jr.

CASSEROLES

BOILED BEEF IN CASSEROLE

4 large serving-size pieces of boiled beef
2 C. brown sauce (see below)
4 small boiled onions
4 small boiled carrots
2 T. butter
1 t. salt
1 t. sugar
8 potatoes, small

Place meat in casserole; cover with brown sauce. Cook onions and carrots 3 or 4 minutes in hot butter, season with salt and sugar, and add to casserole. Cook in hot oven (400°) 25 minutes. Baste meat frequently with sauce. Add potatoes and continue cooking until done. Serves 4.

BROWN SAUCE

1/3 C. beef suet
1 onion, chopped
1 carrot, diced
1/3 C. flour
1½ C. stock or bouillon
1 C. canned tomatoes
1½ C. red wine
2 sprigs parsley
1 stalk celery, chopped
1 bay leaf
¼ t. thyme
1 clove garlic
½ t. salt

Melt suet, cook onion and carrot 3 or 4 minutes. Add flour, stir and cook until browned. Add stock, tomatoes and wine. Bring to a boil, stirring continually until flour and fat are well mixed with liquid. Add herbs, garlic, and salt. Reduce heat and cook gently. Skim when necessary. After 2 hours, sauce should be well thickened. Strain Makes 2 cups.

MRS. HELMUT WINKLESTRATER.
Wuppertal, Germany

CHICKEN LIVER CASSEROLE

¼ C. butter
3 t. minced onion
15 oz. pkg. precooked rice (1-1/3 C.)
½ lb. chicken livers cut in 1-inch pieces (more could be used and left whole)
Seasoned flour (salt-pepper to taste)
1 can condensed cream of chicken soup, undiluted
½ C. milk
1 T. chopped parsley
Pinch dried basil

Melt butter and add onion. Add this to rice which has been cooked by directions on package. Roll chicken livers in flour. Saute in butter. Combine all in 1½ quart casserole. Bake until hot and bubbly. (375° for 30 minutes).

MRS. FRED BREWER

CHICKEN ROLL

2 C. flour	1 stick margarine or
3 t. baking powder	butter (soft)
¾ t. salt	2/3 to ¾ C. milk

Sift together dry ingredients and blend in half of butter. Knead 20 times. Roll to ½ inch thickness 11 to 12 inches long.

Brush dough with ½ stick melted butter. Make a filling of 2 C. cubed chicken, ½ C. chicken broth, 2/3 t. salt, ⅛ t. pepper. Spread evenly on dough, and roll as jelly roll. Bake on greased cookie sheet 400° 30 minutes.

MRS. BRUCE KIDD

CORN CASSEROLE, MEXICAN

Cook 2 C. corn meal, 3 C. water, salt and pepper in a double boiler for 20 minutes or until batter is firm, but can be poured. Pour into oblong pan. Batter should be about 1½ inches thick. Let batter cool, which takes about 2 hours, or can be left overnight. Cut into 1 inch strips. Mix 1 lb. ground beef, salt, pepper, 2 finely chopped cloves of garlic, 2 finely chopped onions, 2 C. water. Put beef mixture in pan with ½ can of creamed chicken soup, 2½ C. canned whole kernel corn, salt, pepper, 1 onion, chopped fine, 1 clove garlic, chopped fine, 2 doz. large pimento filled olives sliced thin. Line bottom of 8-inch casserole with corn meal strips. Add meat. Top with corn and olive mixture. Crown with strips of green pepper and additional olive slices.

Cook uncovered in 350°F. oven for 2 hours, by which time juices should be simmered down. This can be cooked ahead of time, reheated before bringing to the table and kept warm at the table over candle warmer.

MRS. ALLEN HARRIS, JR.

GRAB BAG CASSEROLE

1 lb. ground beef	Salt and pepper
2 T. shortening	1 No. 2 can cream style
¼ C. chopped onion	corn
1 can tomato soup	¼ C. chopped ripe olive
1½ C. water	1 C. grated cheese
½ 8-oz. pkg. noodles	

Brown meat in shortening. Add onion, cook until golden. Add tomato soup (undiluted), water and noodles. Cook till tender. Stir frequently. Season to taste. Add corn, olives, and ½ C. cheese. Bake 350°F. for 45 minutes. Serve very hot. Serves 6 to 8.

MRS. JOE LUSK

HAMBURGER CASSEROLE

Brown lightly: 1½ lb. ground beef
1 med. onion, chopped
½ green pepper chopped

Add: 2 C. tomato juice
salt and pepper to taste

1 bouillon cube dissolved in
½ cup boiling water
1 C. raw regular rice

Put in casserole and top with cheese and bake covered for 1 hour at 325°F.

MRS. DON KING
Bristol, Tennessee

CHICKEN DINNER

1 C. raw rice
2 oz. jar pimiento
¼ C. mushrooms
½ C. slivered almonds
2 C. cooked chicken (cubed)
¼ C. celery, chopped

2 C. chicken broth
1½ C. French cut
green beans
2 T. flour
salt and pepper

Put rice to steam with 1 cup of water. This will leave it half cooked when steamed dry. Saute' mushrooms (fresh preferred) and almonds in butter. Chop pimiento into rice when it has steamed dry; pour half of rice into buttered casserole, and half of almonds and mushrooms, beans, celery and chicken alternately. Repeat, using all of ingredients. Thicken broth with flour, season it, and pour over all. Top with a few additional almonds. Cover and bake about 1 hour at 350°. Add additional broth during cooking if necessary.

LASAGNA CASSEROLE

1 8 oz. pkg. lasagna noodles
1 lb. ground beef
2 cloves garlic, crushed
2 T. salad oil
1 8 oz. can tomato sauce
1 No. 2 can tomatoes
¼ C. minced onion

1½ t. salt
¼ t. pepper
1½ t. oregano
½ lb. thinly sliced Mozzarella
or American cheese
½ C. Parmesan cheese

Brown beef and garlic in salad oil. Stir in tomato sauce, onions, salt, pepper, and oregano. Cover and simmer 15 to 20 minutes or until slightly thickened. Cook noodles 30 minutes in boiling salted water. Drain. Fill 3 qt. casserole by alternating layer of noodles, Mozzarella cheese, tomatoes, meat mixture, and Parmesan cheese. Bake in moderately hot oven, 350°F., 20 to 25 minutes.

MRS. MAYNARD INGRAM
Port Washington, New York

MACARONI CASSEROLE

1 C. uncooked macaroni	2 chopped pimentoes
1 C. grated sharp cheese	1 C. soft bread crumbs
¼ C. butter	Minced onion to taste

Beat together: **1 C. milk**   **2 eggs**

Cook macaroni and combine with other ingredients. Pour into a buttered baking dish. Make a sauce of 1 small can mushrooms, browned in butter, 1 can of mushroom soup, and a dash of Worcestershire sauce. Pour over the top of the macaroni and bake about 30 minutes at 350°F.

NELLE MacDONALD

MEAT BALLS — GERMAN

1 slice bread soaked in milk	1 T. butter, melted
1 lb. hamburger	¼ c. minced onion
1 beaten egg	

Mix above ingredients. Then add salt, ¼ t. paprika, ½ t. lemon rind, 1 t. lemon juice, 1 t. Worcestershire sauce, garlic salt, 3 T. grated Italian cheese. Mix well. Shape into balls and brown in shortening. Make a brown gravy and pour over meat balls. Serve on mashed potatoes.

MRS. BRUCE KIDD

MEAT MUFFINS

½ lb. ground ham	Add 2 C. cream sauce
½ lb. ground pork	1 unbeaten egg
Add 2 C. cooked macaroni, drained	salt and pepper to taste

Mix well, fill muffin tins and bake 350°F., 25 minutes.

MRS. FRANK L. KNISLEY

MEAT PIE, CHARTREUSE

2 C. ground veal	2 T. finely chopped onion
1 t. salt	1 egg
¼ t. pepper	¼ C. fine crumbs
1 T. chopped parsley or pickle	2 to 3 C. cooked rice

Season the meat and mix with the crumbs and beaten egg. Add enough meat stock to make it pack easily. Line a thoroughly buttered dish with cooked rice. Fill with the meat, cover with cooked rice, cover tightly and steam 45 minutes. Serve with tomato sauce. This recipe doubled fills a melon mold. After steaming, turn out on large platter and surround with tomato sauce.

ADA HORNSBY EARNEST

PORK CHOP CHOW MEIN

5 large pork chops—cook in small amount of fat. Do not brown.
3 C. chopped onions   **2 C. chopped celery**

Cut cooked chops in small pieces. Add **celery and onions and saute.**
Put in heavy pot and add:

1 can Chinese vegetables	1 T. salt
1 C. water	black pepper
1 t. Soya sauce	¼ stick butter
1 can mushrooms	Dash tabasco sauce

Bring to boil and add 3 T. corn starch dissolved in 1 C. boiling water.
Cook about ½ hour. Serve over rice and sprinkle with Chinese noodles.
Serves 6 to 8.

MRS. FRANK TAYLOR

PORK CHOP ONE DISH SUPPER

Use as many pork chops as you want servings. Salt and pepper the
chops well and brown in an iron skillet.

On each chop place a slice of raw onion, and a heaping T. of washed
raw rice. Over this pour a large can of tomatoes. Place in a moderate
oven and cook until rice is fluffy. You may have to add more tomatoes
if it cooks too dry.

MRS. CLEM WILKES

PORK CHOPS, BAKED WITH NOODLES

1 t. salt	1 can condensed tomato soup
4 or 5 medium thick	½ C. water
pork chops	1 pkg. (8 oz.) uncooked
1 C. celery	noodles
1 T. shortening	

Sprinkle salt in skillet and brown chops lightly on both sides. Remove
chops and add shortening. Cook celery until tender. Stir in soup and
water and let simmer. Place the uncooked noodles in an oiled baking
dish. Arrange chops on top. Add celery and tomato mixture. Cover
and bake in moderate oven (350°F.) about 1 hour. Add more warm
water, if too dry during the baking period. Serve at once.

MRS. LILLIAN FIELDS

PORK CHOP SUPREME

Salt, pepper and flour pork chops

Brown in small amount grease. Put 1 can cream of mushroom soup
in casserole and add 1 can water a little at a time. Add pork chops
to soup mixture. Bake in 350° oven 1 hour. Serve with rice.

MRS. J. A. GIULI

SAUSAGE AND CABBAGE (THE EARTHY DISH)

1 lb. sausage (link or bulk) 1 small cabbage shredded
1 No. 2 can tiny new potatoes or 10 tiny boiled new potatoes
1 C. chicken extract — either made from bouillon cubes or
  canned soup
2 T. dehydrated parsley 1 t. thyme
1 t. salt

Brown the sausage in skillet. Remove the sausage and pour off most of the grease. Brown the potatoes and put them in bottom of a low casserole. Add parsley, thyme and salt. Add cabbage and top with sausage. Pour chicken concentrate over all, cover and bake slowly at 350° for about an hour. Long cooking is advised with occasional stirring to keep the top from drying out. This is a hearty dish and will serve four generously. Wonderful for a cold winter supper.

MRS. McKINNON ELLIS

SPAGHETTI CASSEROLE

1 lb. ground beef 1 small can mushrooms
1 No. 2 can tomatoes 4 slices bacon
1 can puree ½ lb. spaghetti
1 medium onion, chopped salt, pepper, grated cheese
1 medium pepper, chopped

Saute pepper and mushrooms. Fry bacon. Remove bacon and brown meat in part of fat. Add all other ingredients. Cook spaghetti in salt water, drain. With large fork mix together. Place in oblong dish. Place in refrigerator over night. Three hours before cooking, remove from refrigerator. Bake 45 minutes with cheese on top.

MRS. JOE MOOREHEAD
Greenville, S. C.

STOHLER'S PIE

1½ lbs. ground beef 1 onion, diced
Mashed potatoes for 6

Brown ground beef in skillet. Add onion. Season to taste with salt, pepper, and mono-sodium glutamate. Add ¼ C. cold water if meat mixture is dry. Put meat mixture in bottom of casserole dish. Top with mashed potatoes. Sprinkle with paprika. Bake in oven 30 minutes at least 325°F. This can stay in oven up to 2 hours if necessary. It makes a very tasty casserole and children especially like it.

MRS. EDGAR STOHLER

SUNDAY NIGHT SUPPER

4 lbs. hamburger
2 medium sized onions
1 can tomato paste
2 cans chicken gumbo soup

3 T. tomato catsup
Worcestershire sauce
garlic, salt, pepper to taste

Brown finely chopped onion in 2 T. fat. Add hamburger and brown. Add tomato paste, chicken gumbo soup, tomato catsup, small clove garlic, finely chopped, dash Worcestershire sauce, and salt and pepper to taste. Simmer over low heat for 1½ hours. Serve on hamburger buns. Serves 16 to 20.

MRS. HUGH GADDIS

HOT TAMALE PIE

1 large onion, chopped
1½ lb. ground beef
1 can condensed tomato soup
1 t. salt
½ t. pepper

1 T. chili powder
¾ C. chopped ripe olives
1 12-oz. can whole kernel
    corn (¾ C.)

Brown onion and meat in hot fat, add remaining ingredients. Pour into greased casserole, and cover. Bake in moderate oven (325°F.) 1½ hours. Pour corn bread batter over the top and bake uncovered in hot oven 425°F., 25 minutes. Serves 8:

CORN BREAD

Sift ½ C. flour, 1 t. salt, 1 t. baking powder and ½ t. soda. Add ¾ C. corn meal and mix well. Add 1 C. buttermilk and 1 beaten egg, then 2 T. salad oil. Bake at 400 degrees for 30 minutes.

MRS. HUGH MOHLER

TAMALE PIE, MEXICAN

1 C.corn meal
4 C. water
1 t. salt
1 medium onion
2 C. ground cooked meat

1 green pepper
3 T. cooking oil
2½ C. cooked tomatoes
Dash cayenne or chili
    powder

Cook corn meal, water, and salt in top of double boiler for 45 minutes. Chop onion and pepper and fry in hot oil, add tomatoes, cooked meat, salt and cayenne or chili powder and cook until thickened. Line greased baking dish with half of the mush, pour in meat mixture, cover with remaining mush and bake in hot oven (375°F.) 30 minutes or until top is lightly browned. Serves 6 to 8.

MRS. FOSTER YOUNG

TEXAS HASH

3 T. drippings

Brown 2 onions and 2 green peppers chopped fine, until
golden brown and tender

Add 1 lb. ground beef, cooked until gray

2 t. salt	1 t. chili powder
¼ t. pepper	1 No. 2 can tomatoes
1 C. cooked rice or spaghetti	

Blend. Put in covered casserole and cook 350°F., oven 45 minutes.

Mrs. Frank L. Knisley

TURKETTI

1¼ C. raw spaghetti broken in 2-inch pieces	1 can cream of chicken soup or cream of mushroom soup
1 to 2 C. cubed cooked chicken or turkey	½ C. chicken broth
¼ C. diced pimento	½ t. salt
¼ C. green pepper	⅛ t. pepper
½ C. peeled onion diced	1¾ C. grated cheese

Cook spaghetti. Put everything in casserole. Add broth and part of
the cheese. Sprinkle rest of cheese on top and bake at 350°F for 45
minutes. Serve alone as a main dish or on chow mein noodles if desired.

Mrs. Hugh Warren

HARD COOKED EGG CASSEROLE

6 T. butter	10 hard cooked eggs, chopped
6 T. flour	
3 C. milk	½ lb. grated sharp cheese
salt to taste	
dash of pepper	1 stack crackers, crushed very finely
1 (2 oz.) can pimentos, chopped	1 stick butter melted

Make a cream sauce using the butter, flour, milk, pepper and salt;
then add pimentos. Put a layer of crumbs on bottom of buttered
dish, add egg slices, cheese and sauce in layers. Top with a topping
made of melted butter and crumbs. Bake at 350 degrees till bubbly
and brown, about 20 minutes.

Mrs. Al Miller

ITALIAN JOY

1 lb. ground chuck	1 small can corn
1 No. 2 can tomatoes	1 large onion
2/3 8 oz. pkg. spaghetti	Cheese

Brown onion in butter, add meat. Season with garlic, chili powder,
salt, pepper, tomatoes. Add cooked spaghetti. Pour in greased pyrex.
Bake 45 minutes at 350°F. Top with sharp cheese.

Miss Emily Beckner

FRANKFURT BARBECUE

¼ C. chopped onion	2 T. vinegar
2 T. fat	¼ C. lemon juice
½ t. salt	3 T. worcestershire sauce
Dash of pepper	½ T. prepared mustard
Dash of cayenne	½ C. chopped celery
2 T. brown sugar	12 frankfurters (1½ lbs.)
1 C. catsup	½ C. water

Lightly brown onion in fat; add combined remaining ingredients, except frankfurters; simmer 30 minutes. Prick frankfurters with fork; arrange in baking dish; pour sauce over. Bake in moderate oven (350 degrees) for 45 minutes. Serves 6.
A tart sauce for chops or ribs, too.   **Mrs. Charles Hillman**

HAMBURGER PIE

1 lb. ground chuck	1 onion, chopped
1 can tomato soup	1 can green beans
Mashed potatoes	salt & pepper to taste

Brown ground beef and chopped onion in fat. Add can of tomato soup and can of green beans. Stir. Mash potatoes and beat an egg into the potatoes. Put meat mixture in casserole and spread mashed potatoes on top. Set dish under heat (broil) until potatoes are brown. Cheese strips can be placed on top of the mashed potatoes.

Mrs. W. H. Conant
Kingsport, Tenn.

HAMBURGER AND WILD RICE CASSEROLE

2½ C. wild rice	2 large bay leaves
2 qts. boiling water	½ t. each: celery salt, pap-
½ C. olive oil	rika, onion salt, curry pow-
¾ C. chopped onions	der, salad herbs, garlic
2 lbs. lean ground beef	powder
2 C. water	4 cans chicken with rice soup
salt to taste	4 small cans mushrooms
	(stems & pieces)

Pour boiling water over rice and let stand 15 minutes. Drain. Saute' onions in olive oil. Add beef, and brown. Add wild rice, soup, mushrooms (liquid, too), water and seasonings. Cover with Italian cheese and bake at 375 degrees for 1 hour. Best made the day before (Serves 16)   **Mrs. Alfred Bolton**

HELEN'S "MALAY" DINNER

Cook one (6 lb.) stewing hen until tender. Cool. Cut in bite size pieces. Use broth to make gravy for sauce and make PLENTY! Use chicken boullion cubes to make gravy more flavorful if necessary. Cook plenty of rice. For on the plate you will follow this order. . . Rice, Chicken, Condiments, and Gravy. Now, you will prepare a bowl full of each of the following: Celery (chopped fine) . . . Hard boiled eggs (chopped) . . . Onion (chopped fine) . . . Sweet Pickles (chopped very fine) . . . Mild cheese (chopped) . . . crushed pineapple (drained) . . . Cashews (chopped) . . . Each guest, after putting the rice then the chicken on his plate, then adds a little of each condiment sprinkled over and tops it off with gravy and is it DEE-LICIOUS! (Serves 20 people)

Mrs. Helen Sheffield
West Palm Beach, Florida

LASAGNA

SAUCE:
¼ C. olive oil
1 lb. ground round
1 large onion, minced
2 cloves garlic, minced
1 can tomato paste

1 can tomato sauce
1 No. 2 can Italian tomatoes
1 t. Italian Seasoning
2 C. water
Salt and pepper

Heat oil in skillet, add meat, onion, garlic and cook until brown. Separate meat into pieces with fork. Add seasoning, tomato sauces and water. Simmer 1½-2 hours.

OTHER INGREDIENTS:
½ pkg. lasagna (1 lb. size)
1 C. grated Italian cheese
(grated Romano and Parmesan)

2 (6 oz.) pkg. provalone cheese

Mix:
1 pkg. cottage cheese mixed with
1 egg, beaten or 1 lb. ricotta cheese without egg

Cook lasagna noodles in boiling salted water until tender - 20 minutes and rinse. Drain. Then put together;

Ladle enough sauce on bottom of baking dish to cover. Add layer of lasagna, spread with cottage cheese then cover with slices of Provolone Cheese. Repeat layers until dish is filled (Should make 3 layers in 9" dish) Sprinkle with grated cheese and bake in 375 degree oven about 30 minutes or until cheese is well melted. This sauce is also good for spaghetti.

Mrs. Bill Kohler

LAURA'S HOT DISH

1 lb. ground beef	2 C. celery, diced
2 small onions, diced	½ C. raw rice
1 can chicken rice soup	2 T. soy sauce
1 can cream of mushroom soup	2 C. water

Mix and bake at 350 degrees for 1 hour, covered. DO NOT SALT.

Mrs. Bill Kohler

MYSTERY SUPPER RING

4 T. oleo	4 T. flour
1 C. mayonnaise	2 C. milk
2 C. diced turkey or chicken	2 eggs
3 chicken boullion cubes	1 can slivered almonds
	1 can chinese fried noodles

Melt oleo, blend in flour, add milk and cubes. Stir over low heat until smooth and thickened. Cool slightly. Add to well-beaten eggs, mix well. Stir in mayonnaise. Fold in turkey, almonds and noodles. Bake in well greased ring mold at 350 degrees for 50-60 minutes.
Let stand for 5 minutes. Unmold and fill center with hot sauce.

SAUCE:
1 can condensed celery soup 1 can mushroom soup

Combine soups, do not dilute, and bring slowly to boiling point. Pour into ring just before serving.

Mrs. Robert Mains

MANDARIN FOO YOO

1 lb. ground pork and beef (half & half)	1 T. soy sauce
1 T. California sherry	1 T. cornstarch
	Salt

Form into meat balls. Brown. Pour sweet and sour sauce over it.

SAUCE:
1 T. cornstarch	½ C. dark brown sugar
⅓ C. vinegar	6 T. pineapple juice
2 t. soy sauce	

Put cornstarch and sugar in pan. Add vinegar, soy sauce and pineapple juice. Bring to boil and simmer 1½ min. Pour over meatballs. Add pineapple chunks (2½ oz. can) and green pepper rings which have been saute'ed till tender-not dark green. Simmer ½ hour.

Serve over rice or Chinese noodles and top with slivered almonds. (Serves 4)

Mrs. William Blackard

QUICHE' LORRAINE (2 Pies)

Line pan with pie crust

36 slices of bacon cooked and crumbled
**36 slices of Gruyere cheese, cut up, Norweigan Jarlsburg
or Swiss**

Fix overlapping layers of cheese and bacon in pie crust. Over cheese sprinkle 1½ t. grated onion (in each pie).

BEAT TOGETHER:

12 eggs	**dash cayenne pepper**
3 T. flour	**freshly ground pepper**
1½ t. salt	**3 cloves garlic, mashed**

(3 wine glasses of brandy) Add lastly to eggs before straining. Add 6 cups light cream (scalded) and stir in 4½ Tbs. melted butter. Strain above mixture over bacon, cheese and bake at 450 degrees for 12 min. then at 300 degrees for 35 min.

Mrs. Al Costner

SOUR CREAM NOODLE BAKE

1 (8 oz.) pkg. med. egg noodles	**2 T. butter**
2 lb. ground beef	**2 (8 oz.) cans tomato sauce**
1 t. salt	**⅛ t. pepper**
¼ t. garlic salt	**1 C. cottage cheese (creamed)**
½ C. chopped green onions	**1 C. sour cream**
¾ C. cheddar cheese, shredded	

Cook noodles according to package directions. Rinse and drain. Melt butter in skillet. Brown meat, add tomato sauce, salt, pepper and garlic salt. Cover and simmer 5 minutes. Fold together the noodles, sour cream, cottage cheese and onion. Spoon half the mixture into bottom of 2½ qt. casserole cover with half of meat mixture. Repeat layers once again. Sprinkle with shredded cheese on top. Bake 25-30 minutes at 350 degrees until mixture is thoroughly heated and cheese melted.

Mrs. Al Costner

STUFFED CABBAGE SURPRISE

Wash 1 medium head of cabbage. Cover with boiling water. Boil 20 minutes. Drain and cool. With kitchen shears or sharp knife remove core and enough of the center part to make a cavity for the meat mixture.

STUFFING:

Saute':.. ½ cup chopped 2 T. diced green pepper
    onion 1 lb. ground beef
    (in a little fat-2 T.)

Remove from heat. Combine with remaining:

1 t. salt ⅛ t. pepper
¼ C. chopped green olives 1 egg, well beaten
½ t. Worcestershire sauce ½ C. bread crumbs

Stuff cabbage with above mixture. Place cabbage upright in baking dish. Cover and bake at 350 degrees for 30-40 minutes.
To serve, cut cabbage into wedges. Serves 4 to 6.

Mrs. Dudley Evans

SWISS RICE BAKE

2 C. shredded Swiss Cheese 1 C. milk
½ stick butter or margarine 1 C. diced cooked chicken
1 (4½ oz.) jar sliced   or ham
   mushrooms drained ¼ t. salt
¼ t. dill weed ¼ t. leaf marjoram
3 eggs, well beaten 1 C. uncooked rice

Cook rice according to package directions. Heat milk and butter in a saucepan. Combine all ingredients. Pour into a shallow 1½ qt. baking dish which has been rubbed with butter. Bake in a moderate oven (350 degrees) about 45 minutes, or until table knife inserted into center of rice comes out clean. Remove from oven. Serve immediately. (Makes 6-8 servings)

Mrs. James W. Gibson

BEEF GOULASH (HUNGARIAN)

Approx. 3 oz. salt pork
1 lb. onions (3-4 medium)
2 to 3 lbs. beef (chuck,
    shoulder, or similar cut)
    cubed
1 T. flour

1 t. vinegar
1 t. pepper
1 t. garlic
1 T. paprika
Salt to taste

Cube and heat salt pork or other fat. Slice and fry onions until yellow. Add meat cubes and brown. Add garlic, paprika, vinegar, pepper and salt. Cook slowly for 2-3 hours, adding as little water as possible. When meat is tender, add flour (sour cream - ½ pt. is optional) and serve with rice, potatoes or dumplings.

Mrs. Walter Fleischmann

BEEF STROGANOFF (GROUND BEEF)

2 T. oil
1 lb. ground beef
1 small onion
1½ C. to 2 C. noodles
½ C. sour cream

1 t. worcestershire sauce
1 t. celery salt
½ t. salt & pepper
2 C. tomato juice

Brown onion in the oil. Add ground beef to onions and cook until it loses its pinkness. Add seasonings and tomato juice. Add uncooked noodles to mixture and simmer slowly covered. This can be simmered for quite a while. Add sour cream before serving.

Mrs. Douglas Sizemore

BRIDGE CASSEROLE

1 No. 2 can artichoke hearts
    or 1 pkg. frozen
1 can (3½ oz.) crab meat
1 can mushrooms

1½ C. med. cream sauce
1 T. worcestershire sauce
¼ C. sherry (dry)
¼ C. parmesan

Put artichokes on bottom of small casserole - cover with crab and mushrooms - pour sauce over all. Cover with Parmesan. Bake 25 minutes at 375 degrees.

Mrs. John Wilson

COUNTRY BAKED BEEF PIE

1 lb. ground beef	1 tomato, chopped
1 carrot, sliced thin or grated	1 med. potato, grated
1 clove of garlic or onion	1 T. A-1 sauce
1 T. worcestershire sauce	Salt and pepper to taste

Brown meat, saute' tomato, carrot, potato, garlic in skillet, add sauces to the meat; cover with a thin cornbread batter. Bake until brown at 400 degrees. (30-40 minutes).

Mrs. Robert L. Hodges, Jr.

CURRIED FRUIT

1 No. 303 can peach halves	1 No. 2 can pineapple slices
1 No. 303 can pear halves	Jar maraschino cherries
1/3 C. butter	with stems
4 t. curry powder	3/4 C. light brown sugar, packed

Day before: 1 - heat oven to 325 degrees. Drain fruits; dry on paper towel; arrange in casserole. 2 - Melt butter, add brown sugar, and curry powder, and stir until blended. Spoon over fruit. 3 - Bake 1 hour uncovered. Cool-Refrigerate. 4 - before serving, reheat casserole of curried fruit in 350 degrees oven for 30 minutes. Serve warm fruit with ham, lamb, poultry, etc.

Mrs. Ben Kelly

SPICED PINEAPPLE CHUNKS

2 cans pineapple chunks	1 C. sugar
1 C. vinegar	2 cinnamon sticks
12 cloves	

Boil the sugar, vinegar, cinnamon and cloves with the syrup from the pineapple for 20 minutes. Add the pineapple chunks and simmer 15 minutes longer. Serve hot with ham or barbecued chicken.

Mrs. James R. McLean

CHEESE & EGGS

BAKED MACARONI AND CHEESE

1 C. soft bread crumbs
1 C. cooked macaroni
1 t. grated onion
1½ C. grated cheese
1½ C. milk

2 eggs
1 T. green pepper
1 T. butter
¼ t. prepared mustard
Salt, pepper and paprika

Combine all ingredients. Season to taste. Pour into greased baking dish. Set in pan of warm water. Bake at 375°F. about 40 minutes

MRS. JACK TANNER

CHEESE FONDUE

Mix: 1 C. soft stale bread crumbs
      ¼ lb. mild cheese (cut fine)

1 C. hot scalded milk
1 t. butter and ¼ t. salt

Add the **well beaten yolks of 3 eggs.**

Cut and fold in whites beaten until stiff and dry. Turn in buttered baking dish. Bake 25 minutes in moderate (350°F.) oven.

MRS. LEONARD HASCHE

CHEESE PUDDING

1 C. grits
⅛ lb. butter
1½ - 2 C. grated sharp cheese

1 C. heavy cream
1 egg, slightly beaten

Cook grits in 4 C. water for 30 minutes. Add remaining ingredients and mix well. Pour into greased casserole and bake for 1 hour in 350°F. oven. Serves 6 to 8.

MRS. T. D. EVANS, III

CHEESE SOUFFLE

3 T. butter
3 T. flour
1 C. milk
½ t. salt
½ t. dry mustard

Pepper to taste
1 C. grated cheese
3 well-beaten egg yolks
3 stiffly beaten egg whites

Melt the butter and blend in the flour. Gradually add the milk and bring to a simmer. Stir constantly for 3 minutes. Add salt, mustard, and pepper.

Cool slightly. Stir in the grated cheese and 3 egg yolks. Fold in the egg whites. Place in a well-greased baking dish or casserole and bake in a 375°F. oven for 40 to 45 minutes. Serve immediately. Serves 4 or 5.

FOOLPROOF CHEESE SOUFFLE

Spread 8 slices of white bread with butter. Cut into ½-inch cubes.
Grate 1 lb. sharp cheese

Grease casserole and put in alternate layers of cheese and bread.

Beat 6 eggs — Mix with
¾ t. salt

3 C. milk
Dash red pepper

Add Worcestershire sauce for flavor.

Pour over cheese and bread. Let stand in refrigerator (covered) several hours or overnight. Bake in 350°F. oven for 1 hour.

MRS. DAN WEXLER, JR.

SCRAMBLED EGGS WITH CHEESE

4 eggs
1 small cake of Philadelphia
    cream cheese
6 strips of bacon, cut
    in small pieces

2 T. butter
¼ C. cream
3 T. olive oil
Salt and pepper to taste

Mash cheese and mix with olive oil in a mixing bowl. Add eggs, salt, pepper and cream. Beat with a fork until all ingredients are thoroughly mixed. Cook the bacon in a skillet until it is almost done. Do not allow it to get crisp. Drain off all but a small amount of grease. Add butter and melt with bacon. Add egg and cheese mixture. Cook over slow heat, stirring constantly until eggs have reached the desired consistency. Before serving, drain off any liquid which may have formed from the cheese. Serves 2.

A variation to this recipe is to place cooked eggs on thin slices of buttered toast. Cover with slices of sharp cheese. Place under a broiler until the cheese starts to melt. Serve hot.

MRS. RICHARD C. MILLER

HAM AND EGG CROQUETTES

1 can mushroom soup
6 hard boiled eggs, chopped
½ t. Worcestershire sauce
½ t. prepared mustard
1½ C. soft bread crumbs

1 C. chopped cooked ham
Dry bread crumbs
1 egg, beaten
1 t. salt

Heat mushroom soup. Combine eggs, salt, Worcestershire sauce and mustard. Add eggs, soft bread crumbs and ham to soup. Heat and cook for 4 to 5 minutes. Chill. Shape into croquettes. Roll in bread crumbs, dip into egg (diluted with 2 T. water) and roll again in crumbs. Fry in hot fat 375°F., two to five minutes or until brown. Drain on absorbent paper. Serves 6.

MRS. FOSTER YOUNG

EGG CUTLET

5 hard boiled eggs   1 C. cream sauce

Melt 3 T. butter. Stir in 3 T. flour. Add 1 C. warm cream and cook over low heat stirring constantly until thick. Chop eggs and add hot sauce. Season to taste and allow to cool. Shape in balls and roll in fine cracker crumbs. Fry in deep hot fat until brown. Drain and serve. Makes 9 cutlets.

MRS. WILLIAM PREAS

GRAPENUT EGGS

Butter a casserole generously. Break one egg into it for each person to be served. Sprinkle over each egg one tablespoon of grapenuts fresh from the package. Add 2 T. of milk for each egg. Be sure to pour the milk over the grapenuts so that they will soften and not become toasted. Salt and pepper to taste. Bake 20 minutes. If desired, a half strip of bacon may be placed on top of the casserole.

The eggs will puff up so they can be lifted out separately.

MRS. JOSEPH RAYMOND HUDSON

EGG NOODLES

2 whole eggs   1 egg yolk
4 half shells of milk

Mix and add flour until it makes a very stiff dough. Divide into **two** portions to roll. Roll very thin. Spread to dry. Cut any width desired after they have dried. This amount of noodles will serve 6.

MRS. FRED DENEEN

BAKED EGG OMELET

6 eggs   6 T. milk
¾ t. salt   4 T. shortening

Preheat oven to 350°F. Grease a heavy skillet, preferably iron, and heat it. Combine all ingredients and beat well. Pour into the hot skillet and bake for 15 minutes. Turn onto a hot platter and serve immediately.

MRS. RICHARD JENNINGS

SCRAMBLED EGGS AND ALMONDS

4 eggs
½ C. almonds, rolled fine
1 medium-sized onion,
     chopped fine
½ C. cream
Salt, pepper and tabasco
     to taste

½ t. chili powder
½ C. ground cooked meat
     (any leftovers)
½ C. soup stock
4 T. butter

Mix all ingredients except eggs in a frying pan. Cook until brown, stirring constantly. (This will burn easily if not stirred.) Mixture should have enough liquid to boil. Pour in eggs and stir constantly until thoroughly cooked into the mixture. Serves 2.

MRS. RICHARD C. MILLER

SPANISH EGGS

1 5 or 6-oz. pkg. (2 C.) noodles
½ C. chopped onion
½ C. chopped green pepper
3 T. fat
1 #2 can tomatoes (2½ C.)

¼ lb. American cheese (1 C.)
¼ C. margarine
¼ C. flour
½ t. salt
6 hard boiled eggs

Cook noodles in boiling salted water until tender; drain. Cook onions and green pepper in hot fat until tender, but not brown. Add tomatoes and simmer 10 minutes; add cheese. Melt shortening, blend in flour and salt. Stir in tomato mixture. Cook and stir until thick. Place ½ of the noodles in a 2 qt. casserole. Slice 3 eggs over the noodles; top with the tomato mixture. Repeat the layers. Bake at 350°F. for 25 min.

MRS. BERNEY SPENCER

FONDUE VANDOISE

1 lb. grated Swiss cheese
1 12-oz. glass of Chablis wine
1 t. prepared mustard
½ t. salt
¼ t. black pepper
1 clove garlic crushed in
 mortar and pestle

1 oz. kirsch
1 t. cornstarch
½ t. baking soda
cubed toasted bread

Rub the inside of a chafing dish, or equivalent, with the garlic. Add wine, mustard, salt, and pepper, and bring to a boil.

Add cheese and stir constantly over a low flame until smooth and bubbling. Add cornstarch and baking soda which have been diluted in kirsch. Pour the latter in slowly, and continue to stir until thoroughly blended. Serve in the chafing dish, and keep hot at the table. Spear cubes of bread with toothpicks and dip in the cheese mixture. Serves 6 to 8.

MRS. RICHARD C. MILLER

HUEVOS RANCHEROS

1 clove garlic, minced
1 small onion, sliced
Cook in 2 T. shortening for about 2 minutes.

½ green pepper, sliced

Blend in:
 1 T. flour
And add:
 1 #303 can tomatoes
 ½ C. pitted ripe olives
 ¼ t. oregano

1½ t. chili powder
¾ t. salt

Pour this mixture into shallow baking dish. Break 6 or 8 eggs directly into sauce. Slip a teaspoon under each so that the egg will sink down into the savory sauce. If you wish, you may put little cubes of cheese between the eggs. Bake in moderate oven (350°) until eggs are set, about 30 minutes. If sauce is made ahead of time, reheat before adding eggs.

MRS. ALLEN HARRIS, JR.

LITTLE OMELETS

The following is an excellent method of making omelets when members of the family come to breakfast one at a time. The mixture will be satisfactory even after standing some time, provided that it is beaten again just before frying.

6 eggs
½ t. salt

¼ t. pepper
1 C. milk

Beat the eggs until light and foamy, using a rotary beater. Beat in the seasoning and milk, and fry a spoonful at a time on a hot griddle or in a small, thin skillet with plenty of butter. Roll each omelet quickly when done, and serve immediately.

MRS. E. L. CAUDILL

MACARONI SOUFFLE

Boil 1 C. of macaroni. Mix with 1 C. of soft fine bread crumbs, ½ C. melted butter or margarine, 3 eggs, slightly beaten, ½ C. grated cheese, 1 T. chopped green pepper, 1 chopped pimento, ½ t. salt, dash of pepper and paprika, 2 T. finely chopped parsley, and 1 C. scalded milk added last. Bake for 20 minutes in a moderate oven 325°F. to 350°F. May be baked in casserole 2 to 3 inches deep, 1½ qt. capacity.

MRS. WILLIAM A. McDONALD

NOODLE CASSEROLE

2 T. butter or margarine
½ lb. ground steak
1 pkg. egg noodles (4 oz.)
1 3-oz. can sliced mushrooms
½ lb. American cheese, grated
½ t. salt
¼ t. pepper
1 8-oz. can tomato sauce
2 onions, chopped

Cook onions in butter until tender. Add steak and cook until redness disappears. Add mushrooms, tomato sauce, seasonings, and let simmer 15 minutes. Cook noodles in salted boiling water. Drain noodles well. Place in well buttered casserole in layers of noodles, sauce, and grated cheese, ending with grated cheese over the top. Bake in 350°F. oven for 40 minutes. Serves 8.

MRS. PAUL FOXX

NOODLES ROMANOFF

½ pkg. noodles
1 carton cottage cheese
½ pt. sour cream
½ C. finely chopped onion
2 T. Worcestershire sauce
2 or 3 dashes tobasco sauce
1 t. salt
1 can of grated Parmesan cheese

Cook noodles 15 minutes and drain. Stir in well the remaining ingredients, topping with grated Parmesan cheese. Cook in a greased casserole 40 minutes in a 350°F. oven.

MRS. GEORGE SPEED

WELSH RAREBIT

1 T. butter
½ lb. soft mild cheese, cut in small pieces
¼ t. salt
¼ t. mustard
Dash of cayenne
1/3 to ½ C. ale or beer
1 egg

Put butter in double boiler and when melted, add cheese and seasonings. As cheese melts, add ale gradually while stirring constantly. Then add egg slightly beaten. Serve on dry toast.

MRS. EDWARD SONNTAG

COOKIES

ALMOND CRESCENTS

Mix together: 1 C. shortening (half_butter)
                 1/3 C. sugar
                 2/3 C. ground almonds

Sift together and work in: 1-2/3 C. flour
                              ¼ t. salt

Chill, then roll with hands into pencil thin ropes. Cut in 2½" lengths, form into crescents and bake on ungreased cookie sheet at 325° F. until set, but not brown (10-15 min.). Cool on pan until only slightly warm, then dip in 1 C. confectioners sugar with 1 t. cinnamon.

MRS. O. M. JONES

BON BONS

Thoroughly cream 1 C. butter and 1½ C. confectioners sugar. Add 1 beaten egg, ½ t. vanilla and almond extract. Beat well. Add 2½ C. flour, sifted with 1 t. soda and 1 t. cream of tartar. Beat thoroughly. Chill one hour. Form into small balls on greased cookie sheet; flatten slightly and center each with a blanched almond. Bake at 375°F. for 10 to 12 minutes.   Makes 5 dozen. (Very delicious cookie—not too sweet.)

MRS. REUBEN TREADWAY

BOSTON COOKIES

3 eggs
2/3 C. melted butter
2 C. brown sugar
1 t. soda, dissolved in ½ C.
    buttermilk
1 t. cloves
2 t. cinnamon

1 lb. raisins, dark
½ lb. pecans, chopped
½ lb. citron
½ lb. chopped cherries
½ t. vanilla
3 C. flour

Beat sugar and eggs together. Add spices to flour and add, alternately, with milk and melted butter. Mix well and add lightly floured fruits and nuts.   Drop on well greased pans far apart and bake in moderate oven, 375°, 10-15 min.

MRS. DOROTHY RICE FRIBERG

BROWN DANISH COOKIES

1½ C. brown sugar
1½ C. butter
½ C. molasses
1 egg
1 t. soda
1 t. baking powder
1 t. ginger

1 t. cinnamon
½ t. cloves
½ t. salt
1 t. vanilla
About 3½ C. flour — or
    more to handle well

Cream butter and sugar, add molasses and egg and mix.   Sift and mix in dry ingredients. Add vanilla. Form in rolls and place in refrigerator over night. Slice thin and bake at 375°F. until light brown.

MRS. RICHARD FENN

BROWN SUGAR COOKIES

2 C. brown sugar (measure
after sifting)
1 C. butter
3 eggs
4 C. flour (sifted)

1 t. soda, dissolved in 2 t.
water
1 t. vanilla
nuts (if desired)

Cream sugar and butter; add eggs, one at a time, and beat well. Add flour and mix well, then add soda. Mix again and drop on greased pan by teaspoonfuls. Bake at 425°F. until golden brown, about 10 minutes.

MRS. G. A. MASENGILL

BROWNIES

4 squares unsweetened
chocolate
2/3 C. vegetable oil
2 C. sugar
4 eggs

1½ C. sifted flour
1 t. baking powder
1 t. salt
1 C. broken nut meats

Preheat oven to 350°F. Melt chocolate in oil over hot water. Beat sugar and eggs, add chocolate, and stir in sifted dry ingredients. Mix in nuts. Spread in well greased oblong pan and bake 30-35 minutes. Cool and cut into squares.

MRS. RENO BURLESON

CHRISTMAS GUMDROP BARS

4 eggs
2 C. light brown sugar
1 T. water
2 C. flour
¼ t. salt
1 t. vanilla

2 t. baking powder
1 t. cinnamon
½ C. pecans
1 C. red and green
gumdrops, chopped

Beat eggs well and add sugar and water. Beat again. Sift dry ingredients and sprinkle some over the pecans and gumdrops. Add the remaining flour to the eggs and sugar. Fold in the nuts and gumdrops and mix well. Spread thin in well greased and floured pans. Bake at 325° for 30 minutes.

MISS ISABEL MARTIN

BUTTERSCOTCH CHEWS

¼ lb. margarine, melted
2 eggs
2 C. flour
2 t. baking powder

2 t. vanilla
¼ t. salt
2 C. brown sugar (packed)
½ C. chopped pecans

Pour melted margarine over sugar. Stir well. Add eggs and beat well. Add vanilla and dry ingredients. Mix well; add nuts and pour into shallow pan lined with wax paper. Bake 300°F. about one hour. Turn out while warm. Cut and roll in powdered sugar.

CAROLYN MARTIN

BUTTERSCOTCH STICKS

¼ C. butter	1 t. baking powder
1 C. brown sugar	¼ t. salt
1 egg	1 t. vanilla
1 C. flour	¼ C. pecans

Cream sugar and butter. Add egg and vanilla and mix well. Add nuts with dry ingredients. Bake in greased pan at 375° F. for 15 or 20 minutes.

ICING

6 T. brown sugar	2 T. butter
4 T. cream	

Boil 1 minute over low heat. Cool for 1 minute. Thicken with sifted powdered sugar to desired thickness and spread on cooled cookies before slicing.

MRS. JACK PITTS

CARAMEL CUTS

A saucepan is used as a mixing bowl when making caramel cuts. Melt in the saucepan ¼ C. butter. Add 1 C. light brown sugar and blend well. While the mixture is still warm, add 1 unbeaten egg and when thoroughly blended, add ½ t. vanilla, ¾ C. flour, 1 t. baking powder and a pinch of salt. Add the dry ingredients with ½ C. finely chopped pecans to the first mixture. Pour into a shallow 7-inch square pan, which is lined with wax paper, and bake at 350°F. for 30 minutes. As soon as taken from the oven, remove the wax paper and when cool, cut into squares.

ELSIE ARTZ

CHINESE ALMOND CAKES

Sift into large bowl:

2½ C. all purpose flour	¼ t. salt
¾ C. sugar	1 t. baking powder

Blend in with pastry cutter: ¾ C. shortening
Beat together and add:
2 T. water	1 egg
	1½ t. almond extract

Mix as you would pastry and when thoroughly blended form into balls about the size of a walnut. Place on cookie sheet and press with heel of your hand to flatten. Press one whole blanched almond into top of each cookie. Brush each with slightly beaten egg white. Bake at 350°F. about 20-25 minutes. About 36 cookies.

MRS. PAUL COLEMAN

CHOCOLATE CHIP SCOTCH BARS

1 C. sifted flour	1 C. brown sugar, packed
½ t. baking powder	1 egg
⅛ t. salt	1 t. vanilla
½ C. chopped nuts	½ pkg. chocolate bits
1/3 C. shortening	⅛ t. soda

Sift flour once and measure. Add baking powder, salt and soda, and sift again. Add nuts and mix well. Melt shortening in saucepan. Remove from heat, add sugar, and mix well. Cool. Add egg and vanilla. Add flour mixture, a small amount at a time, mixing well after each addition. Turn into greased 9x9x2-inch pan. Sprinkle chocolate bits over top. Bake in moderate oven 350°F. for 20 - 25 minutes. Cool in pan. Cut into 24 bars.

MRS. R. H. ELIASSEN

CHOCOLATE MINT STICKS

2 squares unsweetened chocolate	¼ t. peppermint extract
½ C. butter or margarine	½ C. sifted flour
2 eggs	Dash of salt
1 C. sugar	½ C. chopped almonds

Melt chocolate and butter over hot water. Beat eggs until fluffy. Stir in sugar, chocolate mixture, peppermint extract. Add flour, salt and almonds and mix thoroughly. Pour into greased 9" square cake pan. Bake at 350°F. for 20 to 25 minutes. Cool, spread with filling:

Cream 2 T. butter; add 1 C. sifted confectioners sugar, 1 T. cream and ¾ t. peppermint extract. Keep cake in refrigerator while making glaze.

Melt 1 square chocolate and 1 T. butter over hot water. Mix thoroughly and dribble over the cake. Be sure surface is covered. Refrigerate about 5 minutes. Cut into strips 2" by ¾" or smaller. Makes about 50 sticks.

MRS. KENNETH SCHOLL

CONGO SQUARES

2¾ C. sifted flour	3 eggs
2½ t. baking powder	1 C. broken nut meats
½ t. salt	1 small pkg. semi-
2/3 C. melted shortening	sweet chocolate bits
2¼ C. brown sugar (1 box)	

Mix and sift flour, baking powder and salt. Melt shortening, add brown sugar, stir until well mixed and cool slightly. Add one egg at a time, beating well after each addition. Add dry ingredients then nut meats and chocolate. Pour into greased pan 10½x15½x¾. Bake at 350°F. for 20-25 minutes. When almost cool, cut into squares 2x2.

MRS. C. G. McNABB

CREAM CHEESE COOKIES

½ C. flour   1 small pkg. cream cheese
½ t. salt   3 T. corn syrup
½ C. butter   Jam

Cream butter, add cream cheese and mix well. Add syrup, then flour and salt that have been sifted together. Chill dough, then roll ⅛-inch thick and cut with cookie cutter. Top with small amount of favorite jam and bake 10-12 minutes in 350°F. oven.

MRS. RICHARD GRESHAM

DATE DREAM CAKES

¾ C. butter   3 T. white sugar
1½ C. flour

Cream together and spread on buttered 8" pan. Bake 10 minutes in oven 250°F. Mix:

2 eggs   1½ C. dates
1 C. chopped nuts   1 t. vanilla
1 C. shredded coconut   2 T. flour
1 t. baking powder

Mix together and spread over the first mixture and bake ¾ hour. Cut into squares when cool. If recipe is doubled, bake 1 hour at 300°F.

MRS. ROSE MOTTERN

DATE NUT BARS

3 eggs   ¼ t. salt
1 C. brown sugar   1 t. vanilla
1 C. flour   1½ C. chopped dates
1 t. baking powder   1 C. chopped nuts

Beat eggs until fluffy. Add sugar. Sift flour, baking powder and salt over dates and nuts. Mix into egg mixture. Add vanilla. Pour into ungreased pan and bake 20 minutes at 325°F. Cut into bars, sprinkle with powdered sugar.

MRS. FRANK HUMPHREYS

FRUIT BARS

1½ C. sifted all purpose flour   2½ C. uncooked oatmeal
1 t. soda   1½ C. brown sugar
1 t. salt   1 C. shortening (melted)
½ C. chopped nuts

Heat oven to 350°F. Grease 12x8x2 baking dish. Combine first 6 ingredients and add melted shortening. Mix well. Press half of dough very firmly into dish. Spread with filling. Cover with rest of dough and pat down well. Bake about 25 or 30 minutes. Cool in pan. Cut.

DATE FILLING

2—7½ oz. pkg. pitted dates   ¼ C. orange juice
½ C. white granulated sugar   1 T. grated orange rind
¾ C. light corn syrup   ¼ t. salt

Simmer all ingredients, stirring until thick. Cool.

MRS. WALLACE FRANCE

FRUIT CAKE COOKIES

½ C. shortening	½ t. salt
1 C. brown sugar, packed	½ t. soda
1 egg	1 C. chopped pecans
¼ C. buttermilk	1 C. chopped dates
2 C. sifted flour	1 C. candied cherries
½ t. baking powder	(cut in fourths)

Mix shortening, brown sugar and egg. Add buttermilk. Sift together and stir in dry ingredients. Mix in pecans, dates and cherries. Chill dough 1 hour. Drop from teaspoon about 2 inches apart onto lightly greased baking sheet. Top each cookie with a pecan half or half a candied cherry. Bake 10 to 12 minutes at 400°F. Makes 4 doz.

MRS. O. K. GARLAND

GINGERSNAPS

¾ C. shortening	¼ t. salt
1 C. sugar	2 t. soda
¼ C. light molasses	1 t. cinnamon
1 egg	1 t. cloves
2 C. flour	1 t. ginger

Cream shortening and sugar; add molasses and egg and beat well. Add sifted dry ingredients; mix well. Roll in small balls, dip into sugar and place 2 inches apart on greased cookie sheet. Bake in moderate oven 375°F. for 15 minutes. Makes 4 dozen.

MRS. SAM HARDING

ICE BOX COOKIES

1 C. butter	½ t. salt
2 C. brown sugar	2 eggs
1 C. chopped nuts	1 t. soda
3½ C. flour	

Cream butter and sugar. Add eggs and mix well. Add sifted dry ingredients, mix well and add nuts. Shape into a roll, refrigerate over night. Turn onto a floured board, slice very thin, bake in a moderate oven about 325°F., until crisp. This recipe makes about 5 dozen.

GERTRUDE DAVIS

KURABIYE (RICH TURKISH COOKIES)

1 C. melted butter	2 C. powdered sugar
1 egg yolk	

Stir butter and sugar together for 20 minutes until creamy. Add yolk of egg and keep stirring for a minute or so. Fold in enough sifted flour to make a dough firm enough to handle (approximately 1 C.). Roll into tiny marble shapes. Put on greased pan and bake 1 hour or until done at 200°F.

MISS MARGARET FRANCIS
Fountain City, Tennessee

LAYER COOKIES

½ C. butter	1 t. baking powder
1 C. white sugar	½ t. vanilla
1½ C. flour	½ t. salt
2 eggs	

Cream butter, add sugar, eggs and vanilla. Sift flour with baking powder and salt and add to creamed mixture. Spread ½" thick in shallow pan.

SECOND LAYER

1 egg white	¾ C. chopped nuts
1 C. brown sugar	½ t. vanilla

Beat egg whites. Fold in sugar. Add vanilla. Spread mixture over first layer. Sprinkle with nuts and bake 30 minutes at 350°F. Cut into squares.

MRS. RICHARD FENN

LEBKUCHEN (HONEY CAKES)

4 whole eggs	2 oz. citron, cut fine
1 lb. light brown sugar	½ lb. almonds, blanched
2 C. flour	and cut fine
1 t. cinnamon	

Beat eggs well, add sugar gradually and continue beating. Mix flour and cinnamon with nuts and citron and combine the two mixtures. Bake in two flat greased 11"x13" pans in 400°F. oven. When cool, cut into long thin strips. Before removing from pan, frost with:

1 C. confectioners sugar	2 T. cold water
½ t. almond extract	

MRS. GENE TAYLOR, JR.

MOLASSES DROP COOKIES

1 C. white sugar	1 t. salt
1 C. shortening	1 t. cinnamon
1 egg	1 t. ginger
1 C. light molasses	1 t. cloves
1 C. buttermilk	4 C. flour
2 t. soda, added to milk	1 C. raisins (optional)

Cream sugar and shortening. Add ingredients in order given with sifted dry ingredients last. Bake at 350°F. on greased and floured cookie sheet about 12 minutes.

MRS. HARRY MYRON, JR.

NUT COOKIES

2 C. brown sugar	1-1/3 sticks butter (melted)
1 C. flour, heaping	2 t. vanilla
½ t. baking powder	2 eggs
1 C. pecans, heaping	

Mix sugar, eggs and melted butter. Add vanilla, nuts and sifted dry ingredients. Spread in well greased pan. Bake 30 to 40 minutes at 300°F. Let cool in pan and cut in squares.

MRS. TOM CHILD

OATMEAL CRISPIES

1 C. shortening   1 C. brown sugar
1 C. white sugar

Cream these three ingredients together. Add:

2 beaten eggs   1 t. vanilla
1½ C. flour, sifted with   1 t. salt
1 t. soda

Add: **3 C. quick cooking oats and ½ C. chopped nuts**
Form into long rolls. Chill thoroughly. Slice ¼" thick. Bake on ungreased cookie sheet in moderate oven 350°F. for 10 minutes. Makes 5 dozen.

MRS. SAM DOAK

OATMEAL FILLED COOKIES

1 C. shortening   ½ t. salt
1 C. brown sugar   1 t. soda
½ C. sour milk   ½ t. nutmeg
4 C. oatmeal   2 C. flour

Cream shortening with sugar. Add sour milk and oatmeal. Sift dry ingredients and add to mixture. Roll dough ¼" thick and cut with large biscuit cutter. Place spoonful of filling on circles of dough. Cover with another circlet, pinching sides together. Bake in 350°F. oven approximately 8 - 10 minutes. Do not brown. These cookies may be stored in tin container in your freezer.

FILLING

1 pkg. mincemeat   1 T. lemon juice
4 T. wine   1 C. walnuts
1 T. sugar

Combine first four ingredients. Simmer over low heat 30 minutes. Add chopped nuts. Water may be added as needed during cooking.

MRS. JERRY METTETAL

ORANGE SLICE SQUARES

1 C. brown sugar   1 t. baking powder
1 T. butter   ¼ t. salt
2 eggs   10 candy orange slices,
1 C. nuts   chopped
1 C. flour

Cream butter and sugar. Add eggs. Sift flour and baking powder over nuts and candy. Add to other ingredients. Mix and bake in greased pan 25 minutes at 325°F. Cut into squares.

MRS. A. B. ALPHIN

PEANUT BUTTER COOKIES

1 egg, beaten	1 C. peanut butter
½ C. brown sugar	1 C. flour
½ C. white sugar	1 t. soda
½ C. shortening	1 t. vanilla

Cream sugar and shortening. Add beaten egg, then peanut butter. Add sifted flour and soda. Add vanilla. Pinch off small pieces; place on greased sheet and flatten with a fork. Bake at 375°F.

JUDY MYRON

PEANUT BUTTER CRUNCH COOKIES

1 C. shortening	2 eggs
1 C. peanut butter	1 T. milk
½ t. salt	1 t. soda
1 C. white sugar	1 can chopped or crushed
1 C. brown sugar	peanuts
2 C flour	

Combine shortening, salt and peanut butter and mix well. Add sugar and cream thoroughly. Add eggs, milk, flour and soda to mixture, blending well. Add chopped peanuts, if desired. Drop from teaspoon onto greased cookie sheet; press with fork. Bake 15 minutes at 350°F. Children love them.

MRS. BILL LACEY

PECAN CONFECTIONS

Beat **1 egg white** very stiff. Add gradually **1 C. brown sugar** mixed with **1 T. flour** and **⅛ t. salt.**
Fold in **1 C. chopped pecans**

Drop by teaspoon onto greased cookie sheet. Bake 15 minutes in slow oven 300°F. Cool before removing from sheet. Makes 2 dozen.

MRS. JAMES H. PREAS, JR.

PLAIN SUGAR COOKIES

¾ C. margarine	3 C sifted flour
1 C. sugar	1 t. soda
1 egg	½ t. salt
1/3 C. sour cream	2 t. vanilla

Cream margarine and sugar. Add the unbeaten egg and sour cream and beat well. Blend in the sifted dry ingredients and vanilla and mix well again. Chill the dough for a few hours before handling. Then form into small balls and flatten on baking sheet. Bake about 10 minutes at 375°.

PECAN PUFF

2 egg whites, unbeaten	1 t. vinegar
2 C. sifted confectioners sugar	1 t. vanilla
	2 C. whole pecan halves

Heat oven to 300°F. Beat egg whites with electric beater until stiff but not dry. Gradually add sugar. Stir in remaining ingredients. Drop by teaspoonfuls, two inches apart, onto a greased cookie sheet. Bake 12 - 15 minutes. Yields 3 dozen.

MRS. MALCOLM CAMPBELL

RAISIN CHEWS

Crumb Mixture:

¾ C. soft margarine or butter	½ t. salt
1 C. brown sugar packed	½ t. soda
1¾ C. sifted flour	1½ C. rolled oats

Filling:

2½ C. seedless raisins	¾ C. water
½ C. sugar	3 T. lemon juice
2 T. cornstarch	

Cook, stirring constantly, over low heat until thickened about 5 minutes. Cool.

Mix butter with sugar. Add sifted dry ingredients and oats. Press half of mixture into greased pan (13x9x2). Spread on filling. Sprinkle on remaining crumbs. Bake at 400°F. for 20 or 30 minutes. Cut into bars.

MRS. EDDIE COWELL

ROCKS

1 C. butter	½ C. currants
1 C. sugar	1½ t. boiling water with
2¼ C. flour	1 t. soda
1 C. raisins	1 t. cinnamon
1 C English walnuts, chopped	½ t. cloves
	3 eggs, beaten separately

Cream sugar and butter; add eggs. Chop nuts, cut raisins, add flour and mix by hand. Drop ½ teaspoonful 2 inches apart. Bake at 350°F. until brown.

MRS. U. G. JONES

SANDIES

¾ C. butter	¾ C. powdered sugar
2 C. flour sifted	2 t. vanilla
1 C. chopped pecans	¼ t. salt
½ t. ice water	

Mix ingredients well. Cream butter, sugar and ice water. Add flour, vanilla and nuts. Chill at least 6 hours. Mold into small sticks, crescents, balls, etc. Cook at 250°F. Roll in sifted powdered sugar.

MRS. INEZ PAGE
Durham, N. C.

SAND TARTS

2 C. sugar   1 C. butter
4 eggs (separated)

Beat yolks with 1 C. sugar. Cream butter and add 1 C. sugar with 3 egg whites. Mix together and stir in enough flour to make a soft dough— (about 2 C.). Roll thin. Cut into diamond shapes. Beat remaining white of egg enough so that you can brush tops with it. Press ½ almond on top of each and sprinkle with sugar. Bake at 375° for 10 to 12 minutes.

MRS. IVA BIDDLE

SOUR CREAM COOKIES

2¼ C. flour   2/3 C. light brown sugar
1½ t. baking powder   firmly packed
½ t. soda   1 egg unbeaten
½ t. salt   ½ C. nuts (more if desired)
¼ t. allspice   ½ C. raisins
¼ t. nutmeg   ¼ C. sour cream
½ C. butter or margarine

Sift all dry ingredients together. Cream butter and sugar, add egg and beat well. Add dry ingredients, alternately, with sour cream. Bake as drop cookies on greased cookie sheet at 375° for 10-12 minutes.

MRS. ADAM BOWMAN

SOUTHERN PECAN BARS

Sift together: 1½ C. flour   ½ t. baking powder

Blend together: 1/3 stick butter or margarine
                 ½ C. firmly packed brown sugar

Cream well and add the dry ingredients; mix with electric mixer or spoon until mixture resembles coarse meal.

Stir in ¼ C. pecans, chopped fine; mix well. Pat firmly into bottom of well greased 12"x8"x2" or 13"x9"x2" pan.

Bake in moderate oven, 350°F., for 10 minutes before adding the pecan topping.

———◇———

TOPPING

Beat 2 eggs until foamy   3 T. flour
Add ¾ C. dark corn syrup   ½ t. salt
¼ C. firmly packed brown   1 t. vanilla
   sugar

Mix well. Pour over partially baked crust. Sprinkle with ¾ C. pecans coarsely chopped. If desired, fold the chopped pecans into filling before pouring over the crust. Arrange 30 pecan halves over top, one for each bar. Bake in moderate oven 35 to 40 minutes. Let cool in pan; cut into bars.

MRS. LOUIS FRANCIS
Fountain City, Tennessee

TOM THUMB COOKIE BARS

½ C. shortening	2 eggs, well beaten
½ t. salt	2 T. flour
1½ C. brown sugar, firmly packed	½ t. baking powder
1 C. sifted flour	1 can flaked coconut
1 t. vanilla	nuts (optional)

Cream shortening, salt and ½ C. brown sugar thoroughly. Add 1 C. flour and blend. Spread mixture in a greased and floured square pan. Bake in slow oven 325°F. about 15 minutes. Add remaining 1 C. brown sugar and vanilla to beaten eggs and beat until thick and foamy. Add 2 T. flour, baking powder and coconut (and nuts) and blend. Spread over baked mixture. Return to moderate oven 350°. Bake 20-25 minutes. Cool. Cut into squares.

MRS. SAM DOAK

VIENNESE NUT COOKIES

1 C. butter or margarine	1 C. pecans, finely chopped
¼ C. sugar	1 t. vanilla
2 C. all purpose flour	Confectioners sugar

Cream butter. Add granulated sugar, flour, nuts and vanilla. Mix thoroughly. Shape into balls the size of large marbles and arrange on buttered cookie sheet. Bake 35 minutes at 300°F. Roll in confectioners sugar while warm. After cookies have cooled, roll again in confectioners sugar. Makes approximately 36.

MRS. HARRIS HUNTER

WALNUT DROP COOKIES

2 C. sifted flour	½ C. shortening
2 t. baking powder	1 C. sugar
½ t. salt	½ t. vanilla
½ C. chopped walnuts	1 egg
¼ C. milk	

Mix and sift dry ingredients; add walnuts. Cream shortening; add sugar, vanilla and egg. Alternate flour and milk, beating until smooth. Drop from teaspoon on greased baking sheet; bake in moderately hot oven 375 - 400° F., 8 - 12 minutes.

CHOCOLATE DROP COOKIES

Add 2 squares of melted chocolate to the butter, sugar and egg mixture, and increase milk to 1/3 cup. Yields 2½ dozen.

MRS. WARREN VEST

BROWNIES

6 whole eggs	1 C. shortening or margarine
3 C. sugar	4 sqs. chocolate
2½ C. flour (plain)	2 t. vanilla
pinch of salt	

Beat eggs and add sugar. Melt shortening and chocolate, then add to egg and sugar mixture. Add flour. Stir. Add vanilla and salt. Pour into a 9" X 13" pan and bake in a 350 degree oven for 20-25 minutes chewy or 30-35 minutes—done.

Mrs. Earl Weaver

SCOTCH SHORTBREAD

3 C. flour	Dash of salt
4 T. (heaping) powdered sugar	½ lb. soft butter

Mix thoroughly with hands the above ingredients. Roll to about ⅜" thickness on board dusted with powdered sugar. Cut in any desired shape. Place on ungreased cookie sheet and bake at 275°F. for 1 hr. or until cookies are barely golden in color. When kept in a tight tin box, these will keep just as long as you can keep your family away from them!

Mrs. P. W. Alexander

CHINESE CHUZ

Part I—1 stick margarine, 2 cups white sugar. Melt margarine and pour over sugar and cream it. Add 2 whole eggs and 2 egg yolks one at a time. Cream. Sift together 2½ cups sifted cake flour, 2 tsp. baking powder. Pat this mixture into deep pans. Part II—Take the 2 egg whites and beat stiff, and add 2 cups brown sugar, 1 tsp. vanilla; add to top of Part I. Bake 45 min. at 325 degrees to 350 degrees. Cover with foil if the edges brown too quickly. Cook in middle of oven. Cool in pan. Slice and take pieces out with spatula.

Mrs. Alfred Abernethy

CO-COONS

1 C. flour	3 T. sugar
1 stick butter	1 C. pecan meats

Mix all ingredients together. Shape into crescents or balls. Bake on greased cookie sheet at 275 degrees for 20-25 minutes.

Mrs. Joe Lusk

DELICIOUS COOKIES

1½ C. flour (self-rising flour)	½ C. Crisco or oleo
¼ C. brown sugar	½ C. white sugar
½ t. salt	1 egg beaten

1 bag semi-sweet chocolate drops or caramel drops
1 can (No. 2) crushed pineapple-not drained.

Stir and make soft batter; If needed add a few spoons of milk but usually the pineapple juice is enough. Drop from spoon on cookie sheet and bake at 375 degrees for 8 to 10 minutes. Let set on cookie sheet for a minute after cooking to firm up and then remove.

Mrs. R. V. Rainbolt

DIETETIC COOKIES

MIX AND SIFT:

1¾ C. plain flour	and	½ t. salt
1 t. cinnamon		½ t. nutmeg
½ t. cloves		1 t. soda

COMBINE:

1 stick margarine	and	1½ T. liquid sweetener
1 egg		1 C. dietetic applesauce
½ C. raisins		1 C. all bran or oatmeal

Add flour mixture, little at a time. Bake at 375 degrees for 12 minutes on greased cookie sheet. These are very good; you would never know they were dietetic.

Mrs. Roy W. Jones, Sr.

ICEBOX COOKIES (NO BAKING)

Line bottom of large pan or baking dish with WHOLE graham crackers. Melt in saucepan 2 sticks butter. Combine and beat and add to melted butter, bringing to boiling point for 1 minute:

1 C. sugar	and	1 egg
½ C. milk		

Add following to above mixture and blend well:

1 C. nuts	and	1 C. graham cracker
1 C. coconut		crumbs

Pour all of this over the whole graham crackers in baking dish, evenly. Top with more whole graham crackers.

ICE with butter icing:	1 T. milk (more if needed
¾ stick butter or margarine	to spread)
2 C. powdered sugar	1 t. vanilla

Place cookies in refrigerator until well chilled, overnight and slice. This recipe can be made while cooking a meal. Mrs. Herman Carriger

MOLASSES WALNUT COOKIES

3½ C. sifted flour
½ t. salt
1 t. baking soda
¾ C. shortening
½ C. chopped walnuts

1 C. firmly packed brown sugar
½ C. molasses
3 T. water
2 eggs, well beaten

Mix and sift flour, salt and baking soda and then set aside. Beat shortening until creamy; add sugar gradually. Continue beating until light. Stir in molasses and water. Add eggs, beat well. Add flour mixture and nuts to egg mixture. Mix well. Cover. Chill two hours. Set oven for 400 degrees. Drop dough by tablespoons on greased baking sheets, about two inches apart. Bake 10 to 12 minutes. Makes about 60 cookies.   Mrs. Kelver Willis

PEANUT BLOSSOMS

SIFT TOGETHER:
  1¾ C. flour   and   1 t. soda
  ½ t. salt
CREAM TOGETHER:
  ½ C. shortening   and   1/3 C. peanut butter
ADD:
  ½ C. sugar   and   ½ C. brown sugar
Add 1 unbeaten egg   and   1 t. vanilla

Beat well. Shape dough into balls, using a rounded teaspoon for each. Roll balls in sugar. Place on greased cookie sheets. Bake at 375 degrees for 8 minutes. Remove from oven. Top each with a chocolate Hershey kiss, pressing down firmly so cookie cracks around edge. Return to oven for 2 to 5 minutes longer.   Mrs. Ed Parker

DATE REFRIGERATOR PINWHEELS

2¼ C. pitted dates
1 C. sugar
1 C. water
1 C. chopped nuts
1 C. shortening

2 C. brown sugar, firmly packed
3 eggs, beaten
4 C. sifted all-purpose flour
½ t. salt
½ t. baking soda

Combine dates, sugar and water in a saucepan and cook over low heat until thick. About 10-15 minutes. Add nuts and cool. Meanwhile, work shortening with a spoon until fluffy and creamy; add brown sugar - work until light. Add well-beaten eggs and mix well. Add the remaining ingredients sifted together and mix well. Cover and chill thoroughly. Divide the mixture into two parts and roll each part separately into rectangle, a little less than ¼" thick. Spread each with some of the date filling and roll up as for a jelly roll, into 2 long rolls; wrap in waxed paper and chill overnight in refrigerator. Slice into ¼" pieces. Grease cookie sheet and cook at 400 degrees for 10-12 minutes. Makes 5 dozen cookies.   Mrs. J. Eddie Anderson, Jr.

POTATO CHIP COOKIES

2¾ C. flour
½ t. soda
¾ C. shortening
2 eggs
2 C. brown sugar

2 t. vanilla
½ C. milk
1 C. crushed potato chips
1 C. chopped nuts

Mix together flour and soda. Cream shortening and sugar very thoroughly. Add eggs, one at a time, and beat well. Add vanilla. Add flour mixture and milk alternately to the creamed mixture. Fold in crushed potato chips and nuts. Drop by teaspoon on a greased cookie sheet. Bake in a 400 degree electric oven for 10-12 minutes. NOTE: Bacon drippings may be substituted for shortening.

Mrs. Allen Harris, Jr.

SUGAR CUTOUTS

3½ C. flour
1 t. baking powder
½ t. salt
1 C. shortening

1½ C. sugar
2 well beaten eggs
1½ t. vanilla

Cream shortening and sugar; beat in eggs and vanilla. Work in flour with baking powder and salt sifted in. Wrap in foil and chill until firm. Roll a small amount at a time until about ⅛" thick. Cut out with cutters. Bake at 400 degrees for 5-8 minutes. Cool before removing. Yield 6 dozen. Children love to make and eat them. Ice with confectioners sugar, a few drops of vanilla flavoring and milk mixed to spreading consistency.

Mrs. Joe Walker

PUMPKIN COOKIES

1 C. sugar
½ C. shortening
1 C. pumpkin, canned
1 C. raisins
½ C. chopped nuts
2 C. flour

1 t. baking powder
1 t. soda
1 t. cinnamon
½ t. salt
Grated rind of one orange
Vanilla

Cream sugar, shortening, and vanilla. Sift dry ingredients together, add pumpkin. Put a little flour on raisins aud nuts. Add flour, etc. then nuts, raisins and orange rind. Mix well and drop on cookie sheet. Bake at 375 degrees about 12-15 minutes. Ice with confectioners sugar mixed with orange juice and butter. (I always use a tiny amount of yellow coloring in icing.)

Mrs. Bob London

AMBER PAMPEREIS

Crust: Soften ½ C. butter or margarine and one 3-oz. pkg. of cream cheese at room temperature. Cream well and gradually add 1 C. sifted flour. Work with fingers to smooth, well-blended dough. Pinch off small pieces to shape into balls. Place each ball in muffin tins; thumb press dough against cup bottom and sides, lining cups evenly. Fill with pecan custard before baking.

———o———

Filling: Beat 2 whole eggs well, add 1½ C. packed brown sugar, beating well. Add 2 T. melted butter, ½ t. salt, 1 t. vanilla—mix well. Spoon filling over chopped nuts in pastry lined muffin cups, filling cups not quite full. Top the filling with a teaspoon of chopped nuts.

Bake in preheated oven 350°F. for 15 minutes; reduce heat to 250°F., and bake 10 minutes longer. Let cool. Carefully remove from pans.

MRS. EDDIE COWELL

APPLE TREAT

18 graham crackers	1 C. orange juice
¼ t. nutmeg	3 T. cornstarch
¼ C. brown sugar	½ C. brown sugar
½ C. butter	Pinch of salt
8 cooking apples	3 egg whites
1 C. corn syrup	6 t. sugar
½ C. water	

Crush graham crackers and combine well with nutmeg, brown sugar, and butter. Press half this mixture in the bottom of a greased 9-inch pan. Peel and cut apples and simmer in the corn syrup and water until tender. Remove apples, drain and place on top of crumbs. To the syrup add the orange juice, cornstarch, brown sugar and a pinch of salt. Cool until clear and pour over the apples. Beat egg whites with salt and sugar. Place on top. Then add the rest of the crumbs. Bake 30 minutes in a moderate oven (350°F.). Serves 6. Delicious.

MRS. IRMGARD KOCH
Montreal, Canada

BAKED ALASKA

2/3 C. sugar	1 long angel food cake
¼ t. salt	1 pt. strawberry brick
¼ t. cream of tartar	ice cream
4 egg whites	1 pt. chocolate brick
1 cookie sheet (covered	ice cream
with aluminum foil))	

Slice cake lengthwise: put 2 layers of different colored ice cream between the layers. Beat eggs, salt and cream of tartar. Add sugar gradually. The mixture should be very stiff. Ice cake on top and sides well. Brown in oven 3 minutes at 450°F. Slice and serve at once or put in deep freeze and serve cold later. Wonderful to make and freeze for future use!

MRS. TROX MONTGOMERY

CHEESE CAKE SUPREME

1½ C. graham crackers (crushed)

2 T. butter
2 T. sugar

Combine melted butter with the crushed graham crackers. Add sugar and mix well. Pour ½ of this mixture in the bottom of a spring form pan and pack well.

2 lbs. cream cheese

1 C. sugar

Cream the cream cheese and sugar well.

4 T. flour
Pinch of salt

4 egg yolks, beaten well
1 C. coffee cream

Mix together and add these to the cream cheese mixture. Beat 4 egg whites until stiff and fold into batter. Pour batter into spring form pan. Spread remaining graham cracker mixture evenly on top of batter. Bake 1½ hrs. at 300°. After baking leave cake in the oven with the door open until it is completely cooled.

MRS. PAUL BASHOR

CHOCOLATE COCONUT CHIFFON RING

1 envelope unflavored gelatin
1½ C. cold milk
2/3 C. sugar, divided
¼ t. salt
2 sqs. unsweetened chocolate

3 egg yolks, slightly beaten
3 egg whites, stiffly beaten
1 t. vanilla
1 pkg. shredded coconut
½ C. chilled heavy cream
3 T. sweetened cocoa mix

Soften gelatin in milk. Add 1/3 C. sugar, salt, and chocolate. Cook over hot water until chocolate melts and gelatin is thoroughly dissolved. Beat with rotary beater until well blended. Pour slowly over egg yolks. Cook and stir 3 minutes longer. Cool 10 minutes. Add remaining 1/3 C. sugar to beaten egg whites; beat to stiff peaks. Blend in chocolate mixture. Add vanilla and half of coconut. Turn into 1-qt. ring mold. Chill until firm. Unmold. Spread with cream and cocoa mix beaten together until fluffy and thick. Top with remaining coconut. Makes 8 servings.

MRS. GUY CARR

CHOCOLATE MINT BOMBE

3 pts. chocolate ice cream
2 egg whites
½ pt. whipping cream

½ t. mint flavoring
¼ C. sugar
green food coloring

Line the sides and bottom of a greased 2-qt. mold with 2 pts. of ice cream. Place in freezer until hard. Whip the egg whites and whipping cream separately. Add the sugar to the beaten egg whites and fold in whipping cream. Add mint flavoring and food coloring. Fill the lined mold and freeze. When firm, spread the remaining ice cream over the top and refreeze. To serve, unmold and slice.

MRS. TOM HAPPEL

CHOCOLATE ROLL

½ C. sifted flour	4 eggs
½ t. baking powder	¾ C. sugar
¼ t salt	1 t. vanilla
¼ t. soda	6 T. cocoa

Beat eggs and sugar until very thick and light. Sift dry ingredients together three times, and add to the eggs and sugar all at once. Add vanilla. Turn into a 10" x 15" pan that has been greased and lined with waxed paper. Bake 15 minutes in a 350° oven. Turn onto a tea towel that has been sprinkled lightly with powdered sugar. Quickly spread the cooled almond filling to within ¼" of the edge of cake. Roll as you would a jelly roll. Wrap tightly with the tea towel and allow to cool. Frost with your favorite white icing, or slightly sweetened whipped cream.

ALMOND CREAM FILLING

2/3 C. sugar	2 egg yolks
4 T. flour	½ t. vanilla
¼ t. salt	¾ t. almond extract
1½ C. milk	2 T. butter

Mix sugar, flour and salt in top of double boiler. Add milk and cook 10 minutes stirring constantly. Add a small amount of hot mixture to the beaten egg yolks. Return to double boiler and cook 2 minutes. Add vanilla, almond extract and butter. Cool.

MRS. BAILEY WILLIAMS

CRANBERRY DESSERT

¼ C. butter	1 t. baking powder
½ C. sugar	¼ t. salt
1 egg, beaten	1½ C. cranberries, raw
1 C. flour	½ C. milk

Prepare as any cake and bake at 350°F. for 35 - 40 minutes in square brownie pan. Cut in squares and serve with following sauce:

½ C. butter	1 C. sugar
½ C. cream	

Boil this 10 minutes and serve hot on cake.

MRS. GEORGE MILLER

PEANUT BRITTLE CREAM

1 pint heavy whipping cream
½ to ¾ lb. peanut brittle, crushed

Fold crushed brittle into stiffly whipped cream. Pour into refrigerator trays or shallow baking pan. Freeze until firm without stirring. Serve plain or with fudge or caramel sauce.

This is extremely simple to prepare but luscious!

DANISH DATE AND NUT PASTRY

Bring to a boil —
> 1½ C. brown sugar
> 1 T. butter
> 1½ C. water

Mix into a batter —
> 1 C. brown sugar   1 C. flour
> ½ C. milk   1 t. baking powder
>   1 C. chopped dates

Put above batter in 8½x8½x2-inch square pan. Sprinkle 1 C. chopped nuts over batter and pour hot brown sugar syrup over all. Bake 30 minutes in 400°F. oven. Serve with whipped cream. The appearance of this mixture is misleading before being put in oven as the water and batter congeal.

MRS. ROBERT LINCOLN

DATE CUPS

> 3 eggs, separated   2 T. flour
> ¾ C. sugar   1 t. baking powder
> 2 pkgs. dates   1 t. vanilla
> 2 C. nuts

Beat yolks until light. Add sugar and blend thoroughly. Cut dates and break up nuts. Combine baking powder and flour and sprinkle over dates. Add, with nuts, to egg and sugar mixture. Fold in well beaten whites of eggs. Bake in greased muffin tins in a moderate 350°F. oven for 15 - 20 minutes. Serve warm or cold with whipped cream or the following sauce:

> ½ C. butter   1 t. vanilla
> 1 C. light brown sugar 2 T. brandy
> 2 eggs

Cream butter, add sugar and eggs. Beat together until stiff and creamy. Put in top of double boiler and cook over hot water until completely melted and thickened. Flavor with brandy or vanilla.

MRS. GRIFFIN ADAMS

DATE ROLL

> 1 pkg. dates, chopped   juice of 1 lemon
> 10 marshmallows, diced   May add 3 or 4 finely chopped
> 18 - 22 graham crackers   maraschino cherries
> 1 C. finely chopped pecans

Roll graham crackers with rolling pin until they are fine crumbs. Chop dates, marshmallows, pecans and mix with half of cracker crumbs. Add lemon juice. Knead until well blended. Form in shape of roll and roll in remainder of crumbs. Chill for 24 hours. Slice and serve with whipped cream topped with cherry or nut.

MARION CARR
Durham, N.C.

KENTUCKY ICEBOX EGGNOG CAKE

2 sticks butter
5 eggs, beaten separately
1 C. chopped nuts
Whipped cream to ice cake

1 box confectioners' sugar
6 T. bonded whiskey
2 to 3 doz. lady fingers

Cream together, butter and sugar. Add whiskey to well beaten egg yolks. Mix well so that yolks are cooked. Add this to butter and sugar. Next add stiffly beaten egg whites and nuts. Line a mold or square cake pan with waxed paper. Open lady fingers and cover bottom of pan with them, top sides of cake down. Cover with a layer of cake mixture. Do this until there are 3 layers of cakes and 2 of mixture. Last layer should be 3 lady fingers with top sides up. Place in refrigerator for 12 hours. Serve iced with whipped cream, flavored as desired.

MRS. JACK CUMMINS

BUTTERSCOTCH ICEBOX CAKE

Line bottom and sides of spring form with lady fingers. Cream ¼ lb. butter with 2 C. powdered sugar. Add 4 egg yolks, 1 t. vanilla, and 1 pt. of cream, whipped. Cover cake with one third of this. Sprinkle with ground nuts following with ground butterscotch candy. Alternate cake mixture, nuts, and butterscotch candy until all are used. Place in refrigerator for several hours.

MRS. JAY GUMP

CHOCOLATE ICEBOX CAKE

¼ C. water
½ C. sugar
2 sqs. bitter chocolate
4 egg yolks
1 C. butter

1 C. powdered sugar
1 t. vanilla
4 egg whites -
2 doz. lady fingers

Cook water, sugar and chocolate in double boiler until smooth. Add beaten egg yolks and cook one minute more, beating constantly. Remove from heat and cool. Cream butter; add powdered sugar slowly; add vanilla. Add this to cooled chocolate mixture. Beat egg whites stiff and fold in.

Line pan with lady fingers. Alternate layers of lady fingers, with layers of chocolate mixture. Set in refrigerator 24 hours. Unmold and top with whipped cream and nuts.

MRS. CALVIN MORGAN

LEMON ICEBOX CAKE

4 egg yolks
½ C. sugar

juice and grated rind of 1 lemon

Cook in double boiler until thick.

Dissolve 3 T. lemon jello in ½ C. boiling water and add to above mixture while hot. Set aside to cool. Whip ½ pt. cream. Whip the 4 egg whites and add ½ C. sugar. Mix whipped cream and beaten egg whites, and add to egg yolk mixture. Line refrigerator freezing tray with finely-crushed vanilla wafers and pour in lemon custard. sprinkle crushed wafers on top. Freeze. Cut in squares to serve. May garnish with whipped cream.

MRS. GEORGE DOUGHTY

CHERRY PUDDING

2 C. sour, pitted cherries	½ t. salt
1 C. sugar	1 t. baking powder
2 T. butter	½ C. milk
½ C. sugar (for batter)	½ C. boiling water
1 C. flour	

Mix cherries and 1 C. sugar and let stand while preparing batter. Cream butter and ½ C. sugar and add sifted dry ingredients alternately with milk. Pour into greased baking dish, and pour cherries on top of batter, and boiling water over all. Bake for about 30 minutes at 400°.

MRS. FRANK KELLY

CHOCOLATE BREAD PUDDING

2 C. bread crumbs	2 whole eggs
4 C. scalded milk	¼ t. salt
2 heaping T. cocoa	1 t. vanilla
¾ C. sugar	

Add crumbs to milk. Mix cocoa, sugar, salt and vanilla. Stir in eggs; mix well; and add gradually to milk and crumbs. Bake in greased pan 45 minutes to 1 hour.

Sauce:

	3 heaping T. butter
2 C. brown sugar	1 egg

Mix well and heat, stirring until thick. Serve on hot pudding.

MRS. BLAINE SHELL

CHRISTMAS PUDDING

Mix together:

2 C. seedless raisins	½ C. candied cherries
½ C. citron	½ C. candied chopped dates
Grated rind of one orange	½ C. candied pineaple
Grated rind of one lemon	½ C. candied pecans
One large peeled and chopped apple	½ C. orange juice
	1 C. orange marmalade

Let this mixture stand overnight. Next morning beat 3 eggs until very light. Slowly add:

½ C. sugar	1½ C. fine dry bread crumbs
1 C. molasses	1 C. finely cut suet

Then add the first mixture. Sift 1 C. of flour with:

1 t. salt	½ t. allspice
1 t. baking powder	½ t. cloves
1 t. cinnamon	¼ t. soda

Stir this into pudding mixture and put in two well greased quart molds. Cover tightly, steam about three hours. Before serving, steam until thoroughly hot.

CARAMEL SAUCE: Melt 28 caramels with **3 T. of hot water** in double boiler. Cream **1 C. butter** with **1 C. confectioners sugar.** Blend in caramel sauce. Serve on hot pudding.

MRS. WALTER J. MILLER

FRESH COCONUT PUDDING

1 pt. milk or cream	1 t. almond extract
2 T. plain gelatin	2 C. fresh coconut, grated
1 C. sugar	1 pt. heavy cream, whipped

Bring milk to boil; add gelatin soaked in ¼ C. water. Stir until dissolved. Add sugar and almond. Cool until it begins to thicken and fold in coconut and whipped cream. Pour into large ring mold. When ring is unmolded, serve with caramel sauce and sprinkle with coconut.

SAUCE:

1 T. butter	1 C. coffee cream
1 lb. brown sugar	⅛ t. salt
2 egg yolks	1 t. vanilla

Combine egg yolks and cream in pan. Add other ingredients and cook until smooth, about 3 minutes.

MRS. JOE KEEFAUVER

DATE PUDDING

2 C. dates, cut coarsely	2 T. flour
2 C. chopped nuts	1 t. vanilla
2 C. sugar	2 heaping t. baking powder
4 eggs	1 C. milk
1 C. melted butter	

Melt butter and add sugar. Beat until smooth. Add well beaten egg yolks, and milk. Fold in flour, baking powder, nuts, dates and vanilla. Fold in gently the well beaten egg whites. This rises very little and is rather soft. Bake 350° for 40 minutes. Serve topped with whipped cream.

MRS. W. C. PHLEGAR

DATE - NUT PUDDING

5 egg whites	2 t. baking powder
1 C. sugar	1 C. nuts, floured
4 rounded T. soda cracker crumbs	1 C. chopped dates, floured

Beat egg whites very stiff. Fold in sugar mixed with baking powder. Fold in cracker crumbs, nuts and dates. Pour in slightly greased 8" x 12" pyrex baking dish. Bake in slow oven, 300°-325° for one hour. Serve cold with whipped cream.

MRS. J. LAFE COX

LEMON PUDDING

¾ C. sugar	1½ t. melted butter
2 lemons	1 C. milk
1/3 C. flour	2 eggs

Beat egg yolks well. Add lemon juice, rind, sugar and flour. Add milk and melted butter. Add stiffly beaten egg whites. Bake 45 minutes in 350° oven in a dish set in hot water. Pudding will rise to the top, leaving sauce on the bottom.

MRS. REUBEN TREADWAY

MARSHMALLOW PUDDING

1 T. plain gelatin	1 t. vanilla
1 C. cold water	1 C. sugar
4 eggs	chopped nuts
pinch of salt	crystalized pineapple

Soak gelatin in ½ C. water. Stir over heat until dissolved. Add ½ C. water to hot gelatin and cool slightly. Beat egg whites with pinch of salt until very stiff. Add vanilla. Pour cool gelatin very slowly into egg whites, beating constantly. Continue beating as you sprinkle in the sugar. Tint ½ of mixture with food coloring and spread over the bottom of waxed paper lined pan. Sprinkle with nuts and pineapple, and add the remaining meringue. Serve with whipped cream.

MRS. LOUIS RICE

BAKED OZARK PUDDING

1 egg	1 C. chopped apples
¾ C. sugar	½ C. chopped nuts
3 T. flour (heaped)	1 t. vanilla
1¼ t. baking powder	1 C. cream, whipped
⅛ t. salt	

Beat egg well and add sugar, beating until light and creamy. Sift flour, baking powder, salt and add to egg mixture, blend well. Fold in apples and nuts and add vanilla. Pour into greased paper lined dish. Bake in a slow oven 325° for 30 minutes. Serve with whipped cream.

MRS. LEONARD HASCHE

SHERRY PUDDING

1 pkg marshmallows	1 C. almonds, blanched
¼ C. sherry	and chopped
1 C. maraschino cherries, chopped	1 pt. whipped cream

Cut marshmallows into fourths. Pour sherry over marshmallows and let stand overnight. Then whip until light and fluffy. Fold in the cherries, almonds and whipped cream. Chill until ready to serve.

MRS. CHARLES GORDON

BANANA SHERBET

1 2/3 C. sugar	Juice of 2 or 3 lemons
Juice of 2 oranges (juicy)	2 bananas
2 C. milk	

Pour fruit juice over sugar and let stand. Mash bananas with a fork. Pour milk over mashed bananas and mix well. Add to sugar and juices gradually. Mix well. Pour in tray or pan and freeze. Stir well during process of freezing.

MRS. J. W. STONE

BUTTERMILK SHERBET

Combine: **2 C. buttermilk, 1 t. vanilla, dash of salt, 1/3 C. sugar and 1 C. crushed pineapple.** Freeze to mushy stage and beat until smooth.

Add 1/3 C. sugar to 1 stiffly beaten egg white. Fold egg white into frozen mixture. Freeze at #1 temperature and when frozen turn to #3 temperature until ready to serve.

MRS. GEORGE WARNICA

LIME SHERBET

Soak: **1 pkg. of lime jello** in **1 C. hot water and stir. Mix in scant 1½ C. sugar** and **grated rind and juice of 2 lemons.**

Let cool. Stir in 1 qt. homogenized milk. Put in a carton and place in the freezer.

MRS. MOSE JONES

SHERRY DELIGHT

3 eggs
Pinch of salt
½ C. sugar

4 T. sherry wine
½ pt. whipped cream

Separate 3 eggs. Add to the yolks the sugar, salt and sherry. Cook until these ingredients begin to thicken. Let cool, and add whipped cream. Fold in the stiffly beaten egg whites. Line pan with crushed vanilla wafers. Pour in mixture and freeze. Save some crumbs to sprinkle over top of mixture.

MRS. BOB DAVIS
Macon, Georgia

SYLLABUB

1 pt. heavy cream
½ C. sugar

2 egg whites
2 T. sherry or brandy

Add a pinch of salt to the egg whites and whip stiff. Add sugar slowly while beating and fold in the stiffly beaten cream and then the brandy. Serve in par fait glasses with slice of cake. To vary, fold in crystalized fruit.

MRS. JAMES A. WELLER

SCHAUM TORTE

Beat whites of **6 eggs,** very dry. Add slowly 2 C. sugar while beating continously. Beat in **1 T. vinegar and 1 t. vanilla.** Beat the above until very stiff. Bake in large, slightly greased skillet, very slowly for 40 minutes (about 275°). This meringue type dessert will fall slightly when removed from skillet. It is delicious served with crushed, sweetened strawberries and whipped cream. It will serve 8 or 9 persons. Can be served with raspberries, peaches, or any tart fruit or berry.

MRS. HARRY WOLFE

MARSHMALLOW TARTS

1½ C. flour   2/3 C. butter
1 T. sifted confectioners sugar

Cut butter into flour and sugar as you would pastry. Knead it into small rolls. Then press into muffin tins and bake at 325° until golden brown. Cool. Melt 25 marshmallows in double boiler and add ½ banana mashed, 15 chopped cherries. Mix thoroughly and fill shells. Let set, cover with chocolate icing, and top with a nut.

MRS. IRMGARD KOCH
Montreal, Canada

THE TORTE OF THE TOWN

Beat 6 egg whites (room temperature) with ¼ t. salt for 15 minutes. Use an electric mixer at high speed. Gradually sift in 2 C. sugar, beating constantly for 15 minutes. Throughout beating, push mixture from bowl's sides. Add 1 t. vinegar, 1 t. vanilla and ½ t. baking powder. Pile mixture into a 9 inch tube spring form pan which has been lined with brown paper. Bake 1 hour in a very slow oven, 275°. Cool. Loosen from outer side of pan with knife or spatula and remove side. Loosen from bottom and center tube. Place meringue on serving plate and fill center and cover top with sweetened crushed strawberries and whipped cream. Cut in wedges to serve 8.
To bake individual meringues; drop by spoonfuls on brown paper and bake 1 hour at 250°. This makes 30 to 36 delightfully chewey meringues.

MRS. LESTER T. SCOTT

ITALIAN TORTE

2 eggs   ¼ t. salt
½ C. cold water   1 C. sifted white sugar
1 C. sifted cake flour   1 t. vanilla
¾ t. baking powder   ½ t. lemon flavoring
3 t. sweet Italian Vermouth

Have eggs at room temperature. Heat oven to 350°. Line bottoms of 2 8" layer pans 1¼" deep with waxed, greased paper. Separate eggs; place whites in a small bowl; yolks in a large bowl with the water.

Sift flour, baking powder, salt in another bowl. Beat egg yolks and water until fluffy and tripled in volume. Add sifted sugar gradually while beating. Continue to beat until light colored and thick enough to mound slightly (about 10 minutes.) Now stir in flavoring. Add flour mixture **all at once,** folding gently. Beat egg whites until they form moist, stiff peaks. Then fold into yolk mixture until completely blended. Pour into layer pans and bake at 350° for 25 to 30 minutes. After baking, invert cakes on cake rack until cakes are cold. Remove cakes from pans and remove paper carefully. Split cake layers crosswise to form 4 layers. Place one layer on cake plates with cut side up and sprinkle with one quarter of the Vermouth. Spread with 1/3 of frosting. Repeat with the other three layers. Chill at least 4 hours. Keep in refrigerator at all times.

FROSTING FOR ITALIAN TORTE

Whip 1 C. heavy cream until it begins to thicken. Add ½ C. canned chocolate syrup and beat until mixture mounds. Fill layers and frost top of cake. Top with toasted almond slivers or slivered Brazil nuts. Wonderful!

Mrs. Ike W. Greene

SILVER TORTE

½ lb. butter	2 lemons, juice and rind
2 C. flour	1 C. sugar (for gelatin
2 T. sugar	mixture)
1 envelope gelatin	dash of salt
2/3 C. cold water	1 C. sugar (for egg whites)
8 eggs, separated	toasted almonds, slivered

Mix the butter, flour and 2 T. sugar like pastry. Pat into a long cake pan or pyrex dish. Bake at 325° until light brown.

Dissolve gelatin in water. Mix egg yolks, juice and rind, sugar and salt in top of a double boiler. Beat over heat until creamy, thick and light yellow in color. Remove from heat; stir in gelatin and cool. Beat egg whites stiff with 1 C. sugar. Fold the meringue into the cooled mixture and pour into the crust. Sprinkle the almonds over the top and refrigerate.

Mrs. John Brauer
Wisconsin Rapids, Wis.

CHOCOLATE FUDGE CAKE WAFFLES

½ C. shortening	1½ C. flour
¾ C. sugar	½ t. salt
2 sqs. chocolate	¼ C. milk
2 eggs	1 t. vanilla
3 t. baking powder	

Cream sugar and shortening. Add melted chocolate and well beaten eggs. Sift flour, salt and baking powder and add alternately with milk to mixture. Add vanilla. Place in waffle iron, sprinkle with chopped nut meats and bake. Serve hot with vanilla ice cream.

Mrs. William R. Rigell

HOMEMADE ICE CREAM

1 recipe boiled custard (using 1 qt. milk)
3 boxes frozen whole strawberries or peaches, strained
(1½ qts. if fresh fruit is used)
1 pt. coffee cream
½ pt. whipping cream

Foundation for homemade ice cream consists of a good rich boiled custard using 7 or 8 egg yolks. I prepare mine a day, or even two, ahead in order to have it out of the way and to assure its being thoroughly chilled.

In a large bowl pour the boiled custard, coffee cream and whipping cream. Add fruit. Be sure mixture is sweet enough and has sufficient vanilla. Pour in ice cream freezer container. Turn until handle is very difficult to move.

Mrs. T. F. Beckner, Jr.

ICE BOX CAKE

1 can evaporated milk (chilled).
1 C. sugar
juice of 1 lemon
juice of 1 orange

Whip milk, add sugar gradually; add lemon and orange juice. Put vanilla wafer crumbs in bottom of refrigerator tray. Alternate half of mixture with a layer of crumbs. Last layer should be crumbs.

MRS. JOHN IRWIN

SPANISH CREAM

1 T. plain gelatin
¼ C. cold water
2¾ C. milk

3 eggs
½ C. sugar
Salt

Soak the gelatin in the water and add to the hot scalded milk. Separate the eggs and beat the yolks with the sugar and a pinch of salt. When thoroughly blended add to the milk. Cook in a double boiler until it thickens. Beat the egg whites until they form stiff peaks. Pour the hot mixture over the egg whites and fold in thoroughly. Pour into cold mold and chill until firm. Serve with a sauce, preferably a berry sauce.

MRS. WALTER HANKINS

LEMON BISQUE

1 pt. whipping cream
1 pkg. lemon jello
1¼ C. boiling water
1/3 C. sugar

3 T. lemon juice
grated rind 1 lemon
2½ C. vanilla wafers
⅛ t. salt

Whip cream lightly. Dissolve gelatin in boiling water; add sugar, salt, rind and lemon juice. When congealed slightly, fold in whipped cream. Spread ½ vanilla wafer crumbs in bottom of large pan, pour lemon mixture over it. Top with remaining crumbs. Chill in refrigerator 3 to 5 hours. Serve plain or with whipped cream.

MRS. RICHARD BURKE

LEMON FLOAT

2 eggs
1 lemon
½ C. sugar

½ pt. whipping cream
vanilla wafers

To yolks of eggs, add lemon and sugar. Beat well. Whip cream until very thick. Beat egg whites until very stiff. Add beaten whites and vanilla wafers which have been rolled fine. Add lemon mixture, and top with wafer crumbs. Freeze. Cut in squares to serve.

MRS. JOHN HOWREN

MARSHMALLOW DELIGHT

½ lb. marshmallows
1½ C. diced pineapple
2 t. vanilla

½ pt. whipping cream
2 T. sugar

Cut marshmallows in fourths. Add pineapple and place in covered dish in refrigerator overnight. Drain juice from pineapple. Whip cream. Add sugar and vanilla. Fold in pineapple and marshmallow mixture. Pour in freezing trays and allow to freeze thoroughly. Chopped fruits and nuts may be added.

ALICE McKEE

ORANGE MACAROON CREAM

1 pkg. orange jello
½ pt. whipping cream
1 C. boiling water

1½ C. diced oranges
¼ lb. (1 doz.) almond
macaroons

Dissolve jello in boiling water. Add macaroons broken into pieces and chill. Add whipped cream and diced oranges. Mix well. Pour into mold and chill.

MRS. R. L. TILLMAN

PINEAPPLE DELIGHT

½ lb. vanilla wafers
1½ C. confectioners sugar
½ C. butter
2 eggs

1 small can crushed
pineapple
½ pt. whipping cream
1 C. nut meats

Crush wafers very fine. Butter square cake pan. Line with ½ crushed wafers. Cream butter and sugar. Add beaten eggs. Beat until smooth. Pour over crushed wafers. Whip cream and add nuts and drained pineapple. Pour over egg mixture. Top with remaining wafers. Chill over night.

MRS. E. C. PATTERSON, JR.
Chattanooga, Tenn.

PRUNE WHIP

6 egg whites
1 C. sugar
½ C. chopped pecans

½ C. cut-up cooked prunes
1 t. baking powder

Beat egg whites, adding sugar slowly. Fold in pecans, prunes and baking powder. Bake in greased casserole 40-45 minutes in 350°F. oven. Keep at room temperature until served.

MRS. T. D. EVANS

BUTTERSCOTCH SAUCE

1 2/3 C. brown sugar
¾ C. white Karo syrup
½ t. salt

3 T. butter
1 sm. can evaporated milk
1 t. vanilla

Combine sugar, syrup and butter. Boil 3-5 minutes. Cool. Add milk and boil a few minutes longer. Remove from heat and add salt and vanilla.

MRS. WALLACE L. POOLE

LEMON SAUCE

½ C. sugar	2 T. butter
1 T. corn starch	1½ T. lemon Juice
1 C. boiling water	dash of salt and grated nutmeg

Mix sugar and cornstarch. Add water, stirring constantly. Boil 5 minutes. Add nutmeg, salt, lemon juice and butter.

MRS. ALBERT C. MOSKOPP

PUDDING SAUCE

1 C. butter	2 C. granulated sugar

3 eggs, beaten — whites and yolks separate

Mix egg yolks with creamed butter and sugar and stir in ½ C. boiling water, 1 t. at a time. Fold in beaten egg whites till well blended. Flavor to taste.

MRS. ALBERT C. MOSKOPP

"DEEP DARK SECRET" DESSERT

4 egg yolks, beaten with 1 C. sugar

Add:

½ C. sifted flour	1 t. vanilla
1 t. baking powder	1 lb. dates, cut up
¼ t. salt	1 C. chopped nuts

Fold in:

4 stiffly beaten egg whites

Spread batter ½" thick on greased cooky sheet lined with waxed paper. Bake at 350° for ½ hour. Peel paper off cake while it is still warm. Break into bite size pieces.

Next combine:

3 sliced bananas
2 cans mandarin orange sections
Any other fresh fruits in season may be added

Assemble dessert by putting a layer of cake pieces on a large platter, add a layer of the drained fruit and top with the rest of the cake. Make a mound by gently pressing together. Over this mound pour 1 No. 2 can crushed pineapple. As the cake absorbs juices, reshape mound. This should be put aside in a cool place or refrigerator for 2 or 3 hours to blend. When ready to serve, spread whipped cream over all and decorate with maraschino cherries. This amount will serve 12 generously.

MRS. CHARLES HURLEY
Grand Forks, N. Dak.

BLUEBERRY COTTAGE PUDDING

¼ C. margarine	1 C. milk
2/3 C. sugar	4 t. baking powder
2 whole eggs	½ t. salt
2¼ C. flour	1 qt. blueberries

Reserve 1 C. flour and mix with blueberries. Combine other ingrenients. Fold in blueberry-flour mixture and bake in large pan or dish at 350°, about 35-40 minutes.

SAUCE

½ C. butter or margarine	⅛ t. salt
1 C. powdered sugar	½ t. vanilla

Cream these ingredients together. Fold in ½ pint cream, whipped. Serve sauce over warm cake.

MILLIE EGGENA

A FINE DESSERT

1 C. sugar	4 egg whites whipped,
1 C. chopped English	but not dry
walnut meats	¾ C. saltine crackers broken

Add sugar slowly to beaten egg whites. Fold in nuts and crackers. Bake 20 minutes in pie pan at 325°.

TOPPING

1 C. cream whipped	1 C. fruit cocktail, well drained

Fold cream and fruit together and place over above dessert, when cool. Chill and serve.

MRS. L. A. BALLEW, SR.

BOILED CUSTARD

To 3 slightly beaten eggs, add ½ C. sugar, 3 C. milk. Cook in double boiler until mixture coats a silver spoon. Remove immediately from heat. Cool and add 1 t. vanilla, ½ t. lemon extract. The secret in making this custard is to cook no longer than the very minute mixture coats the spoon.

MRS. BEN CARDWELL

CHOCOLATE DELIGHT

1½ C. sugar	3 squares bitter chocolate
1 C. butter	4 eggs
1 t. vanilla	¼ t. salt

Cream sugar and butter. Add melted chocolate, vanilla and eggs, one at a time, beating 3 minutes after each addition. Line dish with crushed vanilla wafers. Pour in mixture and sprinkle top with crushed wafers. Chill 8 hours. Top with whipped cream. Makes 8 generous servings.

MRS. BOB GRUBBS

FRUIT BAVARIAN CREAM

1 T. plain gelatin	½ C. sugar
¼ C. cold water	1½ C. whipping cream
1 C. fruit juice and pulp	pinch of salt
1 T. lemon juice	

Soak gelatin in cold water to soften and place cup in pan of hot water to dissolve gelatin. After it is dissolved strain it into the fruit juices. Add the sugar and salt and stir until smooth and well blended. Set bowl in a pan of ice water and stir until the mixture begins to thicken. Fold in the stiffly beaten cream and pour into a wet mold. Chill until firm before serving.

Canned pineapple, fresh or frozen strawberries, peaches or oranges, or any other preferred fruit could be used for this.

MRS. STEVE LACY

FLOATING ISLAND

4 C. milk	⅛ t. salt
¾ C. white sugar	1 t. vanilla
4 eggs, separated	½ C. sugar (for meringue)

Beat egg yolks with ½ C. milk. Mix 3½ C. milk with the sugar and salt in a pan over low heat. Heat, just to the boiling point, stirring constantly. Do not let it boil! Add egg and milk to hot mixture slowly and continue stirring over the heat until the custard thickens, about 2 minutes. Remove from the heat and stir in the vanilla. While custard cools, beat the egg whites until stiff, adding the sugar, 2 T. at a time. Drop by tablespoonfuls onto cool custard. Chill thoroughly.

MRS. ETHEL DUKE

TINY TIM PLUM PUDDING

3½ C. flour	1 C. cut figs
2 C. brown sugar	2 C. dried citron
¼ t. cinnamon	2 C. currants
¼ t. nutmeg	¼ C. orange peel
¼ t. cloves	¼ C. lemon peel
¼ t. ginger	3 eggs, well beaten
2 C. ground suet	1 C. water
2 C. cut raisins	1 C. orange juice

In large bowl mix flour, sugar, spices, salt and suet. Add fruit, peel, eggs, water and orange juice. Mix well. Turn into 2 to 2½ quart mold or small cans. Place on trivet in deep well or kettle and steam 5 hours. Let stand 5 minutes. Remove, cool, wrap and refrigerate. About 1½ hours before serving, steam in mold 1 hour. Serve with hard sauce.

MRS. CHARLES PISTON

ANGEL FOOD ICE BOX DESSERT

1 stale Angel food cake (bakery)	1 bottle cherries
½ t. salt	2 C. milk
1 C. sugar	2 egg yolks
1 pt. whipping cream	2 small lemon jello
1 (2½ oz.) can crushed pineapple	2 egg whites

Heat the salt, sugar, milk and yolks until hot. Add jello. Cool. Add stiffly beaten egg whites. When it begins to set add 1 pt. whipped cream, pineapple (drained) and cherries (cut) and nuts if desired. Break cake in small pieces and place in 9 X 13 cake pan or larger pan. Pour mixture over the cake pieces and set in refrigerator over-night.

Mrs. S. J. Wetherbee

ANGEL FOOD DELIGHT

Bake an angel food cake. Slice cake through the middle so as to make 2 layers. Whip 1½ pts. of whipping cream until thick. Add enough chocolate sauce to make it a light brown color. Spread whipped cream on first layer of cake. Then shave 2 Heath bars on top of whipped cream. Lay the 2nd layer of cake on top of first layer. Cover entire cake with whipped cream. Then shave 2 Heath bars on top of cake.

Mrs. Burgin Dossett, Jr.

APPLE GOODY

1 can apple pie filling	⅛ T. baking powder
½ C. oatmeal	¼ C. butter
½ C. brown sugar	½ C. flour

Put pie filling in pyrex dish. Mix all other ingredients and crumble on top and bake 1 hr. at 350 degrees.

Mrs. Bill Lancaster

OLD-TIME BROWN SUGAR APPLE CRUMBLE

1 qt. apples, sliced	¾ C. light brown sugar
¼ C. water	A few shakes of cinnamon
1/3 C. butter or oleo	1 C. sifted flour
1 t. salt	½ C. dark brown sugar

Put apples in buttered 10" X 6" baking dish. Add the light brown sugar, water and cinnamon. Blend the flour, dark brown sugar and salt with the butter or oleo to make a crumbly mixture. Spread evenly over the apples. Bake at 350 degrees for about 50 minutes.

Mrs. Ira Williams, Jr.

FIG NEWTON DESSERT

1 lb. fig newtons   ½ C. sherry
½ to 1 C. nuts

Break fig bars in bite sized pieces and soak with sherry. Pour into greased baking dish. Scatter nuts over mix. Chill. Cut into squares and serve topped with whipped cream.

Mrs. Albert Bowen

FROZEN BUTTERSCOTCH DREAM

2/3 C. sugar   1 C. whipping cream,
¼ C. water   whipped
1 unbeaten egg white   1 of 4 oz. pkg. instant
1 t. lemon juice   butterscotch pudding mix
1 t. vanilla   1 C. milk
                            ¾ C. chopped walnuts or
                              pecans

In small mixing bowl, combine sugar, water, egg white, lemon juice, and vanilla. Beat with electric mixer at high speed until stiff peaks form, about 5 minutes. Fold in whipped cream. Combine pudding mix and milk; fold into whipped cream mixture. Add ½ cup of nuts; turn into 10 X 6 X 1½" baking dish. Top with remaining ¼ cup nuts. Freeze 6-8 hours or overnight. Makes 6-8 servings. (This can also be put in a pie crust and served in the form of a pie.) Serve frozen.

Mrs. James W. Gibson

CHOCOLATE RING

1 pkg. Knox gelatin   1 C. cold water
1 C. boiling water   4 eggs
1 C. sugar   Vanilla
Salt   3 sq. melted chocolate

Beat egg yolks and sugar until light. Add melted chocolate. Dissolve gelatin in cold water and add to boiling water and then add to rest of ingredients. Beat thoroughly. Cool. Fold in egg whites last. Put in ring mold. Refrigerate several hours. Serve with whipped cream in center covered with chopped nuts.

Mrs. William Blackard

CHOCOLATE-MINT CREAM PUFFS

½ C. butter   ¼ t. salt
1 C. boiling water   4 eggs
1 C. flour

Melt butter in water and add flour and salt all at once and stir vigorously. Cook, stirring constantly, until mixture forms ball that doesn't separate. Remove from heat and cool slightly. Add eggs, one at a time, beating vigorously after each addition. Drop from tablespoon 2" apart onto greased baking sheet. Bake in oven (450 degrees) 25 minutes. Remove with spatula and cool on rack. When thoroughly cool, cut side of each puff & fill with peppermint whipped cream and pour generous portion of hot fudge sauce over each puff to serve.

FILLING FOR CREAM PUFFS

1 pt. whipping cream   ½ lb. red soft peppermint candy

Whip cream to serving thickness. Crush candy with rolling pin and gently fold into whipped cream just before serving.

HOT FUDGE SAUCE (Never Fails)

3 sq. unsweetened chocolate   2 T. butter or oleo
1 C. evaporated milk   1 t. vanilla
1 C. sugar   ⅛ t. salt

Mix chocolate, milk, sugar and salt. Cook over low heat, stirring constantly until chocolate is melted. Add butter and vanilla. Continue to cook, stirring constantly, until sauce is smooth. Remove from heat. Serve over peppermint cream puffs.

Mrs. Stewart Cannon, Jr.

WHIPPED CREAM CUPS

1 C. whipping cream   ½ C. macaroon cookie
3 t. sherry   crumbs
1 egg white, stiffly beaten   ¼ C. confectioners sugar

Whip the cream and fold in egg white. Add sugar and sherry and crumbs. Pile high in cupcake cups and sprinkle with crumbs on top. Place in freezer and serve frozen. A delicious light dessert to be served after a heavy meal.

Mrs. Jack Seaton

EASY DESSERT

Vanilla ice cream	Crushed salted peanuts
Toasted coconut	Chocolate sauce

Make rounded scoop of vanilla ice cream into balls and freeze balls. Just before serving: Roll in crushed salted peanuts and toasted coconut. Serve with chocolate sauce and or plus cream de menthe.

Mrs. Al Costner

FORGOTTEN DESSERT

Heat oven to 450 degrees.

5 eggs, whites only	1 t. cream of tartar
1½ C. sugar	

Beat egg whites until foamy, add cream of tartar and beat till stiff. Gradually add sugar and beat 10 minutes. Put in well greased 9 X 13 pan. Put your dessert in oven and turn your oven off right away. **Do not open oven.** Let stand overnight. (You may spread on ¼ pt. whipped cream on this in the morning and put in refrigerator, however, it is good without this whipped cream.) Cut in squares and serve with fresh or frozen strawberries, raspberries or other fruit.

Mrs. Bill Kohler

JEWEL DESSERT

1 pkg. cherry flavored gelatin	1 envelope unflavored gelatin
1 pkg. lime flavored gelatin	2 T. cold water
1 pkg. orange flavored gelatin	½ C. hot pineapple juice
4½ C. hot water	2 envelopes whipped topping
1¾ C. crushed vanilla wafers	1 C. milk
½ C. sugar	½ C. sugar
1 stick margarine	1 t. vanilla extract

Dissolve each package of flavored gelatin in 1½ cups water and pour into separate pans to get firm—then cut in small cubes and refrigerate. Put crushed vanilla wafers in large bowl with ½ cup sugar and melted margarine. Combine and spread half of this mixture over bottom of an 8 x 12 inch pan. Dissolve unflavored gelatin in 2 Tbs. of cold water. Let it stand 5 min. then add ½ cup hot pineapple juice. When this gelatin gets cool, beat 2 pkgs. of topping with 1 cup milk, ½ cup sugar, and 1 tsp. vanilla. Whip until stiff, then fold in the cooled unflavored gelatin. Next fold in the colored cubes of flavored gelatin. Sprinkle other half of crumb mixture over top and keep refrigerated. Can be made a day or two before serving.

Mrs. Roy W. Curtis

HELLO DOLLY

1 stick margarine	1 C. graham cracker crumbs
1 C. chocolate drops (semi-sweet)	1 C. frozen coconut
1 can Eagle Brand milk	1 C. pecans

Melt margarine in baking dish, pour crumbs over, but do not stir. Pour chocolate drops over crumbs, then put layer of coconut, then layer of nuts. Pour sweetened condensed milk over all but do not stir. Bake until it bubbles at 350 degrees. Mrs. Edward Steffner

HOT FRUIT DESSERT

3 small cans apricots	3 small cans pineapple pieces
3 small cans peaches	3 No. 2 size cans pitted bing cherries
3 oranges	½ C. light brown sugar
3 lemons	

Grate rind of oranges and lemons into sugar. Spread fruits, layer by layer including oranges and lemons sliced very thinly in baking dish, sprinkle each layer with brown sugar mixture and a sprinkling of nutmeg. Heat all until very hot and serve topped with some sour cream. Mrs. Latham R. Winn

NABISCO TORTE

Cream 1 cup 4X sugar and ¾ cup butter. Add 2 egg yolks and ½ tsp. vanilla and beat. Fold in beaten egg whites. Spread ½ lb. ground Nabisco sugar wafers in bottom of 9 x 13 cake pan. Spread the above top mixture over this and then spread fruit over this (crushed strawberries or drained, crushed pineapple). Then add 1½ cup whipping cream (whipped and flavored). Then crumble another ½ lb. of Nabisco sugar wafers and put on top and place in refrigerator overnight.

OLD-FASHIONED VANILLA ICE CREAM

2 qts. of milk	3 beaten eggs
2 C. sugar	1 T. vanilla
dash of salt	

Heat over low heat one qt. of milk. Stir in, until dissolved, sugar and salt, next add beaten eggs. Beat with beater while cooking over low heat until mixture is thick and smooth. Do not boil. Cool and then add vanilla and 1 qt. cold milk. Pour into freezer and freeze. If you prefer, to have a fruit-flavored ice cream, add 2 cups of crushed peaches, bananas, etc. If you want it richer, add 1 pt. of whipped cream.

Mrs. C. N. Bolding

ORANGE CUP

4 oranges	4 oz. granulated sugar
½ pt. orange juice	¾ pt. heavy cream
2 egg yolks	4 candied cherries or peel
1 t. cornstarch	

Cut off top of oranges about a third of the way down, leaving a nice cup. Extract the flesh and juice. Blend cornstarch with juice, add egg yolks and sugar. Beat over double boiler until it thickens. Pour into orange cups. Chill and decorate with whipped cream and candied peel.   Mrs. Bill Stevens

PRUNE STUFFED ORANGE CUPS

4 large oranges	4 t. lemon juice
½ lb. prunes, cooked	2 C. ginger ale, chilled
1 C. walnut halves	

Cut oranges in halves; gently remove centers, leaving shells intact. Cut orange centers into bit-sized pieces. Remove pits from prunes, leaving them as whole as possible. Combine prunes with orange pieces and walnuts, pile into orange cups. Sprinkle each cup with ½ tsp. lemon juice. Refrigerate. Just before serving, pour ¼ cup ginger ale over each cup. Makes 8 servings.   Mrs. Stewart Cannon, Jr.

RUM PUDDING

¼ t. salt	2/3 C. milk
3 egg yolks	3 T. rum
6 T. sugar	1 C. whipping cream,
1 envelope-1 T. unflavored	whipped
gelatin	

Add salt to egg yolks and beat till thick and lemon colored. Gradually beat in sugar. Soften gelatin in milk. Heat milk till gelatin dissolves, cool slightly. Add milk mixture to egg yolk mixture while beating constantly, add rum. Chill until partially set. Fold in whipping cream and turn into individual molds. Chill until set, about 4 hours; unmold and serve with raspberry sauce.

RASPBERRY SAUCE

¼ C. sugar	1 (10 oz.) pkg. frozen
1 T. cornstarch	raspberries, thawed
1/3 C. cold water	

Combine sugar and cornstarch, stir in berries and water. Cook stirring constantly, until mixture thickens and boils. Boil 2 minutes more. Push through sieve; chill. Makes 1 cup sauce.   Mrs. John Ferenbach

TENNESSEE PUDDING

2 C. white sugar	3½ C. plain flour
2 sticks butter	1 C. chopped pecans
1 t. soda	1 C. chopped dates
½ C. buttermilk	1 C. coconut (fresh or
4 whole eggs	frozen)

Flour angel food cake pan. (Put butter all over pan and sprinkle with flour.)

Cream butter and sugar.

Put soda in buttermilk and let stand until doubled in size.

Break whole eggs into thoroughly creamed sugar and butter, beat until creamed together thoroughly and add buttermilk.

Add flour with a pinch of salt beating by hand until mixed well. Add nuts, dates and coconut.

Bake 1½ hours at 300 degrees or until done. Just before cake is done (about 5 minutes) mix 1½ cups of orange juice (fresh or frozen) with 2½ cups of sugar, heat until sugar is melted. Remove cake and take a kitchen knife pushing all the way to the bottom of cake pan, (all over cake so the orange juice mixture will go all through the cake). Pour mixture over the cake and let stand until completely cool.

Nancy Stalnaker

DRESSINGS & SAUCES

ARGYLE SALAD DRESSING

4 egg yolks	1 t. dry mustard
6 T. vinegar	1 t. butter
2 T. sugar	1 t. salt

Cook eggs, vinegar, sugar, mustard and butter in a double boiler until thick, stirring constantly. When cold, add 1 C. heavy cream, whipped, and 12 marshmallows cut fine. This is delecious served on any kind of canned fruit.

MRS. EDWIN HUNTER

CENTURY OLD DRESSING

¼ C. sugar	1 C. salad oil
½ C. water	½ C. catsup
¼ C. lemon juice	1 small onion, grated
¼ t. salt	½ t. paprika
¼ C. vinegar	

Boil sugar and water for 10 minutes. Add lemon juice and boil 5 minutes longer. Cool in ice water. Add salt, paprika, vinegar, and mix well. Mix oil, catsup, onion, and add cold syrup. Beat until thick. Pour into glass jar, and fasten securely. Shake well before each use to emulsify.

MRS. A. O. WOLFF

COLE SLAW DRESSING

1 C. sugar (scant)	2 t. prepared mustard
2 egg yolks	½ C. vinegar
2 T. flour	1½ C. water
2 t. salt	

Mix all dry ingredients, add vinegar and water, eggs and mustard and stir until smooth. Cook and stir until thick. Chill well.

MRS. C. R. SMATHERS

COOKED SALAD DRESSING

Mix together:

4 egg yolks	1 t. dry mustard
1 T. butter	½ C. milk
1 T. flour	½ C. vinegar
Salt, pepper, sugar to taste	

Boil until thick; remove from heat and beat until cold. When ready to serve, thin with 2 or 3 T. slightly whipped cream.

MRS. E. HAYNES MILLER

FRENCH DRESSING

1 C. salad oil	1½ t. salt
1 C. vinegar	1½ t. pepper
½ can tomato soup	2 T. Worcestershire
1 T. dry mustard	⅛ C. sugar

Combine ingredients in bottle or jar and shake well. One clove garlic and wedge of bleu cheese or Roquefort may be added if desired.

MRS. C. W. SULLIVAN
Atlanta, Ga.

FRENCH DRESSING

2 C. salad oil	3 t. prepared mustard
1 C. vinegar	1 t. Worcestershire sauce
¼ C. brown sugar	Juice of 3 lemons
1 C. catsup	paprika
large onion or clove of garlic	salt and red pepper to taste

Beat with mixer set at low speed for 30 minutes.

MRS. W. S. WILEY
Bristol, Va.

FRUIT SALAD DRESSING

Juice of 1 lemon	1 T. flour
Juice of 1 orange	1 C. sugar
1 egg	1 T. butter

Mix sugar and flour; add egg and fruit juices and cook until creamy in double boiler or over very low heat. Stir constantly. When cooked, add butter. If desired, ½ pt. whipped cream may be added, using ½ in dressing and ½ mixed with fruit.

MRS. BILL HARRELL

GARLIC DRESSING

1-1/3 C. salad oil	5 t. salt
½ C. vinegar	½ t. dry mustard
1 t. sugar	4 garlic cloves, sliced

Combine ingredients in jar and shake thoroughly. Chill several hours.

MRS. B. G. YOUNG, JR.

LEMON SALAD DRESSING

Stir together and cook until thick:

2 whole eggs	4 T. sugar
Juice of 1 lemon	

When ready to serve, add whipped cream to taste.

MRS. E. HAYNES MILLER

OIL AND VINEGAR DRESSING

½ C. sugar (scant)	1 t. paprika
1 t. salt	1 t. onion juice
1 t. dry mustard	1 C. salad oil
1 t. celery salt	¼ C. vinegar

Mix dry ingredients; add onion juice. Add oil, alternately with vinegar, small amounts at a time, the last addition being vinegar.

MRS. WARNER DUBOSE

ROQUEFORT CHEESE DRESSING

1 lb. Roquefort cheese	½ C. salad oil
1 C. buttermilk	1 t. salt
½ C. mayonnaise	juice of ½ lemon

Mix together well, chill and serve.

MRS. C. R. SMATHERS

SALAD DRESSING — ROTISSERIE SAUCE

1 small onion	½ C. salad oil
1 garlic clove, chopped fine	1 T. Worcestershire sauce
1 C. mayonnaise—added last	1 t. black pepper
¼ C. chili sauce	dash of tabasco sauce
¼ C. catsup	dash of paprika
1 t. prepared mustard	2 T. water

Grate onion on fine side of grater. Mix all other ingredients and put into qt. jar. Shake well and keep in refrigerator.

MRS. L. R. DICKENSON
Maryville, Tenn.

DRESSING FOR SHRIMP

1 C. mayonnaise	1 t. minced onion
¼ C. chili sauce	1 T. minced parsley
2 T. minced celery	Salt and pepper to taste
1 t. dry mustard	Very small pieces of ½ to 1
1 T. vinegar	avocado

Mix ingredients together and place in the refrigerator. This dressing can be used for other salads, but especially delicious with shrimp.

MRS. J. R. WOLFF

SOUR CREAM DRESSING

To **1 pt. of sour cream add 4 T. grated onion, 1 t. salt, 1 t. sugar, 2 or 3 dashes of tabasco and 1 T. prepared horseradish.**
Stir together and store in refrigerator. Serve dressing in a bowl and sprinkle generously with paprika.

MRS. ROBERT LONDON

SWEET OR SOUR CREAM DRESSING (GERMAN)

1 C. sweet or sour cream	1 t. salt
2 T. lemon juice	¼ t. pepper
2 T. vinegar	1 t. prepared mustard
1 T. sugar	

Beat cream until smooth, thick and light. Mix other ingredients together and gradually add to cream, beating all the while. Excellent over vegetables.

MRS. GENE TAYLOR, JR.

TOMATO FRENCH DRESSING

1 T. dry mustard	½ t. paprika
1 t. salt	½ C. vinegar
3 T. sugar	1 C. salad oil
Dash of pepper	1 T. grated onion
½ can tomato soup	

Combine dry ingredients, mix with vinegar. Pour into bottle or jar. Add oil, onion and tomato soup, just as it comes from the can. Cover, shake until well blended. Makes 2 cups.

MRS. HORACE DANCE

WINE DRESSING

1/3 C. sugar   1/3 C. sherry wine, chilled
1/3 C. lemon juice   ⅛ t. salt

Stir until sugar is dissolved.

MRS. J. R. WOLFF

MAYONNAISE

1 whole egg   1 egg yolk
3 C. salad oil   ¾ t. salt
1/3 C. lemon juice   ½ t. paprika
½ t. red pepper

Beat eggs well, gradually add oil ¾ t. at a time until oil remains on surface. Increase amount to ¼ C. at a time after using first cup. When all oil has been used and mixture has become thick, add remaining ingredients. Place in refrigerator away from freezing unit.

MRS. T. F. BECKNER, JR.

BARBEQUE SAUCE

For anything. Can be kept in refrigerator a week or so.

¼ lb. butter   1 C. vinegar
½ C. Worchestershire sauce   1 t. red pepper
1 C. catsup   1 t. dry mustard
½ C. chopped onions (fine)

Heat to a boiling point.

MRS. CHARLES GORDON

COCKTAIL SAUCE

¾ C. chili sauce or catsup   1½ T. lemon juice
1 T. Worchestershire sauce   1 T. prepared horseradish
Few drops tabasco   ¼ t. salt
1 t. grated onion

Mix ingredients and chill.

MRS. DAYTON ISAACS

COME BACK SAUCE

3 buttons grated garlic   Worchestershire sauce
1 C. mayonnaise   1 t. paprika
¾ C. chili sauce and tomato   juice of 1 lemon
    juice mixed   1 T. water
½ C. salad oil   salt to taste
1 t. black pepper   dash tabasco
1 t. powdered mustard

Mix well in electric mixer.

MRS. C. W. SULLIVAN
Atlanta, Ga.

CREAMED HORSERADISH SAUCE

Beat until stiff; ½ C. heavy cream. Add slowly, beating constantly, 3 T. lemon juice or vinegar, ¼ t. salt, ⅛ t. paprika and a few grains of cayenne. Fold in 2 T. grated horseradish. This makes 1¼ cups dressing.

MRS. A. O. WOLFF

MOCK HOLLANDAISE

1 C. white cream sauce	6 T. butter
2 egg yolks	1 T. lemon juice

Just before serving stir in egg yolks, 1 T. at a time. Add lemon juice.

MRS. C. R. SMATHERS

MUSHROOM SAUCE

1 can mushroom soup	salt
½ C. grated cheese	2 T. brown sugar
½ C. cream	1 T. Worchestershire sauce

Heat and serve in split baked Idaho potatoes.

MRS. WILLIAM SELLS

PERFECT HOLLANDAISE SAUCE

Juice ½ lemon	¼ t. salt
2 unbeaten egg yolks	dash cayenne
1 stick butter	

Add lemon juice to the egg yolks. Cut butter into thirds. Add one-third butter to the egg yolks and cook over hot, not boiling, water. Stir constantly until butter melts and sauce thickens. Add another third of butter and stir until melted. Repeat with remaining butter and keep stirring until sauce is as thick as mayonnaise. Remove from heat and stir in seasoning and beat with a spoon or wire whisk until shiny (about ½ minute). If sauce curdles, beat in about 2 T. boiling water. Store any left over sauce in tightly covered jar in refrigerator.

MRS. L. A. BALLEW, SR.

TARTAR SAUCE FOR FISH OR SEAFOOD

1 C. mayonnaise	1 T. green pepper, chopped
2 T. chopped stuffed olives	1 T. tarragon
2 T. chopped sweet gherkins	1 t. lemon juice
1 T. minced onion	½ t. salt
1 T. parsley, chopped	½ t. black pepper

Mix ingredients and store in refrigerator.

MRS. RUSSELL CAMPBELL

WHITE SAUCE

Thin:

2 T. butter	salt
2 T. flour	1 C. milk

Medium:

3 T. butter	salt
3 T. flour	1 C. milk

Thick:

4 T. butter	salt
4 T. flour	1 C. milk

Melt butter, gradually add the flour, then milk and cook until sauce thickens.

SAUCE MORNAY

2 T. butter	salt and white pepper to taste
2 T. flour (level)	¼ C. grated Swiss cheese
2 C. thin cream	onion salt and dry mustard,
¼ C. white wine (optional)	as desired

Melt butter, but do not let it brown. Remove pan from heat and blend in flour, salt and pepper. Stir over the heat for about a minute and remove again to blend in the cream, and wine if desired. After blending, put back over the heat and cook for about 3 minutes, while stirring. Stir in cheese and mustard and onion salt to taste. Serve with fish or other seafood.

HOT RAISIN SAUCE

1 T. bacon drippings	1 lemon, juice and rind
¼ C. chopped onion	2½ T. brown sugar
1 T. cornstarch	1/8 t. cinnamon
1½ C. water	1/8 t. cloves
1/3 C. orange juice concentrate	½ C. chopped seedless raisins
¼ t. dry mustard	

Blend all ingredients well, chopping lemon rind with onion and raisins. Bring to boil, stirring constantly. Cook about 2 minutes. Serve hot over ham or duck.

SOUR CREAM GARDEN DRESSING

1 C. dairy sour cream	1 T. salad vinegar
½ C. chopped cucumber	1½ t. horseradish
¼ C. chopped green onions	¾ t. salt
¼ C. chopped radishes	½ t. dill seed

Chop vegetables until very fine; drain off any juice. Combine all ingredients, mix well and chill.

HOT BACON DRESSING

1 T. bacon drippings	½ t. oregano
1 T. vinegar	¼ t. pepper
½ t. salt	4 strips crisp bacon

Boil vinegar and drippings for a minute; sprinkle in seasonings and pour over vegetables. Crumble the bacon over the top. Particularly good over leaf lettuce.

DIETER'S DELIGHT DRESSING

8 oz. can tomato sauce	½ t. salt
2 T. vinegar	½ t. dill seed
1 t. onion juice	¼ t. powdered basil
1 t. Worcestershire sauce	

Combine in a bottle and shake vigorously. Chill.

FLUFFY HOT SAUCE

1 C. whipped cream
Prepared mustard and horseradish to taste

Gently stir ingredients together and chill. Very good with pork.

FRENCH DRESSING

¼ C. wine vinegar	1 C. salad oil
1 t. onion juice	1 t. paprika
1 t. celery seed	1 t. dry mustard
1 t. salt	½ C. sugar

Put all in blender and beat until thoroughly mixed. Makes 1½ cups.

Mrs. William Blackard

CELERY SEED SALAD DRESSING

⅓ C. sugar	1 t. mustard (dry or wet)
1 t. paprika	1 T. grated onion
1 heaping T. celery seed	

Place all in one bowl. Then mix in 1 tsp. vinegar. Add alternately beating well: 1 cup oil and 3 Tbs. vinegar. Beat until thick and smooth. Refrigerate. Use on fruits salads.

Mrs. Alfred Abernethy

HOMEMADE MAYONNAISE

Make with electric mixer on high speed. Makes one Pint.

    1 egg   1 pt. Mazola or Wesson oil

Pour a drop to get it started and then pour very slowly, as it gets started you may pour it faster. After it thickens add:

1 t. salt	1 t. sugar
paprika (dash)	Red pepper (dash)
About ½ t. dry mustard	Capful of garlic wine vinegar
	1 whole lemon (winter), lime (summer) juice. Be sure and strain

Mrs. William Blackard

IRISH WHISKEY SAUCE

¼ C. soft butter	1 egg
2 C. light brown sugar	1 C. light cream
⅛ t. nutmeg	¼ C. Irish Whiskey

In double boiler with mixer, beat butter and sugar until creamy. Beat in egg, cream, nutmeg and beat until fluffy. Cook, stirring occasionally, over hot water, not boiling, until thickened. Remove from heat, gradually stir in whiskey. Serve warm with pudding or over appropriate cakes (like pound or prune cake).

Mrs. John Wilson

TENNESSEE BARBECUE SAUCE

1 C. vinegar
4 t. salt
¼ lb. butter or oleo or
⅓ C. corn oil

2 t. Tabasco
1 T. Worcestershire
Pinch garlic powder

This is great for chicken.

Mrs. James Thompson

DRESSING FOR TOSSED SALAD

1½ C. Wesson oil
½ C. vinegar
½ C. plus 1 T. sugar
1 t. grated onion

½ t. garlic powder
½ t. dry mustard
½ t. salt

Put the above ingredients into a bowl and beat for 10 minutes until thick. Serve on combination salad.

Mrs. Buddy Price

ROQUEFORT CHEESE DRESSING

¼ lb. Blue or Roquefort
cheese, break with fork
¼ C. vinegar
¼ C. oil

½ pt. sour cream
1 t. salt
½ t. pepper

Mix all ingredients. Add slowly ½ cup more of oil. Put in refrigerator.

Mrs. Mark Hicks

BLUE CHEESE DRESSING

¼ lb. Blue cheese
¼ C. Miracle Whip salad
dressing
½ C. light cream or canned
milk
2 T. lemon juice

2 T. parsley flakes
1 t. onion
¼ t. each, Worcestershire,
garlic salt, pepper and
salt
½ t. Accent

Put all together in blender and mix lightly.

Mrs. Vernon Wilson

FRANKLIN CLUB SLAW DRESSING

1 C. sugar
1 C. salad dressing
Add Accent to taste

½ C. vinegar
1 t. salt

Add a little shredded lettuce to shredded cabbage for slaw.

Mrs. Vernon Wilson

HILO MARINATING SAUCE

1 C. apricot preserves   2 T. honey
½ of 8 oz. can tomato sauce 1 T. Mazola oil
⅓ C. vinegar   1 t. salt
¼ C. sherry (cream)   ¼ t. ginger
2 T. soy sauce

Wonderful to spoon over pork roast or chops. Especially good to spoon over sliced hot dogs. Heat for ½ hour in oven and serve in chafing dish for hors d' oeuvres.

Mrs. John Wilson

BARBECUE

¼ C. onion flakes   1 t. chili powder
3 T. brown sugar   2 T. vinegar
1 t. paprika   1 C. tomato juice
½ t. dry mustard   2 T. barbecue sauce

Tear roast into pieces and add to the sauce. Simmer 20 minutes. Serve on hot buns.

Marylou Conant

SWEET AND SOUR SAUCE

3 T. corn starch   1 T. prepared mustard
1 C. vinegar   2 green peppers, cut in large
1 C. sugar   pieces
Few dashes Tabasco   1 red pepper, or pimento
1 T. Worcestershire sauce   1 large can pineapple chunks
                            1½ lb. cooked veal, cut
                               in strips

Mix corn starch with vinegar and then cook with sugar until clear. Add Tabasco, Worcestershire sauce, mustard and pepper. Add pineapple chunks and juice. Cover and cook 15 minutes. Add meat and let simmer in chafing dish.

Mrs. H. B. Cupp, Jr.

SAUCE FOR LONDON BROIL

1 T. salad oil   ⅛ t. garlic powder
3 t. Accent   2 t. chopped parsley
1 t. salt   1 t. lemon juice
⅛ t. pepper

Broil steak 4 minutes on one side and then 4 min. on the other one. Slice diagonally. Flank steak may be used.

Mrs. Bo Abernethy

EAST TENNESSEE FAVORITES

EAST TENNESSEE FAVORITES

The purpose of adding this chapter to SMOKY MOUNTAIN MAGIC is twofold. It is an attempt to preserve recipes which were commonplace in the homes of yesteryear but are growing increasingly scarce in today's homes. It is also an attempt to pay tribute to the women in the past who took great pride in their cooking and for whom the preparation of food was far more complicated and essential than we today can appreciate. It has been difficult to obtain many of these recipes because these women did not cook from written instructions; methods were handed down from generation to generation and dishes varied from family to family. We have obtained the included recipes by patiently questioning some of the few remaining women we know who still cook with "a pinch," "a handfull," "a little bit;" who still consult the signs of the ALMANAC; and who have fed large families and many friends truly delicious dishes from their gardens and smokehouses. We admire and respect these women as cooks as well as for other reasons. We consider their recipes priceless gourmet fare. Should you never attempt to make some of their more elaborate offerings, we feel you nevertheless will enjoy reading them, and we know you will have a renewed respect for an era of cooking now gone. But should you use these recipes, rest assured that we have tested and tasted the included dishes. They are worthy of your time and effort; they are truly SMOKY MOUNTAIN MAGIC!

Patty Smithdeal Fulton

GRAPE WINE

Mash in a stone crock 60 cups grapes. Add 5 qts. boiling water. Cover and let stand 3 days. Strain through a cheesecloth two or three thicknesses and return to jar. Add 10 cups sugar and a whole egg in shell. Cover and let stand until fermented; this takes about 21 days. Skim frequently and strain several times. When the egg goes to the bottom, it is ready to strain and bottle. I believe a bought strainer would do as well and be less trouble.

Mrs. Roy Brumlt

BLACKBERRY OR ELDERBERRY CORDIAL

Set berries over a moderate fire and let simmer until they fall to pieces, strain through a jelly bag and to each pint of juice allow one pound of sugar. Add cinnamon, cloves and mace to taste, boil fifteen minutes and strain a second time. Set away to cool.

When cold, add to each pint of syrup, one wine glass of good brandy. Bottle, cork tight and put in a cool place.

Mrs. W. K. Vance

SASSAFRAS TEA

Dig roots of Sassafras tree, wash and dry or buy in produce department of grocery store. Bring 4 cups water to boil, add two pieces of Sassafras about 3 inches long, cover and let simmer about 30 minutes. Serve hot with a little sugar.

Beulah Rhea

CHERRY BOUNCE

To 1 gallon of alcohol (white spirits) put 2 quarts of water and 5 to 6 quarts of wild cherries. Wash cherries and put in jug with alcohol. Corn cob stopper in jug. After they stand three months, drain off liquor and strain it well, sometimes twice. Make a thick syrup with 1½ lbs. white sugar and water and boil until ropy. Add the syrup to liquor from jug to taste.

HOT APPLE TODDY

5 qts. apple juice	1 t. whole cloves
1 t. whole allspice	1 lb. sugar
4 sticks cinnamon	1 qt. orange juice
1 lemon, sliced very thin	1 lg. can pineapple juice
4 lemons, juice	(optional)
2 qts. 100 proof whiskey	1 qt. apple brandy

Boil 2 qts. apple juice with the spices for 5 minutes. Add this to sugar, then drop in sliced lemon. Boil 1 minute. Cool. Add rest of apple juice, orange juice, lemon juice and pineapple juice (if used). Strain. Add whiskey and brandy to strained mixture. Seal in quart jars. When used, serve hot but do not boil. This is good to have on hand in winter months—especially for those suffering from colds.

HOLIDAY FRUITS

Use a large pottery crock that holds 4 or more quarts. Pour in a bottle of Brandy. Add to this a stick of cinnamon, a few whole cloves, a pinch of nutmeg, also grate in some orange and lemon rind. When strawberries come, add a quart, steamed and washed, plus their weight in sugar. Store covered in a cool place. When raspberries are in season, add a quart of them, plus their weight in sugar; pitted cherries; blackberries; peeled and cut up peaches; apricots; fresh pineapple; red plums - each time adding equal weight in sugar and more spices and brandy as necessary. When crock is full, cover tightly and store undisturbed for a few months. Open the jar for the holidays and use the fruits on top of ice cream, puddings or as a garnish for meats.

TO PREPARE FOWL FOR BAKING

When fowl is killed be sure that it bleeds well. It is best to remove the head.

Scald the fowl in boiling water. Do not leave it in the water more than six seconds for if it is left too long it sets the feathers instead of loosening them. See that the wings and legs are well scalded. Lay it on a board or hang it up while you pick all the feathers off. The hard tail and wing feathers may be thrown away but the softer feathers should be saved for sofa pillows. Wash them and put them in a cloth sack and hang in a warm place to dry and liven up.

After the fowl has been stripped of all its feathers, it should be singed to remove all the hairs that cover its body. Next wash the fowl clean. Use soap and brush in warm water to clean the skin. Rinse in clean, cold water.

Remove the feet at the first joint above the scales. Remove the crop at the neck. Cut off the oil bag on the top of the back at the tail. Cut around rectum and loosen from back and sides. Make an incision under the breast point large enough to allow intestines to be removed. Care must be used not to break any of them or rupture the gall bladder which is located on the side of the liver.

Remove intestine and all glands. Wash out with cold water and salt inside and cut. Remove with intestine the heart, liver and gizzard. Cut the heart to remove all clot blood. Cut the gall bladder off the liver, taking some of the liver with it to insure a safe removal. Open the gizzard by cutting down to the inner lining and pealing open as one might cut a peanut. Wash it thoroughly and then salt.

Any fowl is better when it has been cooled and has taken salt at least 12 hours before cooking.

Mrs. C. E. Burns

GRANNY BYRD'S CHICKEN AND DUMPLINGS

Dress about a 3 lb. fat hen and soak in cold salt water for few hours. Drain. Cook hen in fresh salted water after placing large whole peeled onion inside hen. Simmer, covered, about 3 or 4 hours, or until tender. Remove hen to baking pan. Remove pot from heat. In bowl put about 2 C. plain flour and 1 t. salt. Skim about a cup or two of broth with chicken fat from top of liquid in pot and add to flour, mixing to make dough you can handle. Place on floured board. Meanwhile bring broth in pot to rapid boil. Work flour-broth mixture into dough and roll out thin. Cut into strips with knife and drop into rapidly boiling broth. Cook uncovered about 10 minutes or until dumplings are "set." Reduce heat, season with salt and black pepper, then thicken broth with 2 or 3 T. flour or cornstarch mixed with cold water to make paste. Pour paste into broth, stirring with fork to make gravy around dumplings. Cover pot and simmer slowly for 20-30 minutes, stirring occasionally to prevent sticking. Brown hen in oven. Slice and serve on platter; pass dumplings in bowl. This makes a tender but chewy dumpling that our family loves. If you like the light, fluffy dumplings, use self-rising flour, omitting the salt, and follow the same directions given above.

Mrs. Lyman (Patty S.) Fulton

GRANDMOTHER'S FRIED CHICKEN AND GRAVY

Grandmother would catch a good sized fryer and wring its neck. Pour boiling water over chicken and pluck feathers. Singe chicken to remove remaining hairs. Wash plucked chicken and dress, cutting into pieces for frying. Cut pulley bone from large end of breast before cutting breast in two pieces. Place dressed chicken pieces in large bowl of cold water with plenty of salt and chill. Salt removes blood. Allow about an hour to fry chicken. Heat shortening, lard, bacon drippings or half butter and half shortening on medium heat in iron skillet. Use enough fat to cover half way up on sides of pieces of chicken. Drain chicken and roll in flour. Place in hot skillet and fry until golden brown on both sides, turning once and seasoning with salt and black pepper on both sides. When brown, cover with lid and cook slowly until tender. Remove lid and fry until crisp on both sides. Remove chicken to heated platter.

GRAVY

Pour off all but about 2 T. grease in skillet. Scrape brown crisp crumbs loose from bottom of skillet; stir in 2 T. flour, making a paste with grease, and stir until very dark brown but don't burn. Have medium sized bowl filled with water or milk and pour liquid into skillet, stir rapidly into smooth mixture, reduce heat, cook gravy until thick as you like. Season with salt and black pepper. Stir to prevent sticking. Pour into medium sized bowl and serve over hot biscuits, rice or mashed potatoes with chicken.

Mrs. Lyman A. Fulton

HECKERMAN DRESSING

This is a very old recipe to make a delicious dressing; we think you will want to try it.

2 loaves toasted white bread	3 or 4 stalks celery
2 lb. chestnuts	2 large onions
1 can mushrooms	½ lb. sausage
½ C. cranberry sauce	Thyme to taste
Salt to taste	Pepper to taste

Put this all through a food chopper and mix well afterward. This makes enough for the inside stuffing of 2 large turkeys, so I usually make the whole recipe, use half for the Thanksgiving bird and freeze the other to use at Christmas. It is a real chore to make and once a year is enough. It is most rewarding, however, as everyone just loves it. To toast chestnuts, I cut a cross on the flatter side and roast in the oven for 20 minutes. Then peel the outer hull, and the inside skin.

Mrs. Norman Thomas

PORK TENDERLOIN

Fry tenderloin slices in a little hot fat until golden brown on both sides and tender. Remove to hot serving platter. Use drippings in pan to make cream gravy and pour over tenderloin slices.

TO CURE A COUNTRY HAM

In a cool place such as a smokehouse, salt ham down with Morton's bag salt for six weeks. Then hang ham for 8 weeks. At this time wash ham in boiling Borax water (1 C. Borax to 2-3 gallons of Water). Rinse in plain water and dry the ham thoroughly. Sprinkle ham with red pepper, black pepper, brown sugar and molasses (to hold sugar on ham). Hang to dry. When ham is dry, wrap in brown paper and hang. Cut about July.

Mrs. Andy (Ollie) Kern

FRIED COUNTRY HAM

Slice ham ¼ inch thick
Cut into pieces of serving size
Melt 1 T. shortening in heavy skillet

Put ham slices in skillet and fry slowly. Brown on one side, turn, and sprinkle brown sugar over top of ham. Cook until brown on both sides, about 5 or 10 minutes. Remove to deep heated platter and make Red Eye Gravy.

RED EYE GRAVY

Remove part of grease. Put 3 T. coffee (liquid, strong black) into about ⅓ cup of water. Pour this into hot skillet with grease which has been heated about 1 minute. Pour over ham.

HOMEMADE SAUSAGE

Using fresh shoulder of pork that has not been salted, grind the lean portion in a sausage grinder with enough fat from the pork for frying purposes. Be sure that none of the blood clots that might have been left in the shoulder are ground with the meat and fat. Season the mixture with 1 tsp. salt per lb. and 1 tsp. ground garden sage per lb. Cut pods from hot red pepper with scissors real fine for seasoning also (2 med. pods for 10 lb. of meat). At this point, fry a small piece of the mixture and taste for seasoning to your taste. If you like garlic, grind garlic and add to the mixture (2 pods the size of golf ball for 10 lb. of meat). Fry mixture made out into small patties until well done. Place hot patties with some of the grease in hot sterile jars and seal. At serving time heat sausage thoroughly, and if you like, make sausage gravy with the drippings after removing the patties to a hot serving platter.

Mrs. J. D. Braswell, Sr.
Newland, North Carolina

SOUSE MEAT OR HEAD CHEESE

Purchase a fresh hog's head which has been dressed and cooked in boiling water until meat is tender. Remove all meat from hog's head and grind. Place ground meat in a square of cheesecloth and press out all grease. Season meat to taste with red and black pepper, sage and salt. Pat mixture into loaf pan and store in refrigerator. This meat dish can be served by warming in oven, but it's best served cold and makes a delicious sandwich.

Mrs. J. D. Braswell, Sr.
Newland, North Carolina

LIVER MUSH

Scald pork liver to seal in blood. Cut liver in small pieces. Cook until tender, take out of water and save water it was cooked in; 1 quart or more. Grind liver and put back in pot with water, let come to a boil. Stir in corn meal, as much as it takes to make it very stiff. Cook well and stir all the time it is cooking. Take off stove and put in diced red pepper pod, salt and sage. Taste to see that it has enough seasoning. Press out excess grease. Pack in container you can cover; chill. When cold, slice and fry in bacon grease until golden brown on both sides; you can fry with onion rings if you like. You can also eat liver mush cold in a sandwich.

Mrs. J. D. Braswell, Sr.

PICKLED PIG'S FEET

Place cleaned pig's feet in stone jar, cover with brine (2 lbs. salt to 1 gal. water) and let stand 10 days. Soak in cold water 3 or 4 days. Drop into hot water and cook slowly until tender. Pack into hot jars and cover with boiling spiced vinegar (½ gal. vinegar, 2 T. grated horseradish, 1 bay leaf, 1 small red pepper, 1 t. peppercorns, 1 t. whole allspice) and seal.

SPARE RIBS AND SAUERKRAUT

Sear spare ribs in pork fat and season with salt and pepper. Place in casserole between 2 layers of raw sauerkraut and thinly sliced onions. Cover ingredients with boiling water. Cover closely. Bake in slow oven 1 to 2 hours until done. Backbones can be cooked with ribs.

CINCINNATI CHICKEN

Use a firm piece of salt pork. Slice very thin and place in cold water in pan and bring to a boil. Remove meat from water and roll in flour. In iron skillet have plenty of hot fat and add floured meat. Turn often and fry until crisp and brown on both sides. Cream gravy can be made with drippings in pan and served with meat and hot biscuits.

HOG JOWL AND TURNIP GREENS

Hog jowl, cured and smoked
4 qts. turnip greens, washed

Drop hog jowl into boiling water. Cook for 45 minutes. Add turnip greens and cook for 1 hour. Drain water and serve separately as pot likker. Serve greens with vinegar. Slice jowl. Serve with plenty of corn pone.

WILD GREENS

Equal Proportions of: **Plantains**
Wild mustard greens   **Polk tops**
Dandelions (only a few)   **Cured side pork**
Young leaves of Narrow dock   **Salt**
Lamb's quarter greens

Put aside polk tops. Bring to boil all the rest of greens. Drain and cover with cold water. Add small piece of cured side pork. Season with salt to taste. Cook until tender adding polk tops (preboil 2 minutes and drain) last 20 minutes of cooking time.

Dr. Charles Grasham

POLK GREENS

Polk Greens are edible only in the early spring, late March through April, in East Tennessee.

Cut leaves and stalk when not more than 10 inches high.

Wash. Cover with water and boil for 10 minutes. Drain. Add fresh water.

SEASON WITH: **¼ t. salt per cup**
    1 t. bacon grease per cup

Return to boil. Lower heat and simmer 10 minutes.

Mrs. John (Kay) Washington

POLK SALAD

1 gal. polk greens	⅓ C. bacon drippings
6 eggs	1 t. salt
¼ t. pepper	

Wash polk greens. Parboil greens 2 to 3 minutes. Drain water and rinse greens again through colander. Heat bacon drippings in skillet over medium heat. Add polk greens, salt and pepper to drippings in skillet. Cover with lid and cook 25 minutes, stirring occasionally so will not stick. Put eggs in mixing bowl and beat. Add eggs to polk greens and stir constantly until eggs are cooked. Serves 4 to 6.

Mrs. Mae Smith Yarbro
Decaturville, Tennessee

KILT (WILTED) LETTUCE

Pick tender leaf lettuce, wash carefully. Drain on toweling and pat dry. Break or cut into pieces into a medium sized bowl, filling bowl to top. Slice spring onions over top of lettuce and include the tender part of the green onion tops. Some people like a little sugar sprinkled over the top of the lettuce and onions, but this is optional. Sprinkle salt over top of mixture. Fry three or four pieces of fat back or slab bacon until crisp. Remove meat from skillet and add 3 to 4 T. vinegar to hot liquid and pour over lettuce and onions while good and hot. Serve immediately. The fried meat can be crumbled over top of lettuce but it is often served without meat.

Mrs. Lyman A. (Patty S.) Fulton

YAMS AND APPLES

5 medium apples	½ C. brown sugar
5 yams	½ stick butter
½ C. white sugar	Bread crumbs

Cook yams until done. Peel apples and slice. Cook with white sugar and 1 cup of water until done. Peel yams and cut in slices. Butter a casserole, put a layer of yams, sprinkle some of the brown sugar over the yams, then dot with butter. Next add a layer of apples. Repeat. Add the liquid from the apples. Cover with buttered bread crumbs. Bake at 400 degrees for about 15 to 20 minutes.

Mrs. C. M. Creech

POTATOES AND EGGS

When you get tired of hashed or warmed-over potatoes prepared in the usual way, try this: Put a piece of butter into your frying pan, and when it is melted brown, put into it a small onion, chopped fine. Have some cold boiled potatoes cut in small pieces, put them into the pan, pour over them 1 or 2 eggs, well beaten, season with pepper and salt, and cook until golden brown on both sides, or fold together as you would an omelet. I sometimes add a little chopped cold meat or bacon bits or minced fish to the potatoes.

Mrs. Bob Treadway

PARSNIPS

Peel or scrape parsnips and slice real thin longways. Cook in salt water with a little chopped onion until tender. Drain. Put parsnips in casserole and slice slab bacon over top. Sprinkle with brown sugar and bake in a moderate oven until nice and brown.

FRIED PUMPKIN BLOSSOMS

Pick large blossoms, wash carefully. Coat on both sides with corn meal and fry on medium heat in bacon drippings until golden brown and crisp. Serve hot.

Prepare OKRA the same way, cutting top and bottom from okra before frying. Be sure okra is tender.

GREEN TOMATOES are fixed the same way only use flour to roll. You can improve the taste of tomatoes by using a little sugar with salt and pepper.

Mrs. Molly Braswell

BREAKFAST MOLASSES

East Tennessee homes used to feature molasses which had been homemade; you never tasted anything as good as spooning molasses onto your plate and mashing a pat of country butter up in the molasses with your fork. Twist the mixture around your fork on to a really hot biscuit.

COMMENTS ON CORN BREAD

There are recipes in other chapters of this book for Corn Pone and Corn Bread, Muffins and Corn Sticks. You will have to decide the recipe you and your family like best because the taste of breads varies among the natives of East Tennessee. Much time has been spent discussing whether corn bread should have an egg, but most agree yellow meal and sugar are two ingredients that never go to make up what any respectable person would call corn bread. It should be noted that meals vary in different parts of the country; the meal in our recipes is the coarsely ground white meal we get in our stores in East Tennessee and Western North Carolina. However, you can use the white meals you can purchase in your state even though it isn't the same as we use.

CORN BREAD AND MILK

Fill a milk glass with broken pieces of cold or hot corn bread. Pour cold sweet milk over corn bread and eat with a long handled spoon like the wise old timers of this area.

Lyman A. Fulton, M.D.

GRITTED BREAD

Years ago a gritter was made by taking a piece of tin and punching nail holes in the tin to make it rough enough to "grit" fresh corn on the cob when scraped over the rough side of the tin. The resulting mixture was called gritted meal which was used to make bread. This bread is a cross between corn bread, spoon bread, and has a marvelous taste of creamed corn. You can grit fresh corn by using the large side of today's grater.

2 C. gritted meal	Buttermilk
(fresh corn on the cob, grated)	1 t. baking powder
¼ C. plain flour	1 t. salt
¼ t. soda	1 egg (optional)

Mix ingredients with enough buttermilk to make batter. Have bacon drippings in iron skillet very hot. Pour batter into hot skillet and bake in fast oven until golden brown and crisp.

Mrs. Andy (Ollie) Kern

FRIED MUSH

Cook corn meal in boiling water and salt to taste for mush. Serve with butter. Then refrigerate mush that might be left over. For fried mush, cut cold mush into slices about the thickness of your small finger and fry in hot fat. Do not try to fry too rapidly; medium heat is best. Brown on both sides. When well-browned, serve with syrup or gravy. Excellent during a Depression or if you are just plain ol' hungry!

Mrs. Bill Meredith

BUTTER

Pour cream into churn. Add ½ cup buttermilk. Let stand in warm place until cream slightly thickens. (It takes hours.) Churn. Skim butter off buttermilk into a bowl. Wash with cold water until all milk is gone. Mix in salt. Pack into mold and put in refrigerator. Unmold when firm. Pour buttermilk into jar and refrigerate.

Mrs. Jess Garland

SWEET BUTTER

Pour fresh cream into bowl or blender and whip. Skim off butter and wash. Add salt. Pack into mold and refrigerate. Unmold when firm.

Mrs. David Garland

SMOOTH CHEESE

1 gal. sweet milk

1 gal. clabber milk or equal parts of any amount

Pour into a large enamel pan or pot. Let it turn slowly on low heat. When it becomes spongy, take out of whey and press out excess whey. Add ½ t. salt, 1 T. butter and enough yellow coloring to make the coloring of bought cheese. Heat on top of stove until you can beat it and it will become smooth and elastic. Press into a bowl and let cool. It is good to eat with crackers or you can cook pimento pepper and mix it with the cheese to make sandwiches.

Mrs. Roy Brumit

HOP YEAST

Boil 4 medium-sized Irish potatoes in ½ gallon water with ½ C. of hops tied in a bag. When potatoes are done, take them from the water and mash in a dish. Remove the hops and put potatoes back in the water, adding one cup white sugar and ½ C. salt. When luke-warm add one C. of made yeast.

Set in a warm place to rise for 12 hours. Keep in a cool place. One cup of this yeast makes two quarts of bread.

YEAST

One T. yeast in a large teacup of lukewarm water. When dissolved, add flour to make a stiff batter. After it has risen enough, add corn meal to make a crumbly mass and dry in the shade.

SALT RISING BREAD

Scald 1 C. sweet milk, then add to it ½ t. salt and 2 T. fresh ground corn meal. Mix thoroughly and put it in a warm place to sour. A good place is to put the batter in a pitcher, cover, and set in a pan of warm water, keeping it at the same temperature for 5 to 6 hours. It must be kept much warmer than yeast bread; a good place to put the pan of water to keep it warm is in the ashes of the fireplace.

Scald 1 qt. milk or part milk and part water, and let stand until lukewarm. Add 1 t. salt and stir in enough flour to make a drop batter. Beat vigorously, add the "salt-rising" and continue the beating 8 minutes longer. Cover again and let stand for 2 hours longer. Add 1 T. lard or butter and enough flour to make a soft dough. Knead thoroughly until smooth and elastic. Divide into loaves, mold and place each in a well greased pan, leaving room for them to rise to twice their original size. Cover with a light cloth. Set where they will keep warm and when light, bake in a steady oven. About 350 degrees. NOTE: One great secret in the making of salt rising bread is to keep an even temperature during the time of rising.

Mrs. Jess Garland

DRIED APPLES

Peel apples, slice very thin and dry just like corn. Don't scald apples, use just the raw apples. You can put them in the sun if you have a nice place where flies won't get to them or put them around your stove, in the window with screen wire. Put them on something so the air can get through to them. Dry and use them in the winter for fried pies, stewed fruit or stack cake.

FRIED APPLES

Use the early, thin skinned green apples. Cut in quarters, remove core but do not peel. Place apples in heavy skillet with a little bacon grease and start cooking on low heat. Cover and cook until tender. Add sugar to taste, stirring thoroughly and being careful not to let apples burn after sugar is added. Serve hot. Good for breakfast with homemade sausage.

STEAMED APPLES

Peel, core and quarter apples that won't cook up (Winesaps are excellent). In pot with tight fitting lid, put 1 quart of quartered apples, ½ cup water and 2 cups of sugar. Put lid on pot and cook very slowly, letting the steam cook the apples. Cook until apples are just tender—do not cook long enough to darken apples. Serve hot. Good with fried chicken.

Mrs. Molly Braswell

APPLE BUTTER IN OPEN KETTLE OLD TIMES

Use a brass kettle and a long handle stir. First day: Quarter apples and cook. No need to peel. Then put them through a Foley food mill and make your sauce. Next Morning: Clean the kettle and start a fire, put the sauce in the kettle and start stirring so it can't stick and burn. When it is boiling good, add sugar, (3 to 5 lbs. per gallon of sauce, according to tartness—usually it takes about 5 lbs.) Cook and stir till it turns red and looks thick. To test, dip 2 or 3 spoonfuls in a saucer and invert quickly. If it clings, it is done. If it falls, it needs more cooking. When done, add some cinnamon drops to flavor and dip quickly to jars. Cover with parafin and seal.

Mrs. R. V. Rainbolt

OVEN APPLE BUTTER

Peel and quarter or just quarter your apples. Cook until tender, then put them through a Foley food mill or something similar to make a sauce. Use a canner or a large roaster. Measure your sauce and use as much sugar as you have sauce. Stir until thoroughly mixed, cover and put in oven.

Turn heat until it stays in a slight boil or full of bubbles so it won't burn. Uncover now and then and stir. When it drops from the spoon in flakes or thick it is done. Add a little red food coloring if desired and any flavoring such as cinnamon. The cooking time depends on the kind of apples. Tart apples are best. Fill jars and cover with parafin and seal.

Mrs. R. V. Rainbolt

PEACH BUTTER

Wash a bushel of ripe peaches thoroughly, remove seeds and slice into thin slices without peeling. Use a brass kettle over an open fire, keeping the fire good and steady throughout cooking time. Put 1 gallon of water in kettle then add the peaches. Stir with a long handle stir, about eight feet long. Cook and stir mixture about 2½ hours. Then add 16 lbs. sugar and cook until mixture turns dark red and has a nice glaze, about 1½ to 2 hours more cooking. To test mixture, spoon a little on to a dish and let it set a few minutes. If it has a glaze and no water stands around it, it is ready to can. Seal in sterilized jars.

Mrs. Robert (Bessie) Whisman

HOT JAM

Makes me hungry to remember the delicious hot jam Grandmother served with her tender biscuits on a cold winter's morning—

Bring to a boil a quart of canned blackberries or other canned berries. Season to taste with sugar and thicken with 2 or 3 T. cornstarch mixed with a little cold water and stirred into the berries. When thick, pour into bowl, top with country butter and serve with hot biscuits.

SHUCK BEANS

Select small, tender, full beans such as Cut Shorts, Half Runners, etc. String and wash beans. You can break your beans if you are going to dry them one way given or leave them whole if dried another. Read on and decide. After preparing beans by breaking, spread one layer deep on clean sheets in a hot attic or in a sunny, warm place on newspapers or in a large, flat pan. While beans are drying, stir them several times to be sure they dry all the way through. If drying outside, beans must be brought in each evening to prevent collection of moisture on beans. Total drying time may be a week or more depending on drying conditions. You can also make shuck beans by stringing them, leave whole and string them by running a needle and thread through the middle of the bean and hang the strings on porch where they can dry in the sun. When good and dry, put beans in a clean pillowcase or bag and hang until ready to cook.

To cook shuck beans, take as many as you want to cook out of your bag and soak in water overnight. The next morning, drain water and cook by method given in our recipe for Soup Beans but allow a longer cooking time.

SOUP BEANS

Dried beans cooked almost all day with fat back and water make up a dish called "Soup Beans" and might be any of the various kinds of dried beans—Pinto, Yellow Eye, Great Northern, or October (also called Cranberry).

Look beans to remove any bad beans or small rocks. Wash beans in two or three waters to clean. Soaking beans in water over night will reduce cooking time, but beans can be cooked without soaking. Put a cup or two of beans in a deep pot, cover well with water and add a two or three inch piece of fat back, streaked meat or slab bacon plus a little salt. Taste for salt after beans are almost done. Bring to rapid boil, reduce heat, cover pot and simmer slowly for several hours. Check beans from time to time and add water as they need it, but PLEASE don't stir the beans and make them mushy. Test a bean for tenderness after about 4 or 5 hours of cooking; taste liquid for seasoning and add more salt if necessary. Serve hot in bowl and pass corn bread. Eat beans plain or with raw onions, onions sliced in vinegar, Kilt Lettuce, or Chow-Chow. The soup from the beans is good spooned over corn bread.

Mrs. Lyman A. Fulton

GREEN BEANS AND SHELLIES

Shellies are large brown beans which grow in a light yellow pod with pink streaks on the pods. These pods are not cooked, instead the beans are shelled out and can be cooked fresh; frozen as is; or canned. They can be dried and cooked as Soup Beans. Fresh green beans mixed half and half with shellies and cooked with meat as directed for Soup Beans is a summer treat.

GRANNY DEAR'S BEAN SOUP

Select the large white beans similar to navy beans. One cup will make soup for 4. Wash and cook the beans as for baking. When beans are tender, mash with the potato masher. Add 2 cups of hot water and season with salt, pepper and bacon or ham fryings. A little onion cooked in is good. Serve with cornbread.

Mrs. Bill (Martha Nan) Meredith

DILLY BEANS

String and wash tender green beans, leave whole until you have about 1 gallon of beans. Scald beans in hot water until beans are tender enough to stick with a toothpick (about 10 minutes). Pack beans into sterile jars, pour mixture over and seal.

2 C. vinegar	1 clove garlic
6 C. water	¼ t. red pepper
Salt to taste	1 head fresh dill

Heat this mixture and pour over beans. Makes six pints.

Mrs. Bessie McKinney
Bakersville, North Carolina

PICKLED BEANS I.

Pickled beans should be made from a bean like the one used for Shuck Beans.

For one pan of beans that holds 8 quarts. String, break and wash beans. Cook beans until tender in plain water. Drain and cool. In one gallon of warm water, add 1 C. vinegar; 1 C. salt (no iodine). Dissolve salt in water. Put beans in quart jars. Pour water, vinegar, salt mixture over beans. Finish filling jars up with warm water if needed. Seal tight. Use the zinc tops with jar rubbers.

Mrs. Andy (Ollie) Kern

PICKLED BEANS II.

Before starting to make pickled beans, check the ALMANAC and only make them if the signs are in the heart or the head. The salt used in this recipe must be pickling salt—do not use salt with iodine. Select tender fresh green beans, string and break them, wash thoroughly and then cook in water until tender. Use any amount of beans you desire. When the beans are tender, rinse in cold water and drain. In the bottom of a 5 gallon crock, sprinkle ½ cup salt, then put about 1 gallon of beans and sprinkle another ¼ cup salt. Continue these layers, depending on the amount of beans you want to pickel. Then pour cold water into the crock to cover all the beans. Weight the beans down to keep them covered with the liquid—you can use a plate weighted with a river rock. Leave at room temperature. In about a week, brine, will begin to form. At this time take the skim off the top of the water—this skim looks like "mother" that forms on vinegar. When the beans taste sour, take them out of the crock, pour off the brine, and using fresh water, bring the beans to a boil and let them boil for about 5 minutes. Fill hot sterile quart jars with the beans and water to cover. Seal jars. At serving time, remove beans from jar, rinse in cold water and place drained beans in a little bacon grease and serve when heated thoroughly. If your beans do not sour and form brine after about a week in the crock, take 3 or 4 ears of corn, cook it on the cob, then cut the corn off the cob and mix with the beans in the crock. The corn will make the beans ferment and can be left with the beans, canned, and eaten along with the pickled beans.

Mrs. J. D. Braswell, Sr.
Newland, North Carolina

DRIED CORN

Boil corn on the cob until the milk in corn is firm enough to cut off cob. Cut and scrape the cob and place corn in pans and put in oven not too hot and stir once in a while. When dry, place in thin cloth bags or jars; hang bag in cool place. Soak corn before using. Cook same as other corn—water, butter, salt and pepper for a corn dish with a very good, sweet taste.

PICKLED CORN

Cook corn on cob; when done, cool. Then place in stone jar. Pour cold water over corn; add enough salt to taste. Put weight on it and place in a very warm place. It will pickle in about two weeks. If a scum comes on it, take it off. Leave corn in the same water and use right out of the jar—heat and serve.

Mrs. Molly Braswell

HOMINY

In the years gone by, ashes from the wood fires were put into an ash hopper. Water was poured over the ashes in the hopper and a crock placed to catch the water as it dripped through the ashes. This was lye water. Today you can make hominy using lye you can purchase.

In a crock put 2 T. lye to 1 gallon of water.

Shell hard corn and put in the water in the crock and let set overnight.

Next morning, drain the water and husks which have come off the corn and wash and drain the hominy grains that are left. Wash thoroughly. Fry hominy in bacon grease until good and hot, season with salt and serve.

Mrs. Andy (Ollie) Kern

CHOW-CHOW I.

4 or 5 lb. cabbage
Several green tomatoes
2 or 3 red or yellow
　sweet peppers

5 or 6 cucumbers past eating
　stage
2 or 3 onions
1 hot pepper

Peel cucumbers and cut out seeds, trim tomatoes and put with cucumbers. Hack fine, pour over hot water and let stand a few minutes, then drain off all water. Hack cabbage, onions and peppers. Add cucumber mixture and add 1 tbs. salt, 1 cup sugar, 1½ cups vinegar. Boil slowly for 15 to 20 minutes and then put in jars and seal.

Mrs. R. V. Rainbolt

CHOW-CHOW II.

2 doz. sweet peppers (green)
2 med. heads cabbage
6 red sweet peppers
2 qts. cider vinegar
1½ doz. whole cloves
⅓ cup celery seeds

2 doz. med. onions
½ cup salt
1 T. Tumeric
5½ cups brown sugar
1½ doz. whole all-spice
½ cup mustard seed

Chop coarsley the peppers, onions and cabbage. Add salt and drain in a muslin bag over night. After draining, add red peppers and tumeric. Mix together the remaining ingredients and cook until sugar is dissolved. Add vinegar mixture to pepper mixture. Reheat and cook 20 minutes. Put into sterilized jars and seal.

Mrs. Jack Seaton

HOMEMADE KRAUT

Kraut must be made when the sign in the ALMANAC is in the heart or the head. Salt used must be pickling salt—no iodine. You must use large solid heads of crisp cabbage (some call this "Kraut Cabbage"). Soak cabbage heads in cold water for about 3 hours to get it good and crisp. Wash, then chop cabbage real fine—do not chop stalk.

METHOD I.—In the bottom of the large crock put ½ cup salt. On top of this pack firmly a pan of finely chopped cabbage. Sprinkle a little more salt over cabbage, and continue layers of cabbage and salt, packing firmly until you have the amount of kraut you want to make. If you like, you can add a little finely chopped red pepper and the whole cabbage stalks. DO NOT ADD ANY WATER. Weight top with plate or rock or board. Leave at room temperature. It will take at least two weeks in a warm house for kraut to ferment. Taste to check and see if kraut is seasoned to your taste. Heat kraut to boiling point and seal in hot sterile jars.

METHOD II.—In the bottom of a quart fruit jar put 1 tsp. of salt. Pack firmly finely chopped cabbage, holding a silver knife in center of cabbage, pour boiling water to fill jar. Put jar ring on jar and screw type lid leaving lid loose. Place jars in a pan and let kraut "work"—water will come out of jars and run down the side. When this foam quits coming to the top, add more boiling water to fill jar to the top, seal jars and store in a cool place.

Mrs. J. D. Braswell, Sr.
Newland, North Carolina

PICKLED ONIONS

1 qt. small white onions 10% brine solution
1 C. sugar 1 qt. white vinegar
½ long, red, hot pepper pod ⅛ bay leaf
3 cloves (without heads) 1 T. coarse salt

Cover onions with water in dish. Add one tbs. of coarse salt. Let onions soak for 2 hrs. Remove outer skins of onions. Now soak onions for 48 hours in 10% brine solution. Drain onions well. Bring to boiling point 1 qt. of white vinegar and 1 cup of sugar. Add onions and simmer for 3 minutes. Place onions at once in sterilized jars and cover with white vinegar used to simmer onions with. Add to jars ½ of a long, red hot pepper pod, ⅛ bay leaf, 3 cloves without heads. Seal and process for 30 minutes in boiling water bath.

Mrs. Mae Smith Yarbo
Decaturville, Tennessee

SOUTHERN FRIED APPLE PIES

1 pkg. dried apples

Put apples in sauce pan, add only enough cold water to cover apples. Bring to boil, cover and cook over low heat until apples are soft and water cooked out. Stir occasionally. Add sugar to taste. (approx. 1-1½ cups). Add while apples are hot. Place in refrigerator until chilled.

PASTRY FOR PIES

3 C. flour   ½ t. salt
¾ C. shortening   ½ C. cold milk

Let stand an hour or overnight in refrigerator to make dough easier to handle.

On lightly floured board place pinched off piece of dough to roll about ⅛ inch thick and size of saucer. On half of this, spoon about 2 tbs. of apples. Dampen edge of pastry with cold water, and bring other side over and press edges together, making pies half-moon shape.

Fry in very lightly oiled skillet on medium heat until golden brown, turning only once. (Use only enough cooking oil to keep pies from sticking).

Mrs. Ray Chalker

OLD FASHIONED STACK CAKE

CREAM:
1 C. shortening and 1 C. sugar

ADD   1 C. buttermilk
⅔ C. molasses   2 eggs, beaten well
1 t. soda   ½ t. baking powder
½ t. allspice   ½ t. salt
½ t. cloves   ½ t. cinnamon

Add enough flour to make a dough that can be rolled thin. Cut in rounds the size of cake layers, by using layer cake pan. Bake in hot oven around 375 degrees. Spread layers out to cool.

Stew dried apples and season well with spices. When almost cool, spread on layers one at a time and stack one on top of the other. There should be six or more layers. Let season for 8 hours before serving.

Mrs. J. D. Thomas

HUCKLEBERRY ROLY POLY

2½ C. flour	2 T. shortening
4 t. baking powder	½ C. sugar
1 t. salt	1 C. sweet milk
1 egg	

Sift together flour, baking powder and salt. Cream together shortening and sugar. Add the milk slowly, then stir in dry ingredients. Lastly add egg, well beaten, and mix thoroughly. Roll to a thickness of about ½ inch. Spread surface with butter then cover with huckleberries. Roll up, handling lightly. Place in center of buttered baking pan, spread shortening or butter over top and sides. Bake in hot oven (400 degrees). As soon as brown, reduce heat and continue baking until done. Serve with hard or soft sauce.

Mrs. Bill (Marjorie London) Dyer

CHESS PIE

½ cup butter (melted)	3 eggs
1½ cup sugar	5 T. milk
1 T. corn meal	1 t. vinegar
½ t. salt	1 t. vanilla

Beat sugar, corn meal, salt and eggs. Stir in milk, vinegar and vanilla. Stir in melted butter. Pour into a 9 inch pastry lined pie pan. Bake at 400 degrees for 35 to 40 minutes or until firm.

Mrs. Harry N. Waggoner

VINEGAR PIE

1 C. sugar	¼ C. vinegar
½ C. flour	1 T. butter
¼ t. salt	2 T. lemon juice or extract
1¼ C. boiling water	3 egg yolks

Mix sugar, flour, salt and vinegar and stir into boiling water. Beat egg yolks and stir a little hot mixture into them. Add lemon and butter. Cook until smooth and thick, stirring often. Cool. Pour into cooled baked pie crust. Beat egg whites, add 3 T. sugar and beat until it stands in peaks. Spread on pie and bake at 350 degrees 10-15 minutes.

Mrs. Roy Brumit

OLD FASHIONED TRANSPARENT PIE

Make crust for one pie. Beat 6 whole eggs until fluffy. Add 2 cups white sugar, ⅔ cup melted butter. Mix and beat well. Add 1 t. lemon extract and bake in a slow oven.

Mrs. Roy Brumit

PEACH COBBLER

2 C. sliced fresh peaches   1 T. lemon juice
½ to ⅔ C. white sugar   1 T. butter
2 T. flour   ¼ t. Almond extract
                               (optional)

Place peaches in greased glass baking dish. Mix flour and sugar, sprinkle over peaches. Add juice and extract. Dot with butter. Cover with your favorite pastry. Slash in several places to allow steam to escape. Bake in hot oven, 450 degrees for 15 minutes or until pastry browns, reduce heat to 325 degrees for about 25 minutes or until peaches are done.

CHERRIES may be used, 2 C. canned sweet cherries
¼ C. sugar
½ t. cinnamon
Omit almond and lemon juice
Proceed as above

APPLES may be used
2 C. apples
¼ C. brown sugar
¼ to ½ C. white sugar depending on tartness of apples
½ t. nutmeg
¼ t. cinnamon
Proceed as above

PASTRY

1 C. sifted flour   ¼ t. salt
½ C. shortening   3 T. ice water

Mix flour and salt. Work in shortening. Add ice water, a spoon at a time. Work just to workable paste. Be careful not to add too much water. This is a rich pastry. Handle as little as possible. Chill, then roll. This makes a single crust pie. For a 2 crust pie, double the recipe.

Mrs. C. M. Creech

COCONUT TRANSPARENT PIE

¾ C. white sugar	1 C. cream or rich milk
¾ C. brown sugar	3 egg yolks
3 T. flour	2 T. butter
1 t. vanilla	1 C. coconut

Mix dry ingredients and add to other mixture. Pour into a pie crust and bake in a slow oven until golden brown, about 1 hour. It needs no topping.

Mrs. Roy Brumit

STICKIES

Many children in this area have enjoyed this treat, often made from scraps of pastry left over from the making of a fresh fruit cobbler or other pie.

Roll pastry out into thin squares. Spread top of pastry with softened butter and sprinkle generously with light brown sugar. Roll pastry as for jelly roll and cut into ¼ inch slices. Place slices in baking pan and bake in moderate oven until brown. Remove from pan with spatula while hot and transfer to waxed paper.

Mrs. John Anderson

JELLY ROLL

4 eggs, separated	¾ C. sifted cake flour
¾ C. sugar	¾ t. baking powder
1 t. vanilla	¼ t. salt

Beat egg yolks until light. Add sugar gradually and then flavoring. When blended, add flour that has been sifted with baking powder and salt. Last, fold in egg whites that have been whipped until stiff but not dry.

Line a 15 x 10 pan with heavy buttered paper. Pour in batter and bake in moderate oven for about 6 to 12 minutes.

While cake is hot, trim hard edges, spread cake with jelly, jam or a cake filling, and roll it with a tea towel which has been sprinkled with powdered sugar or granulated sugar.

STRAWBERRY SHORTCAKE

Make short pastry and press two or more rounds of pastry into circles on baking sheet. You can make as many layers as you want, depending on amount of berries used but have at least two layers of pastry. Bake pastry in hot oven and when you take it from the oven, while still hot, rub tops with butter and sprinkle with sugar. Alternate layers of fresh sweetened strawberries and pastry— starting with pastry and ending with berries. Slice and serve in a bowl with rich sweet cream poured over top or with sweetened whipped cream. The little wild strawberries found in the mountains of East Tennessee are delicious this way.

Mrs. Lyman A. (Patty S.) Fulton

VIRGINIA'S BOILED CUSTARD

½ gallon sweet milk
8 eggs (keep out whites of 2)
1 teacup full of sugar
1 round T. cornstarch

½ t. salt
½ t. nutmeg
1 t. vanilla

Put milk in double boiler.   When milk is hot (DO NOT LET IT BOIL), add sugar, salt, and cornstarch which have been well mixed. Stir constantly from bottom, to cook cornstarch, then add the well beaten eggs, vanilla and nutmeg and stir about 4 or 5 minutes or until it starts to thicken. Remove from heat and add the two egg whites which have been beaten until dry; add a tablespoon at a time, folding into custard. Pour custard into a large bowl, cover bowl with a large plate, set bowl in another bowl of hot water and let stand until water cools. Chill and serve. This is the kind of boiled custard that you drink.

Mrs. Joe Smithdeal
Elizabethton, Tennessee

MOLASSES TAFFY

Pulling taffy was one way grandmother entertained her children on winter evenings; couples "courted" pulling taffy—

1 C. molasses
2 C. brown sugar
1 C. water

3 T. vinegar
3 T. butter

Put molasses, sugar, water and vinegar into saucepan and stir; boil until very brittle when dropped into cold water; add butter and pour on buttered platter. When cool enough to handle, butter hands and pull until light brown. Pull into oblong strips and cut with scissors.

PLANTING CHART

East Tennessee pioneers consulted the ALMANAC to determine the best time to plant as well as the best time to can certain foods. Should you wish to subscribe to their planting methods, you will appreciate the following chart:

Plant on the dark of the moon—first quarter of moon.

When the signs are in the feet, bowels, head or heart—do not plant.

When the signs are in the legs, neck, arms, knees or thighs—good time to plant.

If you purchase your plants, you can set them in the ground anytime. Planting by the signs applies to the planting of seeds.

GRANNY BRUMIT'S COUGH SYRUP I.

Scrub scaly Bark Hickory and break into 3 inch pieces. Boil and strain. Add 1 C. brown sugar, 10-12 sticks horehound candy, a pinch of ginger and cook until it makes a syrup.   Mrs. Roy Brumit

COUGH SYRUP II.

Mix whiskey and rock candy in bottle. Use as needed for cough.
Mrs. David Garland

CURE FOR TOOTHACHE

Tablespoon of any kind of spirits, tablespoon of vinegar, teaspoon of common salt; mix and put in mouth. It gives great relief.
From Knoxville Register, 1820

SALVE FOR POISON

A handfull of the inner bark of Alder, one of Hyssop, and one of the roots of parsley and plantain each, stew slowly in a pint of lard, strain, and it is fit for use.

LYE SOAP

11 C. fat, melted lard	½ C. borax
5 C. cold water	½ C. sugar
1 can lye	4 t. oil of sassafras
½ C. household ammonia	

Heat fat and strain. Dissolve the sugar in 1 C. of the water. Add to rest of water. Add rest of ingredients and stir till lukewarm. Add all of this to the fat. Stir until creamy. Smooth out into container. Cut after 36 hours.   Mrs. I. W. Garland

MEATS

BARBECUED BEEF OR PORK

3 or 4 lb. beef or pork roast

To 2 C. broth in which meat was cooked add:

1 C. catsup	1 t. celery seed
2 T. Worcestershire	salt
1 T. chili powder	red pepper
1 T. ground allspice	

Chop meat fine and add to sauce. Let simmer a few minutes. Serve on buns with following relish:

½ small cabbage chopped fine
1 chopped green pepper
½ C. (or more) chopped sweet pickle
vinegar and sugar

MRS. PHIL CARR

BARBECUED BEEF BRISKET

Buy 8 lbs deboned beef brisket.
Mix 2 T. salt, 2 t. pepper, 2 t. paprika, 2 T. chili powder and 2 t. garlic salt.

Rub into meat. Bake on rack at 350° 6 hours. Slice and serve hot or cold.

MRS. M. L. GOLDSTEIN

BARBECUED SANDWICHES

1 med. onion	3 T. Worcestershire sauce
2 T. butter	½ T. mustard
2 T. vinegar	1 C. water
2 T. brown sugar	1 C. chopped celery
4 T. lemon juice	Salt and red pepper to taste
1 small bottle catsup	

Brown chopped onion in melted butter. Add the remaining ingredients and let simmer until celery is tender. Add about 3 cups (more or less as desired) chopped well done roast beef or pork roast. Serve hot on hamburger buns.

MRS. JULIUS HOBBS
Indianapolis, Indiana

JONNIE MOUSETTI

3 lbs. hamburger	1 can tomato soup
1 lb. onions, chopped fine	1 can mushroom soup
2 large stalks celery, chopped	2 cans tomato sauce
1 clove garlic	1 can tomato paste
2 green peppers, chopped	

Fry meat slowly without adding any fat. Cook next 4 ingredients together in a small amount of water for about 15 minutes. Add to meat with remaining ingredients. Cook 1 large package of noodles, and drain. Pour meat mixture over the noodles and cover with grated sharp cheese and sliced stuffed olives. Bake 1 hour at 350°.

MRS R. A. LACY, JR.

BEEF ROLLS

6 portions round steak. Pound in ½ C. flour, 1 t. salt and ½ t. pepper.

Brown in skillet in bacon drippings or margarine:

½ C. chopped celery	¼ t. salt
½ C. chopped onion	1 t. sage
2 C. soft bread crumbs	½ t. pepper

Roll dressing in pieces of steak. Tie rolls and brown in heavy skillet. Cover with 1 C. water and 1 C. beef bouillon and ½ C. sliced stuffed olives. Simmer 1 hour.

MRS. WILLIAM SELLS

RICE MEAT BALLS

1 lb. ground meat	salt and pepper
¾ C. rice (uncooked)	½ can tomato sauce
1 t. chili powder (optional)	

Mix together, shape into balls. Use remaining ½ can of tomato sauce and ½ can water to pour over meat balls. Bake 45 minutes at 400°.

MRS. J. H. VARNELL

MEAT BALLS WITH SOUR CREAM AND DILL

Mix well:

2 lb. ground steak	½ t. garlic salt
2½ t. salt	¾ C. heavy sour cream
¼ t. pepper	

Shape into walnut size balls and brown well in butter in a hot frying pan. Transfer balls to baking dish when browned and make sauce in drippings in pan. Use 1 C. heavy sour cream, seasoned with a pinch of garlic salt, ½ t. sugar and about 2 t. dried dill seed. Stir until hot and pour over meat balls. Bake at 300° 15 minutes.

NORWEGIAN MEAT BALLS

Prepare a soup of beef stock with celery, onion, salt and pepper to make about 3 quarts. Let stand overnight. Grind together 3 times:

2 lbs. beef	1 lb. veal
1 lb. pork	

Add:

4 beaten eggs	½ t. nutmeg
1 qt. milk	¼ t. ginger
2 t. salt	1 grated onion
2 t. pepper	

Mix together so there are no lumps. Divide soup stock into 3 pans and heat to simmering. Drop meat mixture by ½ T. into the hot stock. Cook about 7 minutes. As balls are cooked remove from stock and put in a roaster. Strain remaining stock and add 4 dissolved beef bouillon cubes. Thicken with flour and pour over meat balls. Bake at 350° for 1½ hours.

MRS. JOHN WILSON

SWEDISH MEAT BALLS IN SOUR CREAM

2 lbs. ground steak	flour
1½ C. rye bread crumbs	½ stick butter
2 C. light cream	¼ C. olive oil
salt & pepper	2 C. sour cream or 2 cans
1 T. Beau Monde Seasoning	beef gravy

Combine steak, crumbs, cream, salt, pepper and Beau Monde seasoning. Mix thoroughly but lightly until blended, and shape into 1-inch balls. Divide butter and olive oil into 2 skillets and roll the balls in flour and brown. Transfer to casserole. Add sour cream or canned gravy to drippings in skillet and pour over meat balls. Put in hot oven to heat thoroughly. If sauce separates, strain it off and repeat heat.

MRS. PHIL CARR

CABBAGE ROLLS (SLAVIC)

1½ lb. ground beef	1 egg
½ C. raw rice	salt & pepper to taste
1 large onion (chopped))	12 large cabbage leaves

Wilt cabbage leaves with boiling water (put into a large bowl and cover with a plate).

While leaves are wilting mix other ingredients together for stuffing leaves. Divide into 6 portions and stuff leaves. Secure leaves with heavy string. Place rolls in heavy pan and cover with tomato sauce as follows:

3 T. bacon drippings	3 to 4 T. brown sugar
3 T. flour	

Add a No. 2 can of tomatoes to the above and salt and pepper to taste. Cook cabbage rolls in sauce until meat is done, approximately 45 minutes. Serve with sauce.

MRS. GILBERT RANNICK

VEAL SUPREME

2 lbs. veal (cut from between shank and cutlet), cubed
1 C. mushrooms, preferably fresh, cut up and saute'ed in butter

3 T. butter	1 C. milk and mushroom
1 t. minced onion	stock and paprika to taste
¼ C. flour	3 drops Worcestershire sauce
1 C. cream	

Cook veal until tender and break up in small pieces, removing any fat or gristle. Make a sauce of butter, flour, onion and liquid. Add meat, mushrooms and seasonings. Pour in greased baking dish and cover with buttered and seasoned bread crumbs. Bake at 400° for 30 minutes. Serves 6 to 8.

MRS. WALTER HANKINS

CORNED BEEF

Place in crock: 5 lbs. of de-boned brisket of beef and cover with water. To each qt. of cold water used, add 3 T. salt, not iodized, 1 t. salt petre, 3 cloves garlic, and 1 T. mixed whole pickling spice with red pepper. Be sure water solution covers meat, if not, add more water. Refrigerate for 10 days. When ready to cook, wash meat thoroughly and cook in plain salted water on low heat for 2 hours or until tender.

MRS. SIDNEY LICHT

GOULASH WITH SAUERKRAUT

2 lbs. veal or beef cut in
   1½ in. squares
4 T. beef suet or butter
1½ C. sliced onion
1 clove garlic, chopped
1 t. salt
½ t. pepper

1 C. canned tomatoes
1 C. sour cream
2 t. paprika
2 t. caraway seeds
1 lb. sauerkraut
2 or 3 T. parsley, chopped

Saute meat in hot beef fat or butter until lightly browned. Add onions and cook 5 minutes. Add garlic, salt, pepper, tomatoes and enough water to partly cover the mixture. Cook slowly until meat is almost done and the sauce greatly reduced, about 45 minutes. Stir frequently. Add sour cream, paprika, and caraway seeds. Simmer ½ hour longer. Heat sauerkraut arrange alternate layers of goulash and sauerkraut in a warmed serving dish. Sprinkle top with parsley. Serves 8 or more.

MRS HELMUT WINKLESTRADER
Wuppertal, Germany

ITALIAN HAMBURG LOAF

1 lb. lean beef, ground
½ lb. cheese, grated
1 small onion, minced
1 green pepper, chopped

1 t. salt
pepper to taste
4 eggs, well beaten

Mix thoroughly all ingredients and shape into loaf. Bake in moderate oven, 300°, for 45 to 50 minutes. Serves 6.

MRS. JOE GREEN

ITALIAN SPAGHETTI

Cover bottom of large frying pan with olive, corn or peanut oil. Add 2 large onions and 3 cloves of garlic, chopped fine. Brown slowly and add ½ green pepper, chopped fine. Cook slowly, about 5 minutes, and then add 1 lb. ground steak and brown well. Prepare the tomato sauce by using 2 small cans prepared tomato sauce and 1 can of tomato paste. Add equal amounts of water; stir well and simmer while the meat is browning.

Combine the meat and tomato sauce in the frying pan and simmer for at least ½ hour. Add 1 T. sugar, 1¼ t. salt, ¼ t. black pepper, a dash of red pepper and 4 or 5 leaves of sweet basil (1 or 2 bay leaves). 1 t. chili powder **may** be added. Stir these seasonings in well and let the mixture set overnight before serving. To serve: heat and add 1 C. mushrooms, broiled in butter. Heat a few minutes longer and serve with hot spaghetti and top with parmesan cheese.

MRS. GILTZ W. CROLEY

ITALIAN SPAGHETTI

1½ lb. ground meat, primarily beef
2 medium onions, minced

Brown in skillet in **2 T. fat.** Add the following to meat:

2 cloves garlic	¼ t. oregano
2 cans tomato paste	1 t. paprika
1 #2½ can of tomato juice	¼ t. sage
1 T. Worcestershire sauce	¼ t. dry mustard
1 T. salt	3 bay leaves
1 T. chili powder (optional)	¼ t. red pepper
¼ t. tumeric	¼ t. cloves

Simmer for 4 to 4½ hours. Serve hot with spaghetti.

MRS TOM POTTER, JR.

MEAT LOAF

1 lb. ground beef, very lean	2 t. salt
¼ lb. ground pork, very lean	¾ t. dry mustard
1 egg	⅛ t. pepper
1 C. bread crumbs	1 T. butter
1 C. canned tomatoes	2 T. chopped onion
½ C. milk	

Mix all ingredients thoroughly. Put in loaf pan and bake at 350° for 1½ hours.

MRS. FLORENCE OVRON

MINCE AND HAM ROLL

1 lb. ground beef	2 t. salt
1 lb. ground ham	1 t. nutmeg
2 C. bread crumbs	1 well beaten egg

Mix all ingredients thoroughly. Place in greased covered casserole and steam in a pan of simmering water for 2½ hours.. Leave in steamer until quite cold. To make the roll especially attractive, arrange hard boiled eggs in the loaf in a pattern so that the yellow rounds will show when the loaf is sliced. In Scotland this is a favorite supper dish for Hallowe'en.

MRS. P. W. ALEXANDER

BEEF IN PEPPER CUPS

8 green peppers	1 C. soft bread crumbs
1½ lbs. ground beef	2 t. salt
2 T. finely chopped onions	1 t. oregano
2 T. fat	¼ t. pepper
2 C. chopped fresh tomatoes	1 C. grated American cheese

Cut off tops of green peppers and remove seeds. Simmer peppers in water about 5 minutes. Drain. Brown meat and onion in hot fat and add tomatoes, bread crumbs and seasonings. Stuff peppers. Stand peppers upright in greased pan. Cover and bake in moderate oven (350°) 25 minutes. Uncover; top peppers with grated cheese and return to oven for 5 minutes. Serves 8.

MRS. W. RAY MOSS
Memphis, Tenn.

SAUERBRATEN OR POT ROAST WITH POTATO DUMPLINGS

3 lbs. round steak or
    sirloin tip roast
1 T. salt
½ t. pepper
2 onions, sliced
1 carrot, sliced
1 stalk celery, chopped
4 cloves

1 pint red wine vinegar
2 bay leaves
2 T. fat
6 T. butter
5 T. flour
1 T. sugar
8 or 10 gingersnaps

Season meat with salt and pepper. Place in enamel, glass, or earthenware bowl. Combine onions, carrot, celery, cloves, vinegar and bay leaves and pour over meat. Cover and put in refrigerator 4 days. Remove from refrigerator, drain and saute in fat. Add 1 T. butter in same kind of utensil until seared on all sides. Add marinade liquid and bring to boil, lower heat and simmer about 3 hours.

Melt remaining 5 T. butter in a pan. Stir flour smoothly into it and blend in sugar. Let brown to nice dark color. Add to meat mixture. Cover and continue cooking until meat is tender, about 1 hour. Remove meat to a warmed serving platter. Stir crushed gingersnaps into pot juices and cook until thickened. Pour gravy over meat. Serves 6 or more.

—o—

POTATO DUMPLINGS

2 lbs. raw potatoes
4 slices white bread
1 t. salt
¼ t. pepper
1 onion, grated

1 t. minced parsley
2 eggs, well beaten
¼ C. flour
1½ qts. boiling salted water

Grate potatoes. Soak bread in a little cold water and squeeze out as much as possible. Mix bread, salt, pepper, onions and parsley. Add potatoes and eggs and mix well. Form into balls. Roll lightly in flour and drop into salted boiling water. Cover pot tightly. Boil 15 minutes. Remove from water and serve.

MRS. W. W. MILLER, JR.

SAVORY BEEF WITH NOODLES

1½ lb. left over or frozen
    slices roast beef
½ C. cooking oil
2 C. sliced onions
1 3 or 4-oz. can mushroom
    with liquid
1½ t. salt

¼ t. pepper
1 8-oz. can tomato sauce
1 C. left over or frozen
    beef gravy
½ C. thick sour cream
6 C. hot cooked noodles

Cut meat slices into strips 1-in. wide. Heat fat in skillet; brown onions and drained mushrooms. Stir in mushroom liquid, salt, pepper, tomato sauce and gravy. Cook uncovered over low heat 10 to 15 minutes. Add meat, cover and cook 15 minutes or more. Stir in sour cream. Serve over noodles.

MRS. BERNIE ANDREWS

SEMUR

1 lb. round steak ½   2 minced garlic cloves
    inch thick   ½ t. sugar
1 T. solod oil   ⅛ t. pepper
1 large sliced onion

Cut meat in ½ in. squares. Saute in 1 T. salad oil until brown. Set beef aside. Add other ingredients to skillet and cook until onion is golden brown. Return meat to skillet and simmer 1 hour adding ½ C. water and 2 T. soy sauce. Nice with mashed potatoes (rice or noodles.) Serves 4.

MRS. CARROLL REECE

STEAK COUNTRY STYLE

Preparation time 1¼ hours.

2 lbs. round steak —   ½ C. water
    seasoned flour   2 T. grated cheese
½ C. butter   1 t. salt
2 medium onions, sliced   dash pepper
½ lb. peeled mushrooms,   ¼ t. paprika
    sliced   ½ C. sour cream

Have steak cut in serving pieces and dredge in flour seasoned with salt and pepper. Melt ¼ C. butter in a large skillet and add onions and mushrooms. Cook until onions are tender and mushrooms are lightly browned. Remove onions and mushrooms from pan. Add the remaining ¼ C. butter and brown steak on both sides. Stir in remaining ingredients. Cover skillet and cook until meat is tender enough to cut with fork. Serves 6.

MRS. A. E. CORNETT

STEAK CUPS

1½ lbs. ground beef   ½ t. salt
¾ C. milk   1 T. horseradish
1 egg, slightly beaten   1 T. mustard
2/3 C. quick cooking oatmeal   6 to 8 T. catsup or
1/3 chopped green pepper   tomato sauce
½ t. monosodium glutamate

Combine all ingredients except catsup. Mix well. Divide meat into 12 equal portions and place in 12 well greased muffin tins. With a tablespoon mold the meat in the muffin cup. Make a small hollow in the center of the meat and fill with the catsup or tomato sauce. Bake 50 minutes in 375° oven.

MRS. JOHN ROSE

ITALIAN STEAK

1½ lbs. arm or round steak,   1/3 C. chili sauce
    cut ¾" thick   ¼ C. water
2 T. shortening or drippings   1 t. salt
1 4-oz. can mushrooms or   ⅛ t. pepper
    ½ lb. fresh mush-   ⅛ t. garlic salt
    roos, sliced   ½ t. Worcestershire sauce
2 T. green pepper chopped   ¼ C. sliced olives
½ C. chopped onion

Add mushrocms, onions and green pepper to melted shortening or drippings. Cook 5 minutes. Blend in chili sauce, water, salt, pepper, garlic salt, Worcestershire sauce and sliced olives. Brown steak in frying pan and then add sauce. Cover and bake in slow oven (300°) 1½ to 2 hours, or until tender. 6 servings.

MRS. HUNT ARCHER

BEEF STROGANOFF

1 can tomato soup	2 T. fat
1 T. Worcestershire sauce	½ C. chopped onion
6 - 8 drops tabasco	1 clove garlic
½ t. salt	1 4 oz. can mushrooms
⅛ t. pepper	1 C. sour cream
1 lb. round steak, ¾" cubes	

Dip meat in flour. Brown in fat. Add rest of ingredients. Simmer about 1 hour. Serve over spaghetti and sprinkle with Parmesan cheese.

MRS. R. W. RUCKEL
Pittsburgh, Pa.

STUFFED GREEN PEPPERS WITH NOODLES

½ C. chopped celery	6 medium peppers
small onion, chopped	2 C. cooked noodles
2 T. shortening	1 t. salt
1 lb. ground beef	1½ cans tomato soup

Heat oven to 300°. Cook celery and onion in shortening until soft. Add meat and cook until pink disappears. Par - boil peppers. Mix meat mixture with ½ C. soup and noodles and stuff peppers. Bake 40 minutes in 300° oven. Heat remainder of the soup and pour it over the peppers 15 minutes before taking from the oven.

MRS. BRUCE CHAMBERLIN

SUKIYAKI

Fry about 1 lb. beef suet in a very large deep skillet. Remove suet and brown 4 lbs. (sirloin or top round) trimmed and cubed to bite size. Add to this 1 large head cabbage chopped, 2 bunches celery chopped, 5 green peppers, chopped, 5 onions, chopped, 1 can bean sprouts, 1 can bamboo shoots, 1 can water chestnuts, and 1 lb. brown sugar. Add 2 6-oz. bottles of soy sauce. Cook together about 45 minutes. Serve over cooked rice. Serves 25.

Pass this sauce to be served on top if desired:

SWEET & SOUR SAUCE

¼ C. vinegar	4 T. cornstarch
1 C. white sugar	1 t. ginger
1 C. beef stock	garlic salt
1 C. soy sauce	

Combine cornstarch and sugar and add slowly to beef stock. Add remaining ingredients and cook until thickened.

MARGARET SELLS
Taipei, Taiwan

TERIYAKI (STEAK MARINADE)

¾ C. soy sauce	1 clove garlic, crushed
1/3 C. sherry	

Make a marinade of these ingredients. Marinate 2 inch cubes of sirloin steak for an hour or longer Thread on skewers and broil to taste (over charcoal if possible).

MRS. COWAN MOSS, JR.

SPICED BEEF TONGUE

1 smoked beef tongue	½ pkg. pickling spices
2 C. vinegar	(tied in bag)
1 C. brown sugar	2 T. chili sauce
1 T. salt	1 clove garlic
2 sticks cinnamon	Water sufficient to cook

Thoroughly scrub tongue, but do not peel off outside skin and roots. Put in kettle with all ingredients and boil until tender. Remove from kettle and allow tongue to cool before removing roots. Trim off nicely and set in ice box to become thoroughly cold before slicing. Delicious served on thin slices of rye or white bread or used as main luncheon dish.

MRS. BERT P. GUMP

BARBECUED FRANKFURTERS

Cook ¼ C. chopped onion in 1 T. butter until clear. Add ⅛ t. pepper, 4 t. sugar, 1 t. mustard, 4 t. Worcestershire sauce, ½ C. catsup, ½ C. water and ¼ C. vinegar. Cut 3 inch slits in frankfurters. Place in flat pan, cover with sauce and bake for 20 minutes.

MRS. HARRY MYRON

FRANKFURTER IN SOUR CREAM

6 franks	2 t. sugar
2 T. olive oil	¼ t. salt
2 t. flour	¼ C. cold water
3 T. chili sauce	1 T. caraway seeds
1 C. sour cream	

Cut franks in ½ inch slices and brown in hot oil. Stir in flour over very low heat. Add rest of ingredients. Heat to boiling point. Serve hot with crackers.

MRS. TOM McKEE

BARBECUED LEG OF LAMB

1 6-lb. leg of lamb, boned and flattened

Marinade

2 T. vinegar	1 t. salt
½ C. olive oil	½ t. pepper
1 clove garlic, crushed	

Combine sauce ingredients and marinate the lamb in this mixture for 2 hours. Broil over charcoal embers for 1½ to 2 hours, turning frequently and brushing every 5 minutes with the hot barbecue sauce.

MRS. ALLEN HARRIS, JR.

BAR-B-Q LEG OF LAMB

1 leg of lamb	salt & pepper
1 t. ground ginger	2 sliced onions
1 t. dry mustard	1 clove garlic (optional)

Sauce to baste:

1 T. Worcestershire sauce	¾ C. chili sauce
1 T. vinegar	sugar to taste
2 T. salad oil	

Wipe lamb with damp cloth, and rub thoroughly with spices mixed together. Dredge well with flour and brown quickly (25 min.) in a hot (400°) oven. Reduce heat to 325° and cover lamb with sauce. Slice onion and garlic on top and baste every 30 minutes, allowing 30 minutes to the pound for roasting. One hour before lamb is done, add 1 C. boiling water to pan. Skim off fat and make gravy.

MRS. CALVIN MORGAN

TOAD IN THE HOLE

Pepper and salt 6 or 8 thick lamb chops ½ in. thick. Put in hot pan well greased with bacon drippings. Pour the batter over the chops. Cook 1 hour at 300°. Baste often with bacon drippings. Serve hot in pan.

BATTER

2 C. flour
2 t. baking powder
1 t. salt

2 eggs, well beaten
1 qt. sweet milk

MRS. ALLEN HARRIS

FRIED COUNTRY HAM SLICES

Soak ham slices in milk for at least one hour if the ham is very salty. Blot slices with paper toweling before frying. Use hot iron skillet so as to sear ham immediately—then turn to low heat and let fry slowly until tender—at least five minutes on each side.

For red gravy pour grease from skillet into gravy boat and add about 2 T. water to pan. Stir until all browned particles melt off bottom of pan. Pour this from pan into grease in gravy boat and mix.

MRS. RICHARD JENNINGS

SAVORY BAKED COUNTRY HAM

10 to 12 lb. country ham
1 T. whole cloves
1 stick cinnamon
3 cloves garlic
1¼ C. vinegar
1 small glass apple jelly
1 C. brown sugar

4 t. dry mustard
¾ C. water
¼ t. powdered cloves
¼ t. powdered cinnamon
2 T. vinegar
1 C. white sugar

Carefully wash the ham and soak in water several hours or overnight. After soaking plunge into large kettle of boiling water, covering ham completely. Put whole cloves, stick cinnamon, garlic, 1 C. vinegar and the white sugar in on ham and simmer gently for 3½ hours or until tender. Turn heat off and let ham stand in hot liquid for at least 4 hours. Remove it from the water and trim off rind. Mix the brown sugar and dry mustard and pat into fat of ham. Whole cloves may be inserted if desired. Add water and ¼ C. vinegar to pan and bake in a slow oven for 1 hour. Don't baste the ham until it is brown. Fifteen min. before removing ham from oven make the following sauce: Mix 1 t. dry mustard and the powdered cloves and cinnamon with 2 T. vinegar. Then add the jelly and heat over a slow heat until the jelly is melted. Add more vinegar if you want the sauce sharper. Slice the ham and pour sauce over slices on platter. Serves 10 to 12. This method and sauce is excellent with sugar cured ham also, but soaking and boiling should be omitted, and baking period extended to 20 - 30 minutes per pound.

MRS. THOMAS POTTER

BARBECUE PORK CHOPS

Pork chops, 1 per serving
brown sugar

catsup

Salt chops and place in baking dish. Cover with sugar (1 t. or more) per chop. Then add catsup and 1 slice of lemon to each. Add whole cloves if desired. Pour small amount of water around edge of chops. Cover and bake in 325° oven for 1½ hour.

MRS. E. H. SILER

LAMB OR BEEF KEBABS

1½ lbs meat (use either beef round or lamb shoulder)
   cut in 1" cubes
½ C. tomato catsup
1 t. salt
2 T. sugar
2 T. beefsteak sauce

2 T. cider vinegar
2 T. Worcestershire sauce
¼ C. water
2 T. salad oil or shortening

Place cubed meat in bowl; combine remaining ingredients in sauce-pan and heat to boiling. Pour over meat; let stand several hours or overnight in marinade. String on skewers and broil over hot coals. Re-heat marinating liquid for sauce. Serves 4. On the skewers alternate the meat with lemon, onion, bell pepper and tomato wedges.

MRS. W. T. MATHES, JR.

PORK CHOPS WITH BARBECUE SAUCE

4 T. minced onion
1 C. tomato puree (can
   tomato sauce)
¾ C. water
3 T. vinegar
2 T. Worcestershire sauce

1 t. salt
1 t. paprika
1 t. chili powder
½ t. pepper
¼ t. cinnamon
dash ground cloves

Combine all ingredients in order listed. Heat to boiling and keep hot until ready to use on chops. Dust pork chops with flour. Sear on both sides until browned, then place 1 T. sauce on each chop. Reduce heat, cover and cook slowly 5 to 8 minutes. Turn chops and place remainder of sauce on them. Cook slowly until tender. About 40 minutes. Enough sauce for about 8 pork chops.

MRS. GERTRUDE SMITH

STUFFED PORK CHOPS (FOR 3)

Dressing:
1 C. bread crumbs
½ t. salt
½ t. pepper
¾ T. minced parsley

½ t. sage
½ T. grated onion
1½ T. milk

Stuff prepared pork chops with mixture
Brown chops in fat
Season with salt, pepper and garlic salt
Add ¼ C. water and
Bake at 350° about 1 hour or until tender.

MRS. FRANK KNISLEY

HAM YUM YUM

1 3" thick slice of raw ham
Brown sugar

flour
1 C. rich milk

Put ham slice on a paper towel and rub into it all the brown sugar and flour that you can make stick to it. Then brown the ham in a hot skillet with butter. When nice and brown, take from stove and add flour and sugar left on the paper. Add milk and cover and bake in 375° oven for 2 hours. Add more milk if necessary to make plenty of rich brown gravy.

MRS. F. L. WALLACE

HAM LOAF

1½ lb. ground ham or	Add 1 medium onion, chopped
1 lb. fresh lean pork, ground	1 C. milk
Mix 1 C. bread and	½ t. black pepper
2 lightly beaten eggs	

Bake in loaf pan 1½ hours at 350°.

SAUCE

½ can whole cranberry sauce	½ C. water
¼ C. white karo syrup	

Cook until thick. Pour over loaf just before serving.

MRS. DAN WEXLER, JR.

HAM LOAF

1½ lbs. cured ham, ground	1½ C. milk
1½ lbs. fresh pork, ground	½ C. brown sugar
1½ C. fine cracker crumbs	1 T. dry mustard
¼ t. pepper	¼ C. vinegar
3 eggs, well beaten	

Combine meat, crumbs, pepper, eggs and milk. Mix thoroughly. Shape into a loaf and place in a baking dish. Mix sugar, mustard and vinegar together and pour over the meat. Bake in a moderate oven (350°) for 1 hour. Baste 2 or 3 times. Serve with Horseradish sauce.

HORSERADISH SAUCE

½ C. whipped cream	½ t. salt
3 T. drained horseradish	

NELLE MacDONALD

COLD HAM LOAF

2 T. gelatin	1 pimiento, finely chopped
½ C. cold water	dash of cayenne, cloves and
1 C. boiling water	nutmeg
2 T. lemon juice	½ C. mayonnaise
1 T. horseradish, drained	2½ C. cooked ground ham
2 t. Worcestershire sauce	(1 lb.)
½ t. onion pulp	

Soak gelatin in cold water and add boiling water. Cool, and add remaining ingredients. When mixture begins to thicken, pour it into a greased loaf pan. Chill until firm. Unmold on a platter and garnish with parsley.

MRS. ROBERT RADER

GLAZED HAM LOAF

½ lb. ground pork	2 T. chopped onion
½ lb. ground beef	¾ t. dry mustard
½ lb. ground ham	¾ C. soft bread crumbs
1 C. milk	1 t. salt
¼ C. catsup	⅛ t. pepper

Mix together and shape into a loaf pan. Bake 1½ hours in 350° oven. Glaze:

½ C. brown sugar	2 t. water
2 T. vinegar	

Boil together 5 minutes. Baste at 10 minute intervals till all is used. Serves 6.

MRS. W. F. SHURTZ

UPSIDE DOWN HAM LOAF

Mix together thoroughly:

1½ lbs. ground smoked ham	2 T. finely chopped onion
1 lb. ground lean pork	2 eggs, well beaten

Add:

1 C. soft bread crumbs	1 C. milk
¼ green pepped, chopped	

Season with salt and pepper. In the bottom of a deep pan, preferably a deep heavy frying pan, arrange slices or "fingers" of pineapple. Sprinkle the pineapple liberally with brown sugar and cover with the meat mixture. Bake in a moderate oven 1½ hours. Turn out on a hot platter upside down and serve plain or with mushrooms or horse-radish sauce. Garnish with pickled peaches.

MRS. MEL SMITH

HAM - CHEESE LOAF

1 lb. boiled ham	¼ t. pepper
1 T. prepared mustard	dash of cayenne
2 T. catsup	1 C. grated cheese

Slice ham in thin slices and spread with mustard, catsup, and pepper mixed well. Place one slice over the other with grated cheese between. Repeat, forming a loaf with cheese on top. Bake 15 minutes at 350°. Remove from oven and cool. Cut in slices to serve. Nice for buffet suppers.

MRS. WILLIAM HENSON

"CHEAPER BY THE DOZEN" SPARERIBS

3 or 4 lbs. spare ribs	½ t. red pepper
2 onions, sliced	½ t. black pepper
2 t. vinegar	1 t. chili powder
2 t. Worcestershire sauce	¾ C. catsup
1 t. salt	¾ C. water
1 t. paprika	

Select meaty spare ribs. Cut into servings or leave uncut. Sprinkle with salt and pepper. Place in roaster and cover with onions. Combine remaining ingredients and pour over meat. Cover and bake in moderate oven (350°) about 1½ hours. Baste occasionally turning spareribs once or twice. Remove cover last 15 minutes to brown ribs. Serves 6.

MRS. MOSE JONES

COLD VEAL LOAF

6 lbs. neck veal   1 T. celery seed
1 large onion

Boil meat with seasoning until meat falls to pieces. Bone meat, remove gristle and grind. Grind 2 large pieces pimento with meat and add desired seasoning to taste.

Boil broth until about 1 pint remains. Strain. Put 2 t. gelatin in a little cold water and then dissolve it in the hot broth. Pour this mixture over the ground meat until it becomes the consistency of soft dough. Press in pan and place weighted pan or plate on top. Chill till firm.

MISS LILLIE TAYLOR

ITALIAN VEAL STEW

1½ lb shoulder of veal, cut in 1½" pieces, brown in
2 T. olive oil in skillet
Combine:

Liquid from 1 4-oz. can button mushrooms
1 8-oz. can tomato sauce   1 bay leaf
½ t. tabasco   ½ C. diced green pepper
1 t. salt   1 minced clove garlic
¼ t. powdered thyme

Add to meat in skillet and cover. Cook over low heat 1½ hours. Add mushrooms and then turn out onto platter. Serve with hot rice.

MRS. E. MALCOLM CAMPBELL

VEAL & MUSHROOMS ITALIAN STYLE

3 lbs. veal or beef round steak, sliced about 1/3" thick
½ C. flour   1 bouillon cube
1½ t. salt   1 8-oz. can seasoned tomato
dash pepper   sauce
2 t. paprika   ¼ C. chopped green pepper
3 T. fat   1 10-oz. pkg. noodles
1 4 to 6 oz. can sliced
mushrooms

Pound meat thoroughly with sharp edged meat pounder. Cut in serving pieces. Combine flour and seasoning; coat meat in mixture. Brown in hot fat. Place in 13x9½x2-inch baking dish. Drain mushrooms, reserving liquid. Add water to mushroom liquid to make 1 C. and heat to a boil. Dissolve bouillon cube in hot liquid and pour over meat. Bake in moderate oven (350°) 30 minutes. Combine tomato sauce, green pepper and mushrooms. Pour over meat and continue baking 15 minutes. Meanwhile, cook noodles until tender in boiling salted water. Drain. Baste meat with the sauce just before serving. Sprinkle with Parmesan cheeses. Serve with hot buttered noodles. Make 8-9 servings.

MRS. W. W. MILLER

VEAL QUEEN ANNE

2 lb. veal round steak, ¾-inch thick

Wipe with a damp cloth and trim the edges. Rub with garlic, then pound the meat well with the edge of a plate or a pounder. Cut surface lightly with criss-cross slices. Cut the meat into serving pieces about the size of a large oyster. Season well with salt and paprika and dip them in rolled cracker crumbs. Then dip in one egg beaten with 2 T. of water and again in crumbs. Brown the slices in butter in hot skillet, then half cover the slices with

1 C. coffee cream	**½ C. stock**
¾ C. queen Anne cherry juice	

Cover skillet with a lid and reduce heat to very, very low heat or place covered skillet in slow oven 300°. Cook meat one hour. Thicken drippings with a little flour.

Stone and drain cherries and cook them in the gravy with the meat for the last 5 minutes.

1½ C. seedless white grapes could be substituted for cherries.

This is really a delicate party dish and always successful.

MRS. ROBERT BOWMAN

VEAL SCALOPPINI

4 T. flour	**1 clove garlic**
½ t. salt	**1 medium onion, sliced**
¼ t. pepper	**½ green pepper, chopped**
2 lbs. thin veal steak—	**1 can mushrooms**
½-inch thick	**1 C. white wine**
¼ C. salad oil	

Combine flour, salt, and pepper and use to coat veal after it has been cut into bite size pieces. Heat the oil in a heavy skillet. Add garlic, green pepper and onion and saute until golden brown. Add veal and brown. Add white wine and mushrooms. Cover and simmer gently until tender. Serve the meat with the sauce.

MRS. JOE WOOD

VEAL SCALOPPINI

¾ lb. boneles veal shoulder,	**1 C. sliced canned mushrooms**
cut very thin	**2 C. cooked or canned**
½ t. salt	**tomatoes**
½ t. celery salt	**2 t. minced onion**
½ t. dry mustard	**½ t. minced garlic**
cayenne pepper, just a sprinkle	**½ t. minced parsley**
3 T. flour	**¼ C. dry sherry wine**
4 T. butter or oleo	**water cress**

Pound to ⅛-inch thickness. Mix salt, celery salt, dry mustard and cayenne with flour. Dredge veal. Brown meat on both sides in butter or oleo in large heavy skillet. Add mushrooms, tomatoes, onion and garlic. Cover tightly and simmer 20 minutes. Add parsley and wine. Simmer 3 minutes. Serve with water cress. Serves 4.

MRS. ELBERT MILLER

BEAN POT BEEF STEW

1½ lbs. lean beef stew
   meat
1 C. diced celery
6 carrots, sliced
1 C. tomatoes
½ T. brown sugar
½ C. soft bread crumbs

3 T. Tapioca dissolved in ½
   C. water
½ C. peas, frozen or fresh
3 med. onions, chopped
1 bouillon cube
2 T. dry sherry
1 t. B. V.

Put all ingredients in a bean pot and cover with foil. Then press lid over foil cover. Bake for 5 hours at 250 degrees in the oven. Serves four generously. Very good over rice since no potatoes are used.

Mrs. Frank Atkinson

COMPANY BEEF STEW

3 lbs. chuck roast stew
¼ t. marjoram
1 small bay leaf
½ t. garlic salt, onion and
   celery salt
3 T. chopped onion
2 green onions

2 T. vinegar
3 T. chopped green peppers
2 tomatoes, cut up
1 clove garlic
2 chopped carrots
1 T. thyme
1½ C. red wine

Brown meat and add rest of ingredients. Cook until meat is tender. To thicken, add 2 Tbs. butter, 2 Tbs. flour-mixed together; stir into stew. Before serving add garnish:

24 white onions
24 mushrooms

1 lemon (juice)
Dab butter and olive oil

To garnish, brown 2 doz. small white onions in 2 Tbs. butter with dash sugar—add a little water, then cover and cook until tender. Brown about 2 doz. fresh mushroom caps in 2 Tbs. each of butter and olive oil. Sprinkle with lemon juice. Cook until tender—about 5 min. Serve stew over rice. Serves 12.

Mrs. John Cavett
Virginia Beach, Virginia

MARINATED BEEF STEW

4 lbs. round steak-cubed
1 C. flour
8 potatoes, quartered
12 carrots, cut
1 C. celery

2 cans onions
4 C. water
1 C. sherry
2 t. each of salt and pepper
12 T. soy sauce

Dredge meat with all the flour. Arrange layers of this and the vegetables, salt, pepper. Mix water, sherry, soy sauce and pour over all. Bake at 325 degrees for 2½ to 3 hours. Serves 16.

Mrs. John Wilson

BEEF BRISKET

1 can tomato sauce	Garlic salt
2 T. catsup	Salt and pepper
Worcestershire sauce	½ C. water
Tabasco	

Ask your butcher to "trim out" a fresh brisket-removing as much fat as possible. Stir the above ingredients together and pour over brisket. Cover and cook 1½ hours at 350 degrees. Take out and cool. With a very sharp knife, slice ACROSS the grain as thin as possible. Put slices back in gravy, cover and cook 1 hour more at 300 degrees. This is even better if done the day before so the meat can absorb the flavors.   Mrs. Bernard Cantor

BARBECUED MEAT LOAF

1½ lbs. ground chuck	salt and pepper
1 C. fresh bread crumbs	½ can tomato sauce
1 med. onion, chopped	1 egg, beaten

Mix all ingredients together and shape into loaf. Pour the following sauce over the loaf:

½ can tomato sauce	2 T. brown sugar
1 can water	2 T. vinegar
2 T. mustard	

Pour over meat loaf. Baste occasionally. Cook at 350 for 1½ hours.

Mrs. W. H. Conant
Kingsport, Tennessee

JULIA'S CHILI

BOIL SLOWLY:
   2 lbs. ground meat in 1 qt. water for 15 minutes
ADD:

2 T. onion salt	2 squirts tabasco
2 T. chili powder	2 large cans red kidney beans
2 12 oz. cans tomato paste	

Simmer for 2 hours. Serves 8 people.   Mrs. B. Cross
Nashville, Tennessee

MEATBALLS

1 lb. ground meat	1 t. salt
⅔ C. apple sauce	½ C. cornflake crumbs

Mix the above ingredients thoroughly and shape into balls. Chop one onion and combine with ½ cup catsup and ½ cup water. Pour this over meat balls and bake one hour at 350-375. These meatballs are very moist and make nice hot Hors d' Oeuvres if shaped into bite size balls, and kept warm in chafing dish.   Mrs. Harmon Monroe

PRESSED BEEF

4 lbs. meaty beef shank   2 t. salt
   or pot roast   ¼ t. pepper
2 qts. water   1 T. powdered sage
6 cloves   1 envelope unflavored
1 onion, sliced   gelatin
1 stick cinnamon   ¼ C. cold water

Cover meat with water; add onion and all seasonings, except sage.
Simmer until meat pulls from bone. Remove meat from broth and tear
with fork until finely shredded. Add sage to liquid; cook down to 3
cups. Soften gelatin in cold water; add to broth. Chill broth until
syrupy and then add meat. Pour in loaf pan; chill until firm. (Makes 8
to 10 servings.) Slice thin and serve with horseradish sauce. Even
better after being frozen.

Mrs. Vernon Wilson

FLUFFY HORSERADISH SAUCE

To 1 carton sour cream add 2 T. fresh horseradish and ⅛ t. salt.

ROUND STEAK SAUERBRATEN

1½ lbs. round steak   3 T. brown sugar
   (½" thick)   ½ t. salt
1 T. fat   ¼ t. pepper
1 envelope brown gravy mix   ½ t. ginger
2 C. water   2 T. worcestershire sauce
2 T. instant minced onion   1 bay leaf
3 T. white wine vinegar

Cut meat in 1" squares. In a large skillet, brown meat on all sides in
hot fat. Remove meat from skillet. Add gravy mix and water. Bring to
boil, stirring constantly. Stir in remaining ingredients. Return meat to
skillet; cover and simmer 2 hrs., stirring occasionally. Remove bay
leaf. Serve meat over hot buttered noodles. Makes 5-6 servings.

Mrs. C. E. Jacobs, Jr.

ANNA SUE'S SISH KABOBS

1½ C. salad oil   2 T. dry mustard
¾ C. soy sauce   1 T. black pepper, scant
¼ C. worcestershire sauce   1½ t. dry parsley
½ C. fresh lemon juice   2 Garlic cloves

Combine all ingredients, marinate 6 lbs. of cubed sirloin for at least 3
hours or overnight. Alternate on skewers with strips of bell peppers,
small tomatoes (or quartered tomatoes) small onions, green olives,
mushrooms and meat.

Mrs. Robert Carter

STUFFED CABBAGE ROLLS

1 large head of cabbage with large leaves	2 large cans tomato sauce
2 lbs. ground beef	1 small can tomato paste
½ C. water	3 T. vinegar
1½ C. minute rice (uncooked)	2 T. brown sugar
1 large grated onion	3 ginger snaps (optional)
	Salt, pepper, garlic salt, ground ginger

Core cabbage and boil about 10 min. Separate leaves and let them sit in boiling water until tender enough to bend without breaking. Season ground beef with salt and pepper to taste—adding about ½ tsp. garlic salt and ¼ tsp. ground ginger. Add water and add rice and mix together well—into meat.

Fill each cabbage leaf with generous helping of meat mixture, fold into envelopes and lay into bottom of dutch oven or roasting pan. Cover with tomato sauce, paste and 1 paste can of water, vinegar, brown sugar and ginger snaps. Cook covered, simmering, for 3 or 4 hours. NOTE: Stuffed cabbage benefits from being made the day before. Just reheat and serve. Unused portion may be frozen and used at a later time.

Harriet Nachman

BROWN SIRLOIN ROAST

Brown sirloin tip roast on all sides slowly in heavy pan. Use no flour and only a little oleo to coat the pan. After browning, cover pan tightly and reduce heat to low. Cook meat about 1 hour, then check moisture. If there are little or no drippings in pan, add ¼ cup water and cover pan. Cook only to medium rare. Remove meat from pan and slice paper thin. Skim off any grease in pan and add 1 or 2 cans of Franco-American Mushroom Gravy to drippings in pan. Mix well, adding a little black pepper. Return sliced meat to pan, cover and simmer about 45 minutes. Serve hot with gravy.

MARY LOU'S POT ROAST

4½ to 5 lbs. pot roast	1 med. onion, chopped
salt	pinch of rosemary
pepper	1 bay leaf
1 celery stalk, including leaves	6 whole allspice or sprinkle of some ground allspice
1 clove garlic minced, or garlic salt	⅔ C. dry red wine (or water)

Put in heavy pot or roaster. Add all ingredients. Cover tightly and allow to bake at 250 degrees for 6-8 hours. If you only have 5 or 6 hours bake at 300 degrees. Good with boiled potatoes.

Mrs. Bill Meredith

ROAST IN FOIL

Dehydrated onion soup in bottom of roaster
Roast
Mushroom soup on top of roast
¼ C. water

Cover with aluminum foil. Don't brown. No salt or pepper. Bake 45 minutes for each lb. at 350 degrees. Chicken (same method). Celery soup on top, ½ can of water. Cook at 350 degrees for 1½ hours. Last ½ hour take off lid and foil.   Mrs. William Preas

SAVORY POT ROAST WITH VEGETABLES

5 lbs. bottom-round beef   **1 bay leaf**
   roast   **6 med. carrots, pared**
2 T. flour   **6 med. potatoes**
1 t. salt   **6 med. onions**
1 T. shortening or salad oil   **1 can stewed tomatoes**
6 whole black peppers

Combine flour and salt; rub into the surface of meat, brown meat in shortening in a dutch oven. Add black peppers, bay leaf and 2 cups of water; simmer 1 hour—covered. Turn roast, add vegetables, simmer 45 minutes or until vegetables are tender. Make pot roast gravy after removing roast and vegetables from pan.

Strain liquid through sieve pressing any remaining vegetables through. Skim off all fat; add water to make 2½ cups. Combine flour with ½ cup water, stirring until smooth. Slowly stir liquid into dutch oven, bring to boil while stirring. Pass gravy with pot roast and vegetables.   Mrs. Herbert Lawson

VEAL SCALLOPINI

1½ lbs. veal cutlets, sliced thin and cut up in medium
   sized pieces
⅓ C. flour   **2 T. chopped green pepper**
1 t. salt   **1 can condensed tomato**
¼ t. pepper   **soup**
⅓ C. vegetable oil   **½ C. water**
1 medium onion, chopped   **½ C. grated sharp cheese**

Roll veal slices in flour, salt, and pepper. Heat oil in large skillet. Saute onion and green pepper until tender. Remove from skillet. Add veal; brown both sides. Pour off excess oil. Add soup mixed with water. Return the onion and green pepper. Cover; simmer 10 minutes or until meat is tender. Sprinkle with cheese and heat until cheese melts. Serve over rice or noodles. Serves 6. This could easily be put in a casserole and put in oven until cheese melts.

                    Mrs. Hugh Warren

BAKED STUFFED PORK CHOPS

4 rib pork chops cut 2" thick, each with pocket	Savory stuffing 1 t. salt

Preheat oven to 350 degrees. Wipe chops with damp towel. Fill pockets in chops with savory stuffing. Stand chops on rib bones on rack in a shallow roasting pan, sprinkle with seasoned salt. Pour water to ½ inch depth in roasting pan; water should not touch rack. Cover pan with foil. Bake 45 minutes. Remove foil and bake uncovered 45 to 55 minutes longer or until tender and brown. Makes 4 servings.

SAVORY STUFFING:

2 T. butter	½ C. dark raisins
½ C. chopped onion	2 T. dried marjoram leaves
½ C. chopped celery	and 2 T. of dried parsley
1½ C. soft bread crumbs	1 t. salt
½ t. pepper	3 T. apple juice

Cook onion and celery in hot butter until tender. Add bread crumbs and brown. Remove from heat. Add raisins, chopped parsley, salt, marjoram, pepper and apple juice; toss mixture lightly to combine.

Mrs. Herbert Lawson

CHINESE PORK CHOP

6 ¾" thick pork chops	Flour
1 T. bacon drippings or fat	⅔ C. soy sauce
⅔ C. vinegar	⅓ C. sugar
½ t. ginger	⅔ C. water

Dredge chops in flour. Heat drippings or fat in heavy skillet. Brown chops on both sides well. Pour off excess fat. Add remaining ingredients and bring to boil. Cover and simmer for one hour.

Mrs. William Blackard

SWEET AND PUNGENT PORK

1½ lb. pork, cubed	3 T. molasses
2 eggs, beaten	3 tomatoes, peeled and
1 C. flour	diced
Oil for frying	2 T. cornstarch
3 green peppers cut in	1 t. salt
strips	1 T. soy sauce
¾ C. brown sugar	Black pepper to taste
1 C. vinegar	1 can pineapple chunks

Combine eggs, flour, salt and ¼ cup water. Add pork cubes and stir until coated. Fry pork in 2 inches of oil at 375° for 5 min. or until brown. Drain pork. Combine peppers, pineapple, brown sugar and vinegar, molasses, black pepper and 1½ cups water. Bring to boil stirring constantly. Add tomatoes and simmer 5 min. Combine cornstarch with ¼ cup cold water and stir into green pepper mixture. Cook until thickened. Add soy sauce and pork. Simmer 15-20 min. Serve with rice. Serves 6.

Mrs. Robert Mains

MEN'S RECIPES

APPLE CRUMB PIE

1 9" pie crust

FILLING:

1 can Comstock apples, drained	1 T. tapioca
1 t. apple pie spice	½ C. sugar

TOPPING:

½ C. brown sugar	4 T. margarine or butter, melted
½ C. flour	½ C. finely crushed corn flakes
1 t. apple pie spice	
¼ t. salt	

Roll out pastry; line pie plate; fill with apples, sprinkle with apple pie ⌐ tapioca and sugar. Combine brown sugar, flour, salt, apple ⌐.⌐e and crushed corn flakes. Work in butter or margarine with pastry blender or finger tips until mixture is crumbly. Spread crumb mixture in even layer over top of apples; pat down lightly. Bake in hot oven (450°) 10 minutes and reduce heat to moderate (350°) and bake 30 to 40 minutes longer or until apples are tender.

R. W. BROWNE

BOILED CUSTARD

Beat 8 whole eggs, gradually add 4 C. sugar. Add one gallon milk and ¼ t. salt. Cook, stirring constantly until mixture coats a spoon. Cool. Add vanilla or other flavoring. Makes about 24 servings.

JACK O. WHAREY

RED BEANS AND HAM

1 lb. dry red beans	2 stalks celery, chopped
2 center slices of ham	2 T. chopped parsley
1 large onion, chopped	1 large bay leaf
1 clove garlic	

Brown the meat in a pan. Cover the beans with hot water in a large kettle and let them soak for a couple of hours. Lift meat into bean kettle. Brown all chopped ingredients in ham drippings—put bay leaf in bean water. Add all ingredients to the beans and cook a couple of hours on top of stove, covered. Cook until thickened. Salt to taste. Serve over hot rice.

E. J. McGARRY
New Orleans, La.

BOWMAN ISLAND SPECIAL

Moisten with vinegar and mash thoroughly 3 cans of Sardines. Add 6 medium onions, minced finely. Add Tabasco, salt and pepper to taste. Serve with crackers. If your taste so desires, make it hot.

W. H. LANCASTER, SR.

PINEAPPLE CHEESE CAKE

1½ envelopes plain gelatin
6 T. cold water
2 eggs, separated
½ C. sugar
1/3 C. pineapple juice
¼ t. salt
1 C. strained cottage cheese
1 3 oz. pkg. cream cheese
1 T. lemon juice
1 t. grated lemon rind

1 C. heavy cream, whipped
½ t. vanilla
1½ C. crushed graham
   cracker crumbs
¼ C. melted butter
¼ t. cinnamon
1 T. sugar
1 small can (9 oz.) crushed
   pineapple drained

Soften gelatin in cold water, about 5 minutes. Combine egg yolks which have been beaten, 1/3 C. sugar, pineapple juice and salt. Cook in top of double boiler over hot water until thick and smooth or until mixture coats the back of a silver spoon. Add softened gelatin and stir until dissolved. Blend together the cottage cheese and cream cheese. Combine with gelatin mixture. Add lemon juice and rind. Chill until partially thick. Beat egg whites until frothy, gradually beat in remaining sugar until stiff and smooth. Fold into cheese mixture with whipped cream and vanilla. Combine cracker crumbs, melted butter, cinnamon and 1 T. sugar. Put all but ½ C. of crumb mixture on bottom of a 7 inch spring form cake pan. Top with drained pineapple. Pour in cheese mixture. Sprinkle remaining crumbs over top. Chill in refrigerator until firm. This serves 6 to 8 people.

C. W. FRIBERG

CHICKEN A LA RAG-OUT

1 frying chicken cut in
   portions
1 clove garlic

½ bell pepper
1 onion
1 small can of mushrooms

Brown all ingredients but chicken in hot fat. Add chicken and 1 can of tomato sauce. Let simmer until chicken leaves bones. Remove bones and serve over hot rice.

RUSSELL CAMPBELL

OSTINDIAN CURRY

1-1/3 lb. pork (no fat) cut into cubes. Knead in 3 T. flour, 1 t. curry and 2 t. salt.
Dice two onions and cook in butter until transparent. Add meat and enough hot water to cover. Cook 1½ hours covered. Serve over hot rice.

BORGE CHRISTIANSEN

ROQUEFORT DRESSING

8 or 9 oz. wedge Roquefort cheese
1 pint mayonnaise

Break cheese in small chunks and mix thoroughly with mayonnaise. Add:

2/3 C. Wesson Oil
¼ C. vinegar — or to taste
dash of A-1 sauce

Mix thoroughly. Delicious served on lettuce wedges.

JOHN IRWIN

FRIED WILD DUCK

Place duck on back on table, or other smooth surface, head away from you. While holding duck between hands, with thumbs press and part skin at breast bone and continue until breast is skinned. With a sharp knife cut along breast bone and remove the two pieces of breast. Then skin the legs by pulling up through the skin.

Soak in salt water for 30 to 45 minutes, drain and dry. Roll in flour that has been salted and peppered. Fry in iron skillet that has a mixture of one half butter and one half shortening, about ¼-inch deep. Fry slowly for about an hour and when half done, dribble a little sherry over each piece and repeat once. Cream gravy made after duck is removed from skillet is excellent.

HAROLD THOMPSON

ROAST WILD DUCK

First, no duck should be eaten earlier than four days after it is killed, but should be refrigerated and not frozen during this time.

Dress as a hen. Stuff with 1 sliced medium apple and 1 whole onion. Sprinkle with salt and pepper and put two strips of bacon on breast of each duck. Add 1 C. water to roaster and baste every five minutes. Cook at 500° for 15 to 30 minutes. (If you like your steak rare, you will enjoy a 15 minute duck).

PETE DOSSER

HAM FRIED RICE ("HAM FLIED LICE")

Prepare:

3 C. cooked (just tender) rice	½ C. diced onion
1 C. diced cooked ham	1 box of mushrooms
1 C. cooked shrimp	fried in butter
1 C. diced celery	4 eggs, beaten
½ C. diced green pepper	

In your largest pan, melt 2 T. butter, 2 T. Wesson Oil. Add onions, celery and stir 2 minutes. Add ham, shrimp and green pepper. Then stir 4 or 5 minutes with spatula. Add rice and continue stirring until hot. Add salt, pepper, soy sauce (to taste), and mushrooms. Finally add 4 beaten eggs and stir just until set. A good "quickie."

ALAN GUMP

SWEET HAM AND PORK LOAF

2 lbs. ground cured ham	1 C. milk
1½ lbs. ground pork steak	1 C. cracker or bread crumbs
2 beaten eggs	Salt and pepper

To the ground meat add the beaten eggs, milk, crumbs and mix thoroughly. Salt and pepper to taste. Make into a loaf. Place in 350° oven and when slightly browned baste frequently with the following syrup:

1½ C. brown sugar	½ C. vinegar
1 T. mustard	½ C. water

Combine the ingredients and cook 5 minutes. Use for basting the meat loaf. Bake 2 hours. Serve hot or cold.

C. N. HEATH

OYSTERS FENNALLI

1 lobster tail, cook with lemon and celery, drain and dice
2 C. crab meat
1 C. shrimp, diced
1 pint small oysters, drained
1 pint whipping cream
Grated Cheddar cheese, medium sharp

Mix lobster, shrimp and crab meat together and add the whipping cream. Season to taste with salt, pepper, tabasco sauce, Worcestershire sauce and small amount of either granulated or powdered garlic. Bring this mixture to a boil, turn to low heat and simmer for 10 minutes. Add just enough cracker crumbs to take up excess liquid The mixture should remain moist, not soupy.

Grease one cup casseroles with butter or oleo. Layer bottom of dish with 6 to 8 small drained oysters. Add ¾ C. seafood mixture. Top with grated cheese. Sprinkle top with very small amount of powdered garlic. Bake approximately 15 minutes at 350° or until cheese is brown.

Refrigerate if made ahead of time. Allow extra cooking to be sure the mixture is heated through. May be wrapped in aluminum foil and frozen. This casserole served with a baked potato and green salad is a very adequate meal.

Dr. Charles Underwood

BROILED RED SNAPPER

Use a filet of red snapper weighing 2 to 4 lbs., wipe with a damp cloth. Roll it in melted butter seasoned with garlic. Then season on both sides with salt, pepper and a few grains of cayenne.

Place fish on well oiled broiling pan and broil 5 inches from the flame. Baste frequently with mixture of butter and white wine. Turn when done on one side. Allow 12 minutes for broiling time of entire fish. Serve on warm platter; garnish with lemon wedges and parsley boiled potatoes.

Lester Ballew, Jr.

ARROZ CON POLLO (CHICKEN WITH YELLOW RICE)

1 fryer	1 onion
2 buttons garlic	1 bay leaf
1 pinch saffron	½ lb. long grain rice
4 oz. shortening	2 green peppers
or ¼ pt. olive oil	2 oz. tomatoes or
1 small can peas	3 fresh tomatoes
2 pimientos	1 quart water
2 t. salt	

Cut chicken in quarters and fry until lightly browned, with onions and garlic. When done add tomatoes and water.

Boil 5 minutes. Add bay leaf, salt, rice, saffron and green pepper. Add small amount of yellow coloring, if a deeper yellow is desired. Stir thoroughly and place in moderate oven until rice is done (about 35 miuutes).

Serve on a heated platter, and garnish with green peas and pimiento strips. With this dish serve a green salad and French bread. Serves 4.

Forster Miller

SALAD, CABBAGE AND FRUIT

grated cabbage
grated celery (2 or 3 stalks)
grated cashew nuts (one can)
crushed pineapple (small can)
1 T. sweetened vinegar or lemon juice
mayonnaise or salad dressing

Mix all ingredients together in order given.

J. M. BURLESON

SEAFOOD COCKTAIL SAUCE

1 part Chili sauce
1 part catsup
⅛ part horseradish

1/10 part of Lea and Perrins
Sauce

Grind peel of an orange, a whole lemon and add to above ingredients.
Add Tabasco sauce, salt and soy sauce to taste. Use for any seafood
sauce.

C. T. UNDERWOOD

STUFFED SUMMER SQUASH

Cut neck off of squash (about 8); hollow out seeds and pack with the
following meat mixture:

1 lb. good ground steak
½ C. raw rice
1 can of tomato sauce
1 small onion, chopped
    very fine

½ small green pepper,
    chopped fine
salt and pepper to taste

Mix well before packing in squashes. Then stand squashes upright
in a casserole. Pour 1 can of tomato sauce and 2 cans water in bottom of casserole. Add salt and pepper and ½ t. Worcestershire sauce
to sauce in dish. Bake in a 350° oven for 1 hour or until tender. Take
lid off to brown. Add water as necessary. Serve with sauce from pan.

CHARLES UNDERWOOD

BRUNSWICK STEW

1 large stewing hen disjointed
1 C. chopped onions
2 #2 cans whole kernel
    white corn
2 #2 cans baby lima beans
2 #2 cans tomatoes

½ bottle Worcestershire
    sauce
Tabasco and pepper sauce to
    taste
salt and cayenne pepper to
    taste

Brown chicken in bacon drippings. Remove to large pot, to which has
been added 4 C. boiling water. Brown onions in drippings and add to
chicken along with the tomatoes, 1 t. salt and cayenne pepper. Simmer covered until chicken falls from the bones. Remove bones and
add vegetables and seasonings. Continue cooking at least 30 minutes.
Serve hot as a hearty soup. Allow 6 hours for cooking. Add more water
if it seems too thick.

TOM HAPPEL

WOODMEN'S STEW

3½ lbs of good beef (select chuck or round) with a little suet
4 good sized onions   4 or 5 potatoes
Head of cabbage (red cabbage is tops)
several carrots
6 whole ripe tomatoes or 2 cans of tomatoes
Fresh corn from the cob or 1 can whole kernel corn
string beans (fresh or 1 can)   1 bunch celery
1 green pepper or several pimientoes
several hot peppers   ½ C. sour cream
Spices—2 bay leaves (important), salt, pepper, sprig of
thyme, 1 clove garlic crushed, sage (if desired), 2 to 3 t.
Worcestershire sauce.

Cut beef into 1½ inch cubes. Place in heavy frying pan; add 2 T.
lard or shortening and 2 T. butter or margarine. Let sizzle until well
browned. Stir to keep from burning. Don't be afraid to brown well;
this gives the natural color to your stew. Take a stew kettle — the
heavier it is the better, and pour meat and fat (scrape all the semi-
liquid out of pan) into the stew kettle. Add the diced onions and 2 C.
of water. Allow to simmer for 30 to 45 minutes. Add vegetables cut
into chunks. Dice green peppers before adding. If pimientoes are
large, cut them up; if small, leave whole. Leave hot peppers whole.
Add spices, salt and pepper to taste. Don't forget the bay leaves for
this makes the stew.

Cook the whole mixture slowly for 45 minutes. Stir only lightly to
keep from burning. Add water from time to time to keep from scorch-
ing and to provide about a quart of liquid. When cooked, add ½ C.
of sour cream, stir in 1 t. of flour and sufficient amount of liquid from
the stew to make a cupful. Stir this mixture well — add to the stew.
Stir lightly and allow to simmer for about 15 minutes.

(Note: The liquid may be poured off the stew before the cream and
flour are added. If you do this, add the cream and flour to the liquid,
let simmer and return to the stew. Caution: if you do this, don't leave
stew without liquid on hot stove or it will scorch.)
Will serve 5 to 6 persons.

EDGAR STOHLER

TENDERLOIN A' LA FIREPLACE

Marinate whole fillet of beef in mixture of Wesson Oil and olive oil
(approximately ¼ inch deep in roasting pan) to which has been added
chopped cloves of garlic. Marinate for at least 30 minutes.

Season with Dash (if desired) and sprinkle generously with Kosher salt.
Place in bed of low burning charcoal (fireplace with grate works fine).
Turn frequently to eliminate burning. Remove when thoroughly brown
(like a charcoal steak) to original pan. Cover with butter slices and
complete cooking in 325° oven. Test for desired doneness.

TOM HAPPEL

UNDARUSK (HUNGARIAN ROOSTER)

1 young rooster, cut up   1 t. paprika
1 large onion, cut up   1 t. salt
2 T. tomato puree

Dredge rooster in flour; brown in butter along with the onion. Add the tomato puree, seasonings and enough hot water to cover. Cover and cook slowly for 1½ hours. Remove the chicken and add ¾ C. cream to the broth. Cook a few minutes.

Serve with potatoes or rice.

BORGE CHRISTIANSEN

VENISON ROAST

Marinate roast for at least 48 hours in apple cider (the longer the better), turning from time to time. Dry the meat and rub with garlic. Then salt, pepper and flour. Brown on all sides in heavy pot over hot flame. Pour the cider it was soaked in over the meat and bake covered in a slow oven (325°) until tender, basting occasionally.

This meat is good on the rare side. The gravy made from the dripping is wonderful.

H. G. RANGE, SR.

HARRIS CANAPE SPREAD

1 small pkg. cream cheese   Worcestershire Sauce
1 small can tuna fish   and tabasco
mayonnaise

Use enough mayonnaise to make spreading consistency, and add the seasoning to taste. Wonderful on crackers.

ALLEN HARRIS, JR.

PIES

COCONUT CREAM PIE

2 egg yolks	1/8 t. salt
2/3 C. sugar	1 t. butter
1 C. milk	1 t. vanilla
3 T. flour	1 baked pie shell

Mix flour and sugar together. Add egg yolks, beaten. Scald milk and add mixture. Cook until thick. Fold in 2 stiffly beaten egg whites. Pour into baked pie shell and sprinkle top with coconut. Brown in hot oven.

MRS. RODNEY SKIPWORTH

BUTTER PECAN PIE

1 C. dark corn syrup	3 eggs, beaten
1/2 C. white sugar	1 t. vanilla
1/2 stick butter	1 C. pecans

Melt butter in saucepan and add remaining ingredients. Beat well and pour into unbaked pie shell. Sprinkle pecan meats over top. Bake in oven at 325° for 45 minutes.

SUE P. WALKER

MACAROON PIE

14 saltine crackers, rolled fine	3 egg whites, beaten
12 dates, cut fine	1/4 t. salt
1/2 C. pecans, cut fine	1 t. almond extract
1 C. sugar	

Mix all ingredients well and fold in beaten egg whites. Bake in buttered 9 inch pie pan for 45 minutes in 300° oven. Serve with whipped cream flavored with sherry and powdered sugar.

MRS. HELEN HALL

APPLE PIE

2 C. grated apples (very tart)	1 C. brown sugar
1/2 C. orange juice — dash of lemon juice	1/4 lb. butter

Mix apples, orange juice, lemon juice, and sugar. Pour into a pastry lined pie pan. Pour melted butter over top. Cover with top crust or twisted pastry strips. Bake in hot oven 425°F. about 45 minutes.

MRS. W. T. MATHES, JR.

RAISIN NUT PIE

Mix together and pour into unbaked pie shell:

2 eggs, well beaten	1/2 t. cloves
1 C. sugar	1/2 t. allspice
1/2 C. melted butter	1/2 C. nuts
2 t. vinegar	1/2 to 2/3 C. raisins
1/2 t. cinnamon	

Bake at 350° about 30 minutes or until set.

MRS. A. B. MARSH

CHOCOLATE ANGEL PIE

2 egg whites
pinch of salt
pinch of cream of tartar
½ C. sifted sugar
½ C. chopped pecans
½ t. vanilla

1 pkg. German sweet
chocolate
3 T. water
1 t. vanilla
1 C. whipped cream

Beat egg whites with salt and cream of tartar until foamy. Gradually add sifted sugar and beat until stiff peaks form. Fold in vanilla and pecans. Grease 8 inch pie plate with salad oil and pour in meringue. Bake at 300°F. 55 to 60 minutes. Let cool.

Melt chocolate in water, then cool. Mix whipped cream with chocolate and vanilla. Pour filling on top of meringue and chill 2 to 3 hours.

MRS. TOMMY GALLAGHER

LEMON MERINGUE PIE

1 C. sugar
¼ t. salt
5 T. cornstarch
2 C. water

3 egg yolks
5 T. lemon juice
2 t. grated lemon rind
2 T. butter

Mix sugar, cornstarch and salt in top of double boiler with ½ C. water. Blend in the rest of the water and stir constantly over low heat until the mixture boils. Cover and cook over low heat 10 minutes. Slowly stir in the egg yolks, juice, rind and butter. Cook one minute longer. Cool before pouring into baked 9 inch pie shell. Make meringue with the 3 egg whites, beaten stiffly with 6 T. sugar. Brown meringue in a 350° oven.

MRS. CHARLES COPAS

FROZEN LEMON PIE

3 beaten egg yolks
¼ C. lemon juice
½ t. grated lemon rind

1/3 t. salt
½ C. sugar

Combine these ingredients and cook until thick, stirring constantly. Beat 3 egg whites until stiff. Whip ½ pt. whipping cream and fold into sauce. Fold in stiffly beaten egg whites. Cover bottom of freezer dish with graham cracker crumbs. Pour cream mixture into it, and cover with graham cracker crumbs. Cover and leave in freezer until ready to use.

MRS. D. M. CHAMBERS, SR.

BUTTERSCOTCH PIE

Pastry for 9" pie:
¾ C. sifted flour
¼ t. salt

¼ C. shortening
2 T. water

Bake 15 minutes at 450°

Filling for pie:
¼ C. cornstarch
1 C. brown sugar (firmly
packed)
¼ t. salt

2 C. scalded milk
3 egg yolks
3 T. butter
1 t. vanilla

Mix cornstarch, sugar, salt and gradually add milk. Cook in double boiler until thick, stirring constantly. Add small amount of hot mixture to slightly beaten egg yolks; stir into remaining hot mixture for a few minutes; cool. Add butter and vanilla. Pour into baked pie shell.

MRS. ROBERT GRIFFITH

HEAVENLY PIE

1½ C. sugar	3 T. lemon juice
¼ t. cream of tartar	1 T. lemon rind
4 egg whites	⅛ t. salt
½ t. vanilla	1 pt. heavy cream
4 egg yolks	

Combine egg whites, cream of tartar, and vanilla. Beat until they stand in stiff, not dry, peaks. Slowly add 1 C. sugar, beating until meringue stands in very stiff glossy peaks. Spread over bottom and up sides of well greased 10 in. pan. Bake at 275° for 1 hour. Beat egg yolks slightly in double boiler top. Stir in ½ C. sugar, lemon juice, rind and salt. Cook, stirring until thick, about 10 minutes. When mixture cools, whip cream and fold custard into it. Put in meringue shell. Chill 12 to 24 hours.

MRS. B. G. YOUNG, JR.

FRENCH CHOCOLATE PIE

Cream: ½ C. butter
Add gradually ¾ C. sugar, creaming well
Blend in 1 sq. bitter chocolate, melted, and 1 t. vanilla
Add 2 whole eggs one at a time, beating 5 minutes after each.
Pour mixture into baked 8 inch pie crust. Chill for 3-4 hours in refrigerator so that it can set well. Decorate edge of pie with whipped cream and with several whole pecans or walnuts.

MRS. EDWIN H. HUNTER

CHOCOLATE CREAM PIE

2½ sq. chocolate	½ t. salt
2½ C. milk	3 egg yolks, slightly beaten
1 C. sugar	2 T. butter
6 T. flour	1 t. vanilla

Add chocolate to milk and heat in a double boiler. When chocolate is melted, beat with rotary beater until blended. Add the combined mixture of sugar, flour and salt to the chocolate mixture. Cook until thickened, stirring constantly. Then cook 10 minutes stirring occasionally. Pour small amount over egg yolks, stirring well. Return to double boiler and cook 2 minutes longer. Add butter and vanilla. Cool and turn into a baked pie shell. Cover with 1 pt. of cream that has been whipped and sweetened. Refrigerate several hours before serving.

MRS. HARRY CRUMLEY

SOUR CHERRY PUDDING PIE

1 C. sugar	1 C. milk
1/3 C. butter or margarine	¼ t. salt
2 t. baking powder	2 C. flour

Cream sugar and butter together. Add dry ingredients alternately with milk. Pour evenly into a 9x12x2 greased pudding pan.

2 C. pitted sour cherries (fresh or frozen are better)
2 C. sugar
1/3 C. butter or margarine, melted
2 C. hot water

Mix all ingredients together until sugar is dissolved and pour over batter in pudding pan. Try to distribute cherries. Bake in 350° oven for 45 minutes. Serve warm with cream or vanilla ice cream.

MRS. J. B. McNIEL

BLACK BOTTOM PIE

35 ginger snaps, crumbled
½ C. butter (or margarine) melted

Mix and pat into 9 inch pie pan; bake 30 minutes at 300°.

2 C. milk, scalded	**2 t. rum extract**
½ C. sugar	**1 T. gelatin**
1½ T. cornstarch	**4 egg whites**
4 egg yolks, beaten	**1 C. cream, whipped**
1½ sq. chocolate, melted	**2 T. sugar**
1 t. vanilla	**bitter chocolate**
¼ t. cream of tartar	

Mix sugar and cornstarch and add to scalded milk. Add beaten egg yolks and cook until thickened. To half this custard add melted chocolate and vanilla. Pour into pie crust. To other half of hot custard add cream of tartar, rum extract and gelatin which has been softened in with 2 T. of cold water. Fold in beaten egg whites and pour this mixture on top of chocolate mixture. Serve with whipped cream topping. Grate bitter chocolate over top of whipped cream. Make the day before needed and keep in refrigerator.

MRS. HAL LITTLEFORD, JR.

WHITE CHRISTMAS PIE

1 T. plain gelatin	**¼ C. water**
½ C. sugar	**4 T. flour**
½ t. salt	**1½ C. milk**
¾ t. vanilla	**¼ t. almond extract**
½ C. whipping cream, whipped	**3 egg whites**
¼ t. cream of tartar	**½ C. sugar**
1 C. moist shredded coconut	

Soften gelatin in cold water. Mix together in saucepan: flour, ½ C. sugar and salt. Stir in milk gradually. Cook over low heat, stirring until it boils. Boil 1 minute. Remove from heat. Stir in softened gelatin and cool. When partially set, beat with rotary beater until smooth. Blend in vanilla and almond extract. Fold in cream. Beat egg whites with cream of tartar until stiff. Gradually add ½ C. sugar and beat until sugar dissolves. Fold meringue into custard mixture. Fold in coconut. Pile in pastry shell. Sprinkle with coconut. Chill 2 hours and serve cold.

MRS. W. W. BALES

PINEAPPLE GRAHAM CRACKER PIE

½ C. butter	**4 T. sugar**
16 graham crackers	**4 T. flour**

Cream butter; add graham crackers rolled fine; add flour. Shape onto sides of the pan as a crust.

Filling:

1 pkg. lemon jello	**1 C. cream, whipped**
1 #2 can crushed pineapple	**2 T. sugar**

Drain pineapple thoroughly. Make the gelatin according to directions on package using the pineapple juice as part of the liquid. Add pineapple. When almost set fold in the whipped cream and sugar. Pour into graham cracker crust and chill for several hours before serving.

MRS. PAUL FOXX

SOUR CREAM RAISIN PIE

3 egg yolks
1 C. sugar
½ C. chopped seedless raisins
1 C. sour cream
1 T. corn starch

½ t. cinnamon
½ t. allspice
½ t. cloves
½ C. chopped nuts
dash salt

Mix sugar and cream. Add remaining ingredients and cook until thick. Cool and pour into baked pie shell. Cover with meringue.

MRS. WILBUR KENNEDY

CHERRY PIE

2 C. canned sweetened
   red cherries
2 T. cornstarch
3 T. sugar

⅛ t. salt
1 C. cherry juice
1 T. butter
1 recipe plain pastry

Drain cherries, saving juice. Mix cornstarch, sugar and salt; add juice gradually and cook slowly until smooth and thickened. Add butter and cherries. Cool. Pour into unbaked pie shell and cover with top crust. Bake at 450° for 15 minutes; reduce heat to 350° and bake for 25 minutes longer.

MRS. O. K. GARLAND

CHESS PIE I

1 C. brown sugar (packed)
½ C. white sugar
1 T. flour
2 eggs

2 T. milk
1 t. vanilla
½ C. melted butter
1 C. pecans

Heat oven to 350°. Mix brown sugar, white sugar and flour. Beat in thoroughly: the eggs, milk, vanilla and butter. Fold in nuts. Pour into pastry lined pie pan. Bake 50 to 60 minutes. Serve slightly warm, plain, or with whipped cream.

MRS. C. C. GOODSON

FUDGE PIE

Melt: 1 stick butter and 2 sqs. chocolate
Sift: ¼ C. flour, dash salt, 1 C. sugar

Beat: 2 eggs. Add dry ingredients and beat well. Add 1 t. vanilla and butter and chocolate to above mixture and pour into greased pie dish. Cook 20-25 minutes in 325° oven. Serve with ice cream or whipped cream. Nuts are optional.

MRS. JACK MILLER, JR.

PECAN DATE PIE

3 eggs	1 C. chopped dates
1 C. white corn syrup	½ C. sugar
1½ C. milk	1 C. chopped pecans
3 T. flour	1 t. vanilla
1 T. butter	

Mix sugar and flour. Add milk, eggs, syrup, butter and dates. Cook until thick. Cool. Add nuts and vanilla. Serve in cooked pastry shells.

MRS. LEON ROWAN
Memphis, Tenn.

PUMPKIN PIE

1 t. ginger	2 eggs
1 t. cinnamon	1 small can evaporated milk
¼ C. hot water	1¼ C. strained pumpkin
⅞ C. brown sugar	2½ T. orange juice
½ t. salt	

Make a smooth paste of the spices and water. Add this, with the sugar, salt and eggs, to the pumpkin. Blend thoroughtly. Then add milk, heated to the scalding point, and orange juice. Pour into unbaked pie shell. Start pie baking in 425° oven. After 15 minutes, decrease to 300° and bake until pie passes the clean knife test. (35 to 45 minutes).

MRS ADA HORNSBY EARNEST

STRAWBERRY PIE

1 qt. fresh strawberries	1 small package cream cheese
1 C. sugar	1 baked pie shell
3 T. cornstarch	½ pint whipping cream

Thin cream cheese with a little cream and spread it in the pie shell. Cover with a layer of nicest berries. Mash remaining berries and cook with sugar and cornstarch until mixture turns thick and clear. Let cool, and pour over berries in pie shell. Top with whipped cream. Chill for several hours.

MRS. JOHN LAWSON

APPLE DUMPLINGS

Pastry: sift together; **2¼ C. sifted flour and ¾ t. salt.** Cut, with pastry knives, **½ C. shortening** into flour until it looks like meal. Cut in remaining **¼ C. shortening** to the sizes of peas. Sprinkle over the mixture **5 T. ice water,** mixing enough to make dough stick together. Round into a ball. Let stand a few minutes to make dough easier to handle. Roll out dough ⅛ inch thick on slightly floured board. Cut in 6 to 7 inch squares.

Now: pare and core **6 medium apples** and place one on each square of pastry. Fill cavities of apples with mixture of:

½ C. sugar	½ t. cinnamon

Dot with **1 T. butter** and pull 4 corners of pastry square up around apple and pinch together at top of apple. Place 2 inches apart in a 9 x 13 x 2 pan.

Sauce: boil together for 3 minutes:

1 C. sugar	2 C. water
4 T. butter	¼ t. cinnamon

Pour over dumplings. Bake 40 to 45 minutes in hot oven, 425°. Baste often. (Children love these.)

MRS. TOM McKEE

BROWN SUGAR PIE

3 C. brown sugar, packed   ½ C. cream
3 eggs   juice of ½ lemon
½ C. butter, melted   1 t. vanilla

Mix sugar, melted butter, eggs, and beat well. Add other ingredients and pour into unbaked pie crust. This makes 2 medium pies. Pecans are good sprinkled over top.

MRS. ADAM BOWMAN

PASTRY SHELLS

2¼ C. flour   ¾ C. shortening
1½ t. salt   4 to 6 T. cold water

Sift flour with salt. Cut in shortening until mixture is granular. Sprinkle water over mixture, blending lightly with fork. Add water sparingly until dough clings together but is not wet. Let stand 5 minutes before rolling. Makes 2 - 9 inch crusts.

MRS. F. B. POTEAT

ANGEL FOOD PIE

1 C. sugar   3 T. cornstarch
1 C. water   2 T. flour
1 small can pineapple   3 beaten egg whites
1 T. lemon juice   ½ pt. whipped cream

Boil together sugar, water, pineapple and lemon juice. Mix with cornstarch and flour and cook until thick. Cool. Add beaten egg whites and pour into baked shell (8 or 9-in.) and chill. Spread top with whipped cream and sprinkle with coconut.

MRS. J. H. THOMPSON

CHESS PIE II

3 beaten eggs   ½ lb. butter (a little less)
1 C. milk   2 T. flour (level)
2½ C. white sugar

Pour hot melted butter over other ingredients. Pour mixture into two medium pie pans lined with uncooked pastry. Pre-heat oven and bake at 400° until pie begins to brown. Reduce heat to 250°. Bake approximately 45 minutes in all.

MRS. W. H. LANCASTER

KEY LIME PIE

A specialty of the Keys is lime pie, made from the famed Key limes, but equally good when made from the limes purchased at the super market or corner grocery.

4 eggs   1 lime rind, grated fine
1 C. sugar   ½ t. salt
1 T. gelatin   2 tsp. Angostura bitters
½ C. lime juice

Beat egg yolks. Add ½ C. sugar, lime juice, and salt. Cook in double boiler until the mixture coats on spoon. Remove from heat and add gelatin (which has been softened in ½ C. cold water), bitters, and rind. Mix well until mixture begins to thicken. Then fold in beaten egg whites to which the remaining ½ C. sugar has been added. Pour into baked pie crust. Spread with whipped cream just before serving.

MRS. RICHARD C. MILLER

FRUIT PIE DELIGHT

Pastry: Make a pastry shell for a 9-inch pie pan and put in refrigerator for 2 or 3 hours before baking. Bake before filling and cool.
Fruit: About ¾ qt. strawberries or other fruit
    1 C. sugar, or sweetened to taste   1 T. lemon juice
    (Save a few whole strawberries for garnish. Halve each remaining berry.)
Add sugar and lemon juice to strawberries and let stand at room temperature for at least two hours. Drain off liquid before adding to filling.
Filling:

1½ C. milk	¾ C. sugar
¼ t. salt	3 T. flour, level
3 egg yolks	1 T. butter
½ t. vanilla	1 pt. whipped cream

Scald one cup of milk over boiling water. Mix sugar, salt, flour, and remaining milk together. Stir into hot milk and cook slowly until thickened, stirring constantly. Cover and cook over boiling water for five minutes. Add mixture slowly to egg yolks and cook one minute longer. Add butter and vanilla. Cool. Pour into baked and cooled pastry shell. Add drained fruit. Top with one pint whipped cream. Top with whole fruit.

MRS. MAURICE D. CARPENTER

PEACH CAKE COBBLER

2 C. sweetened peaches	½ C. milk
fresh, frozen or canned	¾ C. sugar
1 C. flour	2 T. butter or margarine
1 t. baking powder	

Heat fruit in 3 inch baking pan. Make batter of remaining ingredients and pour evenly over fruit. Pour ½ C. boiling water over batter. Bake at 325° until done, 30 to 35 minutes.
Cherries, apples or berries may be used in this cobbler.

MRS. CHARLES BOLTON

PUMPKIN CHIFFON PIE

1 9" baked pie shell
In ¼ C. cold water, soak 1 T. gelatin
Beat slightly 3 egg yolks
Add:

½ C. sugar	¼ t. salt
1¼ C. canned pumpkin	1 t. pumpkin pie spice
½ C. milk	(more or less to taste)

Cook and stir these ingredients over hot water until they are thick. Stir in the soaked gelatin until it is dissolved. Cool. When pumpkin mixture begins to set, stir in the well beaten egg whites to which has been added another ½ C. sugar. Fill the pie shell. Chill for several hours. Serve plain or garnished with whipped cream.

MRS. JAMES HOLMES

MOLASSES PIE

4 eggs	½ C. molasses
½ C. butter	2 T. flour
½ C. sugar	

Mix above ingredients and pour into unbaked pie shell. Bake until firm in 350° oven.

MRS. ROBERT MORRIS

CHEESE PIE

1 (16 oz.) container cottage cheese
½ C. sugar
2 eggs, beaten
1 T. lemon juice
¾ C. milk
1 T. flour, mixed with water
½ T. melted butter
Cinnamon

Strain cottage cheese. Add other ingredients (except cinnamon). Stir thoroughly. Pour into pie shell. Dust with cinnamon. Bake 10 minutes in 325 degree oven; then, 40 minutes in 300 degree oven. It is done when knife, which is inserted in center of pie, comes out clean.

Mrs. C. E. Jacobs

CHOCOLATE CHESS PIE

MELT:
1 stick butter   and   1½ sq. chocolate
ADD:
1 C. sugar
2 beaten eggs
2 T. cream
½ t. vanilla

Pour into unbaked pie shell and place in oven at 350 degrees for 35 minutes.

Mrs. Alfred Abernethy

LEMON CHESS PIE

2 C. white sugar   and   1 T. corn meal
1 T. flour
Toss above lightly
ADD:
4 unbeaten eggs,
one at a time
¼ C. melted butter
¼ C. lemon juice
2 t. grated lemon rind
¼ C. milk

Place in 9" pie shell and bake at 350 degrees for 35 to 45 minutes, or until top is golden brown. Do not let brown too quickly.

Mrs. Sam W. Mitchell

CHOCOLATE LIME PARFAIT PIE

DISSOLVE:
1 C. boiling water   and   1 package lime jello
ADD:
1 t. plain gelatin   1 pt. ice cream, vanilla

Stir until melted. Chill until mixture thickens but not set (about 20 to 30 minutes). Fold in ½ cup grated chocolate. Pour in baked pie shell. Chill. Good with chocolate cookie or graham cracker pie crust.

Mrs. Horace Cupp

GERMAN CHOCOLATE PIE

1 T. flour	2 T. cornstarch
1 C. sugar	¼ C. butter
1 egg	1 t. vanilla
2 T. water	½ C. chopped pecans
1¼ T. cocoa	⅛ t. salt
1 small can evap. milk	½ C. grated coconut

Mix flour, cornstarch, cocoa, salt and sugar. Blend in egg and butter. Mix together vanilla, milk and water; then combine with other mixture with a spoon. Using electric mixer, beat for 5 min. Fold in coconut and nuts. Pour into a 9" unbaked pie shell and bake at 350 degrees for 45 min. Delicious.   Mrs. Hugh J. Warren

MARGIE'S CHOCOLATE BAR PIE

3 broken Hershey with Almond bars	⅓ C. milk
18 marshmallows	½ pt. whipping cream

Melt marshmallows and milk in top of double boiler. Remove from heat. Add chocolate bars. Stir. Let stand and cool. Whip cream and fold in. Pour into 8" cooked pie shell (or graham cracker crust). Refrigerate at least 3 hours.   Mrs. Ballard H. Blevins

CRUNCH PIE

6 C. of sliced fruit (apples or fresh peaches)	1 C. flour
1½ C. sugar	1 egg, beaten
1 t. baking powder	Pinch of salt
	½ C. butter

Fill baking dish with fruit that has been mixed with 1 cup sugar. Combine flour, ½ cup sugar, baking powder and salt. Add beaten egg to dry mixture. Mix until crumbly. Spread over fruit, melt butter and spread over entire mixture. Bake 1 hour at 350 degrees.
                    Mrs. W. H. Lancaster

HOT WATER PASTRY

3 C. flour	1 C. shortening
½ t. baking powder	½ C. boiling water
½ t. salt	

Let shortening melt in boiling water. Cool; beat until creamy. Stir in dry ingredients and mix well. Chill in refrigerator at least 1 hour before using. This will keep in refrigerator as long as two weeks. Will make 3-9 inch pie shells.   Mrs. Carl Jones

GRASSHOPPER PIE

CRUST:

1¼ C. crushed chocolate   and   ⅓ C. melted butter
cookie wafers

Pat into a pie pan and chill.

FILLING:

⅔ C. milk, scalded   and   24 marshmallows

Add marshmallows to milk and melt slowly in double boiler, stirring often.   Cool to room temperature.

ADD:

2 oz. green Creme de Menthe 1 oz. white Creme de Cacao

Whip and fold ½ pt. whipping cream into above. Pour into chocolate crust and freeze. Serve with whipped cream if you wish.

Mrs. Leland Lancaster

OATMEAL PIE

2 eggs, beaten	¾ C. corn syrup
¾ C. white sugar	¾ C. oatmeal
¾ C. coconut	⅔ C. butter
½ C. nuts	

Mix and pour in unbaked pie shell. Bake at 350 degrees until done, about 1 hr.

Mrs. Roy W. Curtis

PEACH CREAM CHEESE PIE

1 baked pie shell	¼ C. lemon juice
1 can Eagle Brand milk	

Mix milk and juice together. Add one 3 oz. package softened cream cheese. Add 2 egg yolks - one at a time and mix well after each one. Beat egg whites for top. Fold into cream cheese mixture 1 cup peaches. Pour into shell, top with egg whites, and bake at 350 degrees till golden brown.

Mrs. Fredrick Brandt

PECAN PIE

1 C. Karo (white)	½ C. sugar (white)
1 T. butter	2 oz. pecans
3 eggs	Pinch salt

Secret to this recipe is in the beating! Combine ingredients and beat with hand mixer at least 5 min. or longer. Pour in 9" unbaked pie shell. Sprinkle pecan meats on top. Baking time 45 minutes to 1 hour. Bake 10 minutes at 325 degrees then lower heat to 300 degrees for remainder of time or until won't shake in center.

Mrs. D. M. Chambers, Jr.

PUMPKIN PIE

1 C. pumpkin	1 t. vanilla
1 C. white sugar	1 t. cinnamon
1 C. evaporated milk	3 eggs
Pinch salt	

Beat all ingredients together with electric mixer. Pour into unbaked pie shell (12" pyrex). Bake at 325 degrees for 10 minutes then at 300 degrees for 35 minutes or until knife comes out clean.

Mrs. D. M. Chambers, Jr.

OLE' FASHIONED TENNESSEE PUMPKIN PIE

1 C. pumpkin	1 C. sugar
2 whole eggs	1 T. flour
1 C. milk	1 T. melted butter
4 T. whiskey	1 t. cinnamon
1 t. nutmeg	1 t. ginger

Mix all ingredients well. Pour into unbaked pie crust. Bake 5 minutes at 425 degrees and then reduce heat to 325 degrees and cook until firm.

Mrs. G. L. Reynolds

STRAWBERRY RHUBARB PIE

3 beaten eggs	½ t. nutmeg
1¼ C. sugar	2½ C. rhubarb-1" (fresh)
¼ C. flour	1½ C. strawberries (fresh)
¼ t. salt	

Combine eggs, sugar, flour, salt and nutmeg. Mix well. Combine strawberries and rhubarb and place in a 9" pastry filled pan. Pour egg mixture over fruit and beat with butter-1 Tbs. or more. Bake in hot oven (400 degrees) for about 40 minutes.

Mrs. Wayne Alexander

RITZ BLITZ

20 Ritz crackers, crushed	½ t. almond flavoring
1 C. sugar	(optional)
1 t. baking powder	½ C. nuts
1 t. vanilla	3 egg whites

Combine all dry ingredients; Fold in stiffly beaten egg whites and flavoring. Put into pie plate and bake 25 minutes at 350 degrees. Cool. Top with 1 cup whipped cream. Chill 2 hours.

Mrs. C. C. Marshall

TOLL HOUSE PIE

Double Toll House Cookie receipe or any good brownie receipe. Bake in two 8" greased pie pans or large pie pan. Don't overbake. Remove from oven and cover pies at once with a lot of minature marshmallows. Next pour warm fudge icing over the top of pies. Serve with vanilla ice cream or just eat plain.

RUM PIE

Soak **1 T. gelatin** in **¼ C. cold water.** Cook until thick in top of double boiler:

1 C. milk
3 slightly beaten egg yolks   **½ C. sugar**

Remove from heat and add gelatin mixture. When cool, add **2 T. rum or sherry** or **1 t. vanilla.** Fold in **3 stiffly beaten egg whites,** to which has been added **¼ t. salt.** Pour into a 9 inch baked pie shell. Chill until set, at least 3 to 4 hours. Top with **1 C. whipping cream** which has been whipped with **3 T. powdered sugar.** Grate **chocolate** over the top.

MRS. HARRY MYRON

OLD FASHIONED EGG CUSTARD PIE

3 C. milk   **¼ t. salt**
3 eggs   **1 t. vanilla**
½ C. sugar   **nutmeg gratings, if desired**

Roll pastry and place in pie plate. Be sure it is flat on the dish so that no air bubbles are beneath. Place in refrigerator for 1 hour. Scald milk. Beat eggs slightly. Add sugar, salt, and vanilla. Slowly add scalded milk to mixture and pour into chilled crust. Bake at 450° for 15 minutes, reduce heat to 325° and bake another 25 minutes.

MRS. D. M. CHAMBERS, SR.

LEMON CHIFFON PIE

1 envelope plain gelatin   **½ t. salt**
¼ C. water   **1½ t. grated lemon rind**
6 eggs, separated   **6 T. lemon juice**
1 C. sugar   **1 C. heavy cream, whipped**

Soften gelatin in 2 T. water. Combine slightly beaten egg yolks, ½ C. sugar, salt, lemon rind and juice and remaining 2 T. water. Cook over boiling water until mixture thickens, stirring constantly. Add softened gelatin, stirring until gelatin is dissolved. Cool until mixture begins to thicken. Gradually beat remaining ½ C. sugar into stiffly beaten egg whites and fold into lemon gelatin mixture. Turn into baked pastry shell and chill until firm. When ready to serve, top with whipped cream.

MS. ALFRED COSTNER

ENGLISH APPLE PIE

MIX:

¾ C. sugar	and	½ C. flour
1 egg		1 t. baking powder

ADD:

½ C. chopped pecan	1 C. apple (chopped) any kind

Mix well and pour into greased pie pan. Bake 30 minutes at 350 degrees. (You just press this mixture into pan - it doesn't matter how you mix it - it always turns out okay).
Serve with whipped cream or ice cream.   Mrs. G. L. Reynolds

BLACKBERRY FAMILY PIE

1 C. flour	½ C. sugar to berries
1 t. baking powder	2 C. sweetened blackberries
½ t. salt	¾ stick butter
½ C. milk	

Make batter of first 4 ingredients. Melt butter in 2 qt. baking dish (oven) and pour in batter, then the blackberries. Cook at 400 degrees until brown. The batter rises to the top to form a crust that has seeped through the berries and flavored by them. Any sweetened berries may be substituted.   Mrs. Jack Seaton

BROWNIE PIE

3 egg whites	½ C. chopped walnuts or
Dash salt	pecans
¾ C. sugar	½ t. vanilla
¾ C. fine chocolate wafer crumbs	Sweetened whipped cream

Beat egg whites and salt till soft peaks form; gradually add sugar, beating till stiff peaks form. Fold in crumbs, nuts and vanilla; spread evenly in lightly buttered 9" pie pan. Bake in slow (325 degrees) oven about 35 minutes. Cool thoroughly. Spread top with sweetened whipped cream; chill well, 3 to 4 hours. Trim with curls of shaved unsweetened chocolate.   Mrs. Ben Kelly

BUTTERMILK PIE

¼ C. butter	2 T. flour
1½ C. sugar	½ C. buttermilk
3 eggs	1 t. almond flavoring
1 9" unbaked pie shell	

Cream butter and sugar together and add eggs one at a time. Sprinkle in flour and then add buttermilk and flavoring. Lemon flavoring may be used instead of almond. Bake at 350 degrees for about 30 minutes in unbaked pie shell until firm to touch.

Mrs. Vernon Wilson

POULTRY & GAME

BRUNSWICK STEW (Very Old)

First get your chickens, wash and cut them
And in an iron pot you put them;
Add water nearly to the top
And in it salt and pepper drop
Boil slowly, now your tomatoes peel
Put in a slim or so of veal.
And for flavor bear in mind
A chuck of middling with the rind.
Next some onions you throw in
The young and tender skin.
And butter beans do not forget
And what is more important yet
The corn; but do not be too fast
This you must grate and add at last
For better than the flour you'll find it'll do
To give a thickness to the stew.
Some lemon peel cut very thin
May now be added and stirred in,
And ere it's taken from the fire
Give it a dash of Worcestershire.
And soon you will hear the praises ring
This is a dish fit for a King.

1 large hen cut up
¼ lb. veal or veal bone

¼ lb. of side bacon (cut up)

Cover with water and add:

¼ t. pepper
1 t. salt
3 small onions

3 tomatoes, peeled
1 pt. green butter beans

Cook until tender; then add:

3 ears of grated corn
small amount of lemon peel,
cut fine

dash of Worcestershire sauce

Serve hot.

MRS. CHARLES PISTON

BRUNSWICK STEW

Take one 3 lb. chicken. Cut up and put over fire with one half gallon water. Let stew until bones can be removed. Add ½ doz. large tomatoes, or one large can, one pint of butterbeans, corn cut from ½ doz. ears, four large Irish potatoes (diced), 1 good sized onion, 1 lb. okra, 2 strips bacon, cut in pieces. Season with butter, pepper and salt. Cook down until thick enough to be eaten with a fork.

MRS. WALTER HANKINS

BAKED CHICKEN IN SAVORY SAUCE

1 2½ to 3½ lb. chicken, quartered and coated with flour that has been seasoned with salt, pepper, paprika, oregano and curry or basil. Melt ¼ C. butter in 2 qt. casserole; add chicken and bake in 400° oven until tender and golden brown.

Make sauce of:

2 T. butter   2. T. flour
2 chicken bouillon cubes in ¾ C. water
½ C. white wine

Top chicken with 2 tomatoes (sliced), scallions, mushrooms and sauce and return to oven for about 20 minutes.

MRS. E. MALCOLM CAMPBELL

BARBECUED CHICKEN

1 fryer — 3 - 3½ lbs.   2 T. brown sugar
¼ C. shortening   3 T. Worcestershire sauce
1 C. chopped onion   2 T. vinegar
½ C. chopped celery   1 t. salt
1 C. water   1½ t. prepared mustard
1 C. catsup   dash red pepper
¼ C. lemon juice

Brown chicken in hot fat. Combine remaining ingredients; simmer 30 minutes. Place chicken in shallow baking dish. Pour sauce over. Bake uncovered in moderate oven (350°F.) 1 hour or until tender. Serves 6.

MRS. BERNIE SPENCER

BARBECUED CHICKEN

Dress as for broiling 2 frying chickens. Dust with flour and pepper. Place in broiling pan with 2 C. water, ¼ C. vinegar, 2 T. Worcestershire sauce, 1 medium sized onion (sliced), juice of 1 lemon, red pepper, salt, and ¼ lb. butter.

Place in oven at 450°F. for 20 minutes. Reduce to 300°F. and cook for 2 hours, basting with sauce frequently. Serve on platter with sauce over it; garnish with parsley and sliced tomatoes.

MRS. C. S. CAMP

CHICKEN A LA KING

In a sauce pan place 2 t. butter, ¼ lb. peeled sliced fresh mushrooms and 1 diced green pepper. Saute about 2 minutes and dredge with 1 T. flour. Add 2 cups of cream, 2 cups diced breast of fowl, 1 t. salt, 1 diced pimiento and season with a little white pepper. Allow to cook until sauce thickens.

Just before serving, take the yolks of 2 eggs and add 2 t. sherry wine. Beat well and add to mixture, not allowing to come to a boil.

Serve in a chafing dish or casserole with fresh toast on the side. Makes 4 generous servings.

MRS. GLENN MILLER

CHICKEN AND ALMONDS

1 (4 lb) chicken	1 C. almonds, quartered
3 small onions	3 t. salt
½ chopped green pepper	4 t. butter
3 C. cooked rice	¼ t. pepper
2 C. tomato juice	pinch of saffron

Cook chicken in boiling water to cover. Add salt, pepper and one onion. Simmer, covered, about 2 hours or until tender. Remove and cool. Strain stock for later use. Separate chicken from bones and cut in small pieces. Chop remaining two onions and saute in butter about 5 minutes. Add green pepper and cook about 3 minutes. Stir in rice, tomato juice, saffron, remaining salt and 1 cup of chicken stock. Finally add chicken and almonds and heat thoroughly. Serve at once with or without Parmesan cheese sprinkled over top.

MRS. C. B. COE

CHICKEN BREASTS BAKED IN WINE

1 package frozen chicken breasts (let thaw if you have time)
1 can cream of chicken soup, condensed
1 can mushroom soup, condensed

4 T. minced parsley	4 T. slivered, blanched
2 cloves garlic, slivered	almonds
	½ C. sherry or white wine

Mix soups together; add sherry and garlic. Place half of the chicken breasts in casserole. Cover with soup mixture and then sprinkle parsley and almonds on top. Add remaining breasts and repeat, having parsley and almonds on top. Cover and cook in oven 1½ hours at 350°F.

Serve with rice and have extra sauce in a gravy boat to pass.

MRS. ALICE FRIBERG

CHICKEN AND YELLOW RICE

2 fryers cut up	½ pt. salad or olive oil
1 onion	2 cloves garlic
1 green pepper	1 bay leaf
1½ qts. water	saffron
1 lb. rice	salt to taste
1 can tomatoes	

Cut chickens and saute in oil with onion and garlic. When done, add tomatoes and water. Boil 5 minutes. Add bay leaf, salt, saffron and green pepper. Pour over rice in baking dish or roaster and cook until rice is done. Garnish with green peas and pimiento strips.

MRS. R. A. LACY, JR.

CHICKEN CASSEROLE

1 C. cooked chicken
1 can cream of mushroom soup
1 can cream of chicken soup
1 small can mushrooms
1 small jar pimiento, chopped
½ C. slivered almonds (save some to sprinkle on top)
2 C. Chinese noodles

1 C. celery, chopped

1 small can evaporated milk

Mix all ingredients together and pour into casserole. Bake about 30 minutes in 350° oven. This can be placed in a pan of water while baking to keep it from getting dry.

MRS. ROBERT DENNIS

CHICKEN COUNTRY KITCHEN

2 fryers
¼ lb. currants
2 onions, medium size
2 small cans of tomatoes
1 large Bell pepper
½ lb. toasted almonds

2 T. curry powder
2 cloves garlic
¼ t. thyme
½ bunch celery
1½ t. salt

Fry chicken in fat. Chop all vegetables. Add seasonings and cook in chicken gravy 15 minutes. Put chicken in roaster with vegetables, half of almonds and currants. Cook over 3 hours. Make rice ring and sprinkle with rest of almonds and currants.

MRS. C. W. SULLIVAN
Atlanta, Ga.

CHICKEN CURRY

1 large onion
3 or 4 lb. stewing chicken
2 large cloves of garlic
1½ T. curry powder
(rounded) or to taste
salt to taste
1 t. ginger

3 T. olive oil
1 t. sugar
3 T. flour
1 large coconut, grated
4 C. milk (3 coconut milk
and 1 plain milk)

Stew jointed chicken with 2 or 3 slices of onion, 2 bay leaves, salt, pepper, and enough water to cover. Cook with tight lid until chicken will slip from bone. Cut in 2 inch pieces. Make coconut cream by pouring 1 C. scalded milk over grated coconut. Set aside 1 hour in warm place. Then squeeze until coconut is dry. Repeat process 2 more times. Discard this coconut.

Peel onion and garlic. Fry all in olive oil until light brown. Add flour mixed with curry powder, ginger and sugar. Cook 5 minutes slowly. Add 1 C. milk, **second** and **third** coconut milk. Let cook in top of double boiler ¾ hour and add chicken. Cook 15 minutes, stirring often. Just before serving, add salt, and **first** coconut cream.

Serve over rice with the following toppings: chutney, pickled pineapple, chopped peanuts, grated coconut, chopped green onion, hard cooked chopped egg and chopped crisp bacon.

MRS. BEN HALL

CHICKEN CHOP SUEY

1 onion, chopped
1 C. chopped celery
1 chicken, cooked and
    chopped
chicken broth

1 t. bead molasses
1 T. soy sauce
1 t. corn starch
1 can chop suey vegetables

Brown onion and celery in chicken fat or shortening. Add meat from chicken and all the broth. Let simmer until onion and celery are tender. Add vegetables. Before serving, add bead molasses and soy sauce which have been blended with the corn starch. Add sauteed mushrooms, if desired. Serve with heated Chinese noodles.

MISS EVINE JENNINGS

CHICKEN DISH

¼ C. chopped green pepper
1 T. grated onion
¼ C. butter
¼ C. flour
1 C. chicken stock
1 C. canned milk
½ t. salt
⅛ t. white pepper

2 T. pimiento
½ t. A-1 Sauce (add last)
½ t. Worcestershire sauce
3 C. chicken (good sized
    pieces)
2 egg yolks, well beaten
½ C. cold chicken stock

Brown green pepper and onion in butter. Blend in flour. Add stock and cream or canned milk. Cook until thick. Stir constantly. Add salt, pepper, pimiento, and chicken. Cook 20 minutes in double boiler. Just before serving, stir in beaten egg yolks mixed with ½ C. cold stock. Add A-1 and Worcestershire. Serve on squares of toasted corn bread.

MRS. FLOYD DOOLEY

CHICKEN IN HORSERADISH SAUCE

1 young hen (5 lbs.), cut in 8 serving pieces
Sauce:

3½ C. cream
1 C. broth
½ C. horseradish
3 T. vinegar

½ stick butter
½ C. flour
3 t. sugar

Cut chicken in pieces. Cover with as little water as possible; cover and cook until tender. When done, remove to a heated platter and cover with sauce.

To prepare the sauce: melt butter; add flour; blend in chicken broth and milk, a little at a time. Mix together sugar, vinegar, horseradish, and salt to taste; add to cream mixture. Cook until thick and pour over the chicken.

MRS. JOHN ROSE

CHICKEN LOAF

Grind or cut finely 3 C. cooked chicken. Add 2 C. crushed crackers, 3 eggs beaten separately and 1 pt. cream. Mix egg yolks with the cream and crackers. Then add ½ C. chicken broth and 2 t. baking powder. Fold in stiffly beaten egg whites.

Steam one hour in a well greased mold.

Serve with a mushroom sauce.

MRS. HANES LANCASTER, JR.

CHICKEN LUZON

1 frying chicken (about 3 pounds)	3 limes
salt and pepper to taste	1/3 C. salad oil
3 T. soya sauce	1½ C. brown rice
	3 C. water

Cut the chicken into serving pieces; salt and pepper and rub with 2 T. of the soya sauce. Slice one lime into thin slices, discarding the end slices. Fry chicken and lime slices in hot salad oil, squeezing the juice of another lime over the chicken as it cooks 40 minutes or until done. Meanwhile steam brown rice in 3 C. water for about 40 minutes. Pour the third tablespoon soya sauce and juice of the other lime over the rice. Serve with chicken. Serves 4.

Although this recipe is unusually simple, you will find one of the few really new taste sensations.

MRS. RICHARD C. MILLER

CHICKEN MAGNANI

Cut and dredge 1 fryer. Heat ¼ C. olive oil and ¼ C. salad oil and brown chicken in oil. Put in casserole. Saute in same oil ¼ C. onion, 3 T. green pepper and 1 clove garlic. Add ½ C. chopped carrots and ½ C. celery. Put on top of browned chicken. Pour over all ½ C. tomato juice. Add small can of peas. Bake in 350°F. oven for 1 hour. Sprinkle chopped olives (green or ripe) and mushrooms over top of baked dish.

MRS. FORREST TRAYLOR

CHICKEN MERINGO

Skin one frying chicken. Season with salt and pepper.

Brown in butter. Slice one good sized onion and brown.

Add: **3 T. flour to butter in skillet**
       3 T. tomato paste
       ¾ C. water

Cover and simmer ¾ hour.
Before serving add ¼ C. sauterne and a large can mushroom caps. Serve with rice.

MRS. J. J. RANGE, II

CHICKEN MANDANAO

2 young chickens, fryer size	1 t. salt
½ C. butter	2 t. powdered ginger
flour, salt, pepper to dredge	1 t. curry powder
3 large sliced onions	2 t. poultry seasoning
2 C. stock	½ t. freshly ground pepper
½ C. soya sauce	juice of 1 lemon

First combine soya sauce, lemon juice, and seasonings. Wash disjointed chicken.   Place in pan and pour this dressing over it.   Do not use
metal pan. Let stand in refrigerator 2 hrs., turning once or twice. Melt
butter in heavy skillet. Drain chicken and after dredging all over with
flour, salt, and pepper, brown each piece evenly in butter. Set in oven
proof dish. Rinse skillet drippings with stock or water and pour over
chicken with rest of the dressing. Cover tightly and cook in 325°F.
oven for 1½ hours. Remove cover for the last half hour. Thicken gravy
in pan very slightly before serving with chicken. Boiled rice and
fried pineapple slices go well with this dish. Serves eight.

MRS. WALTER HANKINS

CHICKEN PIE

Prepare one 5 lb. stewing hen and cook in 3 C. water and 2½ t. salt.
Cook until done. Remove chicken from bones and cut in 1 inch pieces.
Add water to make 6 cups broth.

Make rich pastry:

3 C. flour	1 t. salt
1 C. shortening	ice water

Line pyrex dish, 8 x 12 inches, saving enough pastry to strip top.
Place chicken in dish. Sprinkle with 3 T. flour. Cover with liquid;
add strips of pastry. Pour more liquid over pie and add ¼ lb. of oleo.
Cook at 250°F. for 2 hours. Serve with gravy.

MRS. HORACE DANCE

CHICKEN SAUTE' HOPPER

Dredge pieces of chicken in seasoned flour and brown nicely in almost
½ C. melted butter. Add ¼ C. apple brandy; light and let blaze,
spooning over chicken. Reduce heat; add 1 T. minced parsley, 6
minced spring onions, and 6 T. of Rhine Wine. Cover pan and cook
until tender. Remove chicken to hot platter and add 6 T. of heavy
cream (sour, if you like) to sauce. Bring to a simmer, stirring constantly. Taste for seasoning. This is very good with wild rice.

MRS. JOHN B. McKEE

CHICKEN SPAGHETTI

1 5 lb. hen, cooked until tender	1 lb. almonds
2 packages spaghetti	1 onion, cut fine
1 can tomato juice	4 C. of broth
2 cans mushrooms	1 lb. grated cheese

Cook spaghetti until tender. Drain and add chicken, cut into large
pieces, thickened chicken broth and remaining ingredients. Season to
taste. Cook in double boiler about 2 hours. Have 1 lb. grated cheese
to serve in separate dish. Serves 16.

MRS. R. N. LAWRENCE

CHICKEN SUPREME

For each person use a medium thick slice of broiled hot ham — preferably Virginian. On top of this arrange a cooked breast of chicken. Cover with sauce made by blending:

4 T. melted butter with
4 T. flour

Add:

2 C. rich chicken stock seasoned with
1 t. salt and few grains of pepper

Top with large, plump mushrooms which have been sauteed in plenty of butter. This amount of sauce serves four.

MRS. WALTER HANKINS

CHICKEN TERRAPIN

Prepare one chicken as for salad. Cut in halves and boil one can French mushrooms, keeping them covered until done, and mix with chicken. Bring one pint of cream to a boil and stir in 1 T. flour, and 2 T. butter, creamed together. Stir until this thickens. Remove from stove and drop in quickly, one at a time, the yolks of three eggs, stirring constantly. Season with red pepper, salt, nutmeg, a little chopped onion and chopped parsley. Pour this mixture over chicken and mushrooms in a baking dish and cover with breadcrumbs and bits of butter. Twenty minutes before serving, put into oven and brown well. Serve very hot.

MRS. WALTER HANKINS

CHICKEN RAVIOLI

1 3 or 4 lb. chicken, cooked until tender in about 1 qt. water
½ green pepper, chopped   **¼ lb. sharp cheese, grated**
1 small onion, chopped   **1 large package thin noodles**
1 can mushroom soup
½ small jar pimentoes,
  chopped

Saute pepper and onion and add pimiento. Mix chicken and add other ingredients.

Cook noodles until tender in the chicken broth. Then add cut up chicken, sauteed pepper and onion, pimento and soup to noodles in broth. Before serving, heat to near boiling, remove from heat and toss lightly with the cheese.

MRS. BRUCE CHAMBERLIN

CHICKEN SPAGHETTI

6 lb. stewing hen   **2 large onions**

Stew chicken with onions and salt to season.

Cook 1 8 oz. package elbow spaghetti.Drain and rinse in cold water.

Dice **1 green pepper**   **1 pimiento**
  1 carton fresh mushrooms; simmer these in **½ C. butter** for 10 minutes.

Mix 4 T. flour in above; add 1 qt. chicken broth and 1 pt. milk. Cook until thick. Place large pieces of chicken and spaghetti in 3 qt. casserole. Pour mixture over this. Melt 1 stick butter. Add 12 slices rye bread, cubed. Saute' until bread is thoroughly saturated. Sprinkle on top of casserole and place in 350°F. oven for 45 minutes. This can be made the day before except for the last step.

MRS. R. D. TAYLOR, JR.

CHICKEN TETRAZZINI

2 C. cooked diced chicken, use meat from wings, neck and back primarily
2 C. elbow macaroni or fine noodles that have been cooked in 1 qt. chicken broth
1 or 2 slices bacon, sauteed until brown and crisp with
1/3 C. finely chopped onion
½ C. green pepper, finely chopped

Then add:
¼ C. chopped pimiento
¼ C. toasted slivered almonds
2 C. cooked small peas

Mix everything with the chicken and macaroni (still in broth); pour 1 can of mushroom soup over all; sprinkle with bread crumbs and bake until brown.

MRS. A. E. CORNETT

DAISY'S COUNTRY CAPTAIN

1 hen or 2 fryers
2 or 3 green peppers, chopped
1 pod garlic
2 onions, chopped
1 can tomatoes
1 t. curry powder
2 C. rice (boil until dry)
1 t. thyme

¼ C. raisins to go in sauce
¼ C. raisins to garnish top
¼ C. almonds or other nuts for sauce
¼ C. almonds or other nuts for garnish
1 can mushrooms
salt and pepper to taste

Boil the chicken until done and remove from bone. Make the sauce of cut green peppers, onions, tomatoes, mushrooms, almonds, raisins, thyme, salt, pepper, and curry powder. Add chicken; let simmer on top of stove or in a casserole for one hour. Serve over rice. Garnish with a cup of green peppers, raisins ,nuts. **Sauce should not be too thick.**

MRS. ROBERT COX
Durham, N. C.

DELMONICO CHICKEN

Slice meat of a six pound chicken, after cooking, into long sliver-like pieces. Arrange in a shallow buttered baking dish on a layer of egg noodles, previously cooked in salted water. One six ounce package of noodles is sufficient.

Cover alternating layers of noodles and chicken with a cheese sauce, made by melting:
2 C. American cheese in
2 C. hot milk. Add to
4 T. butter melted and blended well with
2 T. flour
1 t. salt
¼ t. mustard. Stir until well thickened.

Having cheese sauce on top of baking dish, sprinkle with paprika and brown in hot oven 450°F. Serve bubbling hot and sprinkle with grated Parmesan cheese at table. Serves 6.

MRS. WALTER HANKINS

DEVILED CHICKEN

For each 2 lb. chicken:

1 stick butter
2 T. Worcestershire sauce

3 slices garlic
   (pod and a half)
Twist of lemon

Cut chicken in half. Salt and pepper both sides of chicken and place cut side down in bottom of broiler pan. Cut butter on top of chicken and pour Worcestershire over. Slice garlic over this. Add twist of lemon. Bake in oven at 250°F. or 275°F. for 2 or more hours. Baste every twenty minutes.

MRS. FRED LOCKETT, JR.

PRESSED CHICKEN MOLD

Boil one 5 to 6 lb chicken until meat falls from bones. Salt, pepper and strain off broth. Pour off greater part of fat; then cook down broth until reduced to 1 pint. Dissolve in broth 1½ envelopes gelatin (plain). Add ¼ C. vinegar and 1 T. Worcestershire sauce.

Line bottom of ring mold (1 qt. size) or loaf pan with sliced stuffed olives or hard boiled eggs. Add the finely ground chicken, pouring over all the broth. Put in refrigerator to set. Turn out on platter. Serve sliced as meat course or with lettuce and mayonnaise as salad.

MRS. E. A. LANCASTER
Greeneville, Tenn.

CORN STEW

1 stewing hen (2 - 2½ lbs.)
4 to 5 onions
2 to 3 potatoes (medium)

2 dozen ears of corn
salt and pepper to taste

Stew hen, nearly covering with water. Cut potatoes and onions in fairly small pieces, add to hen when half done. When hen is fully done, remove from container and pull all the meat from the bone and cut into small pieces. Return to container with potatoes and onions. Cook 2 to 3 hours. Ten to fifteen minutes before ready to serve add corn which has been cut off. Salt and pepper.

This dish is best cooked slowly and should take about ½ day. Will require little stirring until corn is added. Makes approximately 2 qts.

MRS. BILL BRIDGFORTH

POULET AU VIN

5 broilers split, 2½ lbs. each
3 sticks butter, melted
1 C. sliced scallions

2 bottles sauterne
1 C. chopped parsley

Marinate chicken overnight in sauterne, turning occasionally. Drain sauterne and add to scallions and parsley. Salt and pepper the halves and brown them in a 350° oven, basting with butter. Then pour sauterne mixture over the chicken and cook at 250° for 30 minutes. If a thick gravy is desired, the sauce may be thickened with flour. Serves 10

MRS. GEORGE OLDHAM

CHINESE CHICKEN AND WALNUTS

6 chicken breasts	1 C. diced bamboo shoots
¼ C. butter	2 C. sliced celery
1 C. sliced water chestnuts	½ lb. green beans

Saute strips of chicken in butter. Add next 4 ingredients. Cover with 3 C. chicken stock, ¼ C. soy sauce, 2½ t. salt, 1 t. sugar and 1 t. pepper. Steam for 5 minutes. Blend 2 T. cornstarch with little cold water. Add to mixture and cook until thick and transparent. Saute 1 C. English walnuts in butter until golden and crisp. Serve with rice. Serves 6.

MRS. LYMAN FULTON, JR.

CONGEALED CHICKEN

2 large hens, cooked till tender   **12 eggs, hard boiled**
Combine:

2 pkgs. gelatin	1 C. mayonnaise
4 C. hot chicken broth	

Let this mixture cool.

In a large shallow pyrex casserole place a layer of dark meat, a layer of chopped eggs and a layer of white meat. Pour cooled broth mixture over the three layers. Congeal. Pour cooled tomato aspic on top and congeal. Serves 30.

This can be made the day before serving.

MRS. LEON ROWAN
Memphis

POULET CINTRA

Cut a tender chicken in pieces as for frying. Brown the pieces in butter with a shallot and a chopped clove of garlic. Add ½ C. light port wine, ½ C. dry white wine, a liqueur glass of brandy and a liqueur glass of cherry brandy. When this boils, light with a match shaking the pan until the flame dies. Allow the sauce to simmer down to about half. When cooked, remove the pieces of chicken and keep warm. Finish your sauce with a good cupful of thick cream and 2 egg yolks. Cook until it thickens, taking care not to boil and stirring briskly. Strain; pour over chicken and serve very hot. The wines and liqueur may be domestic and any comparable mixture may be used.

MRS. W. T. SWOYER, JR.

TURKEY MORNAY WITH BROCCOLI

1 pkg. frozen broccoli	½ C. sauterne
¼ C. butter	1 T. Worcestershire sauce
¼ C. flour	2 C. cooked turkey sliced
1 C. turkey broth made by	or coarsely diced
simmering giblets and	Grated Parmesan cheese
neck	Salt and pepper to taste
½ C. light cream	

Cook broccoli until tender and arrange in the bottom of a well greased casserole. With butter, flour, cream, salt and pepper, wine, Worcestershire sauce, make a cream sauce. Add turkey and pour over broccoli. Cover heavily with grated cheese. Bake for 20 minutes at 400°F.

MRS. LESTER BALLEW, JR.

GAME SAUCE

Melt **1½ T. butter** in a saucepan until it is golden brown; add **1 T. flour,** stir until light brown. Add slowly over low heat **1 C. of the hot marinade, the juice of 1 lemon, 1 T. grated lemon peel, 1 T. grated orange peel, a pinch of cayenne, ¾ C. currant jelly**

The marinade consists of the following: 1 carrot and 1 onion cut in rings, 2 shallots cut in half, salt, pepper, a very large bunch of rosemary, and just enough red wine to cover your game. The game is marinated in this for four hours, then the marinade is strained and the game basted with the remaining quantity.

BRAISED GROUSE

1 grouse	¼ C. (4 T.) chopped parsley
¾ lb. salt pork	1 C. chicken broth
1 medium sized onion, minced	½ C. water

Cut 2-inch square pieces off salt pork and place inside the grouse; truss. Cut 3 thin lengthwise slices of salt pork from the remaining piece, then chop the rest in small cubes. Sprinkle the cubed salt pork over the bottom of a Dutch oven and place the grouse on top. Sprinkle with onion and parsley; lay the sliced salt pork over the grouse. Pour in chicken stock. Cover and simmer over low heat for 1 hour and 20 minutes, or until tender.

Remove grouse to an oven proof platter and slide under the broiler for a few minutes to brown. Scoop the salt pork out of the drippings with a slotted spoon; chop the 3 thin slices; place all of salt pork in a frying pan and cook until crisp. Skim fat off the remaining liquid in the Dutch oven; add ½ C. water and simmer 2 minutes. Thicken slightly with a flour-water mixture, then stir in the crisp salt pork. Pass gravy. Serves 3 to 4. The salt pork gives the meat a smoky, sweet flavor. If you desire, soaking the grouse in milk for an hour, turning occasionally, will make it more tender.

MRS. RICHARD C. MILLER

DUCK WITH WILD RICE DRESSING

Ducks may be stuffed with wild rice dressing made by boiling wild rice and seasoning with salt, pepper and chopped onion or any favorite dressing may be used. Salt and pepper the outside of the ducks and place them breast side up in a roaster. Cover the bottom of the roaster with water and cover tightly. Roast at 450°F. for the first 15 minutes then reduce heat to 350°F. Baste every 15 minutes with the liquid in the pan. When almost tender, remove cover from pan (for last 15 minutes or so) to allow skin to brown.

MRS. K. W. CHRISTENBERRY
Knoxville, Tenn.

DEEP FRIED QUAIL

Clean quail thoroughly. Salt and flour each bird then place a lump of butter and a few grains of basil in the cavity. Fry in deep fat, fast at first, until birds are brown all over, then slower for about 20 minutes. Do not cover. Place on brown paper to drain and serve while hot.

MRS. C. C. GREER
Knoxville, Tenn.

DOVE, OR WHITE WING A LA ARIZONA

6 doves or white wings
2 t. seasoned salt
½ C. flour
1 t. salt
½ t. pepper
4 slices bacon

½ C. chopped onions
¾ C. diced carrots
½ C. sliced celery
1 can (10½ oz.) beef
   bouillon
2 C. dry white wine

For best results and tenderer birds, keep birds in refrigerator 3 to 4 days after killing and cleaning. Sprinkle birds with half of seasoned salt and dredge in the flour seasoned with salt and pepper. Cut bacon into small squares, fry, and remove from bacon fat.

Saute birds in bacon fat; then place in casserole and sprinkle with the other teaspoon of seasoned salt. Add small pieces of bacon. In remaining bacon fat, saute onions, carrots, and celery for about three minutes, stirring constantly. Pour whole mixture over birds. Add beef bouillon, previously brought to a boil. Cover casserole and place in a moderate oven (350°F) and bake for 1½ hours; adding 1 C. of wine after the first thirty minutes, the other C. of wine at the end of an hour. When the birds are done, remove them and strain the liquid. Make gravy from the remaining liquid, adding chopped chives and Kitchen Bouquet if desired. Serves 2 or 3. These doves are moist and tender, and do not have the usual dryness.

DUCK WITH BORDELAISE SAUCE

A 3-lb. duck will take about an hour in a preheated 400° oven. Put salt and pepper in cavity. Baste with 4 T. butter. Turn the duck on each of its sides after it has been in the oven ½ hour.

———•———

BORDELAISE SAUCE

Press the liver of the duck and an extra one through a seive and put aside. Put 2 finely chopped shallots with 2 T. butter in a saucepan over low heat. When all the moisture has evaporated, let them cook a few minutes longer to form a glaze. Add ½ C. bouillon in which 1 T. tomato puree has been dissolved and to which 1 T. flour and 1 T. butter has been added. Add 4 T. lighted brandy. Bring to a slow boil; add salt, pepper and a pinch of cayenne. Simmer for 10 minutes. Add ½ C. bouillon. Bring to a boil. Slowly pour half the contents of the saucepan over the two strained livers. Pour into the saucepan and replace over low heat, stirring constantly, but do not allow to boil. Add 4 T. butter. Tip the saucepan in all directions, do not stir. When butter is melted, pour into preheated sauce boat and serve at the same time as the duck.

MRS. RICHARD C. MILLER

PECAN STUFFED PHEASANT

4 T. (½ stick) butter
  or margarine
1-1/3 C. dry bread crumbs
2/3 C. coarsely broken
  pecan meats
2 pheasants
2 T. flour

¾ t. salt
¼ t. pepper
4 T. (½ stick) butter
  or margarine
1½ C. hot water
1/3 C. sherry

Melt the 4 T. butter and pour over bread crumbs; add pecan meats and toss lightly. Stuff mixture into pheasants, then truss birds. Combine the flour, salt and pepper, and lightly sprinkle over the pheasants. Melt the other 4 T. butter in a heavy frying pan; brown each pheasant on all sides, then transfer to a roasting pan. Add hot water and sherry to the browned butter, then pour the mixture over the birds. Cover and bake in a moderate oven (350°F.) for 1 hour. Baste pheasants with the liquid in the pan every 15 minutes. Remove cover and continue baking for 20 minutes, or until the birds are crisp and brown. Remove birds to a platter and keep hot while you thicken drippings for gravy. Serves six.

PHEASANT IN SOUR CREAM

Cut pheasant into pieces for frying. Rub well with salt and lemon juice. Dredge in seasoned flour and brown quickly in fat. Put in casserole with a cover. Chop one medium onion and 1 T. of parsley (if fresh not available use the dehydrated). Add this to 3 T. of the fat and brown onion lightly; then add ¾ C. water and scrape all brown bits from frying pan. Pour this over pheasant· and bake 45 minutes in 350°F. oven. Add ½ pint commercial sour cream and continue baking 30 more minutes.

MRS. J. J. RANGE, JR.

PHEASANT SALMI

6 green onions and tops,
  chopped
3 T. butter or margarine
5 T. browned flour
1 C. stock (made from cooking pheasant bones in
  water seasoned with
  2 stalks celery)
¼ C. (4 T.) sherry

2 T. orange juice
¼ t. grated orange peel
salt
1 C. pecan stuffing or other
  leftover stuffing
2 to 3 C. cooked pheasant
  meat, cut in bite-size
  pieces

Saute onions in butter until lightly browned; add browned flour, and stirring, cook two minutes. (To brown flour, sprinkle into a heavy frying pan and stir; cook over medium heat until it is a light beige). Add the stock, sherry, orange juice, and grated peel; stir; cook until smooth and thickened; taste and add salt if desired. Add stuffing to the gravy mixture along with the meat, and cook just long enough to heat through. Serve over mashed potatoes or split butter biscuits. Serves 4 to 6. Delicious way to use up any left over roast pheasant.

MRS. RICHARD C. MILLER

ROAST DUCK WITH ORANGE JUICE AND WINE

1 duck cleaned (4 to 5 lbs.)	1 C. bread crumbs
1 t. salt	½ C. butter
¼ t. pepper	1 C. orange juice
6 onions cut in small chunks	1 C. dry red wine
6 apples, peeled and cut in small pieces	6 bay leaves
	10 whole cloves
8 or 10 stalks celery, cut in short lengths	2 T. flour

Wash the duck inside and out, and dry with a towel. Rub inside of duck with salt and pepper. Mix onions, apples, celery and bread crumbs to make a very coarse dressing. Stuff inside the duck, and sew it up for roasting. Rub the outside with salt and pepper; and if duck is fat, score the outer surface.

Place the duck in an uncovered roasting pan in a 450°F. oven with a little butter. Turn until the bird is brown. Then reduce temperature to 400°F., cover the pan, and cook for 20 to 25 minutes per pound. After the duck is brown, baste frequently with a sauce of orange juice, red wine, bay leaves and cloves. When the duck is done, remove from the roasting pan and place in a serving dish. Clean out the stuffing, which is not intended to be eaten. Remove bay leaves and cloves from the pan of orange juice, wine, and melted fat. Add 2 T. of flour and the remaining orange juice and wine. Add salt and pepper to taste if necessary. Cook in a saucepan until mixture begins to thicken, stirring constantly. Serve this sauce in a separate gravy boat at the table; use as desired. Serves 4.

MRS. RICHARD C. MILLER

ROASTED QUAIL

Clean quail thoroughly. Salt lightly and place lump of butter inside each bird. Rub birds with mixture of flour and butter. Place in baking pan and bake in slow oven for about 1 hour basting frequently with a little water, melted butter and sherry wine, to which ¼ t. marjoram or tarragon has been added.

MRS. C. C. GREER
Knoxvile, Tenn.

VENISON ROAST

In a skillet fry 3 medium pieces of salt pork. In the rendered fat, brown the roast on all sides. Place meat in roaster and salt. To the frying fat add:

2 C. chopped celery	1 C. catsup
2 C. chopped onion	2 t. Worcestershire sauce
½ C. vinegar	1 C. hot water
½ C. sugar	

Cover meat with mixture and cook at 350°, basting occasionally. Cook for about four hours or until tender (this time usually sufficient for a 6 to 8 pound cut of meat). Before serving taste gravy to determine if any more seasoning is desired. The gravy is excellent served on rice.

MRS. KENT HERRIN

VENISON POT ROAST

6 lb. venison pot roast
3 cloves garlic, slivered
½ lb. salt pork or 1 C.
    bacon drippings
4 T. (¼ C.)flour
½ t. each, salt and sage
¼ t. pepper
3 T. salt pork or bacon
    drippings
4 C. tomato juice
¼ C. wine vinegar

2 bay leaves
2 whole cloves
5 whole black peppers
½ t. each onion salt, garlic
    salt, and celery salt
¼ t. thyme
2 t. Worcestershire sauce
1 can (10½-oz.) mushroom
    soup
6 each onions, carrots, and
    potatoes

Cut all the fat off the meat (in venison the flavor is concentrated in the fat, and if left on, it gives a "gamey" taste to the meat). Wipe the meat with a damp cloth wrung in mild vinegar. Cut slits in meat on all sides and insert slivers of garlic in each slit. Lard with strips of salt pork; or using a pastry brush, coat well with bacon drippings. Mix together flour, salt, sage, and pepper; rub into meat. Heat 3 T. salt pork or bacon drippings in a heavy kettle with a tight fitting cover. Brown meat slowly on all sides. Lift meat out and slip a low rack in the bottom of the kettle. Replace meat, then add tomato juice, wine vinegar, bay leaves, cloves, peppers, onion salt, garlic salt, celery salt, thyme, and Worcestershire. Cover and simmer over low heat for 2 hours. Baste with the liquid 3 or 4 times during cooking. After the meat has cooked two hours, add the mushroom soup and stir until it is well blended with the tomato juice. Peel onions, carrots and potatoes; surround meat with vegetables. Cover and continue cooking for the last hour, or until the vegetables are done to your liking.

If you wish a slightly heavier gravy, pour off sauce and strain; thicken lightly with a flour and water mixture. Pass gravy to pour over the sliced meat. Serves 10.

If you prefer meat with a mild flavor you'll like this recipe. The sauce, which has a flavor of spice and wine, penetrates the meat and makes it moist and tender.

MRS. CHARLES GORDON

DRESSING FOR CHICKEN OR TURKEY

6 C. crumbled bread (part white and part corn bread), a
    little rye bread is a good change
½ C. chopped onion
1 C. chopped celery
¾ C. sliced mushrooms

1 C. coarsely sliced chestnuts
6 T. melted butter

Saute onions and celery until soft, not brown. Mix all ingredients together. Season to taste with ground sage, poultry seasoning, salt and pepper. If dressing is too dry, add a little broth from the cooked giblets. Always stuff fowl lightly.

MRS. MALCOLM CAMPBELL

CHICKEN ALA NAOMI

1 chicken, cut into frying
  pieces (or 6 breast pieces)
1 large can V-8 juice

Dry mustard
2 med. onions
1 t. parsley flakes

Shake chicken pieces in flour as for frying and place in a shallow casserole. Cover completely with V-8 juice and sprinkle with mustard. Slice onions thinly over top and sprinkle with parsley flakes or fresh parsley if available. Cover and bake at 325 degrees for 1½ hours. Serve over rice.
    Mrs. Charles Ray

CHICKEN CASSEROLE

2 C. diced chicken (white
  meat)
1 can Italian Green beans or
  1 pkg. frozen whole green
  beans, thawed and separated

1 can mushroom soup
½ lb. fresh mushrooms,
  sauteed
1 C. (4 oz.) grated
  cheese

Mix and bake 50 minutes at 350 degrees. Remove and cover with 1 can french fried onions. Bake 10 minutes longer. Spoon over toasted English muffins. Serves 4.
    Mrs. Lester Ballew

CHICKEN CHUTNEY

1 C. oil
6 T. vinegar
1 t. salt

2 small cloves - garlic
1 C. chutney
1 chicken cut into frying
  pieces

Blend above ingredients in blender. Rub chicken with butter. Salt and pepper. Broil just to brown about 15 minutes. Turn oven down to 300 degrees and spoon sauce over. Bake 1 hour basting often with sauce.
    Mrs. Malcolm Campbell

CHICKEN GOURMET

4 chicken breasts, boned
4 thin slices cooked ham
4 slices Swiss cheese
1 egg, beaten
1 C. med. white sauce

1 C. fine bread crumbs
Flour
Worcestershire sauce, dash
½ C. oil

On each chicken breast place 1 slice each of ham and cheese, and a dash of Worcestershire sauce. Fold chicken over and secure with toothpick. Flour chicken, dip in egg and roll in bread crumbs. Brown in oil until well browned on both sides. Pour white sauce over this. Bake in 325 degrees oven for 25 minutes.
    Mrs. C. M. Creech

CHICKEN AND HAM CASSEROLE

1 C. flour	2 onions, peeled and
1 T. salt	chopped
1 t. pepper	1 clove garlic, peeled and
1¼ t. powdered savory	crushed
4 chicken breasts, split	2 T. minced parsley
¼ lb. butter	⅛ t. mace
4 slices, thin, precooked ham	½ C. chicken broth
1 lb. mushrooms (or 2 med.	½ C. Sherry
cans)	2 t. brown sugar
1 10 oz. pkg. frozen peas	½ C. orange juice

Place flour, 2 tsp. salt and 1 tsp. pepper and 1 tsp. savory in bag, add chicken breasts which have been skinned and boned, to coat. Brown in ¼ cup melted butter, adding more if needed. When golden brown, remove. Cut ham slices in half, roll up and secure with toothpicks. Brown ham lightly and remove. To same skillet add remaining butter, mushrooms, onion, garlic, parsley, ¼ tsp. savory, 1 tsp. salt, pinch of pepper and mace. Saute until onions are tender. Add chicken broth, sherry and orange juice and brown sugar. Cook stirring occasionally for 5 minutes.

Arrange chicken and ham, (minus toothpicks) in shallow baking dish. Pour mushroom mixture over, cover lightly and bake at 325 degrees for 1 hour. Break peas in clusters over top of casserole-cook 15 minutes more, basting frequently with juices, until peas are done. Serves 6 to 8.

Mrs. Robert Mains

CHICKEN IMPERIAL

8 pieces chicken breast	½ C. parmesan cheese
⅔ stick butter or oleo	1 T. paprika
1½ C. cracker crumbs	2 T. parsley, chopped
(or 1 roll ritz crackers)	Salt & pepper to taste

Wash and dry and skin chicken. Melt oleo. Mix together crumbs, cheese, paprika, salt, pepper, and parsley. Dip chicken in oleo and roll in crumbs. Put on a greased cookie sheet. Bake at 350 degrees for 30 minutes. No turning necessary.

Mrs. William Blackard

CHIVE DUMPLINGS

1½ C. sifted all-purpose flour   1 T. butter or oleo, melted
2 t. baking powder   1 egg, beaten
½ t. seasoned salt   ⅓ to ½ C. milk
2 T. chopped chives

Into medium bowl, sift flour, baking powder and salt. Stir in chives. With fork, stir in butter and egg: Then stir in ⅓ cup milk. (If mixture seems dry, add a little more milk). Drop dumplings on simmering Chicken Fricassee etc. Cook tightly covered (Do not lift lid) 25 minutes or until dumplings are light and thoroughly cooked. Makes about 18 dumplings.

Mrs. Alfred Bolton

CHICKEN WILD RICE CASSEROLE

2 whole broiler-fryer   1 C. dairy sour cream
  chickens (3 lbs. each)   1 med. onion, sliced
1 C. water   1 lb. fresh mushrooms or
1½ t. salt   canned
½ t. curry powder   ¼ C. butter or margarine
½ C. sliced celery   1 pkg. Uncle Bens long grain
1 can (10½ oz.) condensed   and wild rice with herbs
  cream of mushroom soup

Place chicken in a deep kettle, add water, salt, curry powder, onion and celery. Bring to boil; cover tightly. Reduce heat; simmer 1 hour. Remove from heat; strain broth. Refrigerate chicken and broth at once. When chicken is cool remove meat from bones, discard skin. Cut in bite size pieces. Wash mushrooms, pat dry; saute in butter until golden brown (reserve enough to circle top of casserole). Measure chicken broth. Use as part of liquid for cooking rice, following package directions for firm rice. Combine chicken, rice and mushrooms not reserved for top in 3½ or 4 qt. casserole. Blend sour cream and undiluted mushroom soup. Toss together with chicken mixture. Arrange reserved mushrooms in circle on top of casserole. Cover; refrigerate. To heat, bake in a 350 degrees oven for 1 hour.

Mrs. Alfred Abernethy

CHICKEN IN ORANGE JUICE WITH MUSHROOMS

2 lb. chicken, quartered   2 T. salt
⅛ t. pepper   ½ C. butter
½ lb. mushrooms (fresh)   ¼ C. chopped onions
2 C. orange juice (fresh)   1 T. sugar
¼ C. beef consomme

Salt and pepper chicken. Brown in butter in large skillet. Remove to paper toweling. Add mushrooms to same pan and cook until golden. Remove and put aside until later. Stir onions into remaining drippings. Cook a few minutes, then add orange juice and sugar and cook over high heat until mixture is reduced by half. Lower heat and stir in consomme'. Arrange chicken in sauce. Cover and cook over very low heat in oven until tender (about an hour). Add mushrooms during last 10 minutes of cooking. Frozen orange juice and canned mushrooms cannot be substituted.

Mrs. Charles Wofford

PARTY CHICKEN SALAD

1 C. cubed chicken   1 T. chopped sweet pickle
1 T. chopped green olives   ⅜ C. chopped celery
1 T. chopped ripe olives   ¼ C. chopped almonds
1 hard cooked egg, diced   1 peeled apple, diced

Mix all ingredients together with a small amount of mayonnaise.

Mrs. Phil S. Barksdale, Jr.

PARTY CHICKEN

8 very large chicken breasts   1 pkg. chipped beef
(skin and debone breasts)   ½ pt. sour cream
1 can undiluted mushroom   Sprinkle chicken with savory
   soup   salt
8 slices bacon

Wrap each chicken breast with a piece of bacon. Cover bottom of flat greased baking dish (about 8" x 12" x 2") with chipped beef. Arrange chicken breasts over chipped beef. Mix soup and sour cream and pour over all. Cover and refrigerate overnight if possible. When ready, bake at 275 degrees for 3 hours, uncovered. Serves 8.

Mrs. Louis Wexler

CHICKEN BREASTS IN RED WINE

6 chicken breasts	¼ C. butter
1 sliced onion	½ clove garlic minced
2 T. flour	½ T. salt
¼ T. pepper	1 chicken bouillon cube
1 C. hot water	⅓ C. red wine cooking
12 small cooked potatoes	sherry
or rice	Parsley

Saute' chicken in hot butter on both sides until well browned and then add onion, garlic, and simmer 10 minutes. In small bowl combine flour, salt, pepper, and slowly stir in bouillon cube dissolved in hot water. Pour over chicken. Cook slowly, covered, about ½ hour until tender; add wine, potatoes and heat, add parsley. Serves 6.

Mrs. Bo Abernethy

HOT CHICKEN SALAD

3 C. cooked cubed chicken	1 C. chopped celery (raw)
½ C. toasted almonds	½ t. accent'
1 t. salt	2 t. grated onion (more if
2 T. lemon juice	desired)
1 C. mayonnaise	½ C. sharp cheese (grated)
1 C. potato chips	

Mix all ingredients except cheese, almonds, and potato chips. Place in 2 qt. casserole and sprinkle with almonds, then cheese, then chips. Cook in 425 degrees oven for 15 minutes. Serves about 7 to 8 people.

Mrs. Robert Taylor

PUERTO RICAN CHICKEN

Marinate quarters of chicken in mixture of ½ cup olive oil and ½ cup oil, ½ cup white wine, 1 Tbs. grated ginger, 1 minced clove garlic for 1 hour. Broil chicken, basted twice with some of the marinade. Serve with Coconut Chutney, sliced peppers.

Coconut Chutney
Combine equal parts chopped chutney, plum preserves, toasted flaked coconut and brandy to taste.

Mrs. Tom Happel

MAYONNAISE CHICKEN

1 large hen, cooked and cut up (or 2 large fryers)
1 C. celery, chopped
4 hard boiled eggs, cut up
1 C. skimmed chicken stock
2 C. English peas (LeSeur) drained
1 C. sliced almonds toasted
2 C. stiff mayonnaise
2 envelopes gelatin
1 C. cold water
2 C. India Relish

Dissolve gelatin in 1 cup cold water and add to hot stock (last thing). Refrigerate. May be make one day ahead. Serve as salad on lettuce leaf.

Mrs. William Blackard

CHICKEN IN SOUR CREAM

4 or 5 chicken breasts
½ C. pale dry sherry or sauterne
1½ pt. sour cream
1 can mushrooms, stems and pieces
1 can mushroom soup

Mix all above and pour over chicken. Sprinkle paprika heavily over all. Bake uncovered at 350 degrees for 1½ hours. If it begins to dry out, cover with foil.

Mrs. Al Costner

ROAST WILD DUCK

Soak ducks 4 or 5 hours in salt water. Salt inside and stuff with apple, onion and celery. Put in roaster (for best results use a covered pan that is just the right size for number of ducks being cooked. Otherwise sauce will cook too fast and ducks will be dry), with 1" of water. Cover and roast at 375 degrees for one hour. Remove ducks from roaster and throw out all liquid. Return ducks to roaster and pour over them the following sauce:

¼ C. butter	2 T. currant jelly
4 T. flour	¾ C. orange juice
1½ C. consomme	2 oz. Sherry
½ t. salt	Dash of cayenne

Cover ducks and cook 2½ hours longer basting every ½ hour. Last ½ hour turn ducks over and baste backside.

Mrs. Rufus K. Schriber

SOPA ELEGANTE

1½ C. chicken	1 C. celery, finely chopped
¼ C. minced onion	1 C. mushroom soup
¼ lb. almonds or cashews	1 C. chinese noodles
¼ C. sherry or broth	1 large can small peas
2 large cans mushrooms	

Combine all ingredients except half of noodles for top. Toss lightly together and bake for 30 minutes at 325 degrees.

Pat Miller

CRISPY CHICKEN LIVERS

1 lb. fresh chicken livers	1 C. crushed Swiss cheese &
½ t. seasoning salt	ham crackers
¼ C. melted butter	

Clean and cut the livers in half. Mix the crumbs and the salt. Roll the livers in butter; then in crumbs. Arrange in well buttered casserole. Bake at 350 degrees until golden brown. (Cooks in about 20 minutes.) (I usually turn them once.)

Mrs. John Wilson

CHICKEN IN WINE

Roll chicken pieces in flour and fry in one stick of butter. Remove from skillet and brown one small chopped onion.
COMBINE:

2 T. flour	2 T. tomato paste
¼ C. sherry wine	¾ C. water

Return chicken to skillet and pour sauce over chicken with one can drained mushrooms. Cover and let simmer 1 hour.

Mrs. C. C. Marshall

PARTY CHICKEN NOODLE BAKE

8 oz. lasagne noodles
1½ can mushroom soup
1 C. milk
½ t. salt
2 (3 oz.) pkg. softened
cream cheese
⅓ C. stuffed sliced olives
½ t. poultry seasoning

⅓ C. chopped onions
⅓ C. chopped green
peppers
¼ C. minced parsley
3 C. cooked diced chicken or
turkey
1½ C. buttered soft bread
crumbs
1 C. Cottage cheese

Cook noodles in boiling salted water until tender; drain, rinse in cold water. Mix soup, milk, salt and seasoning. Heat. Beat cheeses together. Stir in olives, onion, pepper, chicken, and parsley. Place half the noodles in a 11½ x 7½ x 1½ baking dish. Spread half the cheese mixture, half the chicken, and half the soup mixture. Repeat layers. Top with bread crumbs. Bake in 350 degrees for 30 minutes. Trim with pimento if desired. Serves 10.

Mrs. Carl Childers

POULTRY STUFFING

In stuffing poultry be careful not to fill the crop or body cavity too full or the stuffing will be soggy. Stuffing can be made the day before baking but do not stuff the fowl sooner than an hour or so before it will be baked.

For **bread stuffing,** use one quart of stale bread crumbs, moistened in cold water and then squeezed dry. Add salt, pepper, a little finely chopped parsley, poultry seasoning, ½ C. melted butter and two eggs stirred in but not beaten. A little chopped onion may be added if desired.

An excellent **sausage stuffing** is made with the finely chopped heart and liver of the fowl, ½ loaf of stale bread, crumbled finely and slightly dampened, a little parsley and chopped onion, 6 medium size cold boiled potatoes, ½ lb. pork sausage, ½ t. nutmeg, salt and pepper to taste. Chop all these ingredients together, then mix well with four slightly beaten eggs. This is sufficient for one large chicken. To make **chestnut stuffing with veal** use ½ lb. lean veal, ½ C. melted butter and 1 C. bread crumbs. Blend and if not moist enough add a little broth. Add 4 dozen chestnuts blanched and boiled and salt and pepper to taste.

For an **oyster stuffing,** use equal parts of dry bread crumbs, corn bread and raw oysters and 1 hard boiled egg. Mix well in a frying pan with butter, salt and pepper and any other desired herbs.

PRESERVES & PICKLES

BRANDIED PEACHES

9 lbs. peaches (yellow cling stones)	2 sticks cinnamon
9 lbs. sugar	2 T. whole cloves (heads removed)
1 qt. water	3 pts. brandy

Select large clingstone peaches. Peel and weigh fruit. Boil sugar and water with spices tied in a bag until clear. Drop in peaches a few at a time and cook until tender but not soft. They must remain whole. Repeat until all peaches have been cooked. Place fruit on platter to drain. When syrup has cooled, add brandy and stir well. Place peaches in sterile jars and cover with syrup. Makes about 4 quarts.

LILLIAN YOUNG

CHILI SAUCE

36 tomatoes, medium size	2 T. allspice
6 onions	2 T. cinnamon
4 green peppers	2 t. celery seeds
2 C. sugar	2 t. nutmeg
2½ C. vinegar	2 t. cloves
4 T. salt	

Chop well and bake in oven 250° until thick enough to can. Delicious.

MRS. J. R. SIMMONDS

CHILI SAUCE

30 ripe tomatoes	1 qt. cider vinegar
12 onions	3 T. salt
6 pears	½ T. cloves
6 peaches	1 T. cinnamon
3 red peppers	1 T. allspice
3 sweet green peppers	1 T. celery seed
4 C. brown sugar	

Put all ingredients through grinder. Cook slowly 2½ hours. Bottle and seal.

MRS. G. W. STREET

ORANGE MARMALADE

Sugar	3 lemons
6 oranges	1 C. lemon juice

Wash fruit and slice. Remove seeds. Cover with cold water and let stand overnight. Next morning put on stove and boil for 45 minutes. Take off and cool overnight. Next morning measure pulp and then add 1½ times as much sugar as pulp. Boil 45 minutes. Before removing from heat, add 1 C. lemon juice. Delicious.

MRS. CHARLES PISTON

PEACH NUT CONSERVE

6 C. sliced, ripe peaches
4 C. sugar
1 orange

1½ C. pineapple tidbits, drained
1 C. broken walnuts

Combine peaches and sugar and let stand until juice forms. Put whole orange through food chopper. Chop pineapple and add peaches. Cook slowly, until thick, about 40 minutes. Remove from heat and add nuts. Seal in sterilized glasses.

MRS. COWAN MOSS, JR.

PICKLED PEACHES

7 lbs. peaches
5 lbs. white sugar
1 pt. vinegar

2 T. cloves
2 sticks cinnamon
(broken into pieces)

Peel peaches. Boil sugar, vinegar and spices, tied in a bag, about 12 minutes. Add peaches a few at a time. Cook in syrup until tender but firm. Place in jars, cover with hot syrup and seal.

MRS. GENE TAYLOR, JR.

PEAR BUTTER

16 C. sugar   16 C. ground pears

Cook together for 25 minutes from time of boiling. Add one No. 3 can of crushed pineapple and cook for five minutes more. Add a few drops of lemon juice, if desired.

MRS. HUNT ARCHER

GINGER PEARS

8 lbs. pears
6 lbs. sugar
1 C. water
juice of 4 lemons

4 lemon rinds (cut in strips))
⅛ lb. preserved or candied ginger root, cut into pieces

Use pears that are not quite ripe. Peel and core and cut into thin slices. Simmer until thick. Seal.

MRS. ELMER LUCAS

GINGER PEARS

Peel 10 pounds of pears and cut into small pieces. Add 7 pounds sugar. Cook slowly for 1 hour.

Add 4 lemons, 6 oranges and 1 lb crystalized ginger, cut into small pieces. Let simmer for 3 hours. Put into hot, sterilized jars.

MRS. G. W. STREET

PEAR RELISH

1 peck pears
6 bell peppers (3 red, 3 green)
2 T. mixed pickling spices
    (Remove red pepper if
    desired)

5 medium onions
2 lbs. sugar
4 C. vinegar
1 T. tumeric
1 T. salt

Grind peppers. Drain and discard juice. Grind pears and onions together. Use their juices. Combine with other ingredients. Cook 30 minutes and seal in clear fruit jars.

MRS. FERRELL HANNAH

BREAD AND BUTTER PICKLES

1 gallon medium sized
   cucumbers
8 small white onions
1 green pepper
1 sweet red pepper
½ C. coarse, medium salt
5 C. vinegar

cracked ice
5 C. sugar
1½ t. tumeric
½ t. ground cloves
2 t. mustard seed
2 t. celery seed

Thin slice cucumbers. Add sliced onions and peppers cut in narrow strips. Add salt. Cover with cracked ice and mix thoroughly. Let stand 3 hours; drain. Combine remaining ingredients. Pour over cucumber mixture. Bring to boil and seal in jars. Makes 8 pints.

MRS. JOHN ANDERSON

GREEN TOMATO PICKLES

7 or 8 medium size green tomatoes, sliced medium thin

Soak these for 24 hours in 1 gallon of water and 1 C. pickling lime. Then wash and rinse thoroughly to remove all traces of lime, but handle the slices gently so as to keep them intact.

Cook slices till transparent in syrup made of:

4 lbs. sugar
2 qts. vinegar
4 sticks cinnamon

2 T. cloves
5 t. salt

Lift tomatoes gently into hot sterile jars and pour the remaining syrup over them. Seal.

MRS. ROMA MILLER

BREAD AND BUTTER PICKLES

24 medium cucumbers
10 medium onions

2 handsful salt

Slice cucumbers and soak in ice water to which salt has been added, for three hours.

1 qt. vinegar
2 C. sugar
2 C. water
2 t. celery seed

2 t. tumeric
2 t. ginger
1 t. dry mustard

Bring the above ingredients to a boil. Add to them the sliced onions and cucumbers. Place in jar and seal while hot.

MRS. TOM McCROSKEY

BREAD AND BUTTER PICKLES

4 C. sugar
12 large cucumber pickles, sliced thin (not dill)

Using a gallon jar, arrange a layer of pickle and a layer of sugar until your jar is ½ full. Put in a t. of white mustard seed, 1 t.celery seed, 2 or 3 pieces of garlic, 2 or 3 sticks of cinnamon.

Begin again with layers of pickle and sugar until jar is full. Put 2 T. of olive oil on top. Cover and set aside, turning upside down 2 or 3 times a day, until all sugar is dissolved (about 48 hours). These pickles are sweet and crisp. Children love them.

MRS. THOMAS K. HAPPEL

SWEET PICKLE CHERRIES

Seed red sour cherries and cover with vinegar.

Let stand overnight — drain thoroughly next morning. Use as much sugar as fruit.

Let stand in covered crock and stir every day until all sugar has dissolved.

Heat to a boiling point and put in air tight jars.

MRS. BERT P. GUMP

CRISP 'N CRUNCHY PICKLES

10 medium cucumbers	2 T. mixed pickling spice
8 C. sugar	4 C. vinegar
5 T. salt	

Pour boiling water over cucumbers at night. Drain off the next morning. Use the same procedure for the next three mornings. On the fifth day, drain and slice cucumbers in one half inch slices. Bring ingredients to a boil and pour over sliced cucumbers. Let stand 2 days. Then bring to a boil and seal in jars.

MRS. DON SNYDER

DILL PICKLES

Wash, slice and pack cucumbers in quarts or half gallon jars. In each quart put:

¼ t. horse radish	1 clove garlic, sliced
¼ t. celery seed	1 crown dill

Now you mix together:

1 qt. vinegar	1 C. salt
3 qts. water	1 heaping T. powdered alum

Let come to boil. Pour boiling hot over cucumbers and seal.

MRS. E. J. QUILLEN

KOSHER DILL PICKLES

20-25 four inch cucumbers	1 qt. cider vinegar
⅛ t. powdered alum	1 C. coarse salt
1 clove garlic	3 qts. water
2 heads dill	grape leaves
1 hot red pepper	

Wash cucumbers. Let stand in cool water overnight. Pack into hot sterilized jar. To each quart add above amount alum, garlic, dill and red pepper. Combine vinegar, salt, water; heat to boil; fill jars. Put grape leaf in each jar and seal. Makes 6 to 8 qts.

MRS. LESTER SCOTT

WATERMELON PICKLES

10 lb. watermelon	2 pts. white vinegar
10 lb. sugar	

Tie in cheesecloth or thin bag, 1 oz. ginger root, 1 oz. whole cloves, 2 ozs. stick cinnamon.

Soak rinds in cold water overnight. Cook in water in which it was soaked, until tender (not soft).

Make syrup from sugar and vinegar. Boil until it thickens. Pour in rinds which have been drained, and wiped dry. Let come to a boil. Pour off syrup and reheat for three mornings.

MRS. WARNER DuBOSE

PICKLED OKRA

3 C. vinegar
1½ C. water
7 T. sugar

1 T. salt
3 pts. okra (small)

Cut ends and leave stems. Cook okra and all other ingredients until okra can be pierced with a tooth pick. Add 1 hot pepper pod to each pint jar and seal.

MRS. FRANK THOMPSON

FOURTEEN DAY PICKLES

FIRST DAY: Put 2 gallons of cucumbers, not too small, into stone jar. Add 3 cups of salt and enough boiling water to cover. Let stand 24 hours.

SECOND DAY: Pour off brine. Take cucumbers out of jar and rinse salt out of jar. Put cucumbers back in jar. Add ¼ cup powdered alum, cover with boiling water and let stand 24 hours.

THIRD DAY: Pour off alum water. Cover with clear boiling water and let stand 24 hours.

FOURTH DAY: Boil 1 gallon vinegar with small box pickling spices for 20 minutes. Pour over cucumbers and let stand 9 days.

LAST DAY: Cut cucumbers in round slices and put in jar — layer of cucumbers and layer of sugar, using the same thickness of each. It takes between 8 and 10 pounds of sugar. Leave these in jar until all sugar has dissolved. Then pack pickles in fruit jars and seal.

MRS. J. R. SIMMONDS

ICICLE PICKLES
(Simplified Recipe)

This is a short cut and the result, we think is an excellent pickle.

Put into a large crock, two gallons of cucumbers cut in narrow strips, with seeds removed. Add one pint of salt and one gallon of boiling water. Let stand 24 hours.

Drain off water and add one gallon of boiling water and one chunk of alum, size of walnut (alum makes crisp pickles). Let this stand 24 hours.

Drain water off. Mix 2½ qts. of vinegar, 8 pts of sugar, ¼ C. pickling spices (mixed). Bring to boil. Pour this syrup over pickles which you have placed in clean jars. Seal.

Don't open jars for at least four weeks to serve.

MRS. MACKINNON ELLIS

"PUT UP" RASPBERRIES

Clean and wash red raspberries. Fill half full a glass jar (quart or 2 quart), then on top pour granulated sugar to the top of jar. Cover firmly and put in icebox. Forget about them until Christmas. The sugar will preserve the berries and they will be whole in a clear red syrup.

MRS. CHARLES PISTON

RELISH

2 medium heads of cabbage
8 carrots (medium)
8 sweet peppers (mixed)

12 medium onions
½ C. salt

Chop, mix, salt, and set 2 hours. Then drain. Add 5 C. sugar, 3 pts. vinegar, 1 T. mustard seed, 1 T. dry mustard. Pack in jar.

MRS. J. R. SIMMONDS

COLD RELISH

2 heads cabbage
8 red and green peppers
12 onions
2 bunches of celery
¼ lb. mustard seed

1 t. tumeric
1 qt. vinegar
2 lbs. white sugar
celery seed to taste
salt to taste

Chop cabbage, celery, onions and peppers. Drain. Mix with other ingredients. Heat through. Put into jars and seal.

MRS. ELMER LUCAS

PEPPER RELISH

12 sweet red bell peppers
3 pods hot pepper
1 C. sugar
1 T. salt

12 green bell peppers
9 medium onions
3 T. mixed spices
2 C. vinegar

Chop peppers and onions. Cover with boiling water and let stand 5 minutes. Drain. Cover again with boiling water. Let stand 10 minutes. Drain. Add sugar, seasoning and vinegar. Cook 15 minutes. Pack into hot jars and seal at once; preferably ½ pt. jar.

MRS. LEE HARR

UNCOOKED RELISH

½ peck (1 gallon) tomatoes, not too ripe
2 green peppers   2 large onions

Put through food grinder, or chop very fine. Mix with 1 cup salt. Put in a thin bag and hang to drain for 24 hours. Then mix thoroughly with 1 pint vinegar, 1 pint sugar, 2 T. white mustard seed, 1 t. celery seed, ⅛ t. cayenne pepper.

Do not cook or heat this mixture. It keeps perfectly without sealing. Makes about 3 pints.

MRS. WILLIAM A. McDONALD

STRAWBERRY PRESERVES

1 C. berries   1 C. sugar

Wash berries and drain well on a cloth for several hours. Measure berries and sugar — 1 qt. at a time.

Put into a flat vessel over low heat until juice melts the sugar, then increase the heat and let come to a boil. Boil for 12 minutes. Remove from heat and put into bowl and let stand overnight. Next morning, pour into glass jars and seal. These are grand—berries stay whole.

MIRIAM TATE

STRAWBERRY PRESERVES

1 qt. strawberries   3 C. sugar

Put 1½ C. sugar with fruit and boil 5 minutes. Add remaining sugar and boil 10 to 15 minutes. A watery fruit must be cooked longer.
Turn into earthenware jar and let stand 24 hours. Stir occasionally. Seal cold in sterilized jars.
The small quantity of fruit and short cooking period are the secret of the deliciousness of these preserves.
Of course, you understand that you can "do" as many quarts as the crock will hold, but only 1 quart must be cooked at a time.

MRS. FRANK TAYLOR

HOT PEPPER JELLY

¾ C. bell pepper (about   1½ C. cider vinegar
  3 medium)   1 bottle Certo
¼ C. crushed cayenne or   6½ C. sugar
  red pepper (scant)

Remove seeds from peppers, grind, save juice (or crush in blender). Mix peppers, juice, vinegar, add sugar. Bring to good rolling boil for 5 minutes. Cool 2 minutes; add Certo. Pour into jars. Serve as an hors d'oeuvre with cheese and crackers.

Mrs. David Torbett

LIME PICKLES

7 lb. cucumbers (sliced)   2 C. lime (dehydrated)
2 gal. cold water

Soak above ingredients for 24 hours, stirring often. Drain and wash well. Soak 3 hours in cold water and stir often. Drain again. Mix well solution of:

2 qts. vinegar   2 T. salt
8 C. sugar   1 t. celery seed
2 T. mixed spices

Add cucumbers to this mixture and let stand overnight. Next morning heat to boiling point. Boil for 30 minutes. Cool and can. Chill before serving.

Mrs. Carl Childers

PICCADILLI RELISH

1 gal. chopped green   2 bunches chopped celery
  tomatoes   3 lb. sugar
4 large chopped onions   1 qt. vinegar
½ gal. chopped cabbage   4 T. pickling spices, ground
10 chopped mangoes

Combine all ingredients and simmer 15 minutes. Pack in hot jars and seal. Serve with soup beans.

Mrs. Carl Childers, Sr.

PICKLED OKRA

Wash and drain small okra. Pack in sterilized jars. Make the following solution and pour over okra in jars while boiling hot.

3 C. vinegar   ½ C. sugar
1½ C. water   1 t. salt

Put one hot pepper pod in each jar and add ½ tsp. celery seed to each jar after adding liquid. Seal jars.

Mrs. J. D. Thomas

SALADS

APPLE - SWISS CHEESE SALAD

2 C. cubed red Jonathan apples (or any tasty red apples)
1 C. shredded Swiss cheese
½ C. chopped dates
½ C. chopped celery
1 C. shredded or finely chopped cabbage
1 T. horseradish
2/3 C. mayonnaise

Combine apples, cheese, dates, celery and cabbage. Mix horseradish with mayonnaise and toss gently into salad. Serve on crisp lettuce. Serves 4.

MRS. A. O. WOLFF

ARTICHOKE HEARTS WITH CRAB MEAT RAVIGOTE

Trim artichokes by removing a few outer leaves, the stems, and prickly ends. To avoid discoloration, place them in a bowl of cold water to which has been added the juice of one lemon or two ounces of vinegar. Cook in the same water until heart is tender. Drain by placing upside down. Carefully remove center leaves and the "choke" with your fingers. Fill centers with crab meat, fresh or canned, mixed with Sauce Ravigote.

––––––o––––––

SAUCE RAVIGOTE

1 C. mayonnaise, prepared or homemade
capers
chopped parsley
green onions, chopped
a bit of garlic
tarragon, fresh or dried
dry mustard
salt, paprika
lemon juice
artichokes (1 to each person)

Into the mayonnaise mix other ingredients to taste; blend with crab meat. (Serve as a salad or luncheon dish.)

MRS. JAMES R. MacLEAN

RIBBON ASPIC
(Cheese Layer)

1½ t. gelatin
¼ C. cold water
¼ C. hot water
3 oz. pkg. cream cheese, mashed
¼ t. salt
1 t. grated onion
½ C. heavy cream (whipped)

––––––o––––––

(Aspic Layer)

1½ T. gelatin
2 T. vinegar
1 t. sugar
¼ C. cold water
2 C. tomato juice
1 t. minced onion
1 t. salt

Make cheese layer first. Soften gelatin in cold water; then add to hot water and stir. Add remaining ingredients and place in refrigerator until chilled. Make tomato layer next. Soften gelatin in cold water. Bring other ingredients to boil and add gelatin. Cool and pour on top of cheese layer.

MRS. C. F. ARNOLD

ASPARAGUS FISH SALAD

2 C. asparagus tips	½ C. finely diced celery
1 C. shredded tuna fish or salmon	¼ t. salt
¼ t. paprika	½ C. French dressing

Combine fish, celery, salt ,and French dressing. Let stand thirty minutes. Arrange asparagus tips on crisp lettuce. Toss the fish and celery combination lightly on the asparagus. Serve with mayonnaise. Garnish with paprika. 6 servings.

MRS. W. D. GRINDSTAFF

AVOCADO SALAD

1 pkg. lime jello	2 C. hot water

Mash together and add to cooled jello:

1 avocado	1 pkg. cream cheese

When the above has "set," add these ingredients:

½ C. mayonnaise	¼ C. celery, chopped fine
½ green pepper, chopped fine	onion juice
	salt

Mix well and mold.

MRS. R. J. OVROM

RED CABBAGE SALAD

2 C. shredded red cabbage	½ C. chopped celery
2 C. cooked diced potatoes	½ C. chopped onion
4 hard boiled eggs, quartered	

DRESSING

¾ C. mayonnaise	¼ C. parsley
¼ C. French dressing	1 t. chili powder
salt and pepper	

Mix salad dressing but omit parsley and chili powder. Toss together and sprinkle parsley and chili on top.

MRS. DON KING

CAESAR SALAD

Romaine lettuce	¼ C. Worcestershire sauce
salt	½ C. wine vinegar
freshly ground black pepper	¼ C. lemon juice
2 C. French fried bread croutons	2 T. anchovies, cut and drained
1½ C. garlic flavored olive oil	6 T. grated Parmesan cheese
	2 coddled eggs

Place greens in bowl: sprinkle with salt and pepper. Add croutons, which have been sprinkled with finely chopped garlic and toss. Pour on oil, Worcestershire, vinegar, lemon juice and toss. Add anchovies, cheese and toss. Drop in eggs after coddling 1½ minutes. Toss and serve immediately. Fry croutons several hours earlier.

MRS. T. P. McKEE

BING CHERRY SALAD

2 boxes cherry jello
1 can bing cherries
1 No. 2 can crushed
    pineapple
½ C. chopped pecans

1 large or two small pkgs.
    cream cheese
2 6 oz. bottles of cola

Drain juice from cherries and pineapples (2 cups) and heat. Dissolve jello in hot juice. Add cherries, nuts, pineapple and cheese, cut into tiny cubes. Add the two colas. Serves 9 to 12 people.

MRS. EUSTIS A. LANCASTER, JR.

CHICKEN AND CUCUMBER SALAD

1 pkg. lime gelatin
1 pt. hot water
1 C. cucumber, grated
    (less if desired)

1 t. grated onion
1 T. vinegar
dash of paprika

Mold in rings and fill center with chicken salad.

MRS. J. J. BROWN

CHILI CHEESE MOLD

1 envelope gelatin
½ C. hot water
1 C. commercial chili sauce
1 C. cottage cheese

½ C. mayonnaise
½ t. salt
1 C. cream, whipped

Dissolve gelatin in hot water. Combine chili sauce, cheese, mayonnaise and salt. Add gelatin and mix well. Fold in whipped cream. Pour into oiled mold. Cover with wax paper and freeze. Before serving, allow 1½ hours to thaw.

MRS. OWEN CRUTCHER

CONGEALED SALAD

Soften 1 pkg. lime jello and 1 pkg. lemon jello in 3 C. hot water. Stir until dissolved and let stand until it begins to congeal. Add the following mixture:

Blend and add the following ingredients: carton of cottage cheese, 1 scant C. mayonnaise, 1 small can crushed pineapple, 2 t. prepared horseradish, 1 T. lemon juice and pinch of salt. Stir this well before adding to the jello. Serve with mayonnaise on top.

MRS. ALFRED S. TAYLOR

CHICKEN LUNCHEON SALAD

2 C. cooked chicken, cubed
½ lb. sharp cheese, shredded
¼ C. celery, chopped
½ C. slivered, toasted
    almonds

1 C. seedless white or
    green grapes
½ t. salt

Toss lightly with dressing of equal parts mayonnaise and whipped cream with lemon juice and sugar to taste. This salad will make a complete and delicious luncheon when served with a hot vegetable and rolls.

MRS. WALTER McLEOD

CRANBERRY SALAD

½ box cranberries	1 C. sugar
1 apple	1 whole orange (seeded)

Put these four ingredients through food chopper.

chop ½ C. celery and   ½ C. nuts

Mix all together in jello which is made with

1 pkg. cherry jello in 1-1/3 C. boiling water, cooled.

Congeal in refrigerator.

MRS. RICHARD BOOZE, JR.

RAW CRANBERRY SALAD

Grind 1 lb. cranberries and 1 orange rind. Add 1½ C. sugar. Soak 2 envelopes gelatin in ½ C. cold water and dissolve with juice of 3 oranges, heated. Add ½ C. chopped pecans. Mold. Sprinkle pecans on top. Serves 12.

MRS. FRANCES B. CARR

CUCUMBER MOUSSE

3 cucumbers	1 t. Worcestershire sauce
2 envelopes gelatin	1 t. onion juice
½ C. cold water	1½ t. salt
1 T. lemon juice	¼ t. pepper
¾ C. mayonnaise	2 C. cottage cheese

Cut cucumbers in chunks; scoop out seeds. Cook until tender. Drain and put through food mill. Soften gelatin in water and mix with hot pulp; cool slightly and add remaining ingredients. Place in mold and chill overnight.

MRS. GENE TAYLOR, JR.

"DELICIOUS" SALAD

1 envelope gelatin dissolved in	1 large pkg. cream
½ C. cold water	cheese (add to whipped
1 pkg. lemon jello	cream)
1 C. boiling water	1 small can pimiento, chopped
1 C. ginger ale	½ C. celery, chopped
1 large can crushed pineapple	2/3 C. almonds, chopped
	½ pt. heavy cream, whipped
	½ t. salt

Blend jello with boiling water. Add juice of pineapple. Add gelatin and let cool. When cool, add other ingredients.

MRS. R. R. JACKSON

EGG SOUFFLE SALAD

Dissolve 1 pkg. lemon jello in 1 C. hot water. Add ½ C. cold water, 2 T. vinegar, ½ C. mayonnaise, salt and pepper. Blend with rotary beater. Pour into refrigerator tray. Quick chill in freezing unit until firm one inch from edge of tray, but soft in center. Turn mixture into bowl and whip with beaters until fluffy. Fold in 3 finely chopped hard cooked eggs, ½ C. diced celery, and 1 T. each of diced green peppers, diced pimiento and finely chopped onion. Pour into loaf shaped pan. Chill until firm. Especially good with chicken.

MRS. HORACE DANCE

FRUIT SALAD

2 pkgs. lemon jello   1 C. pineapple juice
1½ C. water

Set aside to partly congeal. Add:

2 C. white cherries   2 C. crushed pineapple
2 oranges (sections)   2 C. marshmallows (chopped)
1 C. whipping cream

SAUCE

2 eggs, well beaten   4 T. lemon juice
4 T. sugar   2 T. butter

Blend well in double boiler and cool. Add to jello and fruit mixture. Fold in whipping cream.

MRS. J. EDDIE ANDERSON

GOLDEN GATE SALAD

1 C. crushed pineapple,   1 C. pineapple juice
    canned   1 C. grated carrots
2 envelopes of orange jello 1 C. cold water
2 C. boiling water

Drain the pineapple. Boil two cups of water and dissolve the orange jello. Add one cup of cold water and 1 cup of pineapple juice. Mix well. Fold in pineapple and carrots. Turn into a 1 qt. mold. Chill until firm.

MRS. JOE WOOD

FROZEN GRAPE SALAD

2 3-oz. pkgs. cream cheese 1 No. 2 (2½ C.) pineapple
2 T. mayonnaise   bits, drained
2 T. pineapple juice   1 C. heavy cream, whipped
24 marshmallows, quartered 2 C. Tokay grapes, halved
                            and seeded

Soften cream cheese; blend with mayonnaise. Beat in pineapple juice. Add marshmallows and drained pineapple bits. Fold in whipped cream and halved grapes. Pour into 1 qt. refrigerator tray. Freeze until firm. Cut in squares and serve. Serves 8. Nice to serve at bridge party with crackers.

MRS. LEE WALLACE

BING CHERRIES WITH OLIVES

1 pkg. cherry gelatin
1 large bottle chopped stuffed olives
1 large can bing cherries (pitted)
4 T. sherry
juice of 1 lemon

Dissolve gelatin in 1 C. hot cherry juice. Cool with another ½ C. cold juice to which sherry and lemon juice have been added. After gelatin is cold and starting to congeal, add drained olives and the cherries. Chill until congealed and garnish with chopped almonds.

SUE P. WALKER

JELLO HAM LOAF

1 pkg. lemon jello
½ pt. water
2 T. vinegar
3 or 4 slices of ham, chopped

½ C. pimiento
3 sweet pickles
½ C. walnuts
½ C. cabbage

Prepare jello and let cool. Add vinegar, chopped ham, cabbage, pimiento, pickles, and nuts. Mold.

MRS. MILTON DeVAULT
Kingsport, Tennessee

LAMB SALAD

2 C. diced cooked lamb
1 C. diced celery
3 hard cooked eggs
mayonnaise dressing

1 C. shredded cabbage
½ C. diced cucumber pickles
1½ t. lemon juice or vinegar
salt and pepper

Combine lamb, celery, cabbage, pickles, and lemon juice. Moisten with mayonnaise. Season to taste. Mix lightly. Serve on crisp lettuce. Garnish with slices of hard cooked eggs. If desired beef, pork, or mutton may be substituted for lamb. One half cup asparagus tips or carrots may be added to give variety in flavor. Good for a main dish.

MRS. W. D. GRINDSTAFF

MOLDED LIME JELLO SALAD

Dissolve 1 box lime jello in 1 C. boiling water. Chill and whip. Add:

3 T. grated carrot
3 T. chopped green pepper
1 T. grated onion

1 C. cream, whipped before
adding
1 C. mayonnaise
1 C. cottage cheese

Pour into mold and chill until firm.

MRS. CHARLES HURLEY
Grand Forks, North Dakota

LIME PINEAPPLE SALAD

1 pkg. lime jello
2 3-oz. pkgs. cream cheese
1 C. mayonnaise

1 pt. whipping cream
1 #2½ can crushed pineapple
½ lb. marshmallows

Put 1 C. hot water over jello and allow to cool until it begins to set. Drain 1 C. of juice from the pineapple; add to cheese and work with a fork until smooth. Add pineapple and marshmallows which have been cut into four pieces each. When jello has begun to set, whip the cream and fold into jello with mayonnaise and the other ingredients. Allow to set overnight. Serve on lettuce cups. Serves 16.

MARY D. SISK

LUNCHEON SALAD

1 10½-oz. can condensed
   tomato soup
1½ T. (1½ envelopes)
   unflavored gelatin
½ C. cold water
2 3-oz. pkgs. cream cheese

1 C. mayonnaise
1 C. chopped celery
2 T. chopped green pepper
1 t. minced onion (if desired)
½ C. broken nut meats

Heat tomato soup. Add the gelatin softened in cold water. Cool. Thoroughly combine remaining ingredients and add to the gelatin mixture. Chill until firm. Serves 6 to 8. If desired, add 1 lb. shrimp, cooked, cooled and diced.

MRS. W. J. MILLER

MACARONI SALAD

Cook 1 C. macaroni in boiling salted water until tender. Drain and rinse in cold water. Combine macaroni with:

2 T. chopped onion
2 T. French dressing

1 t. salt

Mix well. Combine 1 t. prepared mustard with 2 T. mayonnaise. To macaroni mixture, add:

¾ C. sliced raw celery
dash of pepper
½ C. chopped green pepper

3 T. chopped sweet pickle
½ C. shredded carrots

Toss lightly and chill until ready to serve.

MRS. KELVER WILLIS

MOON SALAD

Dissolve 1 pkg. lemon jello in 1½ C. boiling water. Add 2 T. vinegar and ½ t. salt. Cool. Place in refrigerator until it begins to set. Then beat until fluffy. Add 1 pt. cottage cheese, ½ C. mayonnaise and 1 T. onion juice. Replace in refrigerator until firm. Serves 6.

MRS. RALPH CROSS

CHICKEN PARTY SALAD

1 T. unflavored gelatin
¼ C. cold water
1 C. mayonnaise
1 C. heavy cream, whipped
½ t. salt

1½ C. diced cooked chicken
   or veal
¾ C. almonds, blanched,
   toasted and chopped
¾ C. Malaga grapes, halved
   and seeded

Soften gelatin in cold water and dissolve over hot water. Cool and combine with mayonnaise, whipped cream, and salt. Fold in chicken, almonds and grapes. Chill in individual molds until firm. Unmold on crisp lettuce and garnish with whole almonds and grapes. Serves 6.

MRS. A. L. COCHRANE

SPICED PEACH SALAD

peaches
1½ C. spiced peach juice
½ C. fresh orange juice

1 box orange jello
¼ t. grated orange rind
1 pkg. (small) cream cheese

Remove seeds from peaches and stuff hole with cream cheese. Place peach in center of mold and fill with jello mixture. Serve at party or bridge.

MRS. HUGH MOHLER

PERFECTION SALAD

2 envelopes unflavored gelatin	1½ C. finely shredded
½ C. cold water	cabbage
2 C. hot water	1 C. chopped celery
½ C. sugar	½ C. green pepper, chopped
1 t. salt	¾ C. tiny peas
½ C. vinegar	1/3 C. pimiento, chopped
2 T. lemon juice	

Soften gelatin in cold water. Dissolve in hot water. Add sugar and salt and stir until dissolved. Add vinegar and lemon juice. Cool. When mixture begins to thicken, add remaining ingredients. Chill until set. Garnish with olives and unmold on lettuce.

DRESSING

2 pkgs. cream cheese	½ t. grated onion
1 oz. blue cheese	¼ t. salt
½ C. ground nut meats	2/3 C. mayonnaise
1 t. Worcestershire sauce	

MRS. W. R. RIGELL

PINEAPPLE SALAD

Combine: 2 well beaten eggs, 2 T. flour, ½ C. sugar, juice from #2 can sliced pineapple. Add enough water to make 1½ C. of mixture. Cook over low heat until mixture thickens and set aside to cool. Combine ½ lb. cheese cut in small pieces, ½ lb. marshmallows, cut up, and 1 #2 can sliced pineapple, cut up. Place pineapple mixture in bottom of dish and pour cooled mixture over the top. Blend slightly and chill.

MRS. WALTER TEAGUE

POINSETTIA SALAD

1 #2 can of pears	3 T. vinegar
½ C. candy cinnamon drops	few drops red food coloring

Drain juice from pear halves. Combine this syrup with candy cinnamon drops and vinegar. Heat the syrup to boiling. Slice each pear half into four slices into the boiling syrup and let simmer for 20 minutes. Chill the pear slices until ready to serve. Then place on a salad plate on a bed of lettuce, arranging the pear slices to represent the poinsettia petals. Grate cheese into the center of each flower and serve with dressing. A few drops of red food coloring may be added to the pears before chilling for a more brilliant red.

MRS. SAM TAYLOR

HOT POTATO SALAD

1 C. milk	1 pimiento
2 T. flour	1 C. diced celery, stalk and
2 T. butter	leaves
1½ t. salt	10 stuffed olives
¼ t. pepper	2 hard cooked eggs
1 qt. diced potatoes	1/3 C. salad dressing

Make a white sauce with milk, flour, butter, salt and pepper. Add potatoes and heat. Just before serving, add remaining ingredients and mix lightly. Serve hot. Serves 6 to 8.

MRS. JOSEPH R. HUDSON

ROQUEFORT CHEESE RING

2 small pkgs. cream cheese
1 C. crumbled roquefort
   cheese
1 t. chopped parsley
2 T. onion juice

1 t. salt
1 envelope plain gelatin
   dissolved in ¼ C. water
½ pt. whipping cream
paprika

Soften cream cheese with ½ C. of plain cream. Mash roquefort with fork and blend with cream cheese. Add seasoning. Melt gelatin over boiling water and cool; add to cheese mixture. Fold in whipped cream and pour in ring mold which has been oiled lightly with salad oil. Grapefruit sections and avocado mixed with French dressing make a good filling. Men love this salad.

MRS. ALFRED ABERNETHY

SIX CUP SALAD

1 C. crushed pineapple
1 C. fruit cocktail
1 C. coconut (grated fresh
   is best)

1 C. sour cream
1 C. cottage cheese
1 C. small marshmallows

Drain all fruit and mix with other ingredients. Chill overnight, if possible, before serving. Serve on crisp lettuce leaves. This makes a fine luncheon salad.

MRS. JACK TANNER
Kingsport, Tenn.

MOLDED SHRIMP SALAD

1 pkg. lemon gelatin
½ C. finely chopped celery
1 C. shrimp
1-2/3 C. hot water

¼ t. salt
¼ C. stuffed olives
¼ C. chopped sweet pickles

Dissolve gelatin in hot water and add salt. Clean shrimp, and add celery, olives, and pickles. Combine with gelatin mixture. Pour into molds and chill.

MRS. PORTER MARSHALL

SLAW AND COOKED DRESSING

½ head cabbage
1 T. grated onion

1 tomato
1 carrot

Shred cabbage and chop other ingredients.

1 egg
½ C. brown sugar
1 dash pepper
1 t. salt
½ C. vinegar

½ C. cold water
1 T. flour
1 t. dry mustard
1 lump butter

Mix dry ingredients. Add wet ingredients. Add egg and stir constantly over low heat until thick. Add butter and strain over slaw.

MRS. C. T. HERNDON

SPINACH SALAD

Combine:—

1 lb. fresh tender spinach	1 box cottage cheese
½ C. pecans	

Mix separately and let stand:

½ C. sour cream	2 t. horseradish
¼ C. sugar	½ t. dry mustard
3 T. vinegar	salt

Toss just before serving.

MRS. ROBERT BLACKSTONE
Washington, D. C.

SUMMER SALAD SUPPER

½ of a 7-oz. box of shell or large elbow macaroni	1 C. celery, diced
	½ C. sliced ripe olives
1 can drained tuna fish	2 tomatoes, quartered
1 small onion, chopped fine	mayonnaise
2 hard cooked eggs, sliced	salt

Cook macaroni as directed on package. Drain; do not rinse. While macaroni is cooking, prepare other ingredients. Combine all with drained macaroni, salting to taste and add enough mayonnaise for desired moistness. Use sliced eggs and tomatoes for garnish. Serves 4. Men like this—use as a main dish.

MRS. GUY CARR

SUPER SUPPER SALAD

1 head lettuce	2 hard cooked eggs
1 cucumber, peeled and diced	2 tomatoes
1 green pepper, cut in shreds	1 C. French dressing
1 C. cooked ham or luncheon meat, cut in shreds	1 T. bleu cheese
	1 T. catsup
1 C. cooked chicken, shredded	

Tear lettuce into bowl, add cucumber, pepper and meat. Blend cheese and catsup with the dressing and toss lightly with the salad. Just before serving, add eggs and tomatoes cut in wedges and toss very gently to distribute. Serve immediately. You might like to omit the bleu cheese and substitute shrimp or flaked tuna for the meat. Can be used as a main dish.

MRS. A. O. WOLFF

TOMATO ASPIC

2½ C. tomatoes	dash cayenne
½ t. salt	1 envelope gelatin
1 stalk celery, diced	1 t. lemon juice
1 green pepper, diced	1 t. minced onion

Boil first five ingredients ten minutes. Add remainder and turn into mold.

MRS. JOHN PLATT

TOMATO - AVOCADO SALAD

Heat 2 C. of tomato juice with a few celery leaves and 1 bay leaf. Keep it at simmering point a few minutes. Do not boil. Strain. Soften 1 envelope unflavored gelatin in ¼ C. cold water. Add to hot tomato juice. Stir until dissolved. Season with 1 t. sugar, 1 T. grated onion, 1 T. vinegar, ½ t. chili powder and salt to taste. Chill until thick but not set. Pour into a six cup mold that has been rinsed in cold water. Chill in refrigerator. Now prepare the avocado part of salad:

Soften 2 envelopes of unflavored gelatin in ½ C. of cold water. Skin and remove pits from three large avocado pears. Puree through strainer. Add 5 T. lemon juice quickly. Season with 1 T. grated onion, 1¼ t. salt, 4 drops of tabasco and ¼ t. Worcestershire. Add ½ C. boiling water to softened gelatin. Stir until dissolved. Cool and fold in avocado and ½ C. mayonnaise. Beat until smooth and pour into mold on top of aspic.

MRS. E. T. BRADING

TOMATO ICE

1 small square cream cheese	½ t. minced onion
1 can tomato soup	½ t. Worcestershire sauce
1 C. mayonnaise	

Soften cheese, cream and add mayonnaise, soup, onion and Worcestershire sauce and freeze. It is better to mix with electric mixer.

MRS. EARL REASOR

MOLDED TUNA FISH SALAD

1 box lemon jello	1 C. diced cucumber
1 C. hot water	1 small can peas
½ C. mayonnaise	1 can tuna fish
½ C. whipping cream	1 T. chopped pimiento

Dissolve jello in hot water and allow to partially set. Whip and add other ingredients. Pour into an oiled mold. Chill in refrigerator several hours before serving.

MRS. HOWARD PATRICK

TWENTY - FOUR HOUR SALAD I

2 C. white cherries, halved and pitted	2 eggs
2 C. diced pineapple	2 T. sugar
2 C. orange sections	¼ C. light cream
2 C. quartered marshmallows	juice of 1 lemon
¼ lb. almonds, blanched and chopped	1 C. heavy cream, whipped

Combine well-drained fruits. Add marshmallows and nuts. Beat eggs until light. Gradually add sugar, light cream, and lemon juice. Mix. Cook in double boiler until smooth and thick, stirring constantly. Cool. Fold in whipped cream. Pour over fruit mixture and mix lightly. Chill 24 hours. Do not freeze. Serves 10 to 12.

MRS. JESSE McGLONE

TWENTY - FOUR HOUR SALAD II

Mix:

1 medium can diced pineapple
½ lb. marshmallows, cut up
¼ lb. almonds, blanched
and split

1 pt. whipping cream
1 small bottle
maraschino cherries

---◦---

DRESSING

3 egg yolks
3 T. sugar
1 t. salt

¾ C. pineapple juice
1 T. flour
3 T. vinegar

Beat egg yolks and add the other ingredients. Cook in double boiler until mixture coats spoon. When cool, add to the salad mixture. Then whip cream and add to cold salad. Place in molds or dish, let stand 24 hours in refrigerator. Excellent served with tea, coffee and crackers. Can be used as a dessert.

MRS. ELNA H. McAFEE

WHITE SALAD

1½ C. shredded cabbage
1 C. sliced pineapple (cut
in small pieces)

1 C. coconut
½ C. marshmallows
½ C. chopped almonds

Mix cabbage, pineapple, coconut, almonds and marshmallows together with 2 T. salad dressing. Blanch and skin almonds before using.

MRS. TOM WEBB

VEGETABLE AND HERB SALAD

6 to 8 C. halved and peeled boiled new potatoes
½ C. light tarragon vinegar
2/3 C. white wine
¼ C. finely chopped parsely
¼ C. finely chopped chives
1 T. sugar
2 t. salt

1 t. seasoned salt
¾ t. freshly ground pepper
¼ C. salad oil
3 medium tomatoes,
cut in wedges

Combine wine and vinegar in saucepan and bring to a boil. Pour over the potatoes in a large bowl. Add the chives and parsley, sugar, seasoned salt, salad oil and half of the salt and pepper to the potatoes. Mix well, but gently. When cool, refrigerate. Sprinkle the tomatoes with the rest of the salt and pepper and refrigerate. Chill both of these thoroughly and just before serving toss together. Green peas can be tossed with this salad for added flavor and color. French cut green beans, cooked or canned, which have been marinated in French dressing, can be served on the platter with this salad also.

This recipe, which originally was copied from a magazine, has had individual changes added to suit family tastes and has become a great favorite.

ANNE MAE'S CUCUMBER SALAD

1 pkg. lime jello   ¾ C. hot water
              (Dissolve jello in water)

ADD:

¼ C. lemon juice   1 t. onion juice
¼ t. salt
              (Chill until thickened)

FOLD IN:

1 C. chopped cucumber   1 C. commercial sour cream
                              (whipped in mixer)

Pour in oiled molds. Chill until set. Serve on THICK SLICES TOMATOES with lettuce and mayonnaise. Keeps for days.

Mrs. T. D. Evans

APRICOT NECTAR SALAD

1 can apricot nectar (12 oz.)   Juice of one lemon
1 pkg. lemon jello

Combine lemon and apricot juice; add water to make 1 pint; heat and pour over lemon jello. Can be served plain or have 1 can of combined grapefruit and orange sections added. Pour into individual molds and congeal. Serves 4 to 6.

Mrs. W. S. Sells

CONGEALED SALAD

2 small pkg. lemon Jello   1 C. boiling water

Dissolve Jello in boiling water and let partially set in refrigerator
ADD:

1 C. chicken and rice   1 C. chopped celery
  soup, undiluted   2 T. grated onion
1 C. chicken gumbo soup   2 C. flaked tuna or 1 C. crab-
  or cream of chicken soup,   meat and 1 C. lobster
  undiluted   1½ T. lemon juice
1 C. mayonnaise
4 T. chopped green peppers

Fold in 1 cup whipped cream. Mix as any congealed salad and put in mold. Bundt pan is perfect.

Mrs. Charles Gordon

CRANBERRY SALAD

1 pkg. lemon jello   1 pkg. orange jello
2¼ C. boiling water
(Mix well and let cool)

COOK:
    2 C. fresh, whole cran- and 2 C. sugar
      berries (cooked as on   1½ C. water
      pkg.)

MIX:
    1 C. crushed pineapple   and ½ C. black walnuts

Let cranberries cool, then mix cranberries, jello, pineapple and nuts in a mold and let set.

Mrs. Charles Smith

LIME SALAD

MIX AND LET GET SYRUPY:
    1 pkg. lime Jello   1 C. boiling water
    1 small can crushed pineapple

ADD:
    1 C. cottage cheese (small   1 C. marshmallow cream
      curd)
    (Whip into above mixture, let set)

ADD:
    ½ pt. cream, whipped   ½ C. chopped nuts

Will serve 12 average or 8 large servings.

Mrs. E. T. Brading

PINK ARTIC FREEZE SALAD

2 (3 oz.) cream cheese (softened)

ADD:
    2 T. salad dressing and   2 C. whole cranberry sauce

MIX WELL:
    ½ C. chopped nuts   1 (9 oz.) can drained crushed
      (pecans or walnuts)   pineapple

FOLD IN:
    1 C. whipped cream

Pour into 9" x 9" pan; freeze at least 6 hours. Cut in squares and serve on lettuce.

Mrs. J. W. Birdwell

RASPBERRY SALAD

1 pkg. raspberry jello   1¼ C. hot water

Dissolve Jello in water. Add 1 package frozen raspberries (slightly thawed). Let this set up a little and add 1 small can crushed pineapple (drained), 1 large sliced banana, ¼ cup walnuts (chopped).

TOPPING

½ pt. sour cream   1 heaping t. confectioners
Squeeze of lemon   sugar

Mrs. John Wilson

RHUBARB SALAD

1½ C. hot rhubarb   1 pkg. raspberry or
1 C. finely diced tart apple   strawberry Jello
1 C. unsweetened pineapple 1 C. chopped pecans
   juice   1 T. lemon juice

Cook frozen or fresh rhubarb to mushy stage with 2 Tbs. sugar. Pour over gelatin, stir and cool. Add remaining ingredients and put into molds.

Mildred Thomas

STRAWBERRY SALAD

12 x 8 x 2 baking dish   2 large pkg. strawberries
2 small or 1 large pkg. of 8½ oz. can crushed
   strawberry Jello   pineapples
1 C. boiling water   3 med. bananas, sliced
1 pt. sour cream (can use   1 C. chopped nuts
   Philadelphia cream cheese)

Pour ½ mixture in bowl, let firm, then spread sour cream over it evenly. Spoon remainder of mixture over cream, then chill.

Mrs. James H. Miller

SUMMER SALAD

1 pkg. lemon Jello   1 med. cucumber, grated
1½ C. water   1 large carrot, grated
½ C. mayonnaise   1 carton cottage cheese
1 small onion, grated

When Jello begins to congeal, add mayonnaise and beat well. Add cottage cheese and other ingredients. Pour into mold and congeal.

Mrs. Bailey Rice

SUNSHINE SALAD

1 pkg. lemon Jello	2 C. boiling water
1 pkg. orange Jello	1½ C. cold water

Combine the above ingredients and let set until it begins to congeal. Then add: 40 miniature marshmallows, 1 No. 2 can crushed pineapple, 2 large bananas, chopped. Let set till firm.

SAUCE

½ C. sugar	1 C. pineapple juice
1 T. flour	1 pkg. dream whip (whipped)
1 egg (well beaten)	1 (8 oz.) pkg. cream cheese

Combine sugar and flour in small saucepan; slowly add pineapple juice. Cook this until mixture begins to thicken. Add about ½ cup of this mixture to well-beaten egg. Then finish cooking until thick. Cool. Have cream cheese at room temperature and combine it with this mixture. Fold in dream whip and spread over salad.

Mrs. D. M. Chambers, Jr.

WHIPPED CREAM SALAD

1 No. 2 can crushed pineapple	1 small can pimento
1 box lime Jello	1 C. celery
1 box lemon Jello	1 C. chopped nuts
1 large size cream cheese	1 pt. whipping cream

Heat crushed pineapple and dissolve the two packages of Jello in it. Mix cream cheese, pimento, celery and nuts. Add to gelatin mixture. Whip cream and fold into gelatin mixture. Chill. Serves 12 to 16.

Mrs. Latham R. Winn

CABBAGE SLAW

1 med. green cabbage, shredded
1 med. onion, chopped
½ C. chopped celery
¼ C. chopped green pepper

1 or 2 ripe tomatoes, cubed
1 large handfull cheese Ritz crackers, crushed
1 C. grated cheddar cheese
Salt, pepper, paprika

Enough mayonnaise to make mixture have consistency of slaw. Approximately 4 to 5 heaping Tbs.-use your own preference. Combine ingredients.

Mrs. Bill Stevens

CALICO SALAD

1 lb. can Kraut (washed and drained)
1 med. onion (1½ c.)

2 pimentos, chopped
¼ C. sliced radishes
1 small green pepper (¼ C.)

POUR OVER:

½ C. vinegar
½ C. sugar
¼ C. oil
1 t. salt

½ t. black pepper
½ t. garlic salt
1 t. celery seed

Refrigerate for 24 hours before serving. Keeps several days.

Ann Young

COLE SLAW

1 small head lettuce, chopped
1 green pepper, diced
3 tomatoes, diced
1 small onion, grated fine
1 t. salt
½ C. vinegar

1 C. mayonnaise
1 small head cabbage, chopped or grated
2 nice carrots, grated
1 C. diced celery
1 C. granulated sugar
½ t. black pepper

Put together in large bowl and mix well before serving. Add mayonnaise last.

Mrs. Dan Wexler, Jr.

KRAUT SLAW

1 (No. 2½) can Kraut, chopped
1½ C. sugar
½ C. vinegar

1 med. chopped onion
1 med. chopped bell pepper
½ C. Italian (Kraft) salad dressing

Mix all except salad dressing. Let stand 24 hours. Then drain and add dressing. Put in jars and refrigerate. Will keep well.

Mrs. John Wilson

CHEF'S SALAD

¾ head hearts lettuce
½ C. julienne baked ham
⅓ C. julienne tomato

½ C. julienne chicken
1 T. chopped pickle

SALAD DRESSING

1 t. finely chopped chives
3 T. mayonnaise
3 T. Olive or Wesson oil

1 chopped boiled egg
2 T. vinegar or less
1 T. Worcestershire sauce

A touch of garlic can be added. 395 calories to one portion.

Mrs. Alfred Abernethy

A MOST UNUSUAL SALAD

2 C. torn head lettuce
2 C. torn romaine lettuce
1 med. red or white onion, thinly sliced
1½ C. drained peas

2 C. curley endive
6 T. mayonnaise
1 C. julienne strips Natural Swiss Cheese
6 slices bacon, crisp crumbled

Method: Place ⅓ of salad greens into bowl; dot with several tablespoons of mayonnaise and top with ⅓ onion; sprinkle with sugar (about 1 tsp.); dash salt (about ¼ tsp.); and freshly ground pepper. Add ⅓ of peas and cheese. Repeat layers—seasoning each. Do not TOSS-cover-chill 2 hours. Just before serving top with bacon and toss. Makes 6 servings. It mellows and makes its own dressing. If these greens are not available, use anything you like. I often use fresh spinach.

Mrs. A. E. Miller

DAY-BEFORE SALAD RING

1 envelope unflavored
    gelatin
¼ C. boiling water
1 avocado, sliced fine
2 T. green pepper, chopped
    finely
1 C. whipped cream

¼ C. cold water
1 can asparagus tips, cut in
    pieces
12 stuffed olives, sliced
1 C. mayonnaise
2 hard-boiled eggs, chopped

Soak gelatin in cold water; dissolve in boiling water. Mix all ingredients together. Mold and let stand in refrigerator until set-
preferably overnight. Fill center with shrimp, lobster, crab meat, or
tuna. Fills one quart mold.

Mrs. John Wood, Jr.

MOLDED ASPARAGUS SALAD

**Heat liquid from large can (303) Asparagus (1 cup)
Dissolve 1 envelope gelatin in ¼ C. cold water
Stir together and set aside to cool.**

Blend:

½ C. mayonnaise
½ C. sour cream
2 T. lemon juice
1 t. salt

1 t. vinegar (or to taste)
Pinch of sugar
½ C. slivered almonds

Add to gelatin mixture. Put in refrigerator and when it begins to set,
add asparagus and almonds. Serve with small amount of mayonnaise.

Mrs. Sam Doak

BEAN SALAD

1 can green beans
1 can kidney beans
1 large onion, sliced or
    chopped coarsley

1 can wax beans
1 can lima beans
1 green pepper, diced
    coarsley

Marinate 24 hours in dressing made as follows:

Simmer ¾ cup sugar in ½ cup salad oil and ¾ cup vinegar, until
sugar is dissolved.

Add salt & pepper to taste. Combine this mixture with 1 bottle
Catalina dressing and pour over beans, onions and pepper.

Mrs. C. E. Jacobs

POTATO SALAD WITH SOUR CREAM DRESSING

6 C. diced cooked potatoes	½ C. chopped celery
¼ C. sliced green onion	½ C. mayonnaise
1 C. sour cream	1 t. prepared mustard
¼ C. vinegar	1½ t. salt
4 hard cooked eggs, chopped	½ t. pepper

Combine ingredients and serve.

Mrs. Wesley Bates

VEGETABLE SALAD (FRENCH)

Any kind of cooked vegetable may be used to combine this salad. (For example: peas, carrots, cauliflower, corn or green beans). The following vegetables are essential: red beets, raw apple, raw celery and pickles. All vegetables are cooked (except ones specified "raw"), cut into small pieces and mixed.

Dressing: Equal parts of sour cream and mayonnaise. Salt, sugar, and lemon juice to taste. Add small amount of beet juice to make salad pink. This salad should be prepared several hours before the meal. It will keep for one or two days in the refrigerator.

Mrs. Walter Fleischmann

SLICED TOMATOES IN HERBED FRENCH DRESSING

4 t. salt	¼ t. black pepper
1 t. basil leaves	1 t. paprika
¼ t. garlic powder	1 C. salad or olive oil
½ t. dry mustard in 1½ t. water (let stand 10 min.)	3 T. fresh lemon juice
	4 large ripe tomatoes, sliced
1 T. sugar	2 T. red wine vinegar
2 t. chopped onion or chives	

Mix all ingredients, pour over sliced tomatoes and onion. Let stand at least one hour.

Mrs. Hanes Lancaster

CHICKEN-ALMOND SOUFFLE' SALAD

1 pkg. lemon Jello	¼ t. salt
1½ C. water	Dash of pepper
3 T. lemon juice	½ C. mayonnaise

Freeze 15 minutes until firm around edges. Turn into bowl and whip until fluffy.

Fold in: 1 cup diced chicken
　　　　½ cup grapes
　　　　⅓ cup slivered almonds

Mrs. Louis Rice

HOT CHICKEN SALAD

2½ C. diced, cooked chicken or crab-meat	1 C. mayonnaise
2 C. thinly sliced celery	2 T. lemon juice
½ C. chopped toasted almonds	½ C. grated cheese
	1 C. crushed potato chips
2 t. grated onion	½ t. salt

Combine all ingredients-except cheese and chips. Pile lightly in 9 x 9 pan or (sea-shells)-sprinkle with cheese and chips-Bake at 450 degrees for 15 minutes.

Mrs. J. W. Birdwell

JELLIED HAM OR SHRIMP SALAD

2 envelopes plain gelatin	¼ C. green pepper finely chopped
½ C. cold water	1 T. grated onion
1 can tomato soup	1 C. mayonnaise
3 (3 oz.) pkgs. cream cheese	1 (5 oz.) can shrimp or
¾ C. chopped celery	1 C. ground ham

Heat canned soup and add the dissolved gelatin-add cream cheese and beat until dissolved. Let cool and add remaining ingredients. Serve on salad greens.

Mrs. John Wood, Jr.

SEAFOOD

CRABMEAT AU GRATIN

1 C. cream	2 egg yolks
3 T. butter	½ to 1 C. mild cheese,
2 C. fresh or frozen crabmeat	grated
¾ t. salt	2 T. sherry
1 T. cornstarch	

Heat cream. Do not boil. Melt butter in a saucepan. Add cornstarch and mix well. Add crabmeat, salt and cook for 1 minute. Add cream. Stir until sauce is boiling and then reduce heat. Add beaten egg yolks. Mix well and pour into individual casseroles. Sprinkle grated cheese over the top and bake in 350° oven for 25 minutes. Add sherry just before serving. Serve with toast tips.

MRS. LEE WALLACE

CRABMEAT CASSEROLE

1 can crab meat	1 t. chopped onion
½ pt. (1 C.) mayonnaise	1 t. Worcestershire sauce
3 hard cooked eggs, chopped	1 t. chopped parsley
½ C. milk	salt and pepper to taste
2 C. fresh bread crumbs,	
(save some for top)	

Mix well. Put in buttered casserole. Sprinkle with crumbs. Dot with butter. Bake at 350° for 20 to 30 minutes. Serves 6.

MRS. BRUCE KIDD

CRABMEAT CASSEROLE

1 lb. crabmeat	½ t. salt
4 T. butter	dash of pepper
3 hard cooked eggs	2 egg yolks, slightly beaten
4 T. flour	1 small onion
4 T. vinegar	1 C. heavy cream
2 t. prepared mustard	2 egg whites, beaten
2 T. Worcestershire sauce	½ C. buttered crumbs

Pick over crabmeat to remove cartilage. Melt butter in double boiler. Separate hard cooked eggs and mash yolks in butter. Add flour, vinegar and seasonings and stir well. Chop egg whites and add together with beaten egg yolks and grated onion. Pour in cream and cook until mixture is very thick. Add crabmeat. Remove from heat. Fold in well-beaten egg whites. Fill crab shells or casserole and cover with buttered crumbs. Bake in 350° oven for 20 to 25 minutes. Serve at once.

MRS. FORREST MORRIS

STUFFED FISH

Have a large plank fish deboned at the butchers. After cleaning well, stuff with the following:

Browned bread crumbs	salt and pepper
Sour cream, enough to moisten	½ C. chopped ripe olives
lightly	stuff and sew

Brown one side in long pan, about 20 minutes. Then turn and place on plank with whipped potatoes outlining plate. Next to fish place tomatoes stuffed with well seasoned bread crumbs and sprinkled with sharp grated cheese. Place back in oven and brown other side and serve at once.

MRS. ADAM BOWMAN

CRABMEAT SOUFFLE

1 lb. crabmeat (white or dark)	2 T. prepared mustard
2 T. onion juice or 1 onion, grated	1 C. mayonnaise
1 C. chopped celery	few drops tabasco, Worcestershire, and salt to taste

Make sandwich spread of above ingredients

1 lb. N. Y. sharp grated cheese	2 C. milk
	4 eggs

Trim edges from sandwich bread. Butter deep baking dish. Butter one side of bread. Make very thick sandwiches. Place layers of sandwiches in bottom of dish, cover with cheese and place another layer of sandwiches and cheese (two or more layers deep). Mix beaten eggs and milk. Pour over sandwiches and put in refrigerator; for at least 2 hours or overnight. To cook, put baking dish in pan of water and cook for 1 hour at 325° Serves 6 to 8.

MRS. ROY CORMONY

FISH SOUFFLE

1 C. thick rich white sauce	1 C. finely flaked cooked fish, perch or trout better
3 eggs, separated	paprika
1 t. wine vinegar	

Prepare white sauce and cool. Stir in slightly beaten egg yolks. Marinate fish with vinegar and allow to stand a few minutes. Combine fish and sauce and blend. Fold in stiffly beaten egg whites. Bake 350° 45 to 50 minutes. Serves 6.

MRS. WELCH GALLOWAY

FISH STUFFED GREEN PEPPERS

6 green peppers	2½ T. butter
6 C. flaked fish	2 T. bread crumbs
2 C. boiled rice	¾ C. strained tomatoes
1 C. strained tomatoes	salt and pepper to taste
1 T. grated onion	

Remove stem and seeds of peppers. Mix fish, rice, 1 C. tomatoes, onion and seasonings. Fill peppers with mixture; place in baking dish. Cover with mixed bread crumbs and butter. Bake 25 minutes in 350° to 400° oven, basting frequently with the ¾ C. tomatoes.

MRS. WELCH GALLOWAY

LOBSTER WITH CHEESE SAUCE

Saute **1 medium onion, finely chopped, in butter.** Remove from skillet. Make medium cream sauce with cheese, leave in saucepan for time being. Cook **1 can lobster** for 3 minutes in butter. Add **2 T. brandy** or **sherry,** cook 1 minute longer. Add onions, cream sauce, ½ t. salt, **pepper, 1 small can mushrooms, nutmeg, and cayenne.**

Thin to proper consistency with rich cream. Serves 4.

MRS. BILL BRIDGEFORTH

LOBSTER SALAD

1 pkg. lemon gelatin	juice of ½ lemon
1 C. hot water	½ C. mayonnaise
½ C. cold water	¾ C. finely chopped celery
¼ t. salt	1 can lobster

Dissolve gelatin in hot water. Beat in ½ C. mayonnaise, salt and congeal. Add lemon juice to lobster. Whip gelatin mixture and add lobster and celery and pour into well-oiled mold. Let congeal for several
hours.

MRS. BRONCE McCLAIN

LOBSTER WITH WINE SAUCE

Melt 4 T. butter in a pan over direct heat. Add 1 T. chopped onion
and 1 lb. boiled lobster meat, cubed. Simmer until meat turns red.
Sprinkle with paprika and add ½ C. sherry wine. Simmer until wine
practically evaporates. Place pan over water and add 4 beaten egg
yolks mixed with 1½ C. thin cream. Blend. Just before serving,
stir in 1 T. brandy. Serve on buttered toast. Serves 5 or 6.

MRS. LESTER BALLEW, JR.

NEVER FAIL OYSTER SOUFFLE

4 T. butter	3 egg yolks, beaten
5 T. flour	¾ C. sifted bread crumbs
1 C. milk	½ pt. oysters
1 t. salt	3 egg whites, beaten stiff
dash pepper	

Make a sauce of the shortening, flour, milk, salt, and pepper. Pour
over egg yolks, beating constantly. Add bread crumbs and oysters
which have been cleaned and cut in half. Cool, but do not allow to
set. Fold in egg whites and pour into ungreased baking dish. Cook
in moderate oven 325° about 1 hour. Serves 6 to 8.

MRS. WELCH GALLOWAY

OYSTER BATTER

1 or 2 whole eggs	1 t. baking powder
½ C. flour	¼ C. milk
plenty of salt	saltine crackers

Drain oysters. Crush crackers for crumbs. Dip oysters in batter, then
roll in cracker crumbs. Place on cookie sheet in ice box on the morning before dinner. Fry in deep fat.

MRS. EDDIE BAYLOR

MINCED OYSTERS

1 qt. minced oysters	¼ C. melted butter
2 C. toasted bread crumbs	1 t. chopped onion
2 beaten eggs	4 T. chopped celery
salt and pepper to taste	

Cook celery and onion in melted butter until tender. Add oysters and
cook until edges curl. Add rest of ingredients and bake in oblong pan
about 25 minutes at 350°. Serves 12. A little poultry seasoning adds
zest to dish.

MRS. F. L. WALLACE, SR.

SALMON ROLL

1 C. flour	¼ t. salt
2 t. baking powder	½ C. milk
1 C. medium white sauce	2 C. salmon, flaked
2 T. butter	1 egg, slightly beaten

Sift flour and measure. Then sift flour with baking powder and salt. Blend with butter and milk. Mix thoroughly. Turn on lightly floured board. Knead lightly. Roll in sheet 2/3 as wide as long. Combine salmon, white sauce and egg, spread on dough. Roll as jelly roll, brush with milk and bake in hot oven 400° Makes 4 servings.

MRS. E. L. CAUDILL

BROILED SHRIMP

With every 16-ozs. boiled shrimp use:

¼ C. butter	dash red pepper
juice ½ lemon	salt to taste
½ clove garlic, chopped	garlic salt may be used

Melt butter in skillet; add garlic and cook for a few minutes. Add shrimp, lemon juice and seasonings. Stir until shrimp are well coated with butter. Place skillet under broiler for 3 or 4 minutes. Stir occasionally to lightly brown all shrimp. Overcooking will toughen shrimp.

MRS. TOM HAPPEL

SHRIMP WIGGLE CASSEROLE

Make sauce:

4 T. butter   2 T. flour   1¼ C. milk

When sauce is boiling add:

1 C. shrimp.   1 C. drained peas, paprika, celery salt·to taste

Lower heat and stir in (until thickened):

1 egg yolk   salt if needed   1 T. sherry

Serve the wiggle on rounds of hot buttered toast or place in a greased baking dish and cover with buttered bread crumbs or cornflakes. Brown under the broiler. Serves 4 to 6.

MRS. STANLEY BLACK

SHRIMP CURRY

2 lbs. shrimp	¾ C. water
1 C. sliced onion	2 cans condensed tomato
3 T. fat or salad oil	soup
¼ t. salt	1 T. meat sauce or extra T.
3½ t. curry powder	Worcestershire
1 t. vinegar	1 T. butter
1 t. sugar	6 C. cooked rice
1 t. Worcestershire sauce	

Saute onions in fat until brown and tender. Stir in next 9 ingredients. Simmer uncovered for 10 minutes. Add cooked shrimp and cook thoroughly Serve with rice.

MRS. CHARLES SHERROD, JR.

HAWAIIAN SHRIMP CURRY

6 T. butter or margarine	1 T. curry powder
1 t. minced onion	2 t. ginger
6 T. flour	1½ T. lemon juice
2 C. milk	1½ C. uncooked rice
1 C. coconut milk or use	shrimp, cooked and deveined
1 C. milk plus 1 T. sugar	

Melt butter in top part of double boiler over direct heat. Add onion and saute' until limp and golden. Stir in flour. Add milk and coconut milk and cook, stirring constantly, until sauce is thick and smooth. Blend curry powder, ginger, and lemon juice together and stir into sauce. Last, add shrimp and cook over boiling water for at least 30 minutes before serving. Meantime, boil or steam the rice until tender and prepare about 2/3 C. each of the following relishes:

*Ground or chopped roasted peanuts
*Chopped crisp bacon, or bacon and raw onion mixed
*Mango or apricot preserves, or orange marmalade
*Chopped hard cooked eggs

Shredded coconut	chopped green pepper
Chopped green or ripe olive	chopped preserved ginger

To serve, place a portion of the rice on each plate, ladel some of the steaming curry sauce over the rice, and pile it all high with a spoonful of each relish.

Note: *These relishes essential. The rest are optional.

MRS. ROBERT W. SUMMERS

SHRIMP ROCKEFELLER

½ lb. fresh spinach, (or	1½ stalks celery
1 pkg. frozen)	1 clove garlic
6 small green onions	½ C. parsley
½ head lettuce, chopped	

Dry all the above in a towel. (Very important).
Heat:

½ C. butter	1 T. flour
2 t. anchovy paste	⅛ t. tabasco sauce

Add chopped greens to mixture and simmer for 10 minutes. Add ½ C. lightly toasted bread crumbs. Spread sauce over the bottom of a shallow baking dish and cover with 2 lbs. cooked shrimp. Make a medium cream sauce, using:

3 T. flour	3 T. butter	1½ C. milk
¼ t. Worcestershire sauce	¾ t. salt	

Pour over shrimp in casserole and add buttered bread crumbs. Bake 20 minutes at 350° until sauce bubbles.

MRS. LEWIS COSBY

SHRIMP ROLLS

1½ C. medium white sauce made with thin cream
2 C. cooked shrimp   8 rye rolls

Combine white sauce with shrimp. Heat rye rolls, cut open, scoop out some of center and fill with creamed shrimp. Serves 8.

MRS. CLEM WILKES

DEVILED SHRIMP

2 t. minced onion	1/3 C. flour
1/4 C. butter	2 C. milk
1 t. paprika	1 T. lemon juice
1 t. prepared mustard	2 C. cooked shrimp
1/2 t. salt	dash cayenne

Saute onion in butter and seasoning. Gradually add flour. Add milk and cook until sauce boils and thickens, stirring constantly. Add lemon juice and shrimp. Heat and serve over rice or chow mein noodles.

MRS. THOMAS ELLIS

LOUISIANA GUMBO

1 T. butter	1 pt. water
2 T. flour	2 qts. chicken stock
1 C. diced celery	2 small bay leaves
1 minced onion	1 t. thyme
2 cloves minced garlic	2 t. salt
1 lb. shrimp	1/2 t. pepper
2 C. crabmeat	1/4 t. cayenne
1/4 lb. diced ham	2 T. minced parsley
2 chopped green peppers	1/2 t. file powder
1/2 can tomato paste	

Brown flour in melted butter. Add celery, onion, and garlic. Cook over low heat until ingredients become transparent. Add shrimp and crabmeat and cook 5 minutes. Then add ham, green peppers, tomato paste, water, chicken broth and seasonings, except file and parsley. Simmer 1 hour. Just before serving stir in file and parsley. Serve with dry rice. Serves 8. The file powder can be found on the spice or fancy food counter of any large market.

MRS. TODD TILLMAN

TUNA BUNS

1/4 C. cubed cheese	3 t. chopped stuffed olives
1 can tuna	2 t. pickle relish
3 chopped hard boiled eggs	1/2 C. mayonnaise
2 t. minced onions	6 buns

Combine the ingredients and stuff in buns. Wrap in foil paper and refrigerate. Bake in foil for 15 minutes at 350°.

MRS. DON KING

TUNA LOAF

Separate 1 lb. tuna pieces by flaking with fork.
Add 2 C. soft bread crumbs

1/2 t. paprika	1 T. chopped onion
1 T. chopped parsley	1/2 t. salt
1 T. melted margarine	2 well beaten eggs
	1 C. tomato juice

Mix ingredients and pour into greased loaf pan. Bake at 350° about 30 minutes.

MRS. RAY SMITHEY

TUNA CREOLE

2 T. butter or margarine	1 large eggplant (about 1 lb.)
1/3 C. chopped onions	1 6 or 7-oz. can tuna
1 green pepper (diced)	2 T. chopped parsley
1-1/3 C. canned tomatoes	1 t. salt
½ C. water	dash of paprika

In skillet, melt butter over low heat; add onions and green pepper and saute 5 minutes. Add tomatoes and water and bring to boil. Cut unpeeled egg plant into ½ inch cubes. In large casserole, combine eggplant with tomato mixture and add tuna; sprinkle with parsley and salt and paprika. Cover and cook in moderately hot oven 400° about 25 - 30 minutes. Cover with bread crumbs and brown.

MRS. STANLEY BLACK

DEEP SEA DELIGHT

2 C. spaghetti, rice or noodles, cooked
1 can tuna fish or other sea food, cooked
1 can asparagus or frozen peas, drained
1 can condensed cream of mushroom soup

Grease casserole. Place spaghetti in bottom. Add fish, vegetable, and soup, putting dots of butter and grated onion throughout. Grate sharp cheddar cheese over the top and place in moderate oven for about 30 minutes. Serves 6.

MRS. ALF W. TAYLOR

TUNA POT PIE

1. Cook until tender in juice from 1 can of peas:
   1½ C. diced carrots   1½ C. diced potatoes
   3 T. chopped onions
2. Drain off liquid in saucepan and add to it:
   Oil from 7 oz. can tuna (chunk), and enough
   milk to make 2 C. liquid
3. Add to liquid:
   ¼ C. melted margarine   ¼ C. flour
4. Cook over medium heat, stirring constantly, until thickened.
5. Pour sauce over vegetables and add:
   1 C. canned peas   1 7 oz. can tuna
   salt and pepper to taste
6. Turn into greased 1½ qt. casserole and cover with pie crust, biscuit dough or buttered crumbs
7. Bake at 425° about 20 minutes or until dough is done.

MRS. E. O. THOMPSON

BAKED SALMON LOAF

2 C. soft bread crumbs	1 C. milk
1 small onion, chopped	1 T. lemon juice
2 T. butter	½ t. salt
¼ C. chopped celery	dash pepper
2 T. chopped pimiento	1 T. parsley
2 eggs, beaten	1 lb can salmon, flaked

Saute onion in butter. Combine with celery, salt, pepper, parsley, pimiento, lemon juice, and salmon. Combine eggs and milk and pour over bread crumbs Add to other ingredients. Shape into greased mold. Bake at 350° 30 to 35 minutes.

MRS. HARRIS HUNTER

CREOLE SHRIMP

2 T. butter	½ large green pepper,
1 T. flour	finely chopped
1 large onion, finely chopped	½ box fresh mushrooms
1 lb. frozen shrimp, cooked	or small can
and shelled	½ t. oregano
1 small can tomatoes	salt and pepper to taste
1 C. celery, cut in small	
pieces	

Melt butter in heavy skillet, work in flour, add onions and saute until lightly colored. Add rest of ingredients, except mushrooms, and cook slowly about 20 minutes. Add mushrooms and cook another 20 minutes. Serve with cooked fluffy rice. May be made the day before and reheated.

MISS EDITH McQUILKEN

ESCALLOPED OYSTERS

½ C. butter or margarine	1 qt. oysters
½ C. flour	1 onion
1½ t. paprika	½ green pepper
¼ t. black pepper	1 t. lemon juice
dash cayenne	1 t. Worcestershire
¼ C. cracker crumbs	

Melt butter, add flour and cook for 5 minutes or until light brown, stirring constantly. Add paprika, salt, pepper, cayenne. Cook 3 minutes. Add onion and green pepper which have been chopped fine. Add finely minced garlic. Cook slowly for 5 minutes. Remove from heat and add lemon juice, Worcestershire sauce and oysters, which have been picked over and heated in own liquid. Pour into dish and sprinkle cracker crumbs over top. Bake in oven 400° for 30 minutes.

MRS. DOROTHY R. FRIBERG

FILET OF SOLE

Use enough filet of sole for 4 servings and cover with water in shallow pan. Then add 2 pieces thyme, a sliced lemon, sliced carrot, dash pepper, ½ t. salt and 2 T. white wine. Boil gently for 15 minutes. Remove fish and save broth. Serve with sauce.

SAUCE: Heat to boiling point:

1 C. cream	2 finely chopped hard boiled eggs
¼ t. pepper	4 t. fish broth

Add, while stirring: **1 well-beaten**   ½ t. chopped parsley
     egg yolk

Pour sauce over fish while hot.

MRS. EDDIE BAYLOR

HOT - CRAB SALAD

4 hard boiled eggs, sliced	1 pimiento, cut fine
1 lb. can crab meat	salt and pepper to taste
(or frozen crab meat)	1 can cream of celery soup
½ C. almonds	(undiluted)

Combine all ingredients. Put in greased, glass baking dish. Cover with buttered bread crumbs. Bake at 375° for 25 minutes. Serve on head lettuce with ripe olives and tomato wedges.

MRS. SAMUEL L. BROOKSHER

WEST INDIES SALAD

1 lb. lump fresh crabmeat	4 oz. salad oil
1 large onion, chopped	4 oz. vinegar
Pepper to taste	4 oz. ice cold water

Place ½ of onion in bottom of bowl. Top with all the crabmeat. Put rest of onion on top of crabmeat. Pour liquids over this, only in the following order.

     a. 4 oz. salad oil
     b. 4 oz. vinegar
     c. 4 oz. ice water

Do not mix this—Cover. Marinate 4 to 8 hours in refrigerator. Mix before serving. Note: This is a great summer meal.

Mrs. David Hicks

HICKORY SMOKED FISH FILLETS

1 med. sized fish	1½ lemons
½ stick butter	Cheddar cheese, grated

Cut fish in two and remove bone, place fish skin side down on grill and do not turn over. Cook over charcoal to which hickory chips have been added. Baste fish with lemon sauce and butter. After fillets have cooked about 3 minutes, cover with cheddar cheese and continue basting until done.

Mrs. Preston Cobb

OYSTERS ON THE ROCKS

1 pint of select oysters (about 30) enough rock salt to cover a cookie tin. Drain oysters and spread on towel to dry and bring to room temperature. Put cookie tin with salt in oven for ½ hour at 400 degrees or until thoroughly hot. When ready to serve place 4 or 5 oysters on sea shell or oyster plate which has been covered with hot rock salt. Serve with lemon butter sauce.

SAUCE

4 T. butter	Large dash of Tabasco
⅓ C. lemon juice	

Mrs. Adam Bowman
Mrs. William E. McElveen

BAKED RED SNAPPER

2½ to 3 lbs. red snapper	Juice from 1 or 2 lemons
1 stick butter	¼ C. white dry wine
Salt	1 small onion
Paprika	Basil or Rosemary

Prepare fish for cooking. Wash well. Put in baking dish or boiler pan. Place whole onion inside of fish and then dot fish with butter, salt, paprika and basil. Pour lemon juice and wine over fish. Cover with foil. Bake 1 hour to 1 hour and 15 minutes basting fish often at 325 degrees.   Mrs. Alfred Bolton

BAKED SEAFOOD CASSEROLE

½ lb. crab meat	1½ C. finely chopped celery
½ lb. lobster meat	½ t. salt
1 lb. cooked and deveined shrimp	1 T. Worcestershire sauce
	2 C. crushed potato chips
1 C. mayonnaise	Paprika
½ C. chopped green peppers	¼ C. minced onion

Mix ingredients all together as though making a salad. Fill baking pan and completely cover with crushed potato chips. Sprinkle with paprika and bake at 400 degrees for 25 minutes. Serves 12.

Mrs. Latham R. Winn

EASY SALMON BAKE

Chill well 1 tall can salmon. Carefully cut into 4 rounds. Place each round on a square of aluminum foil. Add bit of bay leaf, salt, pepper, a bit of lemon juice, a dash of Tabasco and a slice of lemon to each round. Fold into 4 neat little packages. Bake at 350 degrees for 30 minutes. You'll be surprised.   Mrs. T. Dudley Evans

IRENE'S SALMON CROQUETTES

BEAT: 1 egg	½ C. cracker crumbs
¼ t. soda	Add: ⅓ to ½ C. buttermilk
	2 T. chopped onion

Mix with salmon. Drop by big spoonfuls in hot Wesson Oil and fry slowly.   Mrs. H. C. Seaton

SALMON CROQUETTES

2 cans salmon	¼ t. celery seed
1 C. med. white sauce	1 t. Worcestershire sauce
1 t. chopped parsley	½ C. dry bread crumbs
2 t. grated onion	

Roll into croquettes. Let chill and dip in beaten egg and then roll in biscuit crumbs (if available) or dry bread crumbs. Let chill again. Saute' in oil until golden brown.   Mrs. Sam W. Mitchell

SALMON LOAF

1½ T. butter	2 eggs (slightly beaten)
1½ T. flour	1 t. lemon juice
¾ C. milk	2 C. flaked salmon
Salt, pepper to taste	(fresh or canned)

Make sauce of butter, flour and milk; add seasonings and remove from fire. Slowly add beaten eggs; stir well and add fish and lemon juice. Grease baking dish, pour in fish mixture, cover top of dish. Set dish in container of boiling water; bake in 350 degree oven about an hour. Remove from oven to platter; decorate with hard boiled egg, parsley, and sections of lemon or serve cold on lettuce leaves with cucumber and mayonnaise. Good in sandwiches, too.

Mrs. Alfred Bolton

SCRAMBLED SALMON

6 slices bacon	2 T. chopped onion
1 7 oz. can salmon	4 eggs
salt and pepper	Parsley sprigs, or flakes
paprika	

Fry bacon crisp, drain and keep hot. Add onion to fat and fry till transparent. Pour off most of fat. Keep 1 Tbs. fat and fry onion in pan. Add salmon, stir until coated with fat and hot. Add beaten eggs and scramble as usual. Season and serve with bacon and freshly chopped parsley and sprinkle with paprika.   Mrs. Alfred Abernethy

DOUBLE SHRIMP CASSEROLE

4 oz. (3 C.) med. noodles	1 can frozen condensed
¾ C. milk	shrimp soup
½ C. mayonnaise or salad	¼ C. diced celery
dressing	1 T. chopped green onion
¼ t. salt	⅓ C. shredded natural
1 C. cooked shrimp	cheddar cheese
¼ C. chow mein noodles	

Cook noodles according to package directions. Thaw soup; combine with milk, mayonnaise, celery, onion, and salt. Mix well. Stir in cheese, shrimp, and cooked noodles. Pour in 1 or 2 quart casserole. Bake, uncovered, at 350 degrees for 30 to 35 minutes. Top with Chow Mein Noodles. Bake 10 more minutes. Makes 4-6 servings.

Mrs. Allen Harris, Jr.

FRIED SHRIMP

Wash and devein shrimp; place in ice water until ready to fry. Salt and pepper a small amount of buttermilk. Dip shrimp into buttermilk and roll in self-rising flour. Fry until brown in hot grease.

Mrs. Tom Mitchell

SHRIMP BISQUE

1 C. Pet milk
2 C. chicken stock
1 C. homog. milk
1 T. butter
1 T. flour

1 (10 oz.) pkg. frozen
cooked shrimp
1 (8 oz.) can tomato sauce
or puree

Blend shrimp in blender with part of chicken stock. Add flour and butter. Heat in saucepan with remaining ingredients. Season to taste with salt and pepper. I also use Spice Islands, Spice Parisienne and Saute' style onions.　　　　Mrs. Tom Happel

SHRIMPBURGERS

1 can shrimp, cleaned and
cut fine
Mayonnaise to make
spreading consistency

1 T. green pepper (finely
chopped)
1 T. onion (finely chopped)
1 T. celery (finely chopped)

Split hamburger buns, butter, spread with shrimp mixture. Top with ½ slice of cheese, place under broiler until bubbly and slightly browned. Serves 3-4.　　　　Mrs. T. A. Webster

SHRIMP JUBALAI

2 lbs. fresh shrimp
2 T. peanut oil
3 med.-sized onions
3 small cloves garlic
8 stalks pascal celery
1 green pepper
1 No. 2½ can tomatoes
4 bay leaves

1 t. thyme
2 t. chili powder
Salt
Pepper
1 (4 oz.) can mushrooms
1 small can pimento
1½ C. uncooked rice

Into a fairly large skillet with a close-fitting cover put 2 Tbs. peanut oil. When oil is hot, add garlic, peeled and sliced and 3 medium sized onions chopped. When onions are yellow and tender, add ¾ of the chopped celery (including all the leaves). Next, put into the mixture 1 chopped green pepper, and cook over medium heat for 5 minutes. Now put into the mixture a No. 2½ can tomatoes, along with 4 bay leaves, 1 tsp. thyme, 2 tsp. chili powder, salt and pepper to taste. Put lid on skillet and cook for 10 minutes. Next add washed and shelled shrimp and contents of 4 oz. can mushrooms and small can pimentos. Cook about 7 minutes. Add rest of celery and cook about 3 minutes longer. Serve over 1½ cups rice.

Mrs. Kent Herrin

DEVILED CRAB

1 lb. lump crab meat	2 eggs, beaten
½ C. minced onion	1 hard-boiled egg, chopped
¼ C. minced celery	1 T. white wine vinegar
¼ C. minced green pepper	1 t. Worcestershire
1 garlic clove, minced	¼ t. thyme
1 T. chopped parsley	Tabasco sauce
½ C. butter	1 t. salt
2 C. soft bread crumbs	½ C. heavy cream

Saute' onion, celery, green pepper, garlic and parsley in 6 Tbs. butter for 10 minutes. Cool. Combine 1 cup bread crumbs, cream, raw and cooked eggs, vinegar, Worcestershire, thyme, a few drops of Tabasco and salt with sauteed vegetables. Add crab meat and toss lightly to mix. Spoon into 12 scallop shells or individual baking dishes. Melt remaining 2 Tbs. butter and toss with remaining 1 cup bread crumbs. Top crab mixture with buttered crumbs. Place shells in shallow baking pan. Put ¼ inch water in bottom of pan. Bake in hot oven 450 degrees for 10 minutes, or until browned and hot. Serves 6.

Mrs. Al Miller

HOT CRAB MEAT SANDWICH

Day before..drain and remove bones from two 7¼ oz. cans crab meat. Pull apart and add 4 stalks celery chopped fine, 2 tsp. onion flakes, salt and pepper to taste and add about 2 T. mayonnaise. (Chill overnight). Cut crusts from 16 slices bread. Make sandwiches with crab salad. Cut sandwiches in half. Place in bottom of 13 x 9 x 2 pyrex dish. Beat 2 eggs and 1 pint of milk together; add 1 tsp. parsley flakes. Pour over sandwiches. Bake 325 degrees for 30 to 45 minutes.

Mrs. J. W. Conrey

IMPERIAL CRAB CASSEROLE

1 lb. crab meat	3 T. chopped green pepper
1 egg	¼ t. dry mustard
Dash of pepper	½ t. salt
1 C. mayonnaise	

Mix ingredients, stirring in crab last. Place in buttered casserole; top with buttered bread crumbs. Cook 25 minutes at 350 degrees.

Mrs. Charles Harvey

SHRIMP MOUSSE

1 can tomato soup	2 (3 oz.) pkgs. cream cheese
1½ T. gelatin	1 C. celery finely chopped
½ C. cold water	2 T. chopped green pepper
1 C. mayonnaise	2 small cans shrimp
1 t. onion	(3 oz.)

Heat soup and add gelatin which has been dissolved in cold water — cool. Combine rest of ingredients. Use individual molds if desired.

Mrs. William Blackard

TUNA ARTICHOKE CASSEROLE

1 can artichoke hearts	¼ C. chopped green pepper
1 can cheddar cheese soup	¼ C. chopped onion
1 can white tuna	

Put artichokes in bottom of casserole. Cover with ½ can soup, flaked tuna, onion and pepper. Then add the rest of the soup. Crush potato chips and cover the casserole with them. Bake at 350 degrees for 35 minutes.

Mrs. John Wilson

TUNA FISH PIE WITH CHEESE ROLL CRUST

½ C. sliced green pepper	½ t. salt
2 slices onions	3 C. milk
3 T. butter	1 can tuna
6 T. flour	1 T. lemon juice

Melt butter, add pepper and onion. Cook until soft. Add flour. Stir until well blended. Add salt, milk, slowly stirring, until thick and smooth. Bring to boil, boil 2 minutes. Add remaining ingredients. Pour into large baking dish and cover with cheese rolls.

CHEESE ROLLS

1½ C. flour	3 T. shortening
3 t. baking powder	½ C. milk or half milk and
½ t. salt	half water
Few grains cayenne	¾ C. grated cheese
2 pimentos chopped	

Sift together flour, dry ingredients, add shortening. Mix in thoroughly with fork. Add liquid to make soft dough. Toss lightly on floured board until outside looks smooth. Roll out into sheet 8 by 10. Sprinkle with cheese and pimento. Roll up like jelly roll. Starting at short side with sharpe knife cut 8 slices, flatten slightly and lay on top of creamed mixture. Bake in hot oven at 375 degrees for about 30 minutes.

Mrs. Alfred Bolton

BAKED FISH

1 3 - 4 lb. fish	6 slices onion
3 slices bacon	

Sauce:

1 C. catsup	1 t. prepared mustard
1 T. sugar	1 T. Worcestershire sauce
2 T. lemon juice	½ C. water
½ t. tabasco sauce, if desired	½ t. horseradish

Slit fish crosswise and insert slices of onion and bacon in slits. Pour sauce over fish and place in oven at 400°. Baste fish with sauce, adding water as needed. Cook until done. Approximately 1 hour.

MRS. CARROLL REECE

CRAB IN SHELLS

1 can crab or 1 C. fresh crab meat	1 small can mushrooms, stems and slices
1 egg	1 T. lemon juice
1 t. Worcestershire sauce	1½ C. white sauce
paprika, salt, pepper to taste	2 T. sherry

Mix all ingredients together. Butter shells and fill with mixture. On top of each, put a slice of lemon. Bake in moderate oven until slightly browned, 350° about 15 minutes.

MRS. PERRY HUNTER

CRAB GUMBO

1.
½ C. bacon fat	1 medium onion
1 garlic clove	1 small section green pepper (minced)
1 lb. diced fresh okra	
3 stalks celery (diced)	

Mix ingredients in large skillet and add 4 heaping T. flour and stir. This mixture burns easily. Let cook ½ hour covered, stirring ocassionally.

2. Add large can of strained tomatoes and 2 bouillon cubes dissolved in 4 C. soup stock. Then add 1 ½ T. chili powder. Let cook slowly for 1 hour.

3. Add 1 lb. crab meat, 1 can shrimp, and 1 T. Worcestershire sauce, 1 T. lemon juice, and salt to taste. Put salt and a pinch of cayenne pepper in before adding crabmeat. Let cook 20 minutes and serve with rice.

MRS. A. B. ANDERSON

CRAB AND RICE

Cook 2/3 C. rice, drain	¾ C. mayonnaise
add 2 C. crab meat	salt and pepper to taste
1½ C. tomato juice	1 scant t. hot pepper
1 grated medium onion	top with buttered crumbs
½ C. milk	

Bake at 350° 45 to 50 minutes.

MRS. MILTON GRAHAM
Bayside, California

HOT CRAB CROQUETTES

Make thick white sauce:

3 T. butter	1 t. salt
3 T. flour	⅛ t. pepper
1 C. milk	¼ t. Worcestershire sauce
¾ t. dry mustard	

And add:

1 T. minced onion	2 C. flaked crab meat

Mix all ingredients and chill well. Shape into 48 small balls. Roll in fine cracker meal, then in 2 well beaten eggs and into crumbs again. Fry in deep fat 375°. Delicious served as hors d'oeuvers.

MRS. MILTON GRAHAM

DEVILED CRAB

1 medium chopped green pepper	½ t. salt
1 medium chopped onion	dash pepper
1 C. chopped celery	1 t. Worcestershire sauce
1 6½-oz. can flaked crab meat	1 C. mayonnaise
1 6½-7 oz. can flaked shrimp (1 C.)	1 C. buttered crumbs

Combine ingredients. Fill shells or put in a casserole and sprinkle with buttered bread crumbs. Makes 8 shells. Cook 30 minutes at 350°.

MRS. IKE GREENE

Soups

BARLEY SOUP

Select 3 or 4 pieces, about 2 lbs., mostly lean brisket. Cover with water and boil until tender. Salt and pepper. Add:

½ C. uncooked barley	1 T. chopped parsley
1 medium onion, chopped	1 C. chopped celery, leaves
1 small carrott or pimiento,	and all
chopped	1 bay leaf

Cook slowly another 45 minutes. If too thick, add more water.

MRS. W. RAY MOSS
Memphis, Tennessee

CHICKEN SOUP

In a deep kettle **saute 1 C. minced onion, 1 C. chopped celery** in ¼ C. **butter,** until tender. Add ½ t. curry powder, ¼ t. salt, ¼ t. pepper, **1 can tomato soup, 1 can chicken soup with rice, 4 C. water or milk.** Simmer 15 minutes. Any leftover chicken or turkey may be used. A ball of rice topped with chopped almonds floated in soup makes an attractive variation.

MRS. FLOYD DOOLEY

CHICKEN NOODLE SOUP

3 lb. hen or stewing chicken, cut up
2 qts. cold water
Cover and bring slowly to boil. Remove scum. Add:

1/3 C. diced carrots	**1 sprig minced parsley**
1/3 C. chopped celery	**2 T. salt**
1/3 C. chopped onion	

Cover and simmer gently 3 hours, removing scum occasionally. Strain, chill, remove fat and strain again. To each quart of soup add 1 cup noodles and cook 10 to 15 minutes just before serving.

MRS RAY CHALKER

CHILI CON CARNE

1 lb. ground beef	**1 can kidney beans,**
1 medium onion, finely	**finely chopped**
chopped	**1 can tomatoes**
1 green pepper, finely	**2 T. Worcestershire sauce**
chopped	**1 T. chili powder**
1 clove garlic, finely chopped	**1 t. salt**
	⅛ t. pepper

Lightly brown meat, add onion, green pepper and garlic. Add beans, tomatoes and seasonings and simmer slowly one hour. (Even better made several hours early or a day before.)

MRS. H. PHIL CARR

CREAM OF GREEN PEA SOUP

Put 2 C. green peas in 6 C. boiling water in a saucepan over medium heat. Add 1 medium onion, salt, pepper and 1 stalk of parsley. Boil uncovered until peas are tender, about 25 minutes. Prepare small croutons. Mix 3 yolks of eggs with 6 T. cream; add 1 T. chervil. Before serving, remove onion and parsley from water in which peas have boiled. Add, at once ½ C. butter cut in small pieces, do not stir but tip the saucepan in all directions. Pour over cream and eggs. Add croutons and serve.

MRS. RICHARD C. MILLER

CRAB OR SHRIMP SOUP

2 T. butter
2 T. flour
1 C. milk

1 can consomme
salt and pepper

Mix with the soup one can of crabmeat or shrimp. Watercress may be used as a garnish.

MRS. MAYNE MILLER

CREAM OF PEANUT SOUP

Dissolve 2 heaping T. peanut butter in 1 C. hot water. When smooth, add 2 C. evaporated milk, heaping t. corn starch, mixed with 1 C. of water, 1 t. salt, 2 t. minced onions and a dash of cayenne.
Cook 5 minutes. Beat with an egg beater until frothy; strain and serve hot.

MRS. LANNIE HAYNES

CREAM OF POTATO SOUP

1 C. boiling water
2 C. diced raw potatoes
1 T. chopped onion
1 t. salt
1 bay leaf

1/8 t. pepper
pinch of celery salt
3 C. milk
1 T. butter
3 T. flour

Cook potatoes and onions in boiling water until tender. Make thickening, using 3 T. flour, 1/3 C. milk. Add rest of ingredients and simmer for 30 minutes. Makes about 4 servings.

MISS EDITH ROLLINS

EASY DELICIOUS CREAM SOUP

Put in 2-qt. kettle: 2 stalks celery with tops, one medium-sized onion, cut in quarters, some outside leaves from a head of cauliflower, 2 large potatoes and 1 qt. water. Cook over medium heat, covered, until potatoes are tender. Drain and reserve liquid, press vegetables through food mill or sieve, then return to cooking liquid. Add 1 C. light cream or top milk, 3 T. butter, salt and pepper to taste and a little chopped parsley. Serve very hot with buttered croutons.

MRS. ALICE FRIBERG

IRISH POTATO SOUP

Dice potatoes (1 for each serving). Cover with water and add 1 t. salt. Cook till tender. Break egg in bowl, stir flour into egg until you have a mixture of little dry, yellow crumbs; add to potato soup a few at a time and stir. Let boil 3 minutes, add 3 C. sweet milk, 1 T. butter and pepper to taste.

MRS. GUY A. MILLER

MIXED VEGETABLE MINESTRONE

Saute 1 pkg. of frozen mixed vegetables, and 1 small chopped onion, in 1/4 C. diced salt pork, or margarine for 15 minutes. Add 2 qts. boiling water, 1 bay leaf, 2 sprigs parsley, salt and pepper, 1 C. elbow macaroni. Boil 5 minutes. Reduce heat and simmer for 30 minutes. Serve with grated Romano or Parmesan cheese. (Cook uncovered). Six large servings.

MRS. ALICE FRIBERG

MUSHROOM AND SHRIMP CHOWDER

Simmer 5 or 10 minutes in 6 T. bacon fat 2 t. each chopped onions, green peppers, and celery; add 1 can cream of mushroom soup, 1 can cream of shrimp soup, 4 T. chopped ripe olives. Serve in hot cups topped with strips of avocados. Serves 8.

MRS. GEORGE OLDHAM

ONION SOUP

Brown 4 thinly sliced onions in 2 T. butter. In 20 minutes, sprinkle 1 t. sugar over the onions. Add 6 C. boiling water, salt and pepper. Boil covered, for 10 minutes. In a casserole place ½ lb. bread cut in slices 1/3 inch thickness. Cover each piece of bread with very thin slices of Swiss cheese. It will take a little more than a ¼ lb. cheese. Place them in the soup dish and pour over them the contents of the saucepan. The slices of bread will rise to the surface. Sprinkle on the top 4 T. melted butter. Put the casserole in 375° preheated oven for 20 minutes. Serve very hot.

MRS. RICHARD C. MILLER

QUICK BORSCHT

Put into a large pan 2 cans of consomme and 3 cans water; add one bunch beets, salt. Cook slowly until beets are tender. Put all ingredients in blender. Return to pan until ready to serve. Put a serving of whipped cream to which lemon juice has been added on each bowl.

MRS. ALLEN HARRIS, JR.

ROME CHOWDER

¼ lb. ground round steak	1 can tomatoes
¼ lb. ground pork	1 can peas
1 T. melted butter	1 small can pimientos
1 onion	1 small can ripe olives
1½ C. cooked spaghetti	½ lb. American cheese

Melt butter, add onions and cook until brown. Follow with meat, continue cooking 10 minutes on high. Add remaining ingredients. Continue cooking on low heat 2 hours.

MRS. MINNIE BLACK

SPANISH BEAN SOUP

1 pkg. Garbanzo dried beans	salt to taste
1 ham bone	pinch saffron
1 clove garlic, peeled and sliced thin	4 medium potatoes, cubed
1 small salami, sliced	1 large onion, peeled and sliced thin

Soak beans overnight. Cover beans with fresh water, add ham bone, onion, garlic and salt; boil 4 hours. Add potatoes; ½ hour before serving odd salami and saffron.

MRS. LANNIE HAYNES

SWEET-SOUR CABBAGE BORSCHT (SOUP)

Soup Stock:

2½ lbs. beef plate or brisket	¼ C. each onion, carrot
3 qts. cold water	and celery
1 T. salt	1 C. potatoes, diced
¼ t. pepper	1½ C. white lima beans
1 can tomatoes	¼ C. pearl barley
1 small can tomato juice	1 t.. chopped parsley
	chopped green or red pepper

Wipe and salt meat: place in soup kettle with the cold water. Let come slowly to the boiling point. Skim. Let soup simmer 3 hours then add vegetables, skim off fat and add seasonings. To get the desired sweet - sour taste ,add juice of 6 lemons and 1½ C. sugar. Keep simmering until served.

MRS. WALLACE MILLER

TENNESSEE CLAM CHOWDER

1 10-oz. can minced clams	2 T. finely chopped celery
1 diced potato	1 t. salt, pepper to taste
1 T. minced onion	1 C. water
1 grated carrot	1 C. milk

Mix all ingredients except milk and cook for 20 minutes. Then add milk and heat thoroughly. Garnish with chopped parsley. Serves 3.

MRS. LEWIS COSBY

VICHYSSOISE

3 large leeks, cut into	potatoes, cut in chunks
small pieces	3 bouillon cubes
1 medium-sized onion,	salt and pepper to taste
chopped finely	1 pt. cream
½ C. butter	½ C. chopped chives
1¼ lbs. peeled white	

Cook chopped leeks and onion in butter until soft. Do not brown. Place potatoes in saucepan with 1½ qts. boiling water. Add bouillon cubes and leek - onion - butter mixture. Boil for 1½ hours. Strain and press potatoes through a fine sieve. Allow puree to cool and add ½ pt. cream. Sprinkle with a little nutmeg. Chill puree in refrigerator for 24 hours. Remove and beat with rotary beater for 1 or 2 minutes. Strain and combine with other ½ pint of cream. Serve very cold in previously chilled soup cups. Sprinkle each serving with 1 t. of chopped chives.

MRS. RICHARD C. MILLER

VEGETABLE SOUP

1 lb. beef brisket	1 C. diced celery
1 No. 2 can tomatoes	1 large onion, diced
1 small can tomato paste	1 large potato, diced
2 T. Worcestershire sauce	2 carrots, diced
½ t. tabasco sauce	1 small can green peas
½ C. catsup	1 small can corn
2 t. salt	

Cook beef brisket slowly in three cups water one hour. Add other ingredients and simmer two hours or more.

MRS. W. F. PALMER

CUCUMBER SOUP

8 young cucumbers, (peeled and chopped)	2 med. onions, minced
¼ C. chopped parsley	Top leaves from heart of celery, chopped
2 t. salt	8 C. chicken broth
1-⅓ C. flour	½ C. butter
Dash of cayenne pepper	¼ C. cut chives
2 C. light cream	

Place the cucumbers, onions, celery leaves, parsley and 2 tsp. of salt in a saucepan with the chicken broth. Simmer slowly for about 30 minutes, keeping the pot covered, and stirring once or twice. Make a paste of the flour and butter and add it, little by little, to the cucumbers, stirring until perfectly smooth. Cook again GENTLY for about 5 minutes. Cool and pur'ee the soup in a blender or through a sieve. Add more salt if necessary and cayenne pepper to taste, and combine with the cream and HEAT GENTLY. Serves 10 to 12 people.

Alan Gump

NANTUCKET MINESTRONE

1 can minestrone soup	1 can minced clams (7½ oz.)
1 C. water	2 T. chopped parsley

Heat all ingredients. Garnish with sliced green onions and croutons. Makes 2 to 3 servings.

Mrs. Tom Happel

WINTER SONG SOUP

1 can split pea and ham soup	1 can turkey vegetable soup
1½ soup cans water	Pinch rosemary

Heat all ingredients together. Garnish with croutons. 4 to 6 servings.

Mrs. Tom Happel

CLAM CHOWDER

4 No. 2 cans minced clams	1 sweet green pepper
2 carrots	2 large onions
1 large can of whole tomatoes	½ can tomato paste
	Thyme, pepper, salt

Drain clams and reserve liquid. Put the green peppers, carrots, and onions through a meat grinder. Saute' vegetables and clams in butter until onions are just transparent. Add to 1½ qts. fish stock, clam juice, tomatoes, tomato paste, thyme, pepper and salt. Thicken with 1 cup of broken-up soda crackers. Simmer for one hour and if chowder is too thick, add more fish stock. To each serving add one tablespoon of sherry.

Mrs. Malcolm Campbell

GAZPACHOS

BASE: May be frozen.

24 med. tomatoes (fresh)   **4 med. red onions**
4 (4 oz.) jars pimentos   **1 C. olive oil**
¼ C. wine vinegar

Chop tomatoes, onions and pimentos. (I put them through the blender).
Add olive oil and wine vinegar. Stir well and divide into pint con-
tainers. Freeze for future use. One pint of base serves about 8 to 10
people when the other ingredients are added. Add these other
ingredients listed to each pint of base as needed.

TO EACH PINT OF BASE ADD:

¼ chopped green pepper   **½ C. celery stalks and**
½ C. chopped cucumbers   **chopped leaves**
1 small can chopped ripe   **1 clove garlic, chopped**
** olives (about ½ C. or**   **1 can V-8 juice (26 oz.)**
** more)**   **½ t. Beau Monde seasoning**
¼ C. chopped parsley   **or Accent**

HERBS TO ADD:

1 t. thyme   **1 t. dried oregano**
1 t. basil   **1 t. parsley**
1 t. salt   **1 T. sugar**

Procedure:
Chop fresh vegetables. Add to 1 pint of base with olives, V-8 juice,
minced garlic, herbs. Salt, sugar and Beau Monde or Accent'. Stir
well and serve cold. Note: 1 cup of any good Red Wine may be
added to soup. (You may vary herb seasonings to taste.)

Mrs. William Blackard

Vegetables

ARTICHOKES AND SHRIMP

1 pkg. frozen artichoke hearts, cooked and drained
1 can (4 ozs.) sliced mushrooms (drained)
1 T. butter   1 can frozen cream of shrimp soup
¼ C. milk   1 t. Worcestershire sauce
1 T. grated Paremsan cheese   2 T. lemon juice

Place artichoke hearts in buttered 1 qt. casserole. In saucepan brown mushrooms in butter; add soup, milk, lemon juice and Worcestershire sauce. Heat until soup is thawed, stirring now and then. Pour soup mixture over artichokes, top with cheese and a sprinkle of paprika. Bake in 375° oven for 20 minutes.

MRS. E. MALCOLM CAMPBELL

ASPARAGUS CASSEROLE

1 large can asparagus tips   ½ lb. grated cheese
2 C. cracker crumbs   ½ C. almonds or pecans
½ C. butter   1 can mushroom soup

Grate cheese and mix well with cracker crumbs. Add liquid from asparagus to soup. Put layer of crumbs and cheese in bottom of buttered casserole, layer of asparagus and sprinkling of nuts. Cover with mushroom soup. Repeat until all ingredients are used. Put a layer of crumbs and cheese on top. Dot both layers with butter. Decorate with whole blanched almonds. Bake in 350° oven 20 minutes. This can be prepared the day before.

MRS. KATHERINE KIRKPATRICK MEREDITH

ASPARAGUS SOUFFLE

3 T. butter   ½ t. salt
4 T. sifted flour   ¼ t. paprika
1½ C. milk   1 medium size can (No. 303—
3 egg yolks (beaten well)   14½-oz.) all green
2/3 C. grated cheese (yellow,   asparagus (drained)
     mild)   3 well beaten egg whites

Melt butter, add flour. When well blended, add milk. Cook, stirring until thick. Add egg yolks and cheese. Beat 2 minutes. Add asparagus. Mix well. Fold in egg whites. Pour into buttered casserole. Bake 45 minutes in oven 350°. Serve immediately. Serves 5 - 6.

MRS. C. O. FINNE, JR.
Saltville, Va.

DILL BEANS

3 or 4 C. julienne beans (canned), if frozen, cook
2 T. flour   2 T. dill seed
2 large onions, minced   2 T. cream
2 T. minced parsley   2 T. vinegar
4 T. vegetable oil or melted   Salt and pepper to taste
     butter

Drain beans well (save liquid). Add flour to oil and stir in ¾ C. liquid drained from beans. Cook until smooth and add parsley, onions, and cook until thick. Then add dill seed, salt and pepper and cook 5 minutes. Add cream and vinegar, stir and pour over beans. Keep warm over hot water until serving. This recipe can be made the day before if you heat over water.

MRS. H. T. SMITHDEAL

FRENCH BEAN CASSEROLE

2 pkgs. frozen French cut beans	1 can cream mushroom soup (not diluted)
1 can bean sprouts	small can mushrooms
1 can water chestnuts, sliced	1 can French fried onions

Cook beans about 7 minutes. Drain. Wash bean sprouts. Add other ingredients. Put in buttered casserole. Crush one can onion rings and sprinkle over top. Bake 30 minutes at 350°. This casserole may be made the day before it is to be used, except for adding the onion rings.

MRS. J. B. RICHNER
Fort Lauderdale, Florida

KIDNEY BEANS WITH WINE

2 T. olive oil	2 T. onions

Saute' above until soft, not brown.
Add: **1 can of kidney beans**

Put one-half into casserole; then add slice of ham (tenderized raw), cut into 4 servings. Put rest of beans on top. Pour 1 C. sherry wine over casserole. Bake until ham is tender. Serves 4.

MRS. JAMES R. MacLEAN

LIMA BEAN CASSEROLE

Cook, as directed, the number of boxes of frozen lima beans you desire to serve. Season well. For each box used add one can of undiluted cream of mushroom soup. If more mushrooms are desired, use a can of whole buttered mushrooms. Mix soup and limas. Turn into a well-buttered casserole. Top with bread crumbs or packaged poultry stuffing. Place in oven at 350° until baked.

MRS. CLEM WILKES

HAM AND STRING BEAN SAVORY

½ lb. American cheese	1½ C. cooked green beans
2/3 C. milk	½ t. Worcestershire sauce
1½ C. thinly sliced ham, (slivered)	

Melt cheese in top of double boiler. Add milk (warmed) and stir until smooth and well blended. Add ham, beans and Worcestershire sauce; heat thoroughly. Serve over squares of hot corn bread. Serves 4.

MRS. FRANK THOMPSON

SPICED BEANS

4 C. dried beans, navy or pea	¾ t. ground ginger
4 t. salt	½ t. ground cinnamon
1 large onion	½ t. ground black pepper
1/3 C. brown sugar	2 t. dry mustard (powdered)
½ C. catsup	½ lb. salt pork

Wash beans. Cover with cold water and soak overnight. Add salt and onion (cut in half), cover with water. Boil. Lower heat and simmer until tender. Remove onion. Place ½ pork and ½ onion in bottom of casserole. Add beans. Pour remaining pork and onion over beans. Add liquid mixture of seasonings and 3 C. of bean liquid. Bake covered 1¾ hours at 325°F. Remove cover and brown 15 to 20 minutes.

MRS. E. MALCOLM CAMPBELL

VENETIAN PEAS AND RICE

1 T. olive oil	2 C. fresh or frozen peas
¼ C. butter	¾ C. raw rice
1 small onion, chopped	1¾ C. chicken stock
1 T. crumbled crisp bacon	salt and pepper to taste

Brown onion and bacon in melted butter and oil in heavy skillet. Add peas and cook for 5 minutes, stirring frequently. Add the rice and cook and stir for 3 minutes longer, until grains are well coated with butter. Add stock and seasoning and cover. Cook over low heat for 15 to 20 minutes. Before serving toss with 1 T. Parmesan cheese.

MRS. EDWARD OEHMIG

STRING BEANS SUPREME

3 boxes frozen French cut beans	½ lb. American cheese, grated
1 large onion, chopped	juice of ½ lemon
1 stick butter	¼ C. sherry
1 can mushrooms	1 can French fried onions for topping
2 cans mushroom soup	

Cook onion in butter until transparent. Mix with cooked beans and other ingredients. Blend well. Put into greased casserole and top with French fried onions just before heating in 325° oven for 5 minutes.

MRS. LEE WALLACE

ORANGE GLAZED BEETS

¼ C. butter	1 t. cider vinegar
½ C. sugar	1 T. cornstarch
¼ t. salt	2 T. water
2 t. orange rind	3 C. canned beets
½ C. orange juice	

Melt butter. Add sugar, orange rind (grated), orange juice, vinegar and salt. Mix cornstarch and water, and stir into above. Cook until clear; add cubed beets, simmer for 10 minutes.

MRS. GUY A. MILLER

BROCCOLI CASSEROLE WITH ALMONDS

2 pkgs. frozen broccoli	¾ C. grated cheese
2 T. butter	¼ t. pepper
2 T. flour	1 C. chopped almonds
2 C. milk	

Cook broccoli until just tender. Drain and place in greased casserole. Make sauce of butter, flour, milk, cheese, salt and pepper. Mix almonds with broccoli. Then pour cream sauce over broccoli. Place in 350° oven 20 minutes or until bubbling. Serves 6.

MRS. RICHARD GOVAN

BROCCOLI AND ONIONS AU GRATIN

Cook 3 lbs. of small white onions in salted water until tender. Drain. Remove tough ends of 1 bunch broccoli. Slice each stalk lengthwise, then cut into serving pieces. Cook in boiling, salted water until tender. Drain. Make good rich cream sauce with ¾ C. butter, ¾ C. flour, 1 qt. milk and 1 pt. light cream. Season with 1 t. salt and ¼ t. pepper. Mix with onions and broccoli. Pour into casserole. (This dish can be prepared up to this point several hours in advance.) Sprinkle top with ½ C. grated cheese. Bake in medium oven (350°) until bubbly and brown.

MRS. E. D. HALE

BROCCOLI RING

1 C. water	1 C. white sauce
1 C. white rice	1 t. salt
1 C. sharp cheddar cheese	1 t. pepper
1 onion, large	½ t. Worcestershire sauce
1 box chopped broccoli	2 eggs, separated

Cook rice in water for a few minutes. Add grated cheese and browned onion. Add broccoli and cook for ten minutes.

Make cream sauce, add salt, pepper and Worcestershire sauce. Add to broccoli and rice mixture. Combine all with egg yolks. Beat egg whites and fold in when mixture is cold. Put in greased mold and set in refrigerator until ready to cook. Set mold in pan of water and bake 45 minutes at 400°.

MRS. J. B. THOMAS

GARLIC GRITS

4½ C. water	1 roll garlic cheese
1 C. grits	2 eggs
1 t. salt	½ C. milk
¼ lb. butter	1 C. buttered corn flakes

Pour grits slowly into boiling water and cook over low heat until they are well done, 30 to 40 minutes. Cool 15 minutes. Melt butter and ¾ of cheese roll and add to the grits. Beat the eggs with the milk and slowly stir into the grits. Pour into greased baking dish and top with remaining cheese, grated, and the corn flakes. Bake 45 minutes at 350°.

MRS. RUTLEDGE MILLER

BROCCOLI RING

2 pkg. chopped broccoli	1 C. mayonnaise
1 C. thick cream sauce	6 eggs, separated

Mix first 3 ingredients and season to taste with salt, red pepper and onion juice. Beat yolks and whites separately. Mix yolks into broccoli mixture and fold in whites. Pour into greased ring mold. Cook in pan of water in 300° oven until firm, about 45 minutes.

MRS. ROBERT COX
Durham, N. C.

BARBECUE CABBAGE

Cook one head of cabbage in small amount of salted water until tender. Drain. Cut in wedges and serve with sauce—as follows:

Fry 3 slices of bacon — drain
To grease add ¼ C. catsup, 1 t. vinegar, 2 T. water,
1 t. Worcestershire, ¼ t. salt.

Add crumbled bacon and simmer.

MRS. FRANK ERB

CARROT RING

2 lbs. carrots	2 t. onion juice
1 C. light cream	2 eggs, beaten
3 T. butter	1 T. flour
2 t. salt	paprika

Cook carrots until soft (20 to 30 minutes). Mash and add other ingredients. Bake one hour at 350°F. in a buttered dish or ring mold set in pan of hot water. Serve green peas in center.

MRS. ALFRED W. JONES

CAULIFLOWER IN CHIPPED BEEF SAUCE

1 head cauliflower	½ lb. grated cheese
2 cans cream of mushroom	1 T. lemon juice
soup	1 pkg. dried beef

Cook cauliflower as usual and pour over it the following sauce: Cook soup over low heat until bubbly, add cheese and stir until it melts. Add lemon juice and shredded dried beef last.   Serves 6 - 8.

MRS. JOHN WILSON

CAULIFLOWER — TOMATO AU GRATIN

1 head cauliflower	1 can tomatoes
1 C. grated American cheese	1 bouillon cube
2 medium onions	1 T. sugar
5 sprigs parsley	1 t. salt
3 T. butter	dash pepper
3 T. dry bread crumbs	

Start oven at 350°. Cook cauliflower as usual. Drain and toss sections with ¾ C. grated cheese. Chop onions and parsley and cook in butter until limp. To this add tomatoes, bouillon cube, sugar, salt, pepper and crumbs. Cook slowly 5 minutes. Put ½ tomato mixture in bottom of buttered casserole.   Add cauliflower and top with remaining sauce. Sprinkle remaining cheese on top. Bake 30 minutes

MRS. JOHN WILSON

CORN   FRITTERS

1-1/3 C. flour	2/3 C. milk
1 t. salt	1 egg (beaten)
1½ t. baking powder	1 can whole kernel corn

Sift dry ingredients together. Combine milk and egg; beat well. Add to dry ingredients. Mix just until flour is moistened. Stir in corn. Drop batter from tablespoon into deep, hot fat. Fry 2 to 3 minutes until brown. Serve plain or with warm syrup.

MRS. MELTON PRICE MEEK
Lawton, Oklahoma

CORN   PUDDING

1 pt. scraped corn pulp	½ t. salt
2 eggs, separated	1 heaping T. sugar
1½ T. flour	1 good pinch pepper
1 C. milk	1 T. melted butter

Beat egg yolks. Add milk, combined dry ingredients, corn and melted butter. Fold in beaten egg whites. Bake in buttered casserole at 400° 30 minutes or until set in center.

MRS. WILLIAM JEWELL

EGGPLANT

1 medium eggplant, peeled and cut up. Soak in water 30 minutes and then drain

Cook in salt water until tender; drain and mash.

Add:—

1 C. grated cheese	7 crumbled saltines
2 whole, unbeaten eggs	1 C. rich milk
½ onion, chopped	salt and pepper

Bake in greased casserole at 325°F. for 40 minutes.

MRS. TOM McKEE

SCALLOPED CORN

1½ C. whole kernel corn (1 12-oz. can)	2 T. butter
	1 t. salt
¾ C. thin cream or evaporated milk	dash of pepper
	2 eggs, beaten
2 T. flour	½ C. bread or cracker crumbs

Drain liquid from canned corn into measuring cup; to this add thin cream to make one cup. Melt butter in sauce pan over low heat; add flour, salt and pepper; stir until smooth. Add liquid gradually. Continue cooking until thickened, stirring constantly. Add corn mixed with beaten eggs. Pour into buttered baking dish (1 qt. size). Sprinkle top with bread crumbs. Bake at 350°F. for 45 to 50 minutes. Serves 5-6.

MRS. RODNEY SKIPWORTH

EGGPLANT SOUFFLE

1 medium eggplant	3 eggs, separated
3 T. butter or margarine	grated cheese
2½ T. flour	bread crumbs
1 C. milk	

Cook eggplant in boiling water until tender. Mash. Cream butter and flour; add milk gradually. Add beaten egg yolks, and cook in double boiler until thick. Add eggplant and cool slightly. Fold in stiffly beaten egg whites. Turn into greased baking dish and sprinkle with cheese and bread crumbs. Bake in slow oven (325°F.) until browned.

MRS. P. L. FIELDS

SPANISH EGGPLANT

1 medium sized eggplant	1 small onion, chopped
1 beaten egg	1 C. dry bread crumbs
1½ C. canned tomatoes	½ C. buttered bread crumbs
2 T. melted butter	½ C. grated American cheese

Pare eggplant; cut into 1 inch cubes. Cook in salted boiling water 8 minutes; drain. Add egg, tomatoes, butter, onion and dry bread crumbs. Place in greased baking dish. Top with buttered crumbs and sprinkle cheese over top. Bake in oven at 350°F. for 30 minutes.

MRS. W. J. BARTON, JR.

STUFFED EGGPLANT

1 eggplant	1 T. butter
1 can shrimp	1 medium size tomato
1 medium size onion	salt and pepper
1 C. bread crumbs	

Remove a generous slice from top of the eggplant and boil remainder or steam until tender, about 30 minutes. Remove from heat and scoop out meat, separating from the seeds. In meantime, break shrimp in small pieces and soak the bread crumbs in water. Fry the chopped onions in butter and, when well-browned, add finely chopped tomato. Allow to cook 2 or 3 minutes. Add bread, from which excess water has been drained, to the fried mixture. Add shrimp and the eggplant and allow to cook for 10 minutes. Salt and pepper to taste. Turn this into the eggplant shell and cover with buttered bread crumbs. Bake for 15 minutes in hot oven.

MRS. DOROTHY RICE FRIBERG

NOODLE PUDDING (KUGEL)

½ lb. noodles (cooked)   ½ C. brown sugar
2 eggs   ½ C. raisins
¼ C. water   1 C. sliced cooked apples

Mix ingredients. Pour into greased casserole. Bake in moderate oven until brown on top.

MRS. SARAH CANTOR

NOODLE RING

3 C. cooked noodles   ½ t. pepper
½ C. sour cream   1 t. salt
5 T. melted butter   4 eggs

Beat egg yolks; add cream, butter and seasoning. Mix well with noodles. Fold in egg whites. Pour into buttered ring mold. Set in pan of water and bake at 350°F. for 45 minutes.

MRS. C. E. CREGER

RICE-OLIVE CASSEROLE

Prepare 2 C. cooked rice by placing 2/3 C. uncooked rice in sauce pan with 1½ C. hot water. Cover and simmer until rice is tender. Cut one 4½ ounce can of ripe olives from the pits in large pieces. Grate 1¼ C. yellow cheese. Melt ¼ C. butter or margarine in a sauce pan, add ¼ C. finely chopped onion, and cook until transparent. Now add chopped olives, cooked rice and 1 C. grated cheese. Slightly beat 2 eggs, add ½ C. milk, ½ t. salt and ¼ t. pepper. Blend this with the olive-rice mixture, and pour into a greased 1½ quart casserole. Top with remainder of cheese and bake in 350° oven for 30 to 40 minutes. In this dish green olives can be used as well as ripe ones.

MRS. CARL BARRETT
Kingsport, Tennessee

BERMUDA BAKED ONIONS

Parboil 10-16 small onions for 15 minutes
Toast 3 slices bread, butter and cube it
Have ready ¾ C. grated cheese

Arrange layers of onion, bread cubes and cheese in small casserole. Season with salt and pepper. Beat 2 eggs and combine with ¾ C. milk. Pour over the other ingredients. Dot with butter. Bake 35 minutes at 350° in pan of hot water.

MRS. JOHN WILSON

ONIONS SATELLITE

¼ lb. fresh mushrooms, sliced   2 T. butter
½ lb. bulk pork sausage
1 pt. stock (turkey, chicken, or pork — preferably)
2 lb. little pearl onions (50-60 onions)
1 carton sour cream (8 oz.)
4 T. (¼ C.) pistachio nuts or sesame seeds

Saute' mushrooms in butter. Remove and saute' crumbled sausage in same pan until very brown. Remove sausage, drain grease from pan. Pour in meat stock and stir. Add peeled onions, cover and cook slowly until onions are tender and almost all stock has been absorbed (about 30 minutes). Add sausage and mushrooms, mix well. Just before serving mix in sour cream. Top with ground pistachio nuts. Serves 6.

MRS. CHARLES GORDON

PEAS AND ONIONS

1 T. sugar	¼ C. cream
2 small peeled onions	1 T. butter
1 sprig parsley	¼ C. finely chopped parsley
salt to taste	2 lbs. fresh peas

Place peas in sauce pan. Add sugar, onions, sprig of parsley and salt. Add sufficient boiling water to cover peas and cook until tender. Remove onions and parsley. Drain peas. Reserve liquid and cook until ¼ C. remains. Add cream and butter. Pour liquid mixture over peas and garnish with chopped parsley. Serves eight.

MRS. RICHARD MILLER

PINEAPPLE RICE

1 C. brown rice	½ C. brown sugar
1 small can crushed pineapple	½ stick butter

Cook rice until dry and fluffy. Put ½ in small buttered casserole, cover with ½ pineapple and sugar. Dot with butter. Add second layer in same way and bake in moderate oven until slightly brown on top. Serve as vegetable with ham.

MISS EDITH McQUILKEN

GERMAN POTATO CAKES

4 med. raw potatoes	2 eggs, separated
1½ T. flour	2 t. grated onion
½ t. baking powder	2 T. diced fried bacon

Pare and grate raw potatoes (may use blender); add beaten egg yolks, flour, salt, baking powder, onions and bacon. Fold in stiffly beaten egg whites and drop by spoonfuls into skillet of hot fat. Turn when lightly brown. Serve with applesauce. Nutmeg and cinnamon may be substituted for onion and bacon. Serves 6.

MRS. BILL CROOKSHANKS
Jonesboro, Tennessee

SCALLOPED POTATOES SUPREME

8 medium potatoes, sliced	salt and pepper
1 T. butter	1 can condensed
flour	mushroom soup
¼ C. minced onion	1 C. milk

Alternate layers of potatoes and onions in greased baking dish. Dredge with flour, dot with butter and season each layer with salt and pepper. Mix soup and milk and pour over potatoes. Cover and bake at 350°F. for 1¼ hours. Serves 8.

MRS. KENT HERRIN

KARTOFFELKLOESSE — POTATO DUMPLING

Boil 6-7 potatoes and mash with a lump of butter. Add 3 eggs, salt and ½ C. flour to hold them together. Mix and shape into balls. Cook in gently boiling water for 10-20 minutes, until they float. Serve with roast beef.

LIL RUCKEL

POTATOES MOUSSELINES

Bake 2 lbs. potatoes in oven ¾ hour. While hot, remove the skin. Mash through strainer.

Add:

1 t. salt, ¼ t. pepper, pinch nutmeg
¾ C. soft butter, 4 egg yolks. Mix thoroughly with:
½ C. whipped cream

Cover with melted butter, bake 5 minutes at 450°.

Mashed — Potatoes Luxembourgeoise

Mash potatoes in butter and red wine instead of milk.

MRS. RICHARD MILLER

SWEET POTATO PUDDING CASSEROLE

2 C. grated sweet potatoes	¾ stick butter, melted
1½ C. milk	dash of salt
2 C. sugar	3 eggs, beaten

Mix grated sweet potatoes with milk. Add remaining ingredients. Place in greased casserole. Cook slowly at 275° for 1½ hours.

MRS. CHARLES SHERROD

SWEET POTATO PUFF

5 C. mashed sweet potatoes	8 marshmallows
½ t. salt	¼ C. pecan halves
1 9 oz. can crushed pineapple	

Add salt to sweet potatoes. Mix in pineapple and syrup. Place half in 1½ quart size greased casserole. Top with marshmallows. Then add remaining potato mixture. Cover with brown sugar and pecan halves. Cover and bake in moderate oven 350° for 30 minutes.

MRS. BRONCE McCLAIN

RICE CASSEROLE

1 C. wild or white rice	½ C. onion, chopped
1 C. canned tomatoes	1½ C. boiling water
1 C. sharp cheese, cubed	½ C. vegetable oil
1 C. mushrooms (1 small can and liquid)	
1 C. ripe olives (measure before chopping)	

Wash rice thoroughly and let soak 2 or 3 hours. Drain and add all ingredients raw; salt and pepper to taste. Bake in greased casserole in 350° oven for 1½ hours.

BOBBY McELROY

BAKED RICE AND CHEESE

3 C. cooked rice	1 C. grated sharp cheese
1 small jar of chopped pimiento	

Place a layer of rice in a greased baking dish, then the cheese and pimiento and top with another layer of rice. Add a little milk and dot with butter and salt and pepper. Bake 20 minutes in 350° oven.

MRS. JOE WOOD

GREEN RICE

2 C. raw rice	½ t. salt
2 C. grated sharp cheese	1 C. finely chopped parsley
2 C. milk	½ C. melted butter
2 eggs, beaten	1 medium onion, chopped

Cook rice (until fluffy) and rinse. Combine with other ingredients. Turn into 2 large buttered casseroles and bake 45 minutes at 350° until set and slightly brown on top. Serves 16-20.

ORENE GIBSON
Durham, N. C.

RICE RING

Parboil 1½ C. shredded, raw carrots 5 minutes in salted water. Drain thoroughly and add 1 T. chopped onion, 1 C. cooked rice, 1 beaten egg, seasonings, 1 C. American cheese, grated.

Turn into buttered ring. Bake 30 minutes in moderate oven. Unmold and serve hot with cooked peas in center. Serves 4.

MRS. FRANK THOMPSON

RICE AND MUSHROOM RING

1 lb. mushrooms	1 C. rice
2 T. butter	salt

Boil rice and rinse in cold water. Put mushrooms through meat grinder; saute in butter. Add rice and seasoning and let simmer 15 minutes. Put mixture in buttered ring mold; set in pan of boiling water and bake in oven 350° about 45 minutes. Serve with buttered peas.

MRS. JAY GUMP

SPANISH RICE I

¾ C. rice	2 onions
2 T. fat	2 C. tomatoes
5 C. water	

½ C. chopped green pepper or pimientos, salt, pepper and paprika

Fry the rice in fat until brown, then add water and boil until soft. Drain. Saute' onions in a little fat. Mix with tomatoes and chopped peppers or pimientoes, and add to the rice. Add seasonings. Place in a greased casserole. Bake for thirty minutes. 350°F.
Prepare a day or so ahead for best results. Test and season along if needed.

MRS. J. B. LAWRENCE

SPANISH RICE II

Saute' together:

½ C. butter	1 C. chopped onion
½ C. diced celery	6 T. uncooked rice
½ C. diced green pepper	

Add:

¼ C. green olives, sliced	2 t. salt
1 C. tomatoes	1 C. boiling water
1 t. black pepper	

Bake in greased casserole about 1 hour, 350°F. until rice is done.

MRS. GENE TAYLOR, JR.

SPINACH WITH CHEESE

1 large can spinach	2 T. lemon juice
1 C. cream sauce	dash of tabasco
1 C. grated cheese	salt and pepper to taste
2 T. grated onion	bread crumbs

Mix all together. Top with bread crumbs and bake in buttered casserole 25 minutes at 350°.

MRS. DAN B. WEXLER

SPINACH SOUFFLE

Chop coarsely 2 lb. fresh spinach or 1 large can of spinach

1 T. chopped onion	pinch of nutmeg
1 C. thick white sauce	1 T. lemon juice
2 eggs, separated	1 C. grated cheese
salt and pepper to taste	

Add spinach and onion to sauce. When hot, add beaten egg yolks and cook just until yolks thicken. Add cheese and seasonings. Fold in stiffly beaten egg whites. Put into casserole with bread crumbs and butter dots on top. Set in pan of hot water and bake at 375° about 40 minutes or until firmly set in center.

MRS. T. F. BECKNER

SPINACH CASSEROLE

2 boxes frozen spinach	2 eggs
1 C. mushroom soup	2 chopped onions
1 C. mayonnaise	1 C. grated cheese

Boil and drain spinach. Mix all ingredients; place in buttered casserole and dot top with butter and bread crumbs. Bake 45 minutes at 350°

MRS. LYMAN FULTON, JR.

SQUASH SOUFFLE

1 C. milk	1 T. grated onion, if desired
3 egg yolks	1½ C. grated cheese
2½ C. yellow squash, boiled and mashed	½ t. prepared mustard
	salt to taste

Heat milk until warm; add beaten yolks and other ingredients. Beat whites of eggs until stiff, and fold in last. Pour into a well-greased casserole and bake at 350°F. for about 30 minutes.

MRS. ALFRED W. JONES

YELLOW SQUASH CASSEROLE

Wash squash. Place in casserole a layer of sliced squash, a layer of thin sliced onions, salt and pepper and dot with butter. Repeat until filled. Bake until tender in 300° oven. Before serving, roll corn flakes and peanuts and cover top. Brown lightly in oven.

MRS. E. T. WEST

TOMATOES OREGANO

Cut large, ripe tomatoes in half. Place each half with cut side up in baking dish. Sprinkle liberally with oregano, garlic, salt and pepper. In a small bowl moisten soft bread crumbs with melted margarine. Top each tomato with crumbs and Parmesan cheese. Bake 25 to 30 minutes in moderate oven (350°F.)

MRS. MELTON PRICE MEEK
Lawton, Oklahoma

FRIED TOMATOES AND BACON
(A Pennsylvania Dutch recipe)

For 4 people, fry 8 slices of bacon. Then slice 4 tomatoes in thick slices. Flour, salt and pepper, and fry in bacon grease. Remove the tomatoes, pour off all except 2 T. of drippings. Thicken the remaining drippings with flour and add 1 C. milk. Season to taste. Cook to the consistency of cream sauce. Pour over fried tomatoes and top with bacon.

MRS. ROBERT LATZER
St. Louis, Mo.

STICKY TOMATOES

6 large ripe tomatoes or 1 can of tomatoes
1 C. bread crumbs   1 T. butter
1½ C. sugar   dash salt and pepper

Put tomatoes (peeled) in baking dish. Cover with bread crumbs and remaining ingredients. Stir well and put in slow oven. Cook for at least 3 hours.

MARY HAMILTON

VEGETABLE CASSEROLE

6 small onions   4 or 5 large carrots, sliced
6 small potatoes
1 medium size head or 1 pkg. frozen cauliflower

Make about 2 C. of white sauce. Add to this 1 C. grated cheese. Cook all vegetables separate. Drain well. Place in large casserole. Pour one small can of green peas over, then cheese sauce. Sprinkle grated cheese on top. Bake in moderate oven about 30 minutes.

You may use for sauce — 1 can of condensed mushroom soup — diluted with milk.

This is a wonderful luncheon dish with link sausage or crisp bacon and a fruit salad.

GERTRUDE S. JONES
Mountain City, Tenn.

ZUCCHINI AND ONIONS

2 medium tender zucchini squash
1 bunch green spring onions
1½ C. grated dry cheddar cheese
1 C. buttered bread crumbs   1 stick butter

Cook squash in ½ C. water and ½ stick butter, melted, until rind is tender and squash is almost dry. Stir to prevent sticking. Cook chopped onions, including tops, in ½ C. salted water until tender. Drain well and add ½ stick butter and let melt.

Place vegetables in casserole in layers with cheese and crumbs which have been tossed together. Make top layer of cheese and crumbs. Bake at 350°F. until cheese browns, about 20 minutes. Add ¼ C. milk before baking if needed for moisture.

MRS. NEWTON GARLAND

BROCCOLI SURPRISE

1 pkg. frozen broccoli
(cooked as directed and
drained)
1 can of cream of chicken
soup

1 small jar of cheese whiz
2 C. cooked rice
1 can of water chestnuts,
drained well and sliced

Combine cheese whiz with undiluted soup and heat until fairly well melted and mix in other ingredients in casserole; top with buttered cracker crumbs and bake at 350 degrees until bubbling.

Mrs. Herbert Lawson

COLD BROCCOLI MOLD

2 pkg. cooked chopped
broccoli, drained and cooled

2 hard boiled eggs

HEAT:

1 can beef consomme with:
1 T. worcestershire sauce
2 envelopes gelatin
(½ C. water)

3 T. lemon juice
½ t. tabasco

Cool. Mix finely chopped broccoli with 1 cup mayonnaise and very finely chopped eggs. Combine with other ingredients and pour mixture into greased mold. Refrigerate. Turn out of mold on lettuce.

Mrs. Phil S. Barksdale, Jr.

RED CABBAGE WITH CARAWAY SEEDS

Wash 1 cabbage and drain. Cut in shreds. Fry 3 slices of bacon. Remove bacon from grease. Saute' 2 tbs. chopped onion in bacon grease. Add cabbage. Cover and cook for 10 minutes. Chop up two apples and add to cabbage. Add ¼ tsp. salt and ⅛ cup boiling water. Stir. Cover pan and cook slowly 1 hour and 20 minutes. Dissolve 2 tbs. flour in ½ cup vinegar or red wine. Add to cabbage and simmer 10 minutes more. Then add 1 Tbs. caraway seeds.

Mrs. George Brandt

CHEESE-SCALLOPED CARROTS

12 sliced, pared, med. carrots
¼ C. butter or margarine
1 t. salt
2 C. milk
3 C. buttered soft bread crumbs (fresh bread)

1 minced small onion
¼ C. all-purpose flour
¼ t. dry mustard
¼ t. celery salt
⅛ t. pepper
½ lb. sliced process American Cheddar or sharp cheese

Early in the day: cook carrots covered, in 1" boiling salted water until barely tender; drain. Meanwhile, in sauce pan, gently cook onion in butter 2 or 3 minutes. Stir in flour, salt and mustard, then milk; cook, stirring until smooth. Add pepper and celery salt. In 2 qt. casserole, arrange layer of carrots, then layer of cheese. Repeat until all are used, ending with carrots. Pour on sauce; top with crumbs. Refrigerate. About 45 minutes before serving; bake in 350 degree oven 35 to 45 minutes or until hot. Makes 8 servings.

Mrs. Herman Carriger

GOLDEN FLECK CASSEROLE

4 med. carrots, pared
4 med. potatoes, pared
1 med. onion

1 t. salt
2 T. butter
1 can condensed cream of mushroom soup

About 1¼ hour before dinner: Start heating oven to 400 degrees. Thinly slice carrots (on the diagonal), potatoes, onions. Grease 10" x 6" x 2" baking dish. Place vegetables in layers, sprinkling each layer with salt, dotting each with butter and ending with carrots. Beat soup with 1 soup can of water. Pour over vegetables. Bake in covered dish (use foil for baking cover dish) 35 minutes; uncover and bake 20 minutes or until done.

Mrs. Herman Carriger

FRENCH FRIED CAULIFLOWER

1 box frozen cauliflower
2 eggs

Bread crumbs (sifted)

Parboil cauliflower until barely tender. Drain well. Dip in beaten eggs and bread crumbs and fry until brown. Serves 4.

EGGS CREOLE (VIA MURFREESBORO)

8 eggs, hardboiled
1 med. onion, chopped
1 small green pepper,
   chopped
5 celery stalks, chopped
1 stick margarine or butter
Dash of salt, worcestershire
   sauce, and tabasco sauce

1 can tomato soup
1 can mushroom soup
1 small can mushrooms
1 t. chili powder
Grated sharp cheese
buttered cracker crumbs

Saute' celery, onion and pepper in butter. Add tomato soup, simmer 20 minutes. Add mushrooms and mushroom soup and all seasonings. Simmer 5 minutes. Slice eggs and lay in casserole. Pour sauce over these and top with cracker crumbs and cheese. Bake at 450 degrees for 15 minutes.

Mrs. Bill Meredith

FRESH CORN OYSTERS

1 C. corn, fresh, cut from
   cob
2 eggs, beaten
1 T. flour

¼ t. salt
¼ t. pepper
½ t. baking powder
1 t. sugar

Mix well, drop heaping Tbs. in hot (not too hot) oil and cook til golden brown.

Mrs. Sam Mitchell

SCALLOPED EGGPLANT

1 large eggplant (about 4
   C. diced)
½ C. chopped onion
1 can cream of mushroom
   soup

⅓ C. milk
1 egg, slightly beaten
1 recipe cheese topping
¾ C. pkg. herb-seasoned
   stuffing

Cook diced eggplant in boiling water (6-7 minutes), drain; gradually stir milk into soup. Blend in egg. Add drained eggplant, onion and stuffing. Toss lightly to mix. Turn into greased casserole. Top with cheese topping and bake 20 minutes in 350 degree oven.

CHEESE TOPPING:

Crush ½ cup of herb stuffing. Toss with 2 T. melted butter or margarine. Sprinkle over top of casserole. Top this with 1 cup grated American cheese.

Mrs. Clyde Cooper

GREEN BEANS SUPREME

½ C. sliced onion
1 T. minced parsley
4 T. butter
2 T. flour
¼ t. pepper
½ C. dry bread crumbs

2 cans Parisienne Seasoned
Green Beans, drained
½ C. grated sharp cheese
1 t. salt
1 C. sour cream
½ t. grated lemon rind

Cook onion and parsley in 2 Tbs. butter until tender but not brown. Add flour, salt, pepper and lemon peel. Add sour cream and mix well. Stir in beans. Heat and stir. Turn into 10" x 6" x 1½" baking dish. Top with grated cheese. Combine 2 Tbs. butter with bread crumbs. Sprinkle over top. Broil until cheese melts and crumbs brown.

Mrs. Kenneth Scholl

SWISS CHEESE GREEN BEANS

2 cans stems and pieces
    mushrooms
1 T. minced onion
½ C. chopped cashews or
    almonds
½ C. butter
⅓ C. flour

½ T. dry mustard
2 C. milk
½ lb. shredded swiss cheese
⅛ T. tabasco
1 T. lemon juice
3 No. 2 cans green beans,
    cut & drained

Brown mushrooms, onions, and ½ of nuts in butter. Add flour and seasonings and blend. Add milk; stir constantly and cook until sauce is smooth and thick. Add 1 cup cheese, tabasco and lemon juice. Cook over low heat until cheese melts. Add beans. Pour in buttered dish and top with cheese and nuts. Bake 15 to 20 minutes at 350 degrees or until the cheese melts.

Mrs. Frederic Brandt

BAKED STUFFED MUSHROOMS

1 lb. mushrooms (about
    12 med.)
1 C. finely chopped pecans
3 T. chopped parsley
¼ C. soft butter

1 clove garlic, crushed
¼ t. thyme
½ t. salt
½ C. heavy cream

Remove stems from mushrooms, wipe with damp cloth and arrange caps in baking dish, bottom side up. Chop stems and mix with ingredients except cream. Stuff mushrooms, pour cream over, cover and bake at 350 degrees for 30 to 45 minutes, or until tender. Baste occasionally. Serves 6 to 8.

Mrs. W. H. Lancaster

MUSHROOM FONDUE

1 carton mushrooms	2½ slices toast, very crisp
1 pt. Half 'n Half	

Cut toast in triangles and dip generously in melted butter. Layer toast and raw sliced mushrooms in buttered casserole. Salt and pepper to taste. Pour Half 'n Half over top of ingredients. Cover with buttered crumbs. Bake 45 minutes at 350 degrees. Serve immediately.

Mrs. Joe Thompson

MUSHROOM SOUFFLE

1 lb. mushrooms	Dash of tabasco
1 T. chopped onion	¼ t. thyme
6 T. butter	½ t. marjoram
6 T. flour	Salt & pepper
2 C. scalded milk	6 eggs
½ C. grated sharp cheese	½ C. toasted almonds

Wash and chop mushrooms fine. Mix with onion, cook over low heat in 3 Tbs. butter. Cover and let steam 5 minutes. Push mushrooms to one side of pan. To the liquid in the pan add rest of butter, blend in flour; add hot milk gradually, stir all together until thick and well blended. Add grated cheese, tabasco and herbs. Season lightly with salt and pepper. Cool but do not chill. One hour before serving, separate eggs, beat yolks until thick. Fold into mixture. Beat whites until stiff. Fold in carefully. Pour mixture in casserole, sprinkle with almonds-chopped. Bake at 325 degrees for 50-60 minutes. Serve at once. Optional as to whether casserole is placed in water to bake.

Mrs. Alfred Abernethy

FRENCH PEAS

½ t. sugar	2 T. butter
¼ t. marjoram	¼ t. savory
½ C. water	1 T. parsley
⅛ t. pepper	½ t. salt
½ C. sliced spring onions	1 pkg. frozen peas

Saute' onions in butter 5 minutes, do not brown. Add other ingredients and cover and cook over low heat for 10 minutes. Serve.

Mrs. William Blackard

"THOSE POTATOES"

Boil 6 or 7 potatoes until not quite soft. Peel when cold. Grate a layer of potatoes into buttered casserole. Sprinkle with salt and pepper and cover with layer of sour cream. Repeat until all is used. (1 pt. sour cream to 8" x 12" baking dish.) Bake at 350 degrees for 45 minutes.

Mrs. John Wilson

BROWNED RICE

Cook until yellow in 4 Tbs. butter in heavy skillet (iron), 1 cup drained washed rice. Stir in 4 cups chicken broth or consomme' flavored with onion juice, garlic, thyme, salt, worcestershire sauce, paprika, and a small can chopped mushrooms. Cover. Simmer without stirring until rice is dry and flaky. (25 minutes). Serve hot as meat accompaniment. Serves 6.

Mrs. Latham R. Winn

RICE 'N MUSHROOMS

1 C. rice (do not use minute rice)
½ stick butter
2 cans beef consomme or bouillon
1 med. onion, chopped
1 can mushrooms

Combine first four ingredients in casserole and bake at 350 degrees for 30 minutes. Add mushrooms and bake another 30 minutes. Stir occasionally. Serves 6 to 8 people. (For variation, omit chopped onion and add tiny whole onions last 15 minutes.)

Mrs. Charles Ray

WILD RICE SUPREME

1 lb. cut up canned mushrooms
2 C. wild rice, uncooked
1 C. chopped onions
¼ C. water
1 can condensed cream of chicken soup
1 lb. sausage (hot)
½ C. cream
1 t. Lowreys salt
1 t. accent
Tabasco and pepper to taste
⅛ t. oregano, thyme, and marjoram

Cook rice and drain. Saute' sausage for 10 minutes. Drain excess fat. Stir in onions. Cook 15 minutes, stirring well. Cool. Add cream, chicken soup, spices. Mix. Taste. Add more seasoning if necessary. Mix with rice. Add mushrooms. Put into casserole. Bake 20 to 30 minutes at 350 degrees until mixture bubbles. Serves 10 to 12. This may be frozen. Sprinkle toasted almonds on top before serving. (If use wild and long rice do not use spices.)

UNUSUAL SAUERKRAUT

½ C. chopped onions
1 can drained sauerkraut
1 bay leaf
½ t. salt

2 T. vegetable oil
1 (8 oz.) can tomato sauce
½ C. water
⅓ C. brown sugar

Cook onion in oil until lightly browned, then combine other ingredients. Cook covered 10 minutes, uncover and cook 10 minutes.

Mrs. H. B. Cupp, Jr.

BUTTERNUT SQUASH CASSEROLE

2 C. cooked & mashed
   butternut squash
3 eggs

¼ lb. margarine, melted
1 C. sugar
Ginger to taste (½ to 1 t.)

Combine the above ingredients and place in a buttered casserole. Top with cinnamon and nutmeg. Bake at 350 degrees until brown; 45 minutes.

Mrs. C. C. Marshall

SQUASH CASSEROLE

1½ lb. squash
1 grated carrot
1 small onion, grated

1 C. sour cream
1 can undiluted chicken
   soup
½ pkg. Pepperidge Farm
   cornbread stuffing

Cook squash in a little water and salt with soup, grated onion, and grated carrot. Grease casserole and put in all ingredients. Put the ½ pkg. cornbread stuffing over top and bake 30 minutes at 350 degrees in a 9 x 12 dish.

Mrs. J. A. Meredith
Jonesboro, Tennessee

ZUCCHINI SQUASH

2 C. fresh zucchini squash,
   diced unpealed
⅔ C. fresh tomato (diced
   into small pieces)

1 C. fresh corn (cut & scrape
   cob well)
½ C. chopped onions
½ C. chopped green peppers

Mix these ingredients thoroughly.

In sauce pan melt 1 stick creamery butter

ADD to butter in sauce pan

1 T. flour
1 T. salt
½ t. black pepper

1 t. chili powder
1 T. sugar
½ t. hot pepper (optional)

Mix throughly and pour over vegetable mixture. Preheat oven to 400 degrees; bake 20 minutes or until vegetables are done in greased casserole.

Mrs. Tom Mitchell

SWEET POTATO CASSEROLE

3 cans sweet potatoes   3 T. Brer Rabbit molasses
½ C. chopped walnuts   ½ C. brown sugar
¼ lb. butter or margarine   Marshmallows (small)

Drain liquid from potatoes and mash them together, with butter. Add rest of ingredients. Place mixture in 3 qt. casserole. Cover top with marshmallows and dot with butter. Bake in slow oven 325 degrees, covered, for 20 to 30 minutes. Just before ready to serve remove cover and allow marshmallows to brown.   Mrs. Bill Kohler

BAKED STUFFED TOMATOES

6 firm tomatoes, unpeeled   3 stalks of celery
2 onions   1 C. cooked rice
1 bell pepper

Cut slices from stem end of tomatoes, scoop out inside, leaving a shell to be stuffed. Sprinkle with salt and invert to drain while stuffing is being prepared. Chop onions, peppers and celery fine. Fry in butter until tender but not brown. Add tomatoes insides and simmer until tomatoes are cooked to pieces. Add rice and cook until almost dry. Stuff into tomatoes and sprinkle crumbs on top. Put in pan with a little water around them and bake about 15 minutes at 325 degrees. Ground ham, bacon or chicken livers may be added to the stuffing if desired. Serves 6.   Mrs. Bill Kohler

VEGETABLE DISH

1 pkg. large frozen limas   1 pkg. frozen snapped
1 pkg. frozen peas, large   green beans

Start limas first; allow water to return to boiling, then add beans, let water return to boiling and then add peas.

    1 T. Olive Oil
    Salted water
    (Can use vegetables in pouches but omit Olive Oil if do.)

Cook 20 minutes (vegetables), drain in collander. Toss with sauce.

SAUCE:

1 C. mayonnaise   3 hard boiled eggs, chopped
3 T. lemon juice   finely
2 T. minced onion   1 t. worcestershire sauce
1 t. dry mustard   ¼ t. garlic salt
1 dash tabasco   Salt and pepper to taste
½ C. parsley, cut fine,
    (do not omit)

                            Mrs. Hanes Lancaster, Jr.

ASPARAGUS AND EGG CASSEROLE

1 No. 2 can asparagus	1 C. grated cheese
4 hard boiled eggs, sliced	1 T. worcestershire sauce
1 pt. "Medium White Sauce"	1 t. onion juice

Add cheese, Worcestershire sauce and onion juice to cream sauce. Put asparagus, egg and sauce in alternate layers in casserole. Cover top with sauce, sprinkle with buttered crumbs. Bake until top is brown in 325 degrees oven. Serves 8.

Mrs. William Bailey

ASPARAGUS FONDUE

1 lb. fresh or frozen asparagus, cooked, and drained	2 C. milk
	2 C. soft bread crumbs
	½ t. salt
2 well beaten eggs	⅛ t. pepper
1 C. sharp grated cheese	¼ t. paprika
1 T. onion chopped fine	

Combine all but asparagus, cook over low heat, stirring constantly, until cheese melts. Fold in asparagus. Pour into 1½ quart buttered casserole and bake at 350 degrees for 1 hour.

Mrs. James Wetherbee
Marshall, Minn.

BARLEY CASSEROLE

¼ lb. butter	1½ C. pearl barley
2 medium onions	3 pimientos, coarsely chopped
¾ lb. mushrooms	2 C. chicken stock

Melt the butter in saucepan. Saute' the mushrooms and onions until the onions are translucent. Add the barley and cook until golden brown. Transfer the mixture to a casserole. Add pimiento, stock, salt and pepper and cook in a moderate oven for 50 to 60 minutes, until all the liquid is absorbed. Add more liquid if the barley seems dry during cooking.

Mrs. Malcolm Campbell

BROCCOLI CASSEROLE

4 pkg. chopped frozen broccoli cooked as directed

MIX:

4 eggs	½ C. mayonnaise
½ C. whipping cream	1 can mushroom soup

In casserole put layer broccoli, sauce, broccoli, sauce. Take cheese Ritz crackers and crush and put over casserole. Bake at 350 degrees until it bubbles and browns on top slightly.

Mrs. Edward Steffner

POTATO KNISHES

Dough for knishes:

2½ C. sifted flour	2 eggs
1 t. baking powder	2/3 C. salad oil
½ t. salt	2 T. water

Sift the dry ingredients into a bowl. Make a well in the center and drop the eggs, oil and water into it. Work into the flour mixture with the hand and knead until smooth.

Potato filling for knishes:

1 C. chopped onion	1 egg
6 T. chicken fat or butter	1 t. salt
2 C. mashed potatoes	¼ t. pepper

Brown the onions in the fat. Beat in the potatoes, egg, salt and pepper, and continue to beat until fluffy.

There are two ways to fill the knishes. In either case, divide the dough in two parts and roll as thin as possible. Brush with oil. Now you can spread the filling on one side of the dough and roll it up like a jelly roll. Repeat with the other half of the dough. Cut into 1½ inch slices, place on an oiled baking sheet and press down lightly to flatten. As an alternative, you can cut the rolled dough into 2 inch circles. Place a T. of the filling on each and draw edges together; pinch firmly. Place on the baking sheet pinched edges up. Bake in a 375° oven 35 minutes or until browned. This recipe makes about 36.

———————o———————

Knishes, always a great favorite have become enormously popular in recent years as cocktail party snacks. The basic dough can be used with many different fillings to suit the occasion.

Cheese filling:

1½ C. diced scallions or onions	1 egg
4 T. butter	1½ t. salt
2 C. cottage cheese	1/8 t. pepper
	2 T. sour cream

Brown the onion in the butter and beat in the remaining ingredients until smooth.

Meat filling:

½ C. minced onion	1 egg
2 T. chicken fat	1 t. salt
1½ C. ground cooked meat	¼ t. pepper
½ C. cooked rice	

Lightly brown the onions in the fat or butter. Add the remaining ingredients and mix until well blended.

Chicken filling:

1½ C. ground cooked chicken	1 t. salt
¾ C. mashed potatoes	¼ t. pepper
1 egg	

Mix until smooth.

MRS. JULIUS GINSBURG

MASS WEIGHT

1 ounce (oz)	= 28 grams (g)
1 pound (lb)	= 450 grams (g)
1 gram (g)	= .035 ounces (oz)
1 kilogram (kg) or 1000 g	= 2.2 pounds (lbs)

LIQUID VOLUME

1 fluid ounce (fl oz)	= 30 milliliters (ml)
1 fluid cup (c)	= 240 milliliters (ml)
1 pint (pt)	= 470 milliliters (ml)
1 quart (qt)	= 950 milliliters (ml)
1 gallon (gal)	= 3.8 liters (l)
1 teaspoon (tsp)	= 5 milliliters (ml)
1 tablespoon (tbsp)	= 15 milliliters (ml)
1 milliliter (ml)	= .03 fluid ounces (fl oz)
1 liter (l) or 1000 ml	= 2.1 fluid pints or 1.06 fluid quarts
1 liter (l)	= .26 gallons (gal)

CONTENTS OF CANS

Size	Avg. Contents
6 oz.	¾ cup
8 oz.	1 cup
No. 1 (picnic)	1¼ cups
12 oz. (vacuum can)	1½ cups
No. 300	1¾ cups
No. 1 tall	2 cups
No. 303	2 cups
No. 2	2½ cups
No. 2½	3½ cups
No. 3	4 cups
No. 5	7 cups
No. 10	12 to 13 cups..1 gallon

Oven Temperature Chart

Slow—250° to 325° F.

Moderate—325° to 400° F.

Hot—400° to 450° F.

Very hot—450° and above.

EQUIVALENT MEASURES

Dash—less than ⅛ teaspoon

Pinch—approximately 1/6 teaspoon

3 teaspoons—1 tablespoon

2 tablespoons—⅛ cup or 1 oz.

4 tablespoons—¼ cup

5 tablespoons and 1 teaspoon—⅓ cup

8 tablespoons—½ cup

12 tablespoons—¾ cup

16 tablespoons—1 cup

2 cups—1 lb. granulated sugar

2 cups—1 pint

4 cups—1 quart

2 pints—1 quart

4 quarts—1 gallon

8 quarts—1 peck

4 pecks—1 bushel

16 ounces—1 pound

EQUIVALENT AMOUNTS

almonds	4/5 lb. shelled	1 cup chopped
apples	1 lb.	3 cups sliced
apricots	1 lb.	6 cups cooked
beans, dried	½ lb.	1 cup
butter	1 lb.	2 cups
cheese, American	½ lb.	2 cups grated
cheese, cream	3 oz.	6 tbsp.
chocolate	1 oz.	1 square
egg whites	8 to 10	1 cup
egg yolks	14 to 16	1 cup

EQUIVALENT AMOUNTS (Continued)

flour . . . . 1 oz. . . . . 4 tbsp.

flour, all purpose . . . . . . 1 lb. . . . . 4 cups sifted

flour, cake . . . . 1 lb. . . . . 4½ cups sifted

flour, whole wheat . . . . . 1 lb. . . . . 3½ cups

lemon juice . . . . 1 medium . . . . 3 tbsp.

lemon rind . . . . 1 medium . . . . 1 tbsp. grated

marshmallows . . . . ¼ lb. 16

meal . . . . 1 lb. . . . . 3 cups

meat . . . . 1 lb. . . . . 2 cups diced

nuts . . . . ¼ lb. . . . . 1 cup

orange juice . . . . 1 medium . . . . ⅓ cup juice

orange rind . . . . 1 medium . . . . 2 tbsp.

pecans . . . . 1 lb. . . . . 4 cups

potatoes, white . . . . 1 lb. . . . . 3 medium large

raisins . . . . 1 lb. . . . . 3 cups

rice . . . . 1 lb. . . . . 2½ cups raw and
3½-4 cups cooked

sugar, brown . . . . 1 lb. . . . . 2½ cups

sugar, confectioners . . . . 1 lb. . . . . 2½ cups

sugar, granulated . . . . . 1 lb. . . . . 2 cups

tomatoes . . . . 1 lb. . . . . 3 medium

walnuts, black . . . . 5½ lbs. unshelled . . . . . 4 cups

SUBSTITUTIONS

2 tbsp. flour—1 tbsp. cornstarch.

1 cup butter—1 cup hydrogenated fat and ½ tsp. salt.

1 oz. chocolate—3½ tbsp. cocoa and ½ tbsp. butter.

1 cup sour milk—1 cup sweet milk and 1 ⅓ tbsp. vinegar
or lemon juice.

1 tbsp. baking powder—¼ tsp. soda and ½ tsp. cream of
tartar.

TERMS USED IN COOKING

BASTE—to moisten roasting meat or other food, while baking, with juices from the pan or with additional juice.

BLANCH—to pour boiling water over a food, then drain and rinse with cold water.   Used to whiten or remove skins from almonds, or to prepare vegetables for freezing.

BRAISE—to cook meat or vegetables by simmering in a covered dish in a small amount of liquid, either in an oven or over direct heat.

CARAMELIZE—to heat sugar in a skillet until melted and brown, or to heat foods containing sugar until light brown and of caramel flavor.

FRICASSEE'—to stew meats, poultry, etc. in stock or sauce.

GLAZE—to coat with a thin sugar syrup.

MARINATE—to soak in French dressing, vinegar, lemon juice, sour cream or other dressing; usually before cooking.

PARBOIL—to boil food until partially cooked.

RENDER—to free fat from connecting tissue by heating slowly until fat melts and can be drained off.

SAUTE'—to cook in a small amount of fat, turning often.

SCALD—to heat liquid to a temperature just below the boiling point.   To immerse food in boiling liquid for a short time.

SCALLOP—to bake food in an oven-proof dish in layers with sauce and crumbs.

SCORE—to make light cuts or gashes in surface of a food— usually meat.

SEAR—to brown the surface of the meat by the application of intense heat usually in a hot pan or oven.

SHRED—to cut into very thin slices or strips.

SIMMER—to cook in liquid just below boiling point.

SLIVER—to cut or shred into lengths.

STEEP—to cover with boiling liquid, cover and let stand.

STOCK—liquid in which food has been cooked.

TRUSS—to tie a fowl or other meat so that it will hold its shape during cooking process.

Calorie Value of Various Foods is as Follows:

FOOD	AMOUNT	CALORIES
Whole milk	½ pt.	165
Skim milk	½ pt.	90
Buttermilk	½ pt.	90
Cream, coffee	1 Tbsp.	30
Egg	1 (no fat in preparation)	80
Bacon	2 strips	95
Beef roast	3 oz.	340
Beef, corned	3 oz.	180
Hamburger	3 oz.	245
Steak	3 oz.	375
Cheese, cheddar	3 oz.	345
Cheese, cottage (from skim milk)	3 oz.	75
Chicken, broiled	3 oz.	115
Lamb chop, lean	3 oz.	130
Liver, fried	3 oz.	120
Ham, baked	3 oz.	340
Pork chops	3.5 oz.	295
Veal cutlet	3 oz.	185
Fish stick, frozen	1	40
Oysters (13-19)	1 cup	160
Salmon	3 oz.	120
Shrimp	3 oz.	110
Tuna	3 oz.	170
Asparagus	1 cup	35
Green Beans	1 cup	25
Lima Beans	1 cup	150
Beets	1 cup	70
Broccoli	1 cup	45
Cabbage	1 cup	25
Carrots	1 cup	45
Cauliflower	1 cup	30
Celery	1 stalk	5
Corn	1 cup	170
Lettuce	2 large leaves	5
Mushrooms	1 cup	30
Onions	1 cup	80
Green peas	1 cup	110
Green pepper	1 medium	15
Potato, baked	5 oz.	90
Potato, mashed with milk and butter	1 cup	230
Spinach	1 cup	45
Squash, winter	1 cup	95
Sweet potato	6 oz.	155
Tomatoes	1 cup	45
Tomato catsup	1 Tbsp.	15
Turnips	1 cup	40
Apple, raw	1 medium	70
Apple sauce, sweetened	1 cup	185
Apricots, in syrup	1 cup	200
Apricots, water pack	1 cup	80

Calorie Value of Various Foods is as Follows (Continued)

FOOD	AMOUNT	CALORIES
Avocado (California)	1 cup ½ inch cubes	260
Avocado (Florida)	1 cup ½ inch cubes	160
Bananas	1 medium	100
Blackberries, raw	1 cup	80
Cantaloupe	½ melon (5 inch diameter)	40
Cherries, canned soup	1 cup	120
Cranberry sauce, sweetened	1 cup	550
Dates	1 cup	505
Figs, dried	1 large	60
Fruit cocktail, canned in syrup	1 cup	175
Grapefruit	½ medium	50
Grapefruit juice, unsweetened	1 cup	95
Grapes, raw	1 cup	70
Grape juice	1 cup	165
Lemon juice	1 cup	60
Oranges	1 large	70
Orange juice (California)	1 cup	105
Orange juice (Florida)	1 cup	90
Peaches, raw	1 medium	35
Peaches, canned in heavy syrup	1 cup	185
Peaches, water pack	1 cup	65
Pears, raw	1 medium	100
Pears, canned in heavy syrup	1 cup	175
Pineapple, raw	1 cup	75
Pineapple, crushed, syrup pack	1 cup	205
Pineapple juice, canned	1 cup	120
Plums, raw	1	30
Plums, canned in heavy syrup	1 cup	185
Prunes, uncooked	4 medium	70
Prune juice, canned	1 cup	170
Raisins, dried	1 cup	460
Strawberries, raw	1 cup	55
Strawberries, frozen	10 oz.	300
Tangerines	1 medium	40
Watermelon	4 by 8 inches	120
Biscuits, baking powder	1 2½ inch	130
Rye bread	1 slice	55
White bread, enriched	1 slice	60
Whole wheat bread	1 slice	55
Cornbread	1 2¾ inch square	105
Cornflakes	1 oz.	110
Corn grits	1 cup	120
Crackers, graham	4 small or 2 medium	55
Crackers, saltines	2	35
Macaroni, cooked	1 cup	190
Noodles (egg), cooked	1 cup	200
Oatmeal, cooked	1 cup	150
Rice, (white) cooked	1 cup	200
Rolls, enriched	1	115
Spaghetti, cooked	1 cup	155

Calorie Values of Various Foods is as Follows (Continued)

FOOD	AMOUNT	CALORIES
Butter	1 Tbsp.	100
Vegetable fats	1 Tbsp.	110
Margarine	1 Tbsp.	100
Oils, salad or cooking	1 Tbsp.	125
Salad Dressings:		
Blue cheese	1 Tbsp.	90
Mayonnaise	1 Tbsp.	110
French	1 Tbsp.	60
Thousand Island	1 Tbsp.	75
Jams, Marmalades, Preserves	1 Tbsp.	55
Jellies	1 Tbsp.	50
Sugar	1 Tbsp.	50
Bouillon cubes	1 cube	2
Chili sauce	1 Tbsp.	15
Gelatin dessert, plain	1 cup	155
Sherbet	1 cup	235
Soups,		
Chicken	1 cup	75
Cream soup	1 cup	200
Noodle, rice or barley	1 cup	115
Tomato, clear	1 cup	90
Vegetable	1 cup	80
Vinegar	1 Tbsp.	2
White sauce, medium	1 cup	430
Pancakes, baked	1 4 inch diameter	60
Pies:		
apple	1/7 of 9 inch diameter pie	330
cherry	" " "	340
custard	" " "	265
lemon meringue	" " "	300
mince	" " "	340
pumpkin	" " "	265
Pretzels	5 small sticks	20
Fudge, plain	1 oz.	115
Angelfood cake	2 inch section	110
Butter cake, cupcake (no icing)	1 2¾ inch diameter	130
Plain cake with icing	2 inch section	320
Fruit cake	2" x 2" x ½"	105
Almonds and pecans	12 nuts	98
Cashews or peanuts	12 nuts	85
Peanut Butter	1 Tbsp.	105
Coca-Cola	6 oz.	80
Ginger ale	8 oz.	75
Potato chips	12 large	115

Reference: THE YEARBOOK OF AGRICULTURE 1959, the United States Department of Agriculture, Washington, D. C.

When preparing to serve a large number of people the following guide will be of help to you:

Amounts of foods to buy for 50 people:

FOOD	For 50 Servings	Size of Each Serving	FOOD	For 50 Servings	Size of Each Serving
Beverages			**Meat, Poultry, Fish (Continued)**		
Coffee, instant	1 6-oz. jar	¾ cup	Meat, chopped, for meat loaf	12 lb.	¼ lb. meat
Coffee, regular	1-1¼ lb.	¾ cup	Oysters, for scalloped oysters	6 qt.	½ cup scalloped oysters
Cream, for coffee	1¼ qt.	1½ tbsp.			
Fruit-juice concentrates, frozen	9 6-oz. cans	½ cup	Oysters, for stew	6 qt.	2 cups stew
Fruit or tomato juice, canned	4 46-oz. cans	½ cup	Pork, chops	17 lb. (3 to 1 lb.)	1 chop ¾" thick
Lemon, for tea	5 large	1 thin slice	Pork, loin to roast	25 lb.	½ lb.
Lemonade concentrate, frozen	13 6-oz. cans	1 cup	Sausage, bulk or links	12½ lb.	4 oz.
Punch	2 gal.	2/3 cup	Turkey, for dishes, using cut-up, cooked turkey	16 lb. (ready-to-cook weight)	
Sugar, lump	1⅛ lb.	2 lumps			
Tea	¼ lb.	¾ cup			
			Turkey, to roast	35-40 lb. (ready-to-cook-weight)	½ to 2/3 lb.
Meat, Poultry, Fish					
Bacon	6 lb.	2 slices			
Beef, rolled rib roast	25 lb. before boning	½ lb.			
Beef, standing rib roast	35 lb.	¾ lb.	**Vegetables**		
Chicken, to roast	35-40 lb. (ready-to-cook weight)	¾ lb.	Any canned vegetable	14 No. 303 cans; or 11 No. 2 cans	½ cup
Chicken, stewing, for dishes using cut-up, cooked chicken	20-25 lb. (ready-to-cook weight		Asparagus spears, canned	11 No. 2 cans	4 to 6 spears
			Asparagus, fresh	20 lb.	4 to 5 stalks
Fish fillets, frozen	13 1-lb. pkg.	¼ lb.	Cabbage	7 heads	⅛ head
Ham, canned boned	1 14-lb. can	¼ lb.	Carrots (tops off)	16 lb.	1/3 lb.
Ham, bone in, to bake	22-25 lb.	1/3 lb.	Cauliflower (flowerets only)	15 lb.	¼ lb.
Hamburgers	12½-15 lb.	4-to 5-oz. patty	Corn on cob	50 ears	1 ear
Lamb, leg to roast	25 lb.	½ lb.	Frozen vegetables	13-17 pkg. (10 to 12 oz.)	About ½ cup

FOOD	For 50 Servings	Size of Each Serving	FOOD	For 50 Servings	Size of Each Serving
Vegetables (Continued)			**Sandwiches**		
Green or wax beans, fresh	12½ lb.	¼ lb.	Beef, roast, sliced	4 lb. 12 oz.	1 slice
Onions, for creaming	15 lb.	½ cup (3 or 4)	Bread, sandwich	2 3-lb. loaves	2 slices
Potatoes, for creaming	12½ to 15 lb.	½ cup	Ham, baked, sliced	4 lb. 12 oz.	1 slice
Potatoes, frozen French Fries	16 9-oz. pkg.	About 3 oz.	Swiss cheese, sliced	3 lb. 2 oz.	1 slice
Potatoes, mashed	25 lb.	½ cup			
Potatoes, to scallop	12½ lb.	½ cup	**Miscellaneous**		
			Apples, cooking, for sauce	25 lb.	½ cup
Potatoes, sweet, glazed	25 lb.	1 potato	Applesauce, canned	14 No. 2 cans	½ cup
			Brown bread, canned	8 11-oz. cans	1 slice, ½" thick
Relishes and Salads			Bread	5 1-lb. loaves	1½ slices
Cabbage, for slaw	12 to 15 lb.	⅓ cup	Butter or margarine	1 to 1¼ lb.	1 pat, ½" thick
Chicken salad	6¼ qt.	½ cup	Cling-peach halves, canned	7 No. 2½ cans	1 peach half
Cranberry sauce, jellied	6 1-lb. cans	½" slice			
French dressing	1 to 1½ qt.	1½ to 2 tablesp.	Crackers	1 lb.	2 crackers
Fruit salad	9 qt.	¾ cup	Cream, heavy, to top desserts	1 qt.	1 rounded tablesp., whipped
Lettuce, for lettuce hearts	12 medium heads	1/5 head	Fruits, frozen, to top ice cream	13-17 pkg. (10 to 12 oz.)	¼ to ⅓ C.
Lettuce, leaf, for salad	6 heads	2-3 leaves	Ice cream, brick or bulk	2-2½ gal.	1 slice, or 1 large scoopful
Mayonnaise or cooked salad dressing	1 qt.	1 tablesp.			
Pears, for salad	7 No. 2½ cans	1 pear half	Noodles	8 6-oz. pkg.	½ cup
			Pies	9 pies	1/6 pie
Potato salad	6¼ qt.	½ cup	Rice, packaged precooked	6 15-oz. pkg.	¾ cup
Salmon, for salad	8 No. 1 tall cans	½ cup salad	Rolls or biscuits	6½ doz.	1½
Tuna, for salad	16 cans solid pack or chunk style	½ cup salad	Soup, canned, condensed	20 cans	1 cup
Tomatoes, for salad	30 medium	3 slices			

Note: For 25 persons, divide indicated amount by 2. For 100 persons, multiply by 2.

CHEESE AND EGG DISHES

COOKIES
BAR COOKIES

DROP COOKIES

FILLED COOKIES

REFRIGERATOR COOKIES

ROLLED COOKIES

POULTRY AND GAME

PRESERVES AND PICKLES

High South Publications
JOHNSON CITY JUNIOR LEAGUE
P.O. Box 1082
Johnson City, TN 37605

Please send _____ copies of **SMOKY MOUNTAIN MAGIC** at $16.95 each_____
Please send _____ copies of **TREASURES OF THE SMOKIES,**
             Tempting Recipes from East Tennessee at $16.95 each_____
Postage and Handling .... $ 2.00 each_____
Tennessee residents add 8½% sales tax each .... each_____
                                                      TOTAL $ _____

Name_____

Street_____

City _____ State _____ Zip _____
   Proceeds from the sale of these books are used to support community projects.

- -

High South Publications
JOHNSON CITY JUNIOR LEAGUE
P.O. Box 1082
Johnson City, TN 37605

Please send _____ copies of **SMOKY MOUNTAIN MAGIC** at $16.95 each_____
Please send _____ copies of **TREASURES OF THE SMOKIES,**
             Tempting Recipes from East Tennessee at $16.95 each_____
Postage and Handling .... $ 2.00 each_____
Tennessee residents add 8½% sales tax each .... each_____
                                                      TOTAL $ _____

Name_____

Street_____

City _____ State _____ Zip _____
   Proceeds from the sale of these books are used to support community projects.

- -

High South Publications
JOHNSON CITY JUNIOR LEAGUE
P.O. Box 1082
Johnson City, TN 37605

Please send _____ copies of **SMOKY MOUNTAIN MAGIC** at $16.95 each_____
Please send _____ copies of **TREASURES OF THE SMOKIES,**
             Tempting Recipes from East Tennessee at $16.95 each_____
Postage and Handling .... $ 2.00 each_____
Tennessee residents add 8½% sales tax each .... each_____
                                                      TOTAL $ _____

Name_____

Street_____

City _____ State _____ Zip _____
   Proceeds from the sale of these books are used to support community projects.